Competition and the Corporate Society

BRITISH CONSERVATIVES,
THE STATE AND INDUSTRY
1945-1964

Competition and the Corporate Society

BRITISH CONSERVATIVES, THE STATE AND INDUSTRY 1945-1964

NIGEL HARRIS

METHUEN & CO LTD

First published 1972 by
Methuen & Co Ltd
11 New Fetter Lane, London EC4
© *1972 Nigel Harris*
Printed in Great Britain by
The Camelot Press Ltd
London and Southampton

SBN 416 08280 7

Distributed in the USA
by HARPER & ROW PUBLISHERS, INC.
BARNES & NOBLE IMPORT DIVISION

Contents

5

CONTENTS

Acknowledgements

This work has been an inordinate time in the making, and many people have contributed in many different ways to its construction. The original draft – of a study of Conservative postwar economic policy – was presented for a higher degree of the University of London. Professor R. T. Mackenzie's patient advice in the compilation of that thesis made it possible; and it was much assisted also by the stimulating comments of Professor John Smith. Subsequently, Mr Duncan Burn and Mr Kenneth Tite very kindly went through the entire manuscript with great thoroughness and made numerous suggestions for its improvement. The sustained interest of Professor Graeme Moodie prompted a thorough revision of the work for publication. In addition, at successive stages in writing the work, I have had reason to be most grateful for the advice and help of Sir Michael Frazer and Mr James Douglas of the Conservative Research Department, Mr G. D. N. Worswick, Professors Alan Peacock and Jack Wiseman, Mr Edward Cooney and Mr Keith Hartley. Particularly important contributions were made by Mr Michael Kidron, Mr Hal Draper, Mrs Mary MacAuley and Mrs Tirril Harris. Mrs Pat Goldsmith prepared the final manuscript with impressive speed and competence.

It will be clear to many readers that the political views implicit for the most part in this work are quite different from those held by many who have contributed much valuable advice and suggestions to it. For those political views, as for the errors, the author is alone responsible.

Abbreviations

ABCC	Association of British Chambers of Commerce
BISF	British Iron and Steel Federation
BOAC	British Overseas Airways Corporation
Cmd.	Command White Papers and Committee Reports
CPC	Conservative Political Centre
CUCO	Conservatist and Unionist Central Office
Debs.	Parliamentary Debates (Hansard); the date of major debates and Supply Committee discussions, followed by the volume number and column number of the speech or statement cited in the text, is given. For example, 1 May 1948, 533/179, indicates the date of the citation, volume 533, column 179. Dates only are given for Committee and Report Stage readings
FBI	Federation of British Industries
GATT	General Agreement on Tariffs and Trade
HOC	House of Commons Papers
HOL *Debs.*	House of Lords debates
ICI	Imperial Chemical Industries
IDAC	Import Duties Advisory Committee (the May Committee)
MP	Member of Parliament, identified by full name at first reference, and thereafter by surname or name by which the person is commonly known
NEDC	National Economic Development Council
NIC	National Incomes Commission
NJAC	National Joint Advisory Council
NUCUA	National Union of Conservative and Unionist Associations

OEEC	Organization for European Economic Co-operation
NUM	National Union of Manufacturers
PEP	Political and Economic Planning
RHA	Road Haulage Association
TUC	Trade Union Congress

Introduction

The British Conservative party has been one of the most successful political parties in modern history. Despite the minority interests which it has embodied during its career, its political and electoral appeal has been significant enough to secure it the government of Britain for a far longer period than any of its rivals. Even more, it has been able to escape the institutional or political rigidities which led to the destruction of those European parties most closely comparable to it. Despite major changes in British society, major threats from rivals apparently better able to champion popular interests, the Conservative phoenix has always hitherto been reborn from the ashes of defeat.

The success of the Conservatives is partly – but only partly – related to their beliefs about British society and their characteristic responses to the problems faced by successive British governments. The beliefs of Conservatives are in part derived from what they see as the past record of success or failure in coping with the challenges to their survival. This account of Conservatism in this century, and particularly since the Second World War, is accordingly also an account of what Conservatives saw as problems in the evolution of British society. In particular, the problems of the British economy and of British industry were of primary importance. Here, attention is devoted to describing Conservative responses and locating them in terms of British society, rather than in assessing the validity or merit of Conservative ideas.

It might be argued that it makes little sense to identify a peculiar 'Conservative' response to the economic problems of Britain; for both major political parties have usually presented very similar statements of policy, and pursued in office almost identical courses of action. If ideology were no more than a summation of policies proposed or executed, then it would be reasonable to say that Britain has been governed for much of its modern history by one ideological party, and that the Conservatives, as one of the two factions within it, have no peculiar ideology of their own. There is some merit in this argument, although the two parties – Liberal and Conservative or Labour and Conservative – are not strictly symmetrical. Yet many of the basic assumptions of Conservatives are no more than the assumptions of British public life, and radical though the rhetoric may be, its rivals have not very often or for very long been able to escape imbibing many of those assumptions. On the other hand, an examination of Conservative beliefs does provide us with one view of the opinions of those who traditionally command British society, showing the doubts and conflicts that have arisen in response to a given range of problems. The value of the exercise is not lessened by the fact that the political rival competing with the Conservatives for power often had no radically different proposals to make.

One of the proudest Conservative claims is that their party embodies all that is most characteristically British – or English; that there is something called a 'British way of life' which is peculiar and valuable, and which the Conservatives conserve. Conservative historians seek to portray the past in terms of some continuous tradition, protected and enhanced by the Conservative party and its predecessor, the Tory party. The claim to continuity is itself a political belief, for what it is which is continuous, has to be established. In so far as the Britain of the 1780s is similar to the Britain of the 1970s there are obvious 'continuities'. But Conservative historians want also to say that, for example, the way in which the Tories in the eighteenth or early nineteenth century viewed the State and wanted to use it to regulate or shape the economy is the same as or similar to the view held by modern Conservatives. Yet to make this comparison is to ignore the assumptions upon which Tory and contemporary estimates of the role of the State were and are based. In an agrarian society, governed by an established and landed aristocracy both directly – through its ownership of land – and indirectly – through a monopoly of leading public offices – the State was only imperfectly distinguished from 'society'. Indeed, just as the aristocracy was seen as the embodiment of all wisdom, so its instrument, the State, was seen as society in its moral guise.[1] But the State today is pre-eminently the Government, and its complex of public agencies; and as often as not, they are seen by Conservatives as inimical to the full expression of popular freedom. Tolerating or even extending the public sector can hardly be compared to the Tory conception of the mystically unified British State. Similar comments are appropriate in relationship to Conservative attempts to compare the idea of an organic society in the writings of Burke and modern conceptions of collectivism, or the idea of an aristocracy in the eighteenth century and modern Conservative views of leadership. Out of historical context, we are left with little more than a play on words, or truisms. What is continuous in the history of the Conservatives has to be established rather than assumed, for in locating the real continuities we begin more clearly to understand the role of the party in British society.

To understand the role of the Conservatives the behaviour, rather than the rhetoric, is peculiarly vital in this case. For Conservatives pre-eminently defend the existing nature of society, without necessarily being able to identify unequivocally what the essence of the present *status quo* is. They have no 'theory' of the *status quo*, no detailed analysis of present society which indicates what it is that should be defended. What they defend at any given moment of time depends on what is being attacked rather than any prior assumptions. Yet the way in which they defend things, their behaviour, itself indicates certain priorities, and from these one can, as it were, construct an hypothetical theory, the theory Conservatives – or at least some of them – would have if they needed one. The 'at least some of them' is important also. For the Conservative party has always been a coalition of interests, and, as such, has had to have a leadership capable of reconciling contradictory groups. The aura of Conservatism must remain ambiguous, for intellectual clarity – that is, the clear expression of one set of interests before all others – is the enemy of co-operation between diverse groups. The Conservatives only rarely need a theory of society; and they are often positively opposed to theorization because it jeopardizes the collaboration of what could be hostile groups. Some Conservatives in the 1930s favoured the nationalization of the coal industry; some favoured the State forcing cartelization on the industry; yet others were mine owners who regarded nationalization and cartelization – unless they were to inherit the control of the cartel – as more or less disguised forms of Bolshevism. The survival of Conservatism depended upon blurring these distinctions, on not permitting them to come into open conflict.

The rhetoric often embodies the driftwood of a rich and complex history. Few Conservatives probably know the ships from which the driftwood came, the incidents in which the slogans were important. But the terminology is evocative of high events and noble aspiration. The Conservatives, once they freed themselves from a specific Tory identification with the squires of England, sought to make themselves the political voice of the elite groups of British society. Since industrial Britain was in a process of almost continuous change, different elite groups struggled to positions of pre-eminence, while others declined. To make itself the voice of the new was a precondition of Conservative survival. Yet also the Conservatives had, at least for a time, to carry the old. The rhetoric encouraged the loyalty of the old, and was an induction rite for the new. To survive, the party had itself to change. The most traditional party had to be, within certain very definite limits, the most opportunistic. Tory men and Whig measures were not an accident of Disraeli's youth; they were a precondition for a Conservative party in conditions of continuous social change. Disraeli himself has few rivals in Conservative history who understood this more clearly.

The rhetoric, however, confuses a clear identification of Conservatism. It includes contradictory elements, the product of past groups with contradictory aims. And it provides no guide whatsoever to understanding, let alone predicting, Conservative behaviour. Much of it is 'non-operational': it has, despite occasional appearances to the contrary, no implications for Conservative practice. And indeed this is hardly surprising.

A Conservative party seeks to conserve what is, and is impelled to innovate only in order to conserve. It follows that Conservatives normally cannot pursue aims which are radically in conflict with the maintenance of existing society. The ideals expressed by Conservatives are either a summation of what they feel already exists, or they are appropriate to some past phase of Conservative history, or they are simply decorative. The ideals are not related in any necessary way with the continuous changes introduced by successive Conservative administrations. For example, the aim of achieving a 'property-owning democracy' was voiced by Conservatives from the early 1920s. After the Second World War, the slogan was adopted by the party leadership. Yet no single practical action was undertaken by any Conservative administration to pursue unequivocally this general end. Measures there were to increase ownership (for example, housing), but it was never clear that the increases in ownership at all offset the relative concentration of ownership in fewer hands. The measures in any case were undertaken for specific immediate reasons – like a housing shortage, or the pressure of the Conservative party rank-and-file – rather than in pursuit of a long-term end. The trends in ownership seemed to be in the opposite direction, yet this did not appear to worry Conservatives. In the last analysis, some Conservatives suggested that the 'property-owning democracy' already existed or was almost realized. The phrase came to justify current society; it was idealized description, rather than aspiration. The ideal became lost in the real as soon as the radical attack which had prompted the formulation of the ideal faded. The ambivalence between the ideal and the real is important, for it is the ambivalence of a party which simultaneously defends the *status quo*, and yet must foster or accept changes in the *status quo* in order to survive.

Yet the changes which Conservatism had to absorb in order to survive were not random ones. A party of the ruling class reflects in its composition and beliefs the great changes in society as a whole. For the Tories and Conservatives, there were two major phases of transition, which transformed both the party and British society. The first – the transition from a predominantly agricultural society, governed in the main by the owners of land, the aristocracy, with assistance from merchants, bankers, and traders, to a society primarily engaged in urban industrial activities and governed by an entrepreneurial 'middle class' – was obviously much the more dramatic and radical change. From the middle years of Burke to the middle years of Disraeli, Tories grappled with the implications of the transition. Toryism, particularly towards the end of this long period, was in disarray; contradictory purposes surfaced, breaking up the old coalition and, on its margins, creating both those dedicated to the destruction of existing society and those who were scarcely to be distinguished from the Whigs and the Liberals. Indeed, it became increasingly unclear what Toryism was, what was the *status quo* which was to be defended.

The second and lesser transition from an entrepreneurial to a bureaucratic or managerial society (in rather oversimplified terms), did not destroy the Conservative party as the first transition had destroyed the Tories. Yet between the First and the end of the Second World Wars, Conservatism went through a major crisis, the crisis of British – and indeed, world – capitalism. Conservatives were in disarray. The prescriptions for change increasingly diverged from what formerly had been seen as the essence of Conservatism. Out of the flux emerged something different, something still committed to the defence of the *status quo*, but a rather different *status quo*. The working out of this process is the concern of this book.

Between transitions, Conservatives established a firm accommodation to the new *status quo*. It was an accommodation which included an implicit philosophy, an ethics, a code of politics and administration. Conservative history became a microcosm of British public history as seen from the position of the ruler. And the picture of the ideal ruler changed accordingly between phases, from the world of the Landed Interest to that of the Victorian entrepreneur, and to that of the modern corporate manager or owner. For the squire of the eighteenth century, the land was the nation, and ownership of land was the most important single qualification for the leadership of society. For the entrepreneur, his leadership depended not upon land, but upon his ability to secure an increase in output from limited resources, upon his constant drive to minimize costs and maximize output, on his 'flair', his 'risk-taking', his 'enterprise' (a term which came to describe the system within which entrepreneurs operated). But for the managerial business-man – in public or private corporations – his claim to authority rests not upon his ability to gamble or even to work hard, but upon his claimed expertise, his training, education and experience (so that seniority is important), attributes which presuppose not a jungle in which the pioneer, if given enough freedom, can cut out a clearing for himself, but settled and established hierarchies with niches appropriate to the organiza-tion man. The attributes of the ideal leader change in each period, from a stress on culture and leisure, on wisdom acquired in meditative communion with soil and season; to an emphasis on the qualities required to survive in conditions of rapid social change, on the autonomy of 'the individual' who is his own absolute guide, needs no external authority to shape his actions, and who can, out of anarchy, win triumph for the greatest number; to focus on the talents required of those working in large organizations, whose status is explicitly defined in detail within a clearly delineated hierarchy of authority.

In practice, each view was never unequivocally accepted in its respective phase of British history. There were large organ-izations and hierarchies under entrepreneurial capitalism; small businesses continue today. Each of the stable phases had its own conflicts, and in part, some of these conflicts were reflected within the Conservative party. Yet these were not conflicts simply over details. They implied wider disagreements. The language of ordinary politics does not provide a termino-logy accurate or specific enough to identify these wider dis-agreements. Yet for our purposes they must be identified. 'Conservative' is too blunt a term to characterize the different strands of party opinion, particularly in time of crisis when the implicit divergences became explicit and so linked with much wider conflicts. Throughout this account, a series of related dichotomies recur – freedom and order, competitive and functional or co-operative industrial organization, individual-ism and collectivism, conflict and harmony. The first term in each pair can quite directly be related to the core of the nineteenth-century Liberal position, and in particular to the concept of a free competitive market. The second term in each pair cannot be related, with anything like the same ease, to an explicit theory of society and political economy, except if we step outside Britain and consider views developed by other European groups on the Right. This is a legitimate procedure once we see the common process of change affecting all advanced industrial countries in the inter-war years. The problems which created confusion and anxiety among Conservatives in Britain in the 1920s and 1930s were derived from sources which afflicted other industrialized countries, and promoted very similar responses. The responses were usually in direct conflict with the prescriptions of Liberalism.

In this account, the contrast to Liberal thought is identified as corporatism. But even this identification does not accurately capture at least two major separate emphases. On the one hand, radicals saw the State as the main agency for the functional reorganization of society, and stressed the forced expansion of the economy; on the other, many businessmen argued that they themselves should be in charge of the creation or maintenance of the 'corporate society' and were more interested in conserving what they had than forcing expansion. Here these two separate emphases are identified as *'étatiste* corporatism' and 'pluralist corporatism'. The precise content of these terms and their implications will be explored at greater length later in this book.

The framing of terms in this way gives a misleading clarity to what, in practice, is much less clear. Most of the individual members of the Conservative party were consistently neither Liberals nor corporatists; on different occasions, they proposed measures consistent with one or the other major viewpoint, without being necessarily aware of their own inconsistency. Inconsistency it was, for the prescriptions of each position were mutually exclusive and muddle was a method which could achieve the worst of each alternative. The same conflicts arose in other industrialized countries, and the same confusion of purpose produced similar criticisms. The measures associated with the National Industrial Recovery Act in the United States prompted the comment that: 'Such a program might be logically inconsistent and economically harmful. Perhaps, as one critic suggested at the time, it combined the worst features of both worlds, "an impairment of the efficiency of the competitive system without the compensating benefits of rationalized collective action".'[2]

In the inter-war period contradictory responses can be seen with the greatest clarity, but even after the Second World War, the same questions recurred in a different form. The evolution of the industrial structure, the problems generated by the disentanglement of the British economy from its imperial possessions and from a peculiar world economic role, the dual threats of external rivalry and internal challenge, sustained a basic context for Conservative action which entailed the repetition of the same themes as before. The prosperity of the post-war years made the more general questions seem less important, and the coalition character of the Conservative party inhibited serious discussion of what kind of society was being created in Britain. Yet what had been considered on occasions at a general level before the war became more and more important for the detail of policy after the war.

The account which follows tries to describe and explain the changes in Conservative economic thought in the post-war years up to 1964. The scene is set in an introductory study of Conservative thought before 1945, starting with an account of what is called Liberal-Conservatism in the last years of the nineteenth century. This account suggests that the dominant political ideas of the Conservative party up to 1948 continued the main Conservative emphases of the 1930s. But between 1948 and the late 1950s, the party became increasingly influenced by a recreation of certain elements of economic Liberalism. From the late 1950s, the party swung back to a selection of some of the ideas it had abandoned in 1948. The changes were not simply changes in Conservative ideas, but were, rather, broad changes in British political opinion. The changes were as evident – although on a different time scale and with different results – in the drawn-out reappraisal carried out by the Labour leadership as they were in the Conservative party. Of the complex economic, social and political relationships which men identify as the structure of society, certain areas were most decisive for the reappraisal: the State, public ownership, the relationship of government and business to organized labour, and of government to business. Neither party was unequivocal in its attitude, and indeed, neither could in general be unequivocal without taking into account many other circumstances. For the British economy, the international economic scene laid down external priorities which heavily determined the options available to the British Government. However, there were options, and discrimination between them was possible. The absolute pragmatist and the absolute diehard are the inventions of people who are neither, for neither can exist. The pragmatist may choose to conceal his priorities (or, indeed, he may not be aware of his priorities); the diehard behaves in ways and circumstances which inevitably reveal a flexibility not present in his rhetoric (and he may also be unaware of his flexibility). The terms are the stuff of political abuse, rather than categories of analysis. The Conservatives had a limited range of pragmatism with certain, usually unspecified, priorities. The book that follows is an attempt to identify those priorities.

PART I
The Background

I

Liberal-Conservatism

After the repeal of the Corn Laws (1846), the Conservative party was constructed out of the debris of the Tory party. The creation of Conservatism was the result of two related processes: the absorption of Liberal ideas by the aristocratic leaders of the party, and the movement towards a more limited version of Liberalism by increasing numbers of businessmen. The marriage created Liberal-Conservatism.

The role of Disraeli in preparing the ground for this somewhat unlikely evolution can hardly be overestimated.[1] He led the embattled squires of England in their last defensive action against the rise of industrial middle-class power, and then, with consummate opportunism, joined the victors and set about making the new Conservative party an accommodating home for the 'oligarchy of capital'.[2] Having fought one battle to retain protection for the Tories – to retain a tariff on corn imports – he became a defender of free trade.

Disraeli was not alone. No member of the traditional Church of England gentry himself, there were members who followed, tolerated and even encouraged his lead; who abandoned the class of their youth and embraced their old enemies. It was Lord Derby as unchallenged leader of the party who protected Disraeli and eased the continued reform of the party. In 1848 he reintroduced the word so hated by older Tories, 'Conservative'. And his 1849 programme made only marginal concessions to agriculture, the landed interest, to compensate for the abandonment of protection. However, he was a moderate, and restrained Disraeli's demand that free trade be made a party plank (Disraeli's first budget was cheered by the Opposition).

Yet the party could not just wait. It needed a social basis to

23

replace the declining landed interest. Given the Liberal party's monopoly of the middle-class vote, only the lower-middle class remained as new recruiting ground for the Conservatives.[3] The Tories had opposed the 1832 reform and most other attempts to broaden the suffrage, yet now Derby – urged on by Disraeli – began to move towards further reform. Derby's second ministry fell attempting constitutional reform, and his third, despite much opposition within the party, accomplished it. Just before that achievement, the *Quarterly Review*, on behalf of the opposition within the party, promised that 'the Conservatives would forfeit every shred of title to the name which they assume, if they tamper one moment with democracy'.[4]

Lord Salisbury, very definitely an aristocrat, came to play a role not dissimilar to that of Derby. He had opposed the 1867 Reform Bill and resigned from the Derby ministry in protest. But the experience tempered his politics with pessimism and a belief that the trends he witnessed were inevitable.[5] He came to accept that the industrial middle classes should consolidate their power, at least within British political life if not necessarily within the Conservative party itself. His language displayed the terminology of individualism; his views embraced free trade and domestic *laissez-faire*. He even came to accept the desirability of further extensions of the suffrage; he co-operated with the Liberals over reform in 1884.[6]

Disraeli had retained in his programme a stress on the use of the State for an extension of specific popular welfare facilities. This element, derived, it was said, from a Tory tradition, briefly differentiated the two parties, since the Liberals, at least in principle, argued that State welfare provisions circumscribed the freedom of the individual, his ability to help himself. Later in the century, the roles of the two parties tended to become reversed, with the Liberals moving towards advocating State welfare facilities (like the Conservatives earlier, in search of a popular social basis for the party) and Conservatives opposing. By then, the Conservatives were recruiting formerly Liberal businessmen.

In office, Salisbury formally pledged his party to Disraelian welfare aims. But in practice, he devoted himself – as Disraeli had done – to foreign and imperial affairs, and his commitment to welfare was in fact both lukewarm and qualified by a Liberal emphasis on the virtues of self-help – the aid of the State was applied, he said, to encourage independence and thrift. As he grew older, the businessmen who had previously provided a basis for radical Liberalism grew more concerned at the dangers of reform, and, like Salisbury himself, more conservative. The 'classes' that supported the Conservatives, Salisbury advised Lord Randolph Churchill, did not welcome innovation; Conservative legislation must accordingly be conducted 'at less speed, and a lower temperature than our opponents. Our Bills must be tentative, cautious, not sweeping and democratic.'[7] Unlike Disraeli, Salisbury accepted that the Liberals were, and would continue to be, more popular and more radical.

Salisbury's views were not at all clearly differentiated from those of moderate Liberals. He accepted the measuring rod of the 'individual'; and he accepted a changing society; incentives and self-improvement were important. Salisbury offered what was appropriate to an investing, rather than a landowning, audience: 'confidence', 'non-interference' by the State,[8] and no ideological eccentricities. He believed, he said, 'there are no absolute truths or principles in politics'.[9] The defence of the *status quo* was the defence of property, and all property, not just land. The State, for Burke the most important pillar of Christian morality, had become for Salisbury little more than an agency to defend property, an agency which could be used by the wrong people to pillage property. As in a joint stock company, the largest shareholders should control the concern.[10]

During Salisbury's long tenure as leader of the Conservative party, two important individuals offered a challenge to his definition of Conservatism: Lord Randolph Churchill, like Salisbury, an aristocrat; and Joseph Chamberlain, a businessman and the most distinguished former Liberal to cross over to the Conservatives. Both, in different ways, furthered the extension of middle-class power within the party, and further enhanced the creation of a Liberal-Conservatism.

Lord Randolph Churchill was not particularly important for Conservative government, but is significant as a legend in modern Conservatism. He was also more important within the party than without. For he gathered together the new and growing middle-class membership and led its attack on traditional aristocratic control of the party. In July 1884, at Sheffield, his supporters gained control of the National Union. This victory, Churchill commented, proved that 'the Tory party of today is no longer identified with that small and narrow class which is connected with the ownership of land'.[11] It was a sign of the times that the class defended by Burke and by Bolingbroke, the Country party, should have become 'small and narrow'.

Churchill was Conservatism's Grey, and his success, its domestic 1832. The platform created in this struggle, Tory democracy, was a combination of internal party demands and a reiteration of the Disraelian claim that Conservatism must find a popular base from which to defend the *status quo*; the cement to hold the base together was a popular welfare programme. But Churchill's Tory democracy needed a limited franchise, since – with universal suffrage – Conservatism perforce had to 'trust the people'. Democracy, for the Fourth party, denoted attention to 'the people', rather than control by the ruled. It did not entail action to secure universal suffrage: Churchill's programme did not include this. He opposed the Liberal reform plans of 1883 (plans Salisbury accepted). 'Tory Democracy', Churchill explained, 'is a democracy which supports the Tory party.'[12]

The welfare elements in his programme received more sustained attention, grouping together a variety of proposals put forward by members of the party at the time. The programme broadly followed the lines of Disraeli's *sanitas sanitatum*,[13] and was, Churchill said, 'a scheme of social progress and reform . . . (embracing) a social revolution which, passing by and diverting attention from wild longings for organic change', would cover elements of public health, housing standards, national insurance and public amenities.[14] However, the closer Churchill came to power, the more modest became his aspirations. His 1885 programme was explicitly limited, emphasizing administrative competence and measures possible in so far 'as the laws of political economy may permit'.[15] It was this element of Peelite efficiency which was most prominent in his tenure in office, and indeed he resigned over the Gladstonian issue of restraining public expenditure, rather than expanding it to encompass new public welfare responsibilities. Out of office, his demands were again more radical, and at one stage he went so far as to suggest a new national party – with Chamberlain – which might, among other things, foster social reform.

Churchill's ambivalence on reform arose partly because of the shifting significance of Conservatism. Disraeli had argued that Conservatives could survive and be popular if they promoted nationalism and popular welfare. Implicitly, Conservatism would then be supported by a wider mass of the population; explicitly, if there were more support Conservatives ought to promote the extension of the suffrage. But in fact it was the Liberal party which needed to pursue this course of action as the years of the century wore on. The Conservatives were able to lift, not the Liberal clothes (though much of those changed hands also), but many of the rank and file Liberals themselves, the business 'middle classes' who, having attained social pre-eminence, were now growing increasingly conservative. Their conservatism was strengthened both by the growth of domestic challenge – the spread of trade unions, for example – and by increasing foreign competition. Yet such men were still radical enough to respond to Churchill's brand of radicalism, directed at the 'aristocratic oligarchy' which controlled the party. Churchill's ambivalence on reform was one element in the creation of a Liberal-Conservatism, although contrary to what he believed, it was a retreat from, rather than an advance towards, Disraeli's purposes.

The monopoly of world manufacturing, which had been the basis for British free trade, and the optimism and security which went with it, was coming to an end in the last quarter of the nineteenth century. In sectors of heavy production, Germany and the United States overtook Britain in the 1890s. The effects of these changes on domestic political assumptions were far-reaching. The Liberal party, heir to the tradition of economic freedom and opposition to State intervention, began to move towards what seemed to be, by the standards of the time, extreme *étatiste* involvement in the economy and the lives of 'individuals'. The party of Bentham and James Mill, who had lauded the sober reasonableness of the 'middle estate', after the turn of the century adopted a radical rhetoric that seemed to differ little from the stereotype of socialism, and seemed deliberately designed to secure popular, rather than middle-class, support. The Conservatives, who claimed to adhere to a more positive conception of the State, a more consistent demand for strong authority, who claimed to defend the monarchy and constitution, nevertheless adopted a position of diehard resistance to State intervention; in Ireland sought to suspend the Army Act and foment the armed resistance of a minority to the will of the State; urged reform of the constitution to permit a referendum and sponsored a bill to limit the prerogative of the Crown. The Conservatives felt themselves to be faced by a profound challenge, a challenge that threatened the survival of their *pied noir* Anglo-Irish supporters, for example. Faced by such a challenge, much of the rhetoric was stripped from the bone. The constitution became merely another variable in a bitter struggle for power.[16]

For the Conservatives, the times presented two major problems. Externally, the rise of powerful economic rivals to British power rendered the past priorities of free trade less and less effective in sustaining British supremacy. At home, there were signs of a growing industrial, and then political, challenge from the working class. The external problem narrowed itself down to the question of how the traditional Liberal economic philosophy could be modified to 'safeguard' industry against foreign imports in Britain and in the Empire. The second problem was exacerbated by the Liberal appeal to popular radicalism; so that defeating the working-class challenge became defeating the Liberals, defeating their rapid divergence towards 'socialism'.

For the first problem, Tariff Reform was the euphemistic means to qualify free trade. But it also gathered up diverse other aims, which assisted in meeting the second problem. Discriminating against imports into the British Empire would give the Empire some distinct economic form, knitting the imperial territories more closely into dependence upon Britain. Second, a tariff on some imports would give British competitors not only a more secure home market but also a powerful bargaining counter in negotiations with foreign rivals to share markets abroad; this factor affected only some industries or activities, and others – for example, banking, cotton, shipping, merchanting, commodity dealers – consistently opposed protection.[17] Third, and most important for radical Conservatives, the revenue derived from tariff reform could be used to finance social reform without raising domestic taxation; and after the inflation in expenditure during the Boer War, this was a vital consideration.[18] The vague outline of a coherent anti-Liberal position was emerging, a social imperialism.

It was certainly not apparent to most Conservatives in the first instance that tariff reform had this significance. But a central postulate of economic Liberalism could not be amended 'pragmatically' without threatening the entire structure, without – at least, implicitly – creating either a contradictory viewpoint, Liberal-Conservatism, or an explicitly anti-Liberal one. If many Conservatives did not necessarily see the implications of the issue, they were certainly not unanimous in supporting tariff reform. Indeed, the external challenge did not become grave enough to force protection until long after the first discussions of tariff reform.

Joseph Chamberlain, the unlikely heir to Tory radicalism in Salisbury's Conservative party, was ideally suited to lead the campaign for tariff reform. He was specifically from the business middle classes, and his politics unified the colourful rhetoric of imperialism, of social reform without cost, and security to harassed businessmen. His own interests were in social reform and imperialism. What is more, his 'free-trade convictions, even . . . (in his youth) were . . . only skin-deep. . . . *Au fond*, he looked at the problem from the manufacturer's point of view, which welcomes a tariff as an instrument of monopoly.'[19]

The tariff reformers campaigned hard, and, despite the electoral disaster to the party in 1906, succeeded in gaining endorsement from the conference of the National Union in 1907.[20] But Balfour chose to resist this pressure, for tariff reform entailed tariffs on food imports from outside the Empire. Led by the Liberals, popular opposition to taxes on foodstuffs made the demand for protection an impossible one for electoral purposes.

So far as the Liberal programme for social reform was concerned, the Conservatives offered moderate opposition, reserving their full opposition for the financial implications. Earlier, Conservatives had proposed many of the measures now promoted by the Liberals, without raising the question of how the reforms were to be financed. The financial question – the old Liberal 'laws of political economy' – now determined how far the Conservatives were to be reformers. But what really evoked a major storm were the constitutional changes proposed by the Liberals to secure the passage of their reforms through the House of Lords. The controversy over Southern Ireland brought all these matters to a head, driving many Conservatives into their last ditch stand.

The end of Balfour's leadership formally acknowledged what Tory democracy had supposedly striven for. Andrew Bonar Law, a Scottish-Canadian iron-master, replaced him as leader of the English landed party. Bonar Law, it was said, cared little for what were supposed to be the traditional concerns of the party,[21] including the 'mere decline of aristocratic power'. Only two issues in British politics excited him: Ulster and tariff reform.[22] His view of the Constitution was almost a *realpolitik* one: it was either useful for the Conservatives or dispensable.[23] In general, he thought social reform an 'unprofitable line' to pursue,[24] but that the rights of property were a touchstone in political questions.[25]

Liberal-Conservatism stood revealed in its least attractive form. There was little mention now of the organic society nor of the responsibilities of the rich and powerful. The Individual dominated the Conservative view. And the Individual was a peculiarly upper-class person. He was endowed with 'property', over which his rights, as an Individual, must be supreme; the rights of the collection of Individuals, the propertied minority, were of more importance than the constitution, the State, the organic society or some British tradition.[26] Society owed its duty and loyalty to the propertied minority, without whom society as such would dissolve once more into barbarism. And society consisted not in other 'Individuals', but in the 'masses' who, in not having property, had no rights except those voluntarily bestowed upon them by the propertied. It seemed almost as if the majority were outside the nation altogether. Since property was always under threat from barbarism below, the limits of State action and of reform required more emphasis than any potential benefits. Nor was it correct to deplore the ravages of the market, and seek to ameliorate its social effects. For the market established value; it was the source of our estimates of value; it could not itself be challenged upon ethical grounds without thereby jeopardizing the nature of existing society. It was just such a view that the young Disraeli fought with such vigour as all that was worst in Liberalism: the apotheosis of the greed of the industrial middle classes.

The defence of the *status quo* in Liberal-Conservatism appeared to have become wholly negative, suggesting the narrowed room for manœuvre once the Liberals pressed ahead with social reform. The fear that social revolution was not far distant became dominant in Conservative minds.[27] The principles which were supposed to guide Toryism and Liberalism dissolved in a purely opportunistic defence of those who held property. It constituted hanging on, merely surviving, without attempting to shape society or convince the governed that their lot was the best that could be humanly secured. The State, formerly seen as the guarantor of property and order, now seemed to have become a direct threat to property. The constitution, it seemed, inhibited the proper defence of property, and it must therefore be changed or abandoned if 'society' was to survive. The aura of Toryism had faded in the harsh light of capitalism at high noon. The amendments to Liberalism which the Conservatives permitted made it no intellectual substitute for what had been lost. Liberal-Conservatism combined Liberal rhetoric with an opportunistic defence of property. 'Free competition', the guarantor of efficiency and prosperity in the original Liberal scheme, was becoming 'limited or fair competition', the guarantor of nothing except the rights of existing owners; egalitarian harmony was becoming inegalitarian 'equilibrium'; extending the suffrage to all individuals was becoming limiting the suffrage to exclude the dangerous masses and so protect the minority of Individuals. The phrases became convoluted with unspoken exceptions and qualifications, which in sum contradicted the original concepts.

2

Capitalism: Old and New

The difficulties facing Conservatives before 1914 were only the heralds of even graver troubles. The First World War at least solved one range of problems. It temporarily beat back the challenge of external rivals, and it applied a scourge to domestic critics. But if, before the war, there were people who challenged the system, the system itself seemed sound. After the war, it seemed to be the structure itself which was crumbling, and which went on and on crumbling. There could be no satisfaction that each disaster was the last. There seemed always to be worse to come. And even if the revolutionary spirits of workers had been cowed by the magnitude of the disasters, they would not long be kept at bay if the system did indeed continue crumbling. Only a second world war offered unity of purpose and coherent direction to a stagnating society. Catastrophe offered an exit from the disasters of the transition of capitalism.

The two threats to the *status quo* – external and internal – which had plagued Liberal-Conservatism with increasing severity from the last quarter of the nineteenth century, reached a point where Conservatives were forced to undertake measures apparently in contradiction to what had seemed to be their basic assumptions. But even then the effects were only temporary or mild, for the basic problem required an international solution. The problems facing Conservatives certainly had a peculiar national form, but in one way or another they faced all industrialized countries. And the national solutions adopted by each country only tended to worsen the problems of its rivals.

Businessmen themselves attempted, both with and without the assistance of the State, to secure their own survival. But just as national successes tended to make the international problems more acute, so the success of one firm in stabilizing its own position tended to export its difficulties to its competitors and to the national economy. But the successes, such as they were, did slowly begin to change the shape and appearance of the economy, rendering it more and more remote from the model which had been the centrepiece of Liberal thought. The trends towards cartel organization of markets, developing on an *ad hoc* basis in certain important British industries from the 1870s, now accelerated. Production was concentrated, not through the economic logic of the market so much as the political or administrative co-ordination of competition by the competitors, through trade associations, agreements – national and international – to divide markets and share facilities. At home, the aim of such measures was to unify British producers, to create a common front to resist the encroachment of imports and wage a united attack on foreign markets.

At each stage, however, the attempt by some businessmen to control their domestic rivals was radically weakened by the continuation of tariff-free entry for foreign goods to the home market. Local producers had only a very limited incentive to accept the 'discipline' of industrial organization while the foreigner could scoop the home market. In such circumstances, moves towards industrial organization seemed to the smaller producers merely means by the large to eliminate their local rivals, to establish a monopoly at home. As a result, the 'rationalization' of British industry – what was seen as its opportunity to survive – depended upon the success of efforts to achieve protection. And the introduction of protection depended upon the State, upon convincing the government of the day to end free trade. To survive, business had to become involved in politics in a much more extensive way, had perhaps to compel the politicians to accept the high electoral price of a tax on food imports.

Yet even without involvement in the State, important long-term changes in economic structure were taking place. A range of new industries (or what for our purposes here were 'new'), founded just before or after the turn of the century, expanded steadily throughout the inter-war period until they displaced in economic importance what had been the main industries of the preceding phase of the economy. Slump most severely afflicted the older industries – coal, shipbuilding, iron and steel, cotton; the disasters of those industries were the disasters of the British economy. But the newer industries – motors, electrical equipment and radio, chemicals, petro-chemicals, and synthetic materials, oil and parts of light engineering – were often already in part protected from foreign competition by patents or 'safeguarding' duties on infant industries. In time, important differences emerged between new and old. The new utilized a much more advanced technology, and depended much more upon systematic technological innovation. The labour force necessarily was different; it expected and received different rates of return. The units of production, after an initial stage – and sometimes even in the initial stage – tended to be much larger, a greater proportion of production was concentrated in the hands of a few producers. And related to the technological level and the concentration of production, the capital base of such industries was much greater, and grew much more rapidly. But the differences were not merely in terms of the methods of production, for the market priorities were also different. The output of the new, more sophisticated and highly priced, was increasingly suitable for sale on a large scale only in other industrialized countries. The world division of labour of the nineteenth century between relatively poor primary producers and rich manufacturers was directly threatened by the expansion of the new industries, whose orientation was increasingly towards other advanced economies, rather than to the empire or to backward countries.

The increasing size of firms in the newer industries had yet other implications. For power became increasingly vested in small groups, at first the larger shareholders (most often, the nominees of financial institutions, rather than individual owners of stock), but later also including professional managers. The power of the mass of small individual shareholders tended to decline within the firm. But it also declined in society at large; for fierce competition abroad stimulated efforts to increase the rate of domestic investment. Traditionally, Britain had been a source of funds for her competitors although this was of limited significance in the 1920s. The profit – and so the power – of the *rentier* derived from the complete freedom accorded to the international flow of capital funds by the Gold Standard. The end of the Gold Standard robbed the system of the guaranteed security of value for international capital flows; and further measures by the State forced domestic funds into domestic industry. Whatever the priorities of the world market, national capitalism was forced upon the *rentier*. The other side of the coin to that misleading phrase, 'the managerial revolution', was 'the euthanasia of the *rentier*'. As the managers in practice had no simple hegemony of power, so the *rentiers* were not suffocated.

The changes summarized here in an over-simplified form were complex and far-reaching. The need to influence the State grew, and the new aggregations of economic power were better placed to influence the State. The 'growth' industries were partly preserved from the miseries of contraction which faced the older industries and so the economy as a whole. Expansion permitted a more liberal and experimental labour policy (assisted by the problems of union organization in expansive new industries). The size of firms, in some cases their quasi-monopoly position, their dependence on very large concentrations of capital, reduced their 'flexibility' in relationship to fluctuations in the economy – a 'flexibility' permitted to some of the older industries by disastrous variations in the labour force – and necessitated much more elaborate planning and forecasting within the firm. It made such firms also much more interested in State planning, in the overall regulation of the economy so that the planning of the firm could not be rendered ineffective by marginal changes in Government policy. The firms of newer industry, by reason of their growth, could much more clearly perceive the possibility of prosperous stability, could afford optimism and experiment. Their own operations seemed to testify to the merits of large-scale organization, the benefits of monopoly, of functional rather than competitive relationships to the market. Of course, 'new' and 'old' were not always distinct; steel moved from one to the other, and after some hesitation, so did shipbuilding.

Already the dim outlines of an alternative conception and justification of capitalist society were emerging. For although most businessmen in newer industry did not necessarily see themselves as making a revolution, did not see themselves as being anything more than 'pragmatic' in relationship to their inheritance of Liberalism, their amendments constituted a radical rejection of Liberalism. In the transition from Victorian to modern capitalism, two separate conceptions of industrial society, its structure and rationale, emerged: what was left of Liberalism, founded upon the conception of a free market; and a viewpoint based upon the rejection of a free market. The control of the State was critical for the advance of both sides. The Liberal-Conservatives wanted the State both to inhibit its intervention and as a means to compensate them for losses incurred in the market. Their opponents, also in many cases calling themselves Conservative, wanted the State as the agency which would force the reorganization of industry, would direct and plan a national economy. At its crudest, 'individualism' competed with 'collectivism'.

I. THE WAR ECONOMY, MARK I

The conception of a 'functional' organization of the economy was very much a child of war. Two world wars had a decisive impact upon the shape of Western economies. And the inter-war period in Britain was much concerned with unlearning and then relearning the lessons of the war economy. For the First World War offered the model of a capitalism strikingly different from the Liberal view. The measures taken were *ad hoc* and partial, stumbling pragmatism, but what had been achieved at the end was something that seemed quite new. If the blind economic demands of war could achieve this, many post-war radicals argued, how much more ought to be achieved in conscious response to the demands of slump?

State intervention in the First World War developed slowly. But towards the end of the war, the State had succeeded in co-ordinating for the first time the most important sectors of the economy in order to maximize war production.[1] The changes in economic practice received little analysis at the time, but that 'Business as Usual' had been successfully superseded was itself an important step in a different direction.[2]

In particular, the railways attracted sustained attention. They were finally combined and controlled, the Government guaranteeing profit margins. Cotton and jute trading were completely taken over. Even in insurance, the State assumed the major role.[3] By 1918, the Ministry of Munitions – created in 1915 – had become the largest national employer. The State produced the major part of national output.

The State relied throughout on the co-operation of businessmen. Co-operation was usually offered freely (since this guaranteed capacity production and relatively high profits),[4] but if it was refused, it could usually be secured by a mixture of persuasion, pressure or sanctions (for example, the refusal by the State to supply essential raw materials). But pressure was not often required, for the Government was at pains to preserve normal economic incentives, to disturb the structure of business as little as possible. It staffed its control agencies with businessmen; a major shipowner was shipping controller, an important grocer, food controller. Yet inevitably the State treated different firms in different ways. Its purchases went in the first instance to the producers who could guarantee the largest supply. As a result, it was the largest firms which benefited most. And the State was not notably critical about the organization of production and the price of output.

Labour control was an essential element in Government operations, particularly since the war boom along with the drain on manpower into the armed forces created something of a labour scarcity. Indeed, it was said that business was only controlled at all in order to regulate labour.[5] The trade unions were drawn into consultation, although this did not confer any right of permanent consultation.[6] Consultation, appeal and coercion eroded trade union control of standards, in return for a State-sponsored arbitration system. The Government did not seek to institute wage control, although it exercised powerful influence over wage levels to offset the effects of labour scarcity.

The experience of the war powerfully informed proposals for the post-war 'Reconstruction'. In 1916, a committee was appointed to study industrial relations. The Whitley Reports[7] did not propose the creation of a free market in which labour and capital should compete with whatever strength they had for the highest rate of return. They proposed instead the maximum possible co-operation and consultation at all levels of industry between employers and employed. In addition, there should be statutory wage regulation in all 'badly organized' industries, a permanent national arbitration tribunal, and power to a Ministry of Labour to inquire into, and publish reports on, industrial disputes, giving 'an independent and authoritative account of the matters in difference'.[8] Before the end of the war, there were some twenty Joint Industrial Councils in existence. Of the other reconstruction proposals, only two reached the statute book. Labour was rewarded for its loyalty in war with an extension of the suffrage and the Fisher Education Act.

The economic impact of the war was much greater than the State's innovation in industrial organization, for the external prospects of the economy had been rendered much worse. Foreign markets had been lost. The imperial trading links had been allowed to languish. Production – pre-eminently cotton, for example, in India and China – had been allowed to expand to a point where the British could hardly compete on the old scale. At home, the old basic industries had been vastly over-expanded by the demands of war production, had worked obsolescent machinery to the full. After the war, unemployment and high cost production, as industry contracted, threatened the performance of the British economy. Yet if war had exacerbated the condition of older industry, it had stimulated newer industry and protected it from foreign competition.

The dependence of the State upon larger companies, its need to co-ordinate whole industries and the enforced protection of domestic production, all accelerated the trends towards business concentration. And the post-war contraction carried off, in the first instance, the smaller producers rather than the larger. Government policy during the war also became increasingly self-conscious. It assisted in the creation of private associations to control industries. Scarce credit encouraged, and inflation made it possible for, firms to finance their own investment programmes out of large profits, and this also encouraged firms to pool resources and relieve their dependence upon outside sources of finance. After the war, Government factories were sold, again most often to the largest firms.

The trends in business concentration seemed to be vindicated by the record levels of production. Indeed, the benefits of size and non-competitive production seemed to many incontestable. Runciman, a member of the Coalition Cabinet, attributed the success of the war effort to just this organization and industrial co-ordination.[9] Yet, even so, there were many who were dissatisfied with the trends. The alarm was sufficient to prompt the creation of a standing committee in 1918 to examine business concentration. The report concluded that oligopolistic trends existed widely in the British economy and would soon 'control all important branches of British trade'.[10]

2. BETWEEN THE WARS: THE INTERREGNUM

The price of the First World War continued to be paid in the 1920s in the lost hours of adult workers and the constrained consumption of their families. The Great Depression ending this period of stagnation seemed to many to be the *coup de grâce*. It made impossible the previous strategy of trying to return the British economy to its 1914 position, and suddenly crystallized policy and aspirations, although still somewhat half-heartedly, in quite new and anti-Liberal directions.

The old basic industries were particularly reduced by the fluctuations of the 1920s, but even then they were not protected against foreign competition until the events of 1931 swept away the aspiration to free trade. The weight of these industries in the economy curtailed expansion even at times of modest boom. The high cost of production assisted in the steady relative decline of British exports: up to 1929, Cole estimates the absolute decline in British exports at 17 per cent.[11] But the severity of misfortune did not, despite sustained efforts (in coal, shipbuilding, and steel), produce the forms of self-reorganization in the older industries which, it was said, would end the decline. On the other hand, motors and electrical equipment, for example, remained fiercely competitive, and also unable to establish effective price agreements. It was true

39

COMPETITION AND THE CORPORATE SOCIETY

that the larger producers in older industry continued to maintain a vital interest in the decisions of the State, but without protection from imports they could only with difficulty persuade entire industries to collaborate. Much of their energy was directed at influencing the new Federation of British Industries. Formed in 1917, by the 1930s the FBI had become the largest body of its kind in the world and established itself as the authentic voice of British business, represented on Government committees and regularly consulted on a variety of questions.[12] It claimed to have provided the framework for the 1929 Derating Act and to have prompted the introduction of protection in its specific form, the Tariff Advisory Committee.[13]

The Government itself was not averse to assisting reorganization. A 1921 Act compelled the railways to merge into four major – and geographically, not competitively, related – companies. The mines also prompted public intervention, including the provision of Government subsidies to sustain profit margins (or, the argument used to justify it, to keep up wages). But most State intervention of this kind was directed at newer industries where the potential opposition was less because there were fewer producers and so a more favourable political reception. A 1919 Bill empowered the minister to nationalize any electricity unit by Order in Council, and the subsequent Act created State commissioners to co-ordinate the industry. The State merged all existing civil aviation companies in one subsidized public corporation, Imperial Airways. It made broadcasting into a public monopoly. And in 1927, the electricity grid system was nationalized, a measure which evoked backbench opposition.[14] In the case of the older industries, intervention was seen as a once-and-for-all matter, temporary or contingent upon some specific problem. But in the newer industries, the State often determined the model of its future growth in public hands.

In the field of labour, successive governments continued to pursue the aim of co-operation, rather than leaving industrial relations to follow their own logic. Co-operation was envisaged as taking place at all levels, from the plant up to some national, all-industry level. Indeed, even before the First World War, the

40

Liberal Government had temporarily created just such a national, all-industry council.[15] The aspirations behind such attempts were much more persistent than the actual councils created. Somewhere, it seemed, labour and capital would unite their respective corporate bodies in common assembly, and class conflict would be submerged in an overriding concern with something identified as the 'national interest'.[16]

After the war, as part of its execution of the measures implied or recommended in the Whitley Reports, the Coalition Government set up a National Industrial Conference. This body recommended the creation of a permanent council as the government's consultative representative for industry. Accordingly, in 1919 five hundred trade unionists and three hundred employers assembled to formulate proposals to reduce industrial conflict. The Government showed little inclination to accept its views, and with the onset of slump, the pursuit of national collaboration gave way to more immediate problems. In July 1921, the trade union members resigned from the conference.

The coal industry, and the struggle of the miners to stabilize their wages, was the centrepiece of the immediate problems. The undertone of political challenge was a direct threat to the *status quo*. In the early 1920s, backbenchers made numerous attempts to limit statutorily trade union participation in politics.[17] The general strike of 1926 brought these concerns to a head, without resolving them. The general strike made little sense except as the prelude to revolution, yet the TUC saw it as no more than a rather large sympathetic strike. The result was a stalemate, but one which gave the Conservatives the opportunity to pass the 1927 Trade Disputes and Trade Union Act in an attempt to limit political unionism. The passage of the Act acknowledged open conflict rather than co-operation, but in the same year new efforts were made to recreate a mechanism for collaboration. Sir Alfred Mond, an ex-Liberal minister who had become a Conservative, and an industrialist from the most important sector of new industry, chemicals, held talks with representatives of the TUC to foster reconciliation in industry. The Burlington House Conference – the Mond-Turner talks – raised high hopes of a 'new spirit' in industry, or fears of what A. J. Cook called 'National Company Unionism',[18] but nothing concrete emerged. The 'Industrial Parliament' still remained no more than aspiration.

The Depression of 1929 and the ensuing crisis which culminated in the measures of 1931 transformed the situation. In 1931, Britain left the Gold Standard, and introduced extensive protection. The results of protection were not nearly so dramatic for the external balance as had been promised. Between 1931 and 1936, British imports fell by some twelve million pounds, and receipts from import duties increased by seventy-five million pounds or 55 per cent. Exchange control did curb the independent role of finance, and the Government's cheap money policy curtailed its reproduction. In 1928, 60 per cent of available funds went to domestic investment; in 1935, 89 per cent.[19]

However, the curtailment of the stimulus or discipline of the world market raised increasing problems for the domestic economy. If protection made effective the cartelization of industry, and cartels exploited their protected position in the home market, industry would rapidly become monopolized by a few firms and prices would tend to reduce British exports, which in turn would limit the imports required to sustain survival, let alone expansion. To some extent, the Government evaded the problem, at the same time subsidizing some exports and attempting to achieve regulated 'reorganization' of industry. But the Government lacked effective sanctions that it was prepared to use. It was not prepared to tolerate the possible increase in unemployment resulting from the lowering of tariffs in order to discipline home producers. Nor was it prepared to publish and police a set of agreed national objectives which would guide or direct firms in ways consistent with what it saw as the national interest. It was not prepared to plan. And, in any case, it lacked any overriding economic objective of a simplicity and urgency capable of focusing the problems, a set of priorities within which it could order the competing elements of the national economy. Only war had given this central objective, and justified to businessmen the sacrifices in terms of individual initiative required of them.

The Government's first efforts were devoted to establishing tariffs acceptable to the most important sectors of business opinion, and beginning the development of agriculture in order to relieve imports. The Ottawa Imperial Economic Conference was unpromising in the pursuit of 'Empire Free Trade', so that, perforce, the Government had to concentrate on making British protection work.

Making protection work meant using the State to force industrial concentration or co-ordination. State grants and the conditional offer of tariffs were used to try to 'reorganize' home industry. Reorganization remained under the control of the most important businessmen concerned, and while this appeared to aid concentration, it also seemed to be used as a means to restrict production rather than make it cheaper. Steel was an almost notorious example. The Steel Federation of the largest steel producers was created to deal with the Government's Import Duties Advisory Committee (IDAC), and the two established a close partnership which introduced fixed prices for all consumers, the control of capacity to lower output, the subsidization of high-cost production and the control of all development. The resulting inflexibly high prices prompted much criticism from the largest purchasers of steel.[20] Without serious foreign competition, steel producers tended to concentrate on the high price stable domestic market at the cost of exports. The Government, rather than lower tariffs to restore the situation, urged the Federation to join the international steel cartel and establish by negotiation at least a quota of steel exports. As an incentive to the Entente Internationale de l'Acier to accept the Federation's demands, the Government made a temporary increase in the tariff on steel imports to 50 per cent *ad valorem*; once the Federation had joined, the tariff was lowered again.[21]

Efforts were made to reorganize most of the older industries, in particular, shipbuilding, cotton and fishing. Coal, the most bitter symbol of the problems of old basic industry, also symbolized the Government's predicament in offering benefits to an industry before results appeared. The 1929 Labour Government organized quota production in the industry at fixed minimum prices, and a central council to organize the voluntary amalgamation of pits. The commission created to achieve amalgamations almost completely failed in its task in the face of the opposition of the mine owners. To break the deadlock, a Conservative Government in 1938 prepared a bill to nationalize the land on which the mines stood. Long and bitter negotiations, which included a Government offer of a price well above the arbitration valuation of the land, did not persuade the mine owners to accept the bill. The Mining Association, with the support of the major business organizations, campaigned publicly against the bill, and induced some eighty-seven Conservative MPs to refuse the Conservative Whip on the issue. In the event, the Association prompted the Government to accept amendments which neutralized the effect of the nationalization proposals.[22] As if exhausted, the Government refrained from further irritating the mine owners.

In the case of London transport, Labour enforced compulsory amalgamation and created a public monopoly. Two committees examined electricity and gas, and recommended increased State intervention and compulsory reorganization; the two committees were chaired by the chairmen of the two largest private concerns in the country (Sir Geoffrey Heywood of Unilever, and Sir Harry McGowan of ICI). In airways, both the public corporation and a new private rival were subsidized until they were forcibly merged in one State concern in 1939.

The piecemeal innovations revealed a new identification of problems and a disregard for the prescriptions of Liberalism. But they also showed the scale of resistance. The many relatively small-scale producers in older industries were not prepared to be legislated out of existence in favour of their largest rivals, and no amount of pious talk about 'rationalization' and 'self-government in industry' concealed the fact that many would be injured. The opponents of reorganization, defending 'free enterprise' and freedom from State intervention, fought both particular measures, and more general aims like State planning or industrial 'reorganization'.[23]

The Industrial Reorganisation League, which brought together some of the most prominent new industry leaders as well as the largest businessmen in some of the older industries, campaigned to secure Government support for industrial reorganization schemes; if a majority in the industry supported the scheme, the State was to compel the minority to accept it. Parliament was to sanction the procedure by passing an Enabling Bill under which, thereafter, the minister could accept reorganization schemes. In 1934, Harold Macmillan, in the face of the opposition of the platform, secured the agreement of the Conservative Party Conference to a resolution calling for an Enabling Act.[24] In the same year, Henry Mond of ICI, the second Lord Melchett, introduced a Private Member's Bill in the House of Lords to secure an Enabling Act which would cover fifteen major industries.[25]

It still remains to be established how far the consciously directed efforts to reorganize particular industries succeeded, and how far the ordinary working of the economy itself achieved what results there were. But in certain areas, the changes were clear. For example, the coal and shipbuilding industries shrank by a third between 1923 and 1937, and cotton by 28 per cent. Between the same years, electrical engineering and vehicles increased their respective labour forces by over 80 per cent.[26]

The two pressures – from 'free enterprise' and from the 'reorganizers' – found the Government uneasily balanced between. Yet through the 1930s, the Government seemed to lean increasingly towards the second. More might have been possible if the Government had had any clear idea of where it was going, of what central priorities should guide it. As it was, 'rationalization' often seemed no more than outdoor relief for big business.

3. THE END OF THE TRANSITION:
THE WAR ECONOMY, MARK II

The Second World War offered the Government the urgent national priorities it lacked. It also permitted, with great rapidity, the reintroduction of the war economy. The State took up the threads it had relinquished in 1918. And a war economy offered not merely public sanction to cartel and monopoly organization; it punished those who resisted such changes. Much of what remained of overt competition, the discipline of a market, was partly replaced by deliberately functional organization, in which public powers became part of

45

private initiative, and public effort incorporated private production; in which the largest firms assumed public control of entire industries; and in which efforts were made to channel public and private finance to production on output, rather than profit, criteria.

The elaborate structure of controls created in the Second World War welded industry and the State into one whole. The only formal gap in the structure concerned labour. For the Government agreed to try to safeguard trade union authority by not imposing a wage freeze. But the unions fully accepted Government policy for much of the time, so that, like business, the unions seemed also to be part of the system of public administration. Industrial consultation became part of the normal pattern of industrial relations, culminating in a sort of consultative industrial parliament, the National Joint Advisory Council. The unions were also granted privileged access to the Government, and were thus able to influence, for example, the progressiveness of the taxation scale, or the inquiries which culminated in Beveridge's work on social insurance.[27]

War provided the opportunity for reorganization of industry wherever the Government or the largest producers required it, under the auspices of the State and the control of industrialists.[28] Even one of the apparently last strongholds of competition, retail trade, became enmeshed in the structure of trade associations in order to negotiate supplies from the Government.[29] On its side, the Government was entirely dependent on the trade associations which supplied it with the means to wage war.[30] It followed that the resistance to reorganization was eroded by wartime conditions. And as thoughts turned to the post-war order, it was the uncompetitive model that volunteered itself to the minds of many businessmen. In November 1942, for example, some two hundred major industrialists signed *A National Policy for Industry* which recommended a hierarchy of industrial associations under a central council as the organizational plan for the economy after the war. In steel, the young steelmakers' programme accepted that after the war, the Steel Federation must exercise supreme control over all steel production, an aim described in the

Federation's new constitution as 'self-government within the framework of Government policy'.[31]

Part of the explanation for the decline in resistance to plans for reorganization lay in the urgent priorities of war. But it was also true that war drew disproportionately on the output of the new industries. The long phase of growth before and during the period between the wars culminated in very rapid expansion during the Second World War. By 1945, new industry had become the 'commanding heights of the economy', and its ethics and assumptions became much more clearly central to the economy as a whole. The resistance of old industry to its dethronement, even its expropriation by the State, had not disappeared. But it could no longer stand against the tide of change as it had done in the 1930s. Part of the campaign was over, even if it was unclear what form mopping-up operations should take. Of course, for the largest producers in the older industries, there was no question of their elimination. Their interests became slowly disentangled from the mass of their fellow producers, and absorbed into those of new industry. Some, technically, became actually integrated in new industry, as cotton manufacture became increasingly linked to chemicals. Others depended for their consumers upon the now predominant newer industries. One range of issues had been settled.

3

Liberal-Conservatism in Crisis

Two world wars and the 1931 crisis reduced what was left of Liberalism to no more than a shadow. Henceforth, the 'Liberalism' which remained was rather an attitude of generosity and vague progressiveness than heir to a creed which had been remarkable for its intellectual cogency and logical clarity. Without the commitment to free trade, without the interrelated freedom of domestic and world markets, Liberalism lost its primary justification. What before had been thought to flow automatically from the operation of the market – efficiency in production, minimum costs, systematic innovations, consumer sovereignty – now had to be deliberately and consciously introduced if they were to exist at all. What previously had depended upon the 'system', now depended upon the wish, will or perseverance of particular individuals or agencies. Protection and cartelization did not, of course, end competition, but it ended any easy argument that the results of competition – in terms of the growth of some firms and the decline of others – was necessarily in the interests of all. For the giant companies could grow through administrative measures rather than productive efficiency – without foreign rivals constantly curbing the privileges of local monopoly – and the small could disappear, merely because they were small.

1931 is a convenient point of time at which to identify the end of Liberal-Conservatism. For the end of free trade spelled the end of Liberalism. Businessmen who merely resisted the intervention of the State, without opposing protection equally strongly, were not Liberals even though they borrowed the language of Liberalism. Their demand was not one which urged an even more competitive market, it was merely a plea to be left alone to enjoy what they had regardless of any public interest. Indeed, many such businessmen were only too pleased to accept subsidies or subventions from the State where these carried no 'strings', imposed no obligations upon their behaviour. Liberal-Conservatism without free trade constituted little more than a negative defence of the *status quo*, without a positive affirmation of the benefits of competition. Since many Liberal-Conservatives accepted with equanimity the decline of competition, the creation of monopolies or cartels, provided they were left in the unimpeded control of businessmen, we can begin to detect the shadowy outline of a new rationale of the *status quo*. Liberal-Conservatism faded imperceptibly into pluralist corporatism, where the 'corporations' were business firms rather than estates. The critics of this *laissez-faire* position demanded much more conscious and consistent State intervention to curb the dangers to the public interest from the curtailment of competition. But they also accepted the logic of industrial change, the creation of large-scale quasi-monopolies. Their position – and there were many different variations upon the basic theme – is therefore identified as *étatiste* corporatism.

In the 1920s the Conservatives drifted, playing for time in what was not only an apparently hopeless economic situation, but one in which the battle between free traders and protectionists either paralysed the party or destroyed its electoral potential. 1931 at least ended the stalemate over tariff reform. In the 1930s, the Government moved between its pluralist and *étatiste* critics, without satisfying either and without imposing any new coherence or design upon its *ad hoc* measures to reorganize industry. Yet through the 1930s, the Government did appear to be moving slowly towards more deliberate intervention, and the 1938 attempt to nationalize mining royalties showed how far this attempt might go. Backbenchers went much further in denouncing the old model of capitalism, and by comparison with the Labour leaders, some were much more radical in their approach. Whereas Labour claimed that its modest reforms would transform capitalism into socialism, the Conservative radicals claimed that their more radical measures were the only means to ensure the survival of capitalism.

Conservatism in the 1920s was characterized by the man who

led the party for much of the decade. Baldwin, faced with bitter and apparently insoluble problems not only in the world at large, not only within Britain itself, but within the Conservative party, played for time, emphasizing the opinions held in common, the common allegiance of all to some higher purpose – whether it was the rule of law, the nation, or the inheritance of British Conservatism. To survive in conditions where no very persuasive alternatives presented themselves, hanging on with good humour, was perhaps all that was possible for a Conservative leader. It permitted others – for example, the partnership of Neville Chamberlain and Winston Churchill – to get on with the administration. Chamberlain pursued a programme of rationalizing the welfare legislation already passed, and centralizing local government (for example, by the 1928 Local Government Act and the 1929 Rating and Valuation Act), an innovation which led some backbenchers to identify Chamberlain as at heart a Fabian.[1] But intensively as Chamberlain worked, he did not dislodge the impression of lassitude that adhered to the Government. Conservatism fought for essentially anodyne ends – for 'sane common-sense Government' (1924), for leaving things alone (1922),[2] for Safety First (1929).

Part of the explanation for the absence of real innovation lay in the protectionist controversy. It seemed to many that nothing worthwhile could be done until the log jam of free trade had been moved. Before the war, the issue had destroyed one leader of the party; after the war, it destroyed another and very nearly a third. In the 1920s, the protectionist attack was concentrated in three main onslaughts. The first destroyed the Coalition but suffered a severe setback in the 1923 general election. The second, moderated by the relative prosperity between 1926 and 1929, ended in the defeat of the party in the 1929 general election. The third, which nearly dislodged Baldwin from leadership of the party, closed with the 1931 crisis which itself brought in protection.

During the 1920s, different governments extended the *ad hoc* introduction of tariffs, stemming from the 1915 McKenna duties. The 1921 Safeguarding of Industries Act protected parts of newer industry (chemicals, electrical equipment), and in 1925, a committee was created to which industry could appeal for a tariff against 'unfair competition'.[3] By 1929, quite a considerable range of goods had become protected in this way, but in sum, they amounted to only two or three per cent of British imports and did not cover the older, more important and more depressed industries.[4]

No matter what the protectionists did, they seemed unable to dislodge the party leadership's resistance to extensive tariffs. They identified the resistance as the work of the former members of the Coalition or of the Liberal party (like Winston Churchill). Certainly they had seemed to have more success before Churchill assumed importance within the party. The 1920 party conference had pressed for a general tariff, and critics of the Coalition used the Coalition's resistance to the introduction of a general tariff as an argument for the Conservatives leaving it. But the conference was not unequivocally protectionist. In 1921, it seemed as divided as the Liberals had been during the Home Rule controversy of 1886;[5] London and the Home Counties led for protection against the traditionally free trade areas, the North and the Midlands.[6] The following year, Chamberlain was defeated at the Carlton Club, and the Coalition ended. To reunite the party and distinguish it from the Liberals (as well as to pre-empt the possibility of Lloyd George adopting protection for the Liberal party platform, as he had suggested as early as 1912), Baldwin fought the 1923 election on the commitment of the Conservatives to introduce a general tariff. The clear electoral defeat of the party settled the issue for the moment. The Chamberlainites, protesting against the use of the issue in the election, were allowed back into the party by its defeat.

The 1925 Conservative victory at the polls virtually recreated much of the old Coalition, since it included the Chamberlainites and the publicly well-known free trader, Churchill. The Cabinet doomed protectionist hopes. Their pessimism was only further increased by Churchill's reintroduction of the Gold Standard in 1925, a measure which Keynes argued, 'made the market supreme over the industrial system . . . (and) prevented the encroachment of the political government on the industrial system'.[7]

Nevertheless, pressure again built up for an extension of 'safeguarding', and in particular, protection for iron and steel; the industry's application for a tariff had been rejected in 1928.[8]

51

Amery was prominent in the attack, and campaigned at the same time for the removal of Churchill from the Cabinet. In despair he wrote:

> We have cut out small industries (from safeguarding) because they are too small. We have cut out big industries, like iron and steel, because they are too big. We have restricted and twisted the meaning of 'unfair competition' in such a way as to make it impossible to include any of the industries that are left'.[9]

The National Union urged 'more democracy' in the party,[10] and, in July 1928, two hundred MPs petitioned for a discussion of iron and steel in the House. The November party conference urged the maximum safeguarding consistent with existing pledges. To no avail, and Amery was driven to hope that an electoral defeat of the party might dislodge Churchill from it.[11]

The defeat came, and the protectionist attack, no longer restrained by the delicacies incumbent upon the party in office, grew stronger. The financial crisis added sharp edge to the campaign. Some Conservatives formed a separate protectionist party to fight official Conservative candidates,[12] and the leaders of the new party, Lords Beaverbrook and Rothermere, began by attacking Baldwin's 1929 pledge not to increase food taxes. Baldwin himself increased the opposition to his leadership by accepting possible Dominion status for India; the free trade imperialists like Churchill were now opposed to Baldwin. In the event, Baldwin agreed to resign.[13]

Even as the party was in crisis, opposition to protection outside the party was dissolving under the acid of growing economic depression. Bankers urged an extension of imperial trade in August 1930, as did the Associated Chambers of Commerce and that one-time stronghold of free trade, the Manchester Chamber of Commerce. The TUC joined the protectionists, and in October the Federation of British Industries claimed that 96 per cent of its membership favoured protection. But the Commonwealth Conference of the same month held out little hope of a unified imperial 'free trade' which would save free trade faces. Even sections of the Liberal party were now espousing protection: the 'Simonite' Liberals leading, but later followed by Keynes.

Fortunately for Baldwin, his resignation as party leader had been made contingent on the result of a by-election at St George, Westminster. A powerful unofficial candidate was standing against the Conservatives. By some six thousand votes, Baldwin was saved.

The collapse of the Labour Government and the return of the Conservatives to office, at long last settled the tariff reform issue. Within a month, the new Government took Britain off the Gold Standard and began to introduce protection. The power of the free export of capital and the free import of goods now accrued to the State.

For Conservatives, there were few clear guides to assist them in the new era. Liberal terminology, if not Liberal practice, still provided the basic mode of expression, and the world of Conservatives was still inhabited by 'individuals'. But the radicals formulated new qualifications or alternative expressions, part rationalization of the innovations introduced by the Government, part programme for the future. The break in tradition was clear in so far as the Government and its supporters sought 'co-ordinated', 'co-operative' and 'rationalized' industry; praised sheer size in productive units, and denigrated 'cut-throat' competition; at most advocated, and at least accepted, monopoly, oligopoly, deliberate restraints on trade; urged 'self-government for industry', 'planning' by industries and even by the State; and in some cases, pressed the merits of the nationalization of basic industries.* The more romantic

* In the United States, the terminology was even more radically changed:

For a short period . . . New Deal and business spokesmen wrought a virtual revolution in popular symbolism. 'Competition' became 'economic cannibalism', and 'rugged individualists' became 'industrial pirates'. Conservative industrialists, veteran antitrusters, and classical economists were all lumped together and branded 'social Neanderthalers', 'Old Dealers', and 'corporals of disaster'. The time-honored practice of reducing prices to gain a larger share of the market became 'cut-throat and monopolistic price slashing', and those that engaged in this dastardly activity became 'chiselers'. Conversely, monopolistic collusion, price agreements, proration, and cartelization became 'co-operative 'or 'associational' activities; and devices that were chiefly designed to eliminate competition bore the euphemistic title, 'codes of fair competition'.

E. W. Hawley, *The New Deal and the Problem of Monopoly* . . . , Princeton, N.J., 1966, p. 54.

Conservatives, perhaps remembering something of Young England, glimpsed in the new business order a society of hierarchic corporations, a new 'industrial feudalism' where all would be secure.

It was this vision which *The Economist* saw as the apotheosis of Conservative policy in the 1930s. 'We are', it said, 'within measurable distance of setting up a new feudal system, with the British market, instead of British land, parcelled up among the barons.'[14] The Conservatives, it said, had found no middle way between full *étatisme* and *laissez-faire* – 'if *laissez-faire* is ruinous in one way, private monopoly is ruinous in another'.[15] The Conservative programme it described as,

> a set of notions that sees its ideal of an economic system in an orderly organisation of industries, each ruled feudally from above by the business firms already established in it, linked in associations and confederations and, at the top, meeting on terms of sovereign equality such other Estates of the Realm as the Bank of England and the Government. Each British industry, faithful to the prescription, has spent the past decade in delimiting its fief, in organising its baronial courts, in securing and entrenching its holdings and administering the legal powers of self-government conferred on it by a tolerant State.[16]

The Economist remained an isolated voice, loyal to its Liberal origins and thereby eccentric in the new age. More impressive was the slow, sluggish movement of opinion in favour of the new trends. The alarm expressed in 1918 about the growth in 'trusts' gave way to tolerance,[17] or positive approval.[18] Even the Liberals changed their allegiance. Indeed, in the 1920s Keynes had praised the 'socialisation' which he appeared to detect in the growth of 'semi-autonomous corporations'.[19] Two years later, the Liberal party itself, in *Britain's Industrial Future* (1928), called for 'self-governing' industries and the granting of statutory powers to a majority of businessmen in an industry so that they could enforce a collective discipline on the minority. In the 1930s, these scattered observations or recommendations were submerged in activity. Between 1931 and 1948, 'progressive' public opinion remained enamoured with the 'idealogy of Bigness'[20] and sustained almost unlimited faith in the possibilities of State action. Whether public or private – whether nationalized airways or rationalized chemicals – the aims of a functional and integrated monopoly seemed the same. The corporative State seemed to be emerging of its own accord. Indeed, Walter Elliot, a member of the Cabinet, dotted the i's:

> it seems to me to be courting failure to tell people that they have first to dress themselves in black shirts and throw their opponents downstairs in order to get the corporative state. . . . This new economic order has already developed further in England than is generally recognised.[21]

Rank-and-file Conservatives were less assured that the new society was indeed emerging from the old. Their writings – of greater volume than in any other period – are infected with the sense of almost continuous crisis, of apocalypse. The old order was clearly in decay, and the new was not yet clear; revolution might well intervene.

The writers can be divided into those who sought consolation in contemplating past continuities, and those who boldly struck out in new directions, between – as Feiling puts it – 'those whose fathers had followed Salisbury and

> those whose fathers had crossed over with Chamberlain, between men who admired Lloyd George as a second Chatham and men who detested him as a third Jack Cade, between those whose slumber was broken by nightmares of Socialism and those whose policy would not disdain Socialist weapons.[22]

The diagnosis of the nature of the crisis showed the same division. For some, the crisis resulted from bad leadership (corrupted by democracy in some accounts) or the failure of a philosophy (individualism). The antidote lay therefore in a stronger oligarchy of control,[23] in a full critique of democracy, in more power to leadership,[24] or a more powerful State or Monarchy to offset the Commons.[25] At the extreme, measures might have to be undertaken to purge or curb the propensity of the population to resist authority – 'undesirables' must be sterilised,[26] and all disciplined with physical training or service in the armed forces. All agreed that a new morality and a new philosophy must be created to unite society once more.[27]

By contrast, other Conservatives saw the crisis as the result of a breakdown in a particular form of economic organization. It followed that solutions lay in designing a new economic order, in drawing up blue prints.[28] The new organization almost invariably assumed a powerful role for the State within society and the economy, and the corporate organization of industry under professional managers.[29] Just as the State was seen as a neutral force, above the class conflict of society, so also managers were seen as a 'third force' between capital and labour.

If the first group rejected 'collectivism' and planning with vigour, the second powerfully urged both. The former urged balanced budgets and Gladstonian financial management; the latter pressed the case for State control of all investment, State subsidies and investment in industry,[30] the manipulation of interest rates to offset fluctuations[31] in aggregate investment, deficit financing,[32] and counter cyclical taxation; even the nationalization of the Bank of England or industrial insurance.[33] The most radical even went so far as to urge the nationalization of most basic industries, shipping and foodstuffs;[34] one argued that 'the Socialist theory (namely, production of essential commodities for use rather than profit) is being gradually adopted in a practical form by industry itself quite independently of the State,[35] and another that the coal industry 'ought now to be absorbed into the sphere of socialised concerns conducted in the light of wider national considerations – not making its first objective the securing of a profit on its *own* operations but seeking to serve other industries and assist *them* to become profitable.'[36]

In the corporate society, the State had to remain subject to the represented, however. Some writers proposed that an Industrial Parliament should be established, or a representative planning agency where business and the government would meet together; alternatively, more industrial managers should enter the existing Commons. Mond's League of Industry, Petrie's corporatist reform of Parliament, Macmillan's National Industrial Council, Amery's third House of Parliament, Percy's scheme to reform the Commons, all came under this heading.[37]

Industrial monopolies ought to be established throughout the economy. Some writers restricted themselves to praising current cartel and monopoly trends, others urged that statutory powers should be given to industry to compel cartelization or that the State should force amalgamation in order to speed 'the great world movement away from unfettered competition and the conditions of economic anarchy which such competition now brings, towards federation, co-operation and combination'.[38] Harold Macmillan in particular was a tireless advocate of 'industrial reorganization' both in his writings and in his work with Melchett of ICI in the Industrial Reorganisation League.[39]

Trade unions were also to be reorganized into industrial unions, with clear and explicit responsibilities and a defined place in the general corporate structure of industry. Some Conservatives had perceived much earlier the potential role of unions as the organizers of labour for management,[40] as an important instrument of 'self-government in industry'. Now it was proposed that a final bargain be struck with the unions – perhaps offering them the right of a 'closed shop' in return for their agreement to accept certain responsibilities. A Labour charter would summarize this once-and-for-all settlement. It would also outline the means whereby the 'status' of workers could be raised. The relatively new word, 'status', occurred in almost all Conservative writing as the heart of the problem of industrial relations. Status would be guaranteed in an industrial 'partnership', sealed by the attempt to achieve (or, in some writers, the continued maintenance of) a 'property owning democracy'.[41] Indeed, some went so far as to speak of rendering industry consistent with democracy by increasing worker participation in the ownership of capital. Austen Hopkinson carefully qualified this aspiration:

> I see no good reason why he (the capitalist) should not call them (the workers) possessors of the capital if it pleases them; provided he does not surrender to them its control . . . . collective possession of capital means nothing . . . meaning nothing, it can cause no ill effect . . . but

democratic control of capital is a very real thing, and one to be eschewed at all costs.[42]

In almost all cases, Conservatives refused to draw any generalized conclusions about what sort of society they felt should be created or was creating itself. They refused to draw out a general theory which could then be compared and contrasted with the Liberal model rejected. Some did look with approval on foreign experiments, and Petrie explicitly recommended the 'Corporate State' or the 'Ethical State'.[43] But most writers eschewed parallels. They preferred to suggest that what they approved was actually emerging of its own accord and needed no separate and explicit identification. Planning, Macmillan said approvingly, was 'not so much (an idea) among theorists as among those industrialists who see that it is in harmony with what they find it necessary to aim at in the daily conduct of their business'.[44]

But without an explicit analysis, most schemes lacked clear criteria with which to judge actual proposals, and easily degenerated into no more than idle speculation. In particular, the radicals had a bias towards organizational reform. Few sensed the solution which Keynes was to advance, and which hardly required any reorganization of industry (Keynes offered Macmillan a critique of his proposals).[45] Even more, without any general perspective it was difficult to justify the proposals as a whole in terms of the public or popular interest. What 'legitimized' the new society as the unimpeded operation of the market was supposed to legitimize the Liberal model. Macmillan implied that the State would supervise industry, safeguarding consumers and ensuring that the privileges of monopoly were not abused. Popular elections to Parliament to create the Government which would administer the State would then ensure that the popular will was supreme.[46] But, as he admitted, ultimately responsibility for social justice must depend upon the social conscience of those who administered industry. For him this was not problematic for, he argued, 'From my own knowledge of the managerial class in industry, I am confident that in the overwhelming majority of cases, they have a sense of social responsibility and that their interest, like that of most of us, is to do their job efficiently and well'.[47] The word of one man could carry conviction only with those already convinced that the new society was a just one.

The speculation and the frustration of the 1930s was ended by the urgent priorities of the Second World War. Government practice advanced far ahead of the modest perspectives of the pluralist corporatists. But, perhaps because so many of the younger and radical members of the party were away in the armed forces and no general election recruited new men, the party stagnated. The most important members were completely preoccupied with the fighting, and the party as a party tended almost to become obsolete. By 1945, the party seemed much more conservative than it had demonstrated itself to be before the war.

All currents of pluralist – or as it was popularly known, 'die-hard' – opinion did not however disappear. Indeed, on two occasions it expressed itself strongly. The 1943 Catering Wages Bill to create statutory wage regulation in the catering industry prompted some 111 Conservatives to vote against the Government, and 135 to abstain.[48] On the Beveridge Report on social insurance the criticism was even stronger. Ministers had been instructed not to commit themselves to the report, but when the Government did accept it, there was much opposition.[49] Those who had supported the Government over catering wages were among those who pressed the Government to accept the Beveridge Report. Some of them formed themselves into the Tory Reform Committee to pursue research and work for reform as a team. The pamphlets published by the committee represented almost the only consistent attempt within the party to work out reform proposals. The committee stressed the importance of State planning, the control of investment to sustain employment, a pragmatic approach to nationalization, financial help to industry and co-partnership in industrial relations.[50] Its plan for coal rejected nationalization and proposed instead compulsory powers to amalgamate the industry, an international cartel to stabilize world coal trading, and a Miners' Charter.[51]

A month after the consideration of the Beveridge Report, Churchill suggested in a broadcast, that a four-year plan might be appropriate after the war. The casual nature of the suggestion, as well as the fact that what was itemized for inclusion in the plan covered only proposals already made, did not meet the demands of the Tory Reform Committee.[52] But it did represent, even if in a timid form, some sign of change. The Prime Minister said that the State should seek to offset economic fluctuations, and furthermore, that a 'broadening field' existed for State ownership.[53] In the following year, these points were incorporated in a White Paper on employment policy. The paper represented a victory for a modest Keynesianism rather than the reorganizers. It committed the State to seeking to influence the investment level in order to sustain high employment after the war. State expenditure should be used to offset fluctuations in private investment, using the surplus of boom years to compensate the losses of depression. A central staff would undertake the research to make the policy possible. The paper was non-committal about physical planning and industrial location; it accepted the existing level of business concentration, but promised to promote an enquiry into restrictive practices, an excuse, *The Economist* said, for evasion.[54]

Just prior to the White Paper, a party document was published, the first official attempt to define an industrial policy for the party. It was an anodyne document which covered familiar ground with more piety than perception; it praised joint consultation in industrial relations, and suggested a statutory minimum period of notice (one week) to increase the sense of security of workers.[55]

Little of importance was added to the picture during the rest of the war. Up until the end, the magic word, 'planning', still did not feature in any forceful sense in Conservative publicity. Indeed, the nearer the general election came, the more the Conservative leaders seemed to reach back for the language with which they were most familiar, rather than forward to a brave new post-war world. The election campaign was acrimonious and shallow. The Conservatives seemed to have only Churchill to offer, although in terms of their pledges they did not differ so much with their opponents (both accepted, for example, the 1944 statement on employment policy, the welfare proposals, the maintenance of controls, the Reid

Report on coal). The question of private ownership, already considered by some Conservatives to be irrelevant because of managerial control, and of a public adherence to physical planning, alone separated them. 61 per cent of the electorate voted against the party, defeating a major part of the Front Bench. With defeats and retirements, some 60 per cent of the pre-election party was no longer present when the new Commons assembled.

4

Corporatism: Theory and Practice

The economy which emerged from the Second World War shared in the prosperity of an unprecedented boom in the world economy. What had been prepared before the war, was brought to fruition after it. And yet, also, many of the priorities which had seemed self-evident before the war, afterwards either lost their significance or became positive obstacles to growth. What had been 'new' industry was no longer new; it was in essentials the British economy. And the continuing problems of the contraction of old industry no longer dominated the thoughts of those concerned with the British economy. By 1960, motor car exports had attained the same relative position in Britain's export trade which cotton textiles had held in 1913.

The role of the State within the economy grew steadily. The Government acquired more and more responsibilities for guiding, shaping and initiating economic activity, until, it seemed, the Cabinet was really the board of directors of a vast, sprawling conglomerate, the British economy. State capitalism seemed to be slowly superseding private capitalism. Not only did the inherited industrial structure, the problems of the immediate post-war period and after, demand this role of the State. The shadow of war still lay across the world, and the economics of defence exercised a powerful role in making the State even more important.[1] Through its purchases and defence contracts, it was overwhelmingly the largest consumer. In its own public sector, it was the most important employer; it included under its wing what was for much of the period the largest corporation in Europe, the National Coal Board. And it had an even greater stake in the future as the largest financier of research, and systematic research was rapidly becoming one of the most important components in the success of the new capitalism; in 1958, three-fifths of total research expenditure went to the atomic energy, aircraft and electronics industries, and three-quarters of this was financed by the State.

Important as the State had become, it made no attempt to undo the work of concentration and cartelization which had been the response of private businessmen to the inter-war depression. The tariffs which protected those responses continued, even if the fortifications of the national economy were allowed to decay in certain respects. Material on the post-war trends in business concentration gives no clear picture, although there appears to have been no dramatic reversal of the pre-war situation.[2] Large firms continued to grow faster than average, despite the expanding market which increased the number of competitors.[3] Later, mergers became an established part of the industrial scene, and despite hesitant Government efforts to regulate certain 'combinations', particular industries became increasingly dominated by individual firms. Price leadership and collusion between firms (tacit rather than formal after the legislation on restrictive practices) naturally, given the industrial structure, remained important, even if occasionally shamefaced. Trade associations, although expanded on a much more extensive scale under the Labour Government, did not thereafter sustain the same rate of expansion; however, of those that existed, some made their authority much more comprehensive.[4] Even where the substance decayed, the forms were often preserved in case they should be needed in slump.

Internationally, cartelization on a widespread scale was difficult in conditions of expansion with many new competitors. Where the old producers were able to defend their paramount position in an industry, or the problems of inter-producer rivalry were taken over by inter-government negotions, cartels proved more stable. In oil, airways, shipping, textiles and chemicals, for example, international regulation remained very important.

Within the firm, the distribution of power was more clearly tilted against the mass of shareholders. The prerogatives of control were concentrated in the hands of the largest shareholders (most often, financial institutions) and professional managers, but no standard formula fitted all firms: 'Some companies have been manager-led, others large investor led, and in yet others there is a compromise.'[5] If a firm concentrated an industry's production, the concentration of power in a few hands within the firm constitutes a 'double distillation of power'; and if majority control in the firm is held by a holding company, it might well be a 'triple distillation'; indeed, 'as a whole, the *de facto* financial control of the country's manufacturing assets could well be in the hands of three per cent or less of the total shareholders'.[6]

The smaller shareholder had become the parasite he was claimed to be in inter-war 'progressive' writings. Robbed by the oligarchy of managers and financial nominees within the firms, the State also sought to discriminate against him. Taxation on company profits and differential taxes on unearned income made the State itself the great *rentier*. Nor did the relaxation of exchange control permit the shareholder to profit abroad in a way not permitted at home. British capital exports in the post-war period were pre-eminently the direct investment of large companies abroad, rather than *rentier* capital in search of the highest rate of return. These changes were not dramatic, however. They constituted mopping-up operations after the battle had been won. And for that reason they excited relatively little public interest.

State-industry co-operation also reached a new high level in the post-war world. The 1945 Labour Government, in particular, pursued most consistently the 'partnership' themes of the pre-war world. Nationalization relieved the economy of one range of inter-war problems and strengthened managerial power.[7] Controls strengthened trade association power since the Government relied upon these bodies to execute the detail of its policy; the control staff was recruited from the largest firms.[8] Indeed, 'self-government in industry' reached a relatively high level under Labour. 'Labour's one distinctive policy for the private sector',[9] Development Councils, was a State-initiated version of the trade association for 'weakly organized' industries; the membership of the councils 'was representative, almost corporativist, rather than chosen for their special knowledge'.[10] The State also brought representatives of industry into

Government committees. In 1950, the FBI nominated members to some thirty-four major Government bodies, and the TUC to sixty.

The mark of a partner in a firm, Professor Gower notes, is taking a share of the profits. After the war, the State took the largest share of distributed profits 'and to that extent (was) already the senior partner in most firms'.[11] But the boundaries between public and private in any case were becoming increasingly unclear. In the complexity of inter-relationships, it was difficult to detect which was which, and not at all clear that detection served any useful purpose. The private sector, for example, was one of the State's important tax collectors through the operation of PAYE. And if private firms performed public duties, the State appropriated to itself an increasing range of formerly private duties.

As a system, post-war British society accorded in some of its important features to what inter-war corporatist writers had seen as their aspiration. It was perhaps not as close to the corporatist design as mid-nineteenth-century Britain had been to the Liberal model, but in so far as the corporatist design was practicable at all, there were important similarities. Prosperity and expansion robbed most commentators of any sense of urgency in depicting the system, and perhaps it made possible the corporatist structure itself. Without prosperity, the system would have come under challenge, would have thereby created the disharmony it was supposed to make impossible.

But 'corporatism' itself was no single unified doctrine. There were as many versions as writers, and no single political movement to stamp upon the diversity a single pattern. In origin, corporatism began as an explicitly counter-revolutionary doctrine, designed to describe what the aristocracy felt it had lost in the industrial revolution, what the French aristocracy had lost in the French revolution, and what Catholics had lost in the Reformation and in the agnosticism of industrial society. It was a child of the romantics. And it involved a romantic and wishfully inaccurate reconstruction of the medieval fief, ostensibly a little, organic community in which lord and peasant were united in a common society, each expecting and offering clear and unequivocal rights and obligations to the other. The organization of Estates within the wider society embodied the inequalities which were 'organically' accepted as a part of the natural order. The assembly of Estates brought together the component parts of the society in common purpose.

This rationale of sentimental nostalgia might have died a natural death with the spread of industrial society, with the reconciliation of aristocrats to a bourgeois world. The world of de Maistre or of Tour du Pin would then have appeared to be no more than archaic eccentricity. But crisis, the successive challenges to capitalism in the late nineteenth century and afterwards, gave it a new lease of life. Just as Liberal business-men had crossed to the Conservative party as external and internal challenges awoke increasing anxiety – had, as it were, 'joined the aristocracy' – so others also imbibed the aristocratic defence of a society that had passed. In particular, what was claimed as the complete and naturally accepted subordination of the mass of the population in medieval society recommended itself to those worried by recalcitrant workmen and strikes.

Some of the aristocratic corporatists had not unequivocally rejected industrial society. Indeed, some in the Tory 'Young England'[12] group had even considered the mill system of the cotton industry as the new basis for a recreation of the ethics of medievalism. And Tour du Pin had not so much rejected industrialism as the bourgeoisie; he also saw the basis of a new organic society in a reformed factory system and a purged national State.[13] Of course, businessmen had no interest in reversing the industrial revolution, and the 'corporations' which they identified in the world around them were not medieval estates, but Capital and Labour. Yet others, neither businessmen nor aristocrats, searched for an ordered society, one in which 'the anarchy of the market' could be replaced by the guidance of experts, in which hierarchies of rationally organized authority would permit the scientific planning of society. The mysticism of the reactionary had almost imper-ceptibly smudged into the self-proclaimed rationalism of the progressives. What united them was the search for the stable ordered society, for a system where competition, class conflict and political disunity were structurally rendered impossible.

What was taken for granted in all schemes was that there did exist somewhere a 'national interest' which could be revealed and accepted by all members of society, such that they would behave in accordance with it. It was this assumption which lay behind Disraeli's claim to a 'National Idea' and inter-war Conservative pleas for a new philosophy or morality. Voluntary unanimity was seen as being the result of a new nationalism, and that unanimity would immediately overcome 'sectional' interests. The 'corporation' – whether an estate like Capital or Labour, or a business firm – was identified as the first stage in creating unanimity, in encouraging members of the corporation to see that their own interests were fully taken into account by the established order. Eliminating public conflict was an important step forward in achieving the appearance of unanimity. Nationalism exported domestic conflict to the arena where open struggle was still legitimate, the relationships between States.

The different emphases in corporatist writings had different historical traditions. Some were merely traditionalist: their nation-State was a romantic conception of a village writ large, a village united by its hostility to outsiders. Others borrowed on the ideal conception of an army, the militarized State. Some used particular versions of medieval society to identify the source of unanimity; for writers as distant as Coleridge and T. S. Eliot, the creation of a new priesthood, a Clerisy, would allow the formulation of a stable and accepted orthodoxy. For Carlyle, as for Disraeli, the 'charisma' of the hero would elicit a popular loyalty which would obviate the necessity of wider changes.

But on the Left, there were other traditions which stressed the importance of science or the integration, not of businessmen, but of workers in 'self-government in industry'.[14] For the 'scientists', the work of St Simon in describing a society of autonomous economic and social bodies functionally interrelated and ruled by scientific administrators, provided one model. The writings of Comte further developed a 'rationalist' opposition to the market. On the other hand, Sorel and the tradition of anarcho-syndicalism stressed the possibility of a voluntary industrialism. In Britain, guild socialism offered a design for the integration of those who worked in industry, organized in a functional rather than competitive order.

Again, on both sides, the traditions were not much more than speculation or individual meditation in the absence of an external crisis to make them politically significant. Without the events of the 1920s, corporatism on both Right and Left – in its explicit form – would have remained historical flotsam.

But the 1920s added new urgency to the Conservative search for stability and the search of some Socialists for a voluntary reorganization of society. Between the two, others began to identify a new order actually emerging. Walther Rathenau in Germany advanced a plan to reorganize basic industry into complementary trusts working in the public interest; 'the depersonalisation of ownership', he wrote, 'the objectification of enterprise becomes transformed into an institution which resembles the State in character'.[15] As already mentioned, Keynes identified the same process in the 1920s, and recommended a return to 'medieval conceptions of separate autonomies', and 'corporations (as) a mode of government'.[16] For Social Democrats, the 'self-socializing' of private capital seemed to offer a way out of bourgeois society without the necessity of revolution, seemed to offer the hope of a new organic society. For some, the corporatist elements in Fascism and Nazi-ism – the 'Socialist' in National Socialist – rendered them acceptable, or even praiseworthy, as experiments in a new society; and the Strasser element in the Nazi party as well as Mussolini's background as a radical Social Democrat strengthened the attraction.[17] Others found a more 'scientific' version of St Simonian corporatism in the Soviet rhetoric of planning.[18]

The traditions were by no means at all mutually exclusive. They stressed different interests – those of aristocrats, of Christians, of businessmen, of workers, of intellectuals, of experts – but in important respects, they did not necessarily exclude collaboration. The career of Sir Oswald Mosley epitomized the possibility of pursuing consistent ends between what were thought of as inconsistent traditions. Mosley began as a Tory Radical with an interest in social imperialism, became a Left-wing Labour Minister, and finally founded the New Party with another prominent Social Democrat, John Strachey, which became after Strachey's departure an explicitly Fascist party.

By the middle 1930s, the literature of corporatism was already immense. A French observer commented on the scale of Parisian publications: 'A ne retenir que la production des premiers mois de 1935, livres, brochures, articles sur le corporatisme, suffisent à remplir un rayon de bibliothèque.'[19] Such a movement, he went on, must arise from deep causes, and being so deep, could not be eradicated easily. But much of the writing was defensive, what has here been identified as part of 'pluralist' rather than '*étatiste*' corporatism. For Pirou picks out as the key characteristic of the publications 'le caractère conservateur et statique', aiming at the crystallization of existing practices rather than change or progress. It was proposed that the corporation should embody the interests of workers and managers, and should be given supreme rights of internal regulation, constituting finally a 'groupement de droit public'.[20] He comments that corporatism was 'une doctrine qui delibèrement subordonne le point de vue social au point de vue national, et qui accorde au souci de *l'équité entre les classes* moins de poids qu' à celui de la *prospérité* et de la *puissance* de la nation'.[21]

Étatiste corporatism was less speculative, and more related to the specific practice of given governments. In the United States, it received some expression in the later years of the New Deal. In association with the State, 'experts' – unattached radical intellectuals – could play a much more important role than in those situations where the defensive reactions of businessmen dominated the political scene, excluding the experimental. Yet to achieve this situation was itself a long process. Professor Hawley, in his masterly account of the New Deal, identifies in the early years of the National Industrial Recovery Act (1933) three separate and competing groups:

At one corner was the vision of a business commonwealth, of rational, cartelized business in which the industrialists would plan and direct the economy, profits would be insured, and the government would take care of recalcitrant 'chiselers'. At the second was the concept of a cooperative, collectivist democracy, a system under which organised economic groups would join to plan their activities, rationalise their behaviour, and achieve the good life for all. At the third corner was the competitive ideal, the old vision of an atomistic economy in which basic decisions were made in an impersonal market and the pursuit of self-interest produced the greatest social good. As written, the National Industrial Recovery Act could be used to move in any of these directions, to cartelize the economy, establish overhead planning, or attempt to eliminate the market riggers and enforce competition.[22]

The unwillingness of businessmen to pay the price in lost initiative for State-directed cartelization, as well as Roosevelt's response to popular criticism of the attempt of businesses to promote a scarcity – a response embodied in his declaration: 'I am against private socialism of concentrated economic power as thoroughly as I am against government socialism. The one is equally as dangerous as the other; and destruction of private socialism is utterly essential to avoid government socialism'[23] – nudged the New Deal cautiously towards *étatisme* and increased influence for the experts. But the experts, the planners, were not socialists, any more than Harold Macmillan was: 'Their heroes were the engineer, the technician, and the ultimate consumer, not the factory worker. Their central concepts stressed economic balance and unified co-operation, not class struggle and the rule of the proletariat.'[24] The men, the methods and the aims were different. If the pluralists stressed stability and being left free of the State, the *étatistes* pressed the case for expert planning, State direction and expansion.

It was some of the New Deal intellectuals who contributed to the discussion of what kind of society the United States had become in the 1950s. In particular, A. A. Berle wrote extensively on this topic. The writings of Peter Drucker suggested a new rationale for American society, based on the assumption that in terms of structure, Communist and Western societies did not differ, both being dominated by large corporations.[25] The problem was how the corporation could assure 'status and function' for the individual.[26] The answer assumed, in Berle's words, that 'the myth of the market as a self-regulating

mechanism still reigns, although it does not work and is not expected to work'.[27] On the contrary, society was dominated by
relatively autonomous 'non-Statist collectivisms' and could be
called, as a system, 'non-Statist Socialism' or 'People's Capitalism'.[28] Society consisted in a series of quasi-States, a plurality of
corporations. The State, like a king among the barons, is only
primus inter pares. E. S. Mason comments that given that 'politics
inevitably reflect the structure of society, in a society characterized by large organizations, politics will be pressure group
politics'.[29]

Yet the problem noted in connection with Macmillan's
account of what should have been done in inter-war Britain,
remained. How could the system be justified to the mass of the
population? One writer suggested a sort of amended form of
contract – affluence was the reward of discipline and conformity.[30] Rostow argued that the only check on the corporations would have to be the continuation of some competition
between them.[31] Yet others repeated the case, as Macmillan
had done, that the decline of the profit motive meant that
industrial managers could be trusted to pursue socially responsible ends.

The same conclusion appears in the work of the prominent
British Social Democrat, C. A. R. Crosland, in *The Future of
Socialism* (1956); and indeed, the Labour party policy statement of 1957, *Industry and Society*, repeats – as an argument for
opposing further nationalization – that 'under increasingly
professional managements, large firms are as a whole serving
the nation well'.[32]

Berle approached the problem from a different standpoint.
For, he argued, the absence of dissent justified the system. The
lack of dissent rested upon a 'consensus', an agglomeration of
'the conclusions of careful university professors, the reasoned
opinion of specialists, the statements of responsible journalists,
and, at times, the solid pronouncements of respected politicians'.[33] This – as it were – community of acceptable judges is
the nucleus of a new spiritual power which will guide the new
secular power at the head of the hierarchic society.[34] The
conception is drawn from the Middle Ages and a version of the
role of the priesthood, a caste whose function was supposedly

71

to safeguard spiritual values. Medieval society, Berle felt, was the nearest approximation to modern society, and new 'Lords Spiritual' were needed to play the same kind of role today:

> The feudal system was held to a degree of order (when it was) by the countervailing power . . . of the priests, the scholars and divines within the body of the then universal Catholic Church. When that system worked well, the spiritual order erected generally accepted standards or criteria of judgment.[35]

Yet the self-appointed National Clerisy has still to demonstrate that its definition of justice accords with popular wishes so that a democratic vote is no longer required to sanction the acts of authority. Other measures – appointing worker representatives to the management boards of corporations, for example – will hardly bear the weight of this problem. Berle's account of the Middle Ages omits to notice that brute force was also an important element in the maintenance of order. How far the Church, alone and unaided by the soldiers of king and baron, could have regulated society is open to question. The relationship between force and the appearance of unanimity is not settled in the modern, any more than in earlier, corporatist writings: it is assumed. Yet, as Pirou notes in relationship to Italian Fascism and Neumann with reference to the Nazis,[36] corporatism in those countries was not, and could not be, much more than a decorative façade for force. For the harmony which it is assumed is intrinsic to society – if the squabbling cabals can be swept away – can in practice only be reproduced by the use of force. And the use of force directly contradicts the assumption of an intrinsic harmony. In Vichy France and in Salazar's Portugal, overtly corporatist societies, the same comment is appropriate. Corporatism assumes what it is designed to create, and destroys what it seeks to create by pursuing the only practicable means available: coercion.

The fate of Italian Fascism prevented the word 'corporatism' from being widely used, except as a term of denigration. The few Conservatives who had referred to the word before the war did try to defend it, but briefly and with declining enthusiasm. Amery re-argued the case for an Industrial Parliament, and maintained that Fascism was wrong, not for urging an assembly of corporations, but for not creating it.[37] For T. E. Utley corporatism was the only constructive idea of Fascism, and was borrowed from Right-wing thought but never carried out.[38] But in general, Conservatives preserved their unwillingness to theorize, and not having used the word very much before the war, found no need after the war to disentangle it from its associations.[39] Prosperity reduced the need even to begin the attempt.

The same could not be said of practice. Up to about 1947, the leadership of both parties were united in pursuing the aims outlined in *étatiste* corporatist plans of the inter-war period. Backbenchers provided criticisms from pluralist and socialist positions. So far as the division within the Conservatives was concerned, it was consistent on almost all industrial issues. For example, in the field of labour, the *étatistes* favoured a wages policy and integrating the unions into the formal structure of management; the pluralists trusted the market, the result of a contest between free labour and employers. In the nationalized industries, the first favoured an integrated public sector, devoted to supplying the rest of the economy with basic resources even if this entailed a loss to the State; the second urged that each public industry should either be denationalized or should operate independently on straight profit-making criteria – there should be competition between public industries, between public and private, and, in some cases, between the decentralized units of public industry. In finance, some urged that the State should control all investment, supplied to industry at low interest rates on criteria determined by planners; others, that the open money market should decide the distribution of investment.

Yet from 1947, opinion both inside and outside the party began to move in the opposite direction. A neo-Liberalism flourished, reaching its greatest extent in the early 1950s. One commentator in the 1950s noted the surprising change:

> . . . the distrust of the pricing mechanism, widespread in the 'thirties, has all but disappeared even on the Left. Free competition, a dirty word ('cut-throat') in the 'thirties, both to

Labour and Conservative has already been rehabilitated among the Conservatives, and its merits are attested by numbers of Labour Party intellectuals. The rage for bigness – for large-scale enterprise – has been followed by an intellectual passion for the small-scale. Even free-trade is becoming fashionable.[40]

The movement was short-lived, bred on the relatively brief optimism of the 1950s. The troubles of the British economy began slowly and painfully to force a return in the late 1950s.

PART II

The Conservatives in Opposition, 1945–51

5

The Party and the New Order

The tension between *pluralists* and *étatistes* was not resolved in the six years following the Second World War. There were two separate contradictory changes. First, the inter-war radicals (*étatiste* corporatists) united with new recruits to the party from the armed services to lead a 'Tory Democracy' assault on the existing leadership of the party, itself weakened by the electoral defeat of 1945. However, no sooner had the radicals consolidated their position, than they were faced with a broad shift in public opinion which, beginning in 1947, produced a surprising refurbishment of forms of pluralist thought, a 'neo-Liberalism'. Many of the most enthusiastic proponents of neo-Liberalism were just those young Conservatives who had supported the *étatiste* revision of Conservatism up to 1947. Ironically, the Conservative party of 1951 was more Liberal than it had ever been since the 1920s, more 'diehard' in the fashionable terminology of 1945, despite the fact that the old *étatiste* radicals now held positions of influence in the party. 'New Conservatism' embodied the adherence of Conservatives, not to forms of *étatiste* thought but to elements of pluralist thought. The 1947 *Industrial Charter* is less what it is claimed to be – the foundation document of 'New Conservatism' – and more the final expression of the radical *étatiste* thought of the 1930s; it closes rather than opens an era.

The period from 1931 to 1947 is a uniform one in terms of political aspirations. The 1945 Labour Government executed some of the proposals of pre-war Conservative radicals, and pressed further some of the policies of the Conservative and Coalition Governments between 1931 and 1945. In a sense, the 1945 defeat of the Conservative party was fortunate for it. For new men in the party had time to gain experience, to watch

77

Labour's *étatiste* corporatist experiments, and to refine a critique of them. More important, when the tide changed – towards more pluralism – the Conservatives could take it without being constrained by office and by a record of executing an *étatiste* programme.

The 1945 defeat permitted the party to heal its divisions. It quickly removed from the scene a host of names associated with a discredited era. The vacant places in the party were filled by inter-war radicals or newcomers, ex-servicemen. It is scarcely conceivable that R. A. Butler or Harold Macmillan could have played the role they did, or that *The Industrial Charter* could have become part of official party 'ethos', if the party of 1944 had survived the 1945 election intact. A major reform was made possible, in organization, policy and personnel.

The young Conservatives who returned from active military service pressed the leadership hard for a radical answer to Labour's challenge. They also demanded a reform of the party structure, both as part of the Conservative reply to Labour and in order to make room for themselves within the party hierarchy. They chose the slogan for their campaign, 'Tory Democracy', and, as in the earlier use of the slogan, the cry for democracy within the party matched the party's demand, now it was defeated, for democracy in society as a whole. When Lord Randolph Churchill originally used the term, a new rising group within the party pressed for a radical programme; in 1945 the aspirations of the new men included equality of opportunity, progress and expansion; it was a programme simultaneously useful as a weapon within the party and as a platform for the party. In Opposition a general radicalism (where few concrete proposals are specified) tended to appeal to the party, since to conserve society, a change in the *status quo* was required at the very least (namely, the defeat of the government so that the people could triumph). In office, the basis for such radicalism tended to disappear; the demand for democracy implied little democracy existed, and few governments would accuse themselves of this.

However, Tory democracy had other implications in the late 1940s. The stress by its proponents on progress, advancement for all, and popular trust evoked the Liberal memories of Conservatives and matched the neo-Liberal reaction to Government policies. The 1950 general election introduced more young Conservatives to strengthen this reaction and give support to those Conservatives with little property or no strictly traditional high-status background to achieve influence in the party. Neo-Liberalism stressed 'opportunity'; that is, the right of the talented minority to displace or at least share 'room at the top' with traditional occupants. It implied approval of competition and change as opposed to stability and the mere occupation rights of those already established.

Some of the reasons for the creation of a neo-Liberalism by Conservatives are obvious. First, the most important factor was the change in 'public opinion', or at least that part of it exhibited in the national press; this was partly a reaction to the difficulties faced by the Labour Government, but much more the result of a new optimism contingent on relatively continuous British expansion and the end of the fear of a post-war slump. Neo-Liberalism was sustained by conditions of relative prosperity, in this case from 1947, by high employment, by industry working to capacity to fill an expanding market. The stress on stability, discipline, order, accepted status, changed to the demand for more, for progress and change.[1] This seems to have been the basis for New Conservatism, and, indeed, a 'new Socialism' in the Labour party. Second, being in Opposition, the Conservative party tended to emphasize its libertarian traditions and its opposition to State power and 'bureaucracy' on behalf of the 'People'. Third, the two leaders of the party devoted themselves by preference or necessity to foreign affairs, and the formation of domestic policy devolved upon younger men, some of whom were not implicated in the pre-war record and were more responsive to changing currents of non-party opinion. Finally, it could be said, the change was a mere tactic by the party. For example, rather than defend 'planning' (to which the party was broadly committed in 1947) while attacking the Government's practice, it chose to call the Government's practice 'planning' and attack both together. This last explanation, however, underestimates the widespread critique of *étatisme* which developed in the late 1940s.

The period up to 1951, then, is characterized for the

Conservative party first by the victory of the *étatiste* radicals, and
then by the contrary shift to neo-Liberalism. But this is only the
main theme. Pluralist corporatist elements remained vocal
during the first shift, and *étatiste* corporatist elements in the
second. The intellectual tension between the two was never
settled, even if the question of political supremacy was. Indeed,
even in 1951 the party had certainly not evolved a comprehensive political alternative to Labour. In practice, very little of
substance appeared to have changed, despite the apparent shift
in ethos.

Up to 1947, the Conservative party tried to reach some *modus
vivendi* with the forces that had so resoundingly defeated it in
1945. The attempt took different forms in different hands. On
the one hand, the pluralist corporatists urged all-out attack on
State power, with the ultimate hope that the Government
would fall merely because the electorate had tired of it. On the
other, the radicals urged the need for a complete reform of the
party (and this included more or less open attacks on the party
leader) and the definition of a new positive policy for the party.
In the middle, the leadership compromised, sporadically
attacking the Government (on different grounds at different
times) while permitting the radicals to have some say in
domestic policy formulation; increasingly after 1946, Churchill
and Eden concentrated almost exclusively on foreign affairs.

In 1945 the air was full of suggestions as to the future of the
party after the general election, suggestions which continued
into 1946.[2] While this went on, the Opposition attack in Parliament was at first muted to the point of neutrality.[3] Later it
focused almost entirely on the competence of the administration, rather than on its aims.[4] The November Central Council
meeting clarified little, although it clearly demonstrated the
increasing role within the party of R. A. Butler, the demand of
many representatives for 'a new policy', and much dissatisfaction with the party record.[5] The censure of the Government,
debated in early December, seemed overcast by the doubts of
the Opposition concerning its own position, doubts exacerbated
by the concurrent support offered the Government publicly by
the then-president of the Federation of British Industry.

Conservative discussion in public the following year revealed little more unanimity, although it did tend to pinpoint specific issues.[6] Eccles led the campaign for more party democracy and a policy of economic expansion; Macmillan for a new industrial charter to specify the rights and obligations of all members of society, and a merger with the Liberal party under a new name (a suggestion originally made by Churchill himself).[7] The first demand received much support at the party conference which was marked by open conflict between the leadership and the floor; but the suggestion on a change of name was scotched.[8] At the end of the year, however, when *Notes on Current Politics* summarized the party programme, for the first time it placed at the head of the list, planning, including expansion, a wider distribution of power and an attack on restrictive practices.[9]

The indecision within the party was supported by the actual climate of economic opinion. Men still could not escape from the practices designed to combat slump conditions. Many refused to share an optimism which they felt was the mark of those who had helped to make the 1929 slump as severe as it was; they saw post-war full employment as the result of only a temporary boom, liable to collapse as dramatically as the prosperity which followed the First World War. The transition to optimism was still very tentative for those with most to lose. Modified *étatisme* was acceptable, but must not intervene in the prerogatives of businessmen; anything more extreme – a revival of Liberalism, for example – was foolhardy after the inter-war experience.

1947 saw the most dramatic domestic crisis of the immediate post-war period, a major fuel emergency, and, in the summer, the first major dollar crisis. Lt.-Col. Elliot leading for the Opposition gave expression to the pessimism which the fuel crisis engendered: 'I have an uneasy feeling, and so must have anyone who was in Parliament during the period just before the 1930–31 crash, that this is where we see the beginning being run through again.'

But simultaneously, younger Conservatives who had not known the inter-war years were already drawing neo-Liberal conclusions from full employment, whatever the immediate crises. In the short term, terminology concealed the shifts – the young radicals were critical of the party leadership and praised both planning *and* increased economic freedom. *Design for Freedom* showed traces of both elements in February of 1947.[10] The war-torn markets of the world craved supplies from one of the few economies unbroken by war, but the demand to increase supplies conflicted directly with the restrictions created by the inter-war need to curb output.

However, before the full shift took place, the long-promised Conservative statement of positive policy and the most important Conservative document of the period, *The Industrial Charter*, was published (May 1947). It was, in fact, not a statement of policy so much as one of 'ethos',[11] and was subsequently to play no explicit role in Conservative electoral campaigns. It was written, Butler claimed, mainly by Lyttelton, Stanley and Macmillan of the Conservative Front Bench, with a number of younger members of the party.[12] Opposition to the statement cannot have been insignificant[13] although it was rarely as explicit, publicly, as Sir Waldron Smithers' complete rejection of the document as 'milk-and-water' socialism. Churchill is said to have rejected the first draft,[14] as did the British Employers' Confederation, but the representatives at that year's party conference enthusiastically endorsed it. Criticism of the document was perhaps less significant than the fact that for the first time the party had an explicit industrial policy to criticize at all.

The charter was a survey of industrial and economic questions with proposed answers (discussed in later sections). It claimed to offer a synthesis of the benefits of a directed economy and 'free self-development'. The document stressed expansion while maintaining the power of the State, incentives and partnership; the relationship between the 'free' economy and the State was not explored, although the inclusion of both pluralist and *étatiste* elements testifies to the attempt to achieve unanimity. That the elements of a directed economy and a more or less guaranteed status for all citizens were accepted showed, however, the victory of the radicals. 'Between the Wars', Macmillan commented, 'there was always a progressive element in the Party. Now it has seized control, not by force or palace revolution, but by the vigour of its intellectual and spiritual powers.'[15] However, the speeches of the leader and deputy-leader of the party continued to remain true to a much older tradition of orthodoxy than that contained in the charter.[16] Churchill bluntly quoted with approval sentiments he had expressed forty-one years earlier as a member of Asquith's Liberal Government: 'The existing organisation of society is driven by one mainspring – competitive selection. It may be a very imperfect organisation of society, but it is all we have got between us and barbarism.'[17]

The older pluralist tradition, despite the charter and the changed balance of power in the party, tended to merge with the development of neo-Liberalism. The neo-Liberals were also hostile to State intervention but much less ambiguous than the pluralists about, for example, how much 'rationalization' was the same thing as 'restrictive practices'. The Government itself betrayed signs of the trends in its own bill to curb restrictive practices, in the cutting of controls, the modification of the cheap money policy and a re-evaluation of nationalization. In the Conservative party, it was somewhat ironic that *étatistes* had defeated the old guard, only to be transformed themselves into neo-Liberals: that, for example, Macmillan, who had attacked Neville Chamberlain for being insufficiently *étatiste* (although Chamberlain was in practice introducing reforms that could be described as such by many of his followers), should have become one of the leaders of a party more Liberal than Chamberlain's. Many continued to resist the new trends in part or wholly. Macmillan himself criticized the trends towards multilateral trade as a return to nineteenth-century free-trade, and L. S. Amery continued to call free trade 'promiscuous'.

1948 was a year of relative economic growth, a breathing space for the economy and a repudiation of the pessimists. It powerfully strengthened neo-Liberal tendencies. The party seemed to prosper, and the concerns of policy were for the moment shelved. The only check to this consensus came with the loss of a by-election early in 1949. This provided an occasion for re-examining where the party was going.[18] In *The Times*, R. K. Law described Boothby's position as 'an empirical version of Socialism', and Boothby replied by attributing to Law 'undiluted Gladstonian Liberalism'. The party, Boothby said, had to decide whether it was going 'to accept the advent of the managerial society as an established fact, or whether it wishes to make yet another attempt to return to the *laissez-faire* economy of the nineteenth century'. Others entered the fray. Hogg compared the 1945 Labour victory to the 1832 Reform Act, both requiring of Conservatives a more fundamental accommodation than just waiting for the pendulum to swing. The Conservatives must return to the attitude of Peel's Tamworth Manifesto and state their profound acceptance of what he called the 'Social Democratic State'.[19] The controversy came to no conclusion. The demands for a new policy were in part answered by *The Right Road for Britain* in July 1949. This was something of a retreat from the charter. What had there been aspiration (for example, wider ownership) had now become in part mere description of what already existed.[20] As was appropriate to a Liberal position, it was implied that what a government could do was trivial beside what men working for their interests in society could achieve. 'Climate-setting' became the primary function of government rather than making innovations to improve conditions. Vagueness and lack of commitment were criticized by commentators on the new document more strongly than anything actually said in it,[21] but the party conference accepted it with only eight dissenters.

The two general elections of 1950 and 1951 were not marked by great enthusiasm, and the Conservatives fought largely on the demand for lower taxes. The shadow of international crisis in Korea hung over the second contest, tending to dwarf domestic issues. It was not a topic on which the parties were divided. Economic crisis was added, limiting to the minimum what either party was prepared to offer. Observers found few real issues dividing the leadership of both parties, both having converged on common neo-Liberal ground.

However, whatever issues were unresolved, whatever the lack of alternatives, the Conservative sojourn in the wilderness was ended. A workable majority meant that the problems of policy formulation could be shelved in favour of immediate administration.

6

The Heart of the Social Democratic Society: Public Ownership

For *étatiste* radicals, the public appropriation of the declining basic industries was an important advance in economic organization, one which would free the new growth industries for expansion. The pluralists by contrast opposed nationalization as the most extreme expression of the tyranny of the State; an innovation which would destroy the pluralists themselves and the society they defended. Between these two extremes, the broad centre was pragmatic, which, given the political assumptions of the 1930s, involved leaning rather towards the first alternative. But pragmatism provided few clear criteria to justify general policy or the particular nationalization measures undertaken.

With the post-1945 victory of the radicals in the party, the new *étatisme* could not be consolidated properly before neo-Liberalism offered a new critique of nationalization. The critique, nevertheless, broadly accepted much of the Labour Government's nationalization, without any very clear grounds being cited for this. In propaganda terms, the change from one end of the period to the other did not seem great: in 1945 the party had opposed nationalization in principle, while making exceptions in practice; in 1951 it opposed nationalization in practice, but claimed to be pragmatic in principle. Neither position entailed radical action.

However, if this was the appearance of the party in aggregate, individuals continued to put the counter case at all times. In

1945, Lt-Col. J. R. H. Hutchinson maintained in connection with the nationalization of the Bank of England (a measure the party leadership accepted) that wherever nationalization had been tried, it was 'extravagant, where economy is vital; inefficient, where efficiency will be the lifeblood of the country; and unsympathetic in dealings between employers and employed'.[1] In 1947, Sir Herbert Williams explicitly distinguished himself from other Conservatives by saying, 'I am one of those who are opposed to nationalisation of any commercial enterprise on grounds of fundamental principle', continuing that 'there is a strong case for denationalising the telephone, and none for nationalising electricity supply'.[2] By contrast, Lt-Commander Joynson-Hicks put the centrist case on the Bank of England: 'I do not consider, and I do not think anybody else considers, that there is anything inherently wrong in the State running a business, if it can be established that it is more efficient to do so.'[3] And as one of the most consistent *étatiste* radicals, Boothby went even further in 1945 with: 'I think there may be quite a good psychological case for nationalisation of the coal mining industry and quite a good economic case on the basis of the Report published yesterday (the Heyworth Report)[4] for the nationalisation of the gas industry.'[5]

In sum, the party officially did not oppose some nationalization measures, accepted others after opposing them, and pledged itself to denationalize only one industry and part of another. Some members of the party continued to oppose all nationalization on principle, and attacked the leadership for not pledging the party to denationalize all publicly-owned industry.[6] Quite often, other speakers began their speeches pragmatically but subsequently developed cases clearly against nationalization *per se* rather than against a particular measure.[7]

Discussing publicly any criteria for denationalization (which must include, even if only implicitly, criteria for nationalization) offended total opponents of nationalization. *The Industrial Charter* did say that the party broadly accepted what had already been nationalized but did not explain why. Backbenchers mentioned bad labour relations as a justification for coal nationalization, and economic problems for gas.[8] But they would certainly not have accepted the nationalization of all industries which experienced similar problems (for example, cotton or shipbuilding). After a measure had been passed, criteria were sometimes suggested as grounds for accepting it. Lyttelton, for example, accepted that 'common services' should be State owned, but not 'a great industrial interest' like steel,[9] without clarifying the distinction so that it could be used in future cases. Macmillan attempted a broader classification: new growth industries were suitable for 'free initiative and speculation', while those of 'monopolistic middle or old age', without scope for further development, might be suitable for public ownership.[10] This, while interestingly favourable towards new industry (and reminiscent of *The Middle Way*), could not represent the party's view, since an old monopolistic industry, steel, was chief Conservative candidate for denationalization, and three young growth industries, civil aviation, atomic energy and electricity were to remain publicly owned.

There were few other attempts to identify criteria, and the general impression left was that those industries the Conservatives tried to denationalize were merely those where ex-owners exerted maximum pressure on the party, or where implicit or symbolic conventions on the limits of possible nationalization were thought to have been exceeded: the limits being questions of economic or political fashion, rather than related to explicit principles.

If the development of neo-Liberalism did bring a sharper hostility towards nationalization without criteria for accepting some and rejecting other measures, it did also generate new suggestions on organizational reforms for the public sector. As was described earlier, the *étatiste* radicalism of the inter-war period stressed the merits of great size, centralization and non-competitive central direction in industry. From 1947 onwards, the Conservatives came more and more to advocate the benefits of small units, of competition between such units, and of 'decentralization'. The charter confined itself to promising 'reorganization' in the public sector without specifying in which direction. But other Conservative voices were already attacking the centralization of public industries. A resolution was passed at the 1948 party conference specifying 'decentralization' as the *only* way to make State concerns more efficient.[11] By the time of

The Right Road (July 1949), the word had become official policy, incorporating the sale of ancillary operations of public industry, the use of independent Price Tribunals to check the pricing policy of nationalized industries, a clear limit to ministerial power, and the use of the Monopolies Commission to check public on the same basis as private industry. This was the high point of neo-Liberal radicalism, and *This is the Road* (January 1950) was something of a retraction. There were, however, Conservatives who went further than the 1949 policy statement, urging open competition between public industries.[12] There was little trace of the final stage which would have made public industry as close to the Liberal model of private industry as possible: competition between the units of each nationalized industry, and between State and private companies.

'Decentralization' became for the Conservatives what 'co-ordination' had been for Labour before 1947: a word in which the element of possible validity was dwarfed by the attribution of magic qualities to the concept, a magic designed to wish away problems. Apart from Lancaster's work on coal, there is little evidence that much thought was given to the problem of what the word was to mean in detail in given industries. In political terms, the word was a compromise between Liberalism proper (and the demand for complete denationalization) and *étatiste* corporatism (and the view that centralized public industries were a necessary part of the modern economy). It acknowledged the truth of criticisms from the neo-Liberal position but did not entail radical denationalization. It seemed that the Conservatives were becoming properly Liberal by resurrecting the idea of local autonomy, even though 'decentralization' as officially intended did not mean this so much as merely a little loosening in organization. The ambiguity was a necessary element in the political function of the word, and the ambiguity lay in part in not distinguishing between managerial centralization and State centralization. 'Centralization' did not just denote organization, but a sort of organization *by the State*. The State was rejected in terms which permitted both small businessmen and very large-scale managers to unite; the case for decentralization was never intended to imply a forcible decentralization of, for example, *private* steel.

Of the range of measures introduced by the Labour Government, only three can be examined here, although others will be mentioned later. Coal nationalization has been included because it was the first major measure, and was given most detailed attention; transport, because here there was the closest co-operation between the party and affected interests; and steel, because the Conservatives waged their most militant opposition on this issue. However, the broad lines of the discussion here are equally relevant to the other nationalization measures.

I. COAL

The degree of initial centralization in the nationalized coal industry was relatively high, partly to counteract what was said to be the excessive decentralization existing in the pre-nationalization private industry, and partly because this reorganization was one of the final expressions of inter-war *étatiste* thought. Conservatives who shared this last approach advanced as their alternative to Labour's nationalization their most overtly corporatist alternative. Alongside that alternative, pluralists continued to put points of more traditional and general objection. Out of the debate over coal emerged the neo-Liberal idea of 'decentralization', a suggestion that was not made in the actual consideration of the nationalization measure itself.

War organization involving supreme State control provided the model for Labour's intentions.[13] The Conservatives seemed favourably disposed towards nationalization of the industry,[14] although never actually initiating any concrete scheme. The proposals of the Tory Reform Group had included substantial State intervention but stopped short of eliminating private ownership. The Caretaker Government preceding the 1945 general election accepted most of the Reid Report,[15] including the creation of a strong central authority, pit amalgamations, and co-ordination with competing industries (that is, electricity and gas) – in sum, a centralized, cartelized industry operating in statutorily non-competitive conditions.

Despite the widespread impression that the Conservatives would not oppose the nationalization Bill,[16] just before it was published they opted to do so. In practice, opposition was

COMPETITION AND THE CORPORATE SOCIETY

concentrated more on the actual proposals in the Bill than the principle involved. Initially, Eden set the tone by his mild, reasonable approach, asking whether this was really the answer to the aspirations of the miners: a monopsonistic employer unbound by an explicit labour policy.[17] The major part of the Opposition case, however, concentrated on the absence of any scheme for reorganizing the industry, the lack of consumer safeguards and the unfairness of the compensation terms. Others added little to this, and it was unclear what the Conservatives proposed as their alternative. Lancaster thought the State should compete in the industry, but not take it all over.[18] Eccles blamed the coal-owners for not cartelizing sufficiently to render nationalization superfluous.[19] Thorneycroft, one of the earliest and most consistent exponents of a neo-Liberal case, attacked the new organization almost solely because it was a monopoly.[20] Finally, Raikes, the backbencher who moved the official resolution rejecting the Bill, argued that nationalization prevented the State performing its most important role as arbitrator of society,[21] clearly a case against nationalization per se.

Macmillan composited many of these points when he summed up for the Opposition on the second day,[22] although Raikes' argument did not seem to trouble him. Initially, he laid out the case for nationalization in so attractive a form that his opposition seemed paradoxical: the unification of management and primary control would make savings for improved pay and conditions (a particular application of rentier euthanasia); unified selling prices would stabilize markets; heavy Government investment would raise productivity. His alternative followed the lines of the Tory Reform Committee proposals, involving such State intervention and private cartelization that (given he agreed that the ownership question was economically irrelevant) his opposition seemed lukewarm to the point of neutrality. Consideration in committee consisted mainly of attempts to protect coal users[23] by limiting ministerial powers, creating consumer safeguards, and narrowing the area to be nationalized. Amendments were framed to prevent price discrimination, to create an independent Price Tribunal, to prevent the new Coal Board competing with private distributors, to strengthen Consumer Councils, and weaken ministerial control.[24] It was not until the third reading that Colonel Lancaster, leading for the Opposition, suggested for the first time that the Coal Board should usefully be more decentralized,[25] but this was not a point taken up at the time nor explored with concrete proposals, nor did it occur in Macmillan's final summing-up.[26]

The almost unlimited demand for fuel in the immediate post-war years staved off for a time the continued economic decline of the coal industry. Nationalization itself did not impinge directly on the question of the economic future of coal, but fuel in general did continue to be a primary concern of Parliament. In particular, the fuel crisis of the winter of 1947 suggested that the immediate necessity was to maximize fuel supply (rather than minimize its price). But the issue of nationalization was generally accepted as settled,[27] even though some Conservatives were occasionally tempted to blame political interference for the performance of the industry.

The Industrial Charter promised 'reorganization' of the industry, without specifying details. Indeed it was not until late 1947 that Macmillan, for the Opposition, took up Lancaster's point and urged 'decentralization' of the Coal Board's functions to guard against monopoly.[28] Once reiterated, the suggestion rapidly assumed the form of hallowed doctrine, although only Colonel Lancaster pressed on to add any content to the idea.[29] The membership of the party seemed to accept the new aim, but there was no explicit discussion of the underlying criteria. A resolution supporting decentralization appeared before the 1949 party conference,[30] and it proposed that the Board be restricted to the role of landlord, loan corporation, marketing board and research institute, a combination of functions which might seem to tilt the balance towards the aim of centralization rather than that of local autonomy. This impression was confirmed by the only other public proposals, those made by Butler in 1950.[31] Official policy statements of these years merely approved the words without divulging any definitions.

Coal, Eccles said, was 'a necessary . . . symbolic experiment in readjustment'.[32] The Conservatives would not perhaps themselves have nationalized the industry if in power, but they

would have been compelled to tamper with ownership prerogatives more or less extensively to achieve any *modus vivendi* with
the industry. Official policy, before 1947 never very explicit on
this score, seemed directly derived from inter-war corporatist proposals – compulsory amalgamations, rationalization,
centralized self-government and cartelization: that is, it was
open to the same criticisms with which Conservatives scourged
Labour's policies after 1947. The new organization, they said,
involved excessive State intervention, was not 'voluntary', was
centralized and bureaucratic, and established a public monopoly, presumably inferior to a private oligopoly of the most
powerful producers. In practice, the party division amounted to
little more than whether a private profit should accrue to a
minority of coal producers.

Neo-Liberalism offered some sort of political alternative in
the word 'decentralization'. Local autonomy, face-to-face self-
government, was not intended so much as merely some technical
loosening of the organizational structure, with the central
authority retaining the decisive levers of power. Political fervour
seemed to promise the first part of a genuine Liberal renaissance (of which Churchill's Free the People campaign was the
overt political expression). The conservatism of the leadership
restrained itself to the second, where the merits of 'decentralization' were by no means self-evident.

In time the Conservatives accepted coal nationalization, and
concentrated on minimizing the changes involved, on protecting the coal-user along lines suggested by industrial consumers,
on defending or seeking to enlarge managerial as opposed to
ministerial power (an aim in which they were at one with
advocates of Morrisonian nationalization), and on questioning
the relevance of this measure to the solution of industrial conflict. What was not attacked was the lack of any proposed
structure in the industry to foster internal competition. Indeed,
amendments in pricing policy strove to prevent any prospect of
this, and to ensure inter-subsidization between economic and
uneconomic units. The attack on monopoly *per se* was relatively
weak. Further, Conservatives rarely defended the existing
structure of the industry on the grounds that private property
was important, either in its direct or indirect forms (*viz.* to

increase competition, enterprise and initiative). The discussion on both sides assumed a framework of property-less managerial norms, of non-competitive units, and concerned itself with relative technical merits within this framework.

2. TRANSPORT

Coal and railways had had a partly similar experience. The history of both included periods of substantial State intervention (particularly during both world wars), compulsory amalgamations and industrial conflict. Even more so than in coal, some prominent industrialists and politicians favoured nationalization of the railways in order to reorganize the industry and render transport a 'public service', that is, a negligible factor in industrial costs.[33] The development of road transport had complicated the picture by introducing fierce competition to transport from an industry of very small-scale units, much less amenable than railways to national direction. The Liberal rationale of industrial progress, its justification of private ownership, was much more plausibly validated in road transport than in an industry like railways, dominated by geographically monopolistic companies. In addition, the mass of small road-transport entrepreneurs constituted a substantial pressure group that upheld the Liberal rationale, unlike the railways where the distinction between public and private ownership was, in terms of managerial control, largely irrelevant.

The railway companies themselves made efforts to assimilate their new rival, both by purchasing very large holdings in road transport, and by seeking to set up a controlled cartel with road firms. The expansive confidence of road transporters that they could defeat the railways effectively prevented any agreement between the two. Even the 1938 'Square Deal' proposals which permitted some competition between the two, were not accepted, and the end of wartime control left the two industries at logger-heads. However, the election to office of a Labour Government on a pledge to nationalize all transport did what mere negotiation could not do. In July 1946, both industries announced their acceptance of a form of the Square Deal co-ordination proposals.

The Conservatives were drawn in two separate directions over transport – towards transport as a public service, epitomized by the railway cartel, and towards the defence of independent private enterprise in road transport. The compromise between the two positions consisted in only formally opposing rail nationalization, urging the Square Deal as a 'voluntary' scheme, and offering 'strenuous . and uncompromising'[34] opposition to road transport nationalization. However, in the enthusiasm of battle (and possibly to unite the maximum opposition), this tended to become opposition to the nationalization of all transport.

The interests at stake in transport were much more widely dispersed than in many important industries, a circumstance which partly explained the substantial volume of public opposition to nationalization, and necessitated relatively elaborate co-ordination to focus the counter-attack. Well before the publication of the Bill (28 November 1946), business opposition expressed itself in protest meetings, memoranda and published statements.[35] In March 1946, the railways published their alternative to nationalization, modelled on the Square Deal, and these proposals were ultimately accepted by the Road Haulage Association (RHA), and presented, with the support of the FBI and other organizations, to the Minister of Transport.[36] Meanwhile, Conservative speakers increasingly dealt with the issue as one of major importance, suggesting counter-proposals also along the lines of the Square Deal. Indeed, Macmillan went further and promised that a Conservative Government would seek a cartel of *all* transport interests (including air and water transport), and not just road and rail.[37]

The Government announcement that nationalization was scheduled for the coming session caused a flurry of opposition activity and pushed together more closely the political and business elements. The RHA set afoot a campaign of opposition, inaugurated by Macmillan for the party.[38] On the same day, the RHA gave a luncheon for Oliver Poole MP at which he announced that the party, as a token of the importance it attached to the issue of transport, had appointed Sir David Maxwell Fyfe of the Conservative Front Bench to be chairman of the party Road Transport Committee and to lead the

Opposition against the Bill. Two days later, the FBI issued a statement of its opposition to the Bill, and simultaneously combined with other transport-using business groups to create a Central Committee of Transport Users. This body promptly circularized its members on the clauses of the Bill, and subsequently advised the Parliamentary Opposition during the Bill's second reading. Other industrial groups published statements of their opposition.[39] The railway stockholders opened an opposition campaign, and Churchill wired his best wishes, assuring them that 'the Opposition will fight for justice'; Sir Hugh O'Neill MP became vice-chairman of the campaign, and Sir Herbert Williams (a Conservative MP until 1945, thereafter prominent in the National Union) moved the key resolution, supported by Sir John Mellors MP.[40]

The stream of Opposition statements reached its peak to coincide with the beginning of the second reading of the Bill (16 December). In Parliament itself a barrage of memoranda bombarded MPs, peers, ministers and, outside Parliament, interested parties. The deluge was on such a scale that, it is said, the Opposition had one thousand amendments ready for the Bill's committee stage.[41] These were prepared by the party's Transport Committee in consultation with a director of the RHA who was in continuous attendance on MPs during sittings. Where possible, MPs who were members of a relevant trade association, were nominated by the party to put particular amendments.[42] In particular controversies, 'the collective effort of a large number of powerful interest groups' was brought to bear on the problem; for example, in opposition to the 'C' licence clauses.[43] Throughout it all, the Economic League and Aims of Industry tried to mobilize outside opinion through some seven thousand open-air meetings and thirty thousand bus-stop and factory-gate meetings.[44]

The Conservative case against transport nationalization, in essentials, was identical to the case of the extra-Parliamentary transport-users. But differences of emphasis within the party were also apparent.[45] Some attacked the imposition on the industry of a co-ordination that should grow 'naturally';[46] others complained that the Bill contained no plan for co-ordination at all.[47] No one attacked the notion of 'co-ordination' in industry *per se*. In general, the argument on transport was similar to that on coal, with somewhat more emphasis on the need for competition, initiative and freedom from bureaucracy in road transport. It was left to Thorneycroft almost alone to develop a case against monopoly *per se*: 'I happen to be the first Tory to speak in the Debate today', he began unequivocally, and went on, 'A monopoly is in general a racket at the expense of the consumer, and is still a racket, even though it has one or two of His Majesty's Ministers mixed up in it'.[48]

He accused the Government of nationalizing road transport merely to safeguard the railways from competition.[49] Yet still, somewhat inconsistently in terms of the full Liberal case, he did not object to co-ordination in the industry, only that it was imposed.

Committee proceedings were congested and embittered by the introduction of the guillotine (3 March 1947). The main block of amendments covered, as they had done in coal nationalization, efforts to minimize the scope of the Act, of ministerial power (*vis-à-vis* managerial power), and protect existing operators and transport users. The points finally summarized in Maxwell Fyfe's third reading reply for the Opposition covered the 'excessive' power of the Minister, 'overcentralization' in the new organization of the industry (this was May 1947), restrictions on non-nationalized transport, and the compensation terms.[50] By this time, 'decentralization' was becoming an issue, and being contrasted with 'co-ordination'.

The Industrial Charter, the publication of which coincided with the final readings of the Bill, proposed that 'more freedom' should be given to 'A' and 'B' licence-holders, without mentioning denationalization. *The Right Road* (July 1949) was more explicit, saying that no further nationalization of road passenger transport would be permitted, and 'where possible', it would be denationalized; it unequivocally pledged denationalization for road haulage. *This is the Road* (January 1950) officially pledged the party to 'decentralization' in railway organization.

However, individuals within the party had advanced much further in the neo-Liberal case by 1950. Hinchingbrooke urged the profit criterion as the only valid test for transport efficiency, opposed inter-subsidization between services, and argued that the railways must shrink until they either paid or disappeared.[51] Thorneycroft stressed that ancillary operations managed by the Transport Commission must be merged with the railways or sold off; regional units must be autonomous, with a flexible pricing system and subject to competition.[52] Bevins argued that private companies be allowed to compete against public,[53] a proposal that was a startling shift from earlier Conservative fears that public industry would compete 'unfairly' with private firms.

Actual consideration of the Transport Bill spanned the period in which general opinion began to shift towards a neo-Liberalism. The Government's Bill itself partly reflected this since it sought little actual co-ordination between different sectors of transport, despite some Government claims that this was the main purpose of the Bill. The vicissitudes of the dichotomy, 'co-ordination' or 'competition', of the Square Deal cartel proposals or an open market in transport, reflected the evolution of Conservative thinking.

In summary then, during the main consideration of the Bill, the Conservatives did not attack the idea of 'co-ordination' between road and rail *per se*. And to that extent, they did not support the Liberal case for 'free enterprise', but rather the case for private ownership in functionally divided markets with a centralized transport cartel. Only later was this conception changed when 'decentralization' came to the fore as the nearest neo-Liberal version of public industry. However, even this had relatively conservative implications. It did not include the re-establishment of local autonomous units, and so open competition within a nationalized industry, but rather merely increased regional autonomy where, perhaps, neither the benefits of full local autonomy nor those of national centralization were available. No case was presented which unequivocally demonstrated the superiority of increased regional authority.

3. STEEL

The nationalization of the iron and steel industry (like its denationalization) was one of the most curious episodes in modern British political history. The Government proposed drastic ownership changes in an industry for whose economic performance it had nothing but praise; it planned at the same time to retain the existing organization and personnel. Indeed, ultimately, it did not even change the names of the companies operating in the industry. On the other hand, the Opposition defended the industry while accepting the major charges against it (*viz.* that it was a cartel), and defended it on the basis of a case for competition which, it admitted, did not exist, and which it had no intention of introducing into the industry. Indeed, to the degree to which Conservatives defended the existing industry (and, by implication, the record of pre-war governments), they contradicted claims they might have had to defend a new Liberal case for 'free enterprise'.

The defenders, like the attackers, had little option but to concentrate solely on the existence of shareholders in the steel industry, a subject both parties agreed was economically irrelevant. The conflict could only be between a private cartel and a State monopoly, a conflict where the perspectives of neo-Liberalism were only an embarrassment, a ghost at the feast. To defend the private organization of steel, the Opposition perforce had to defend the range of ideas subsumed under the phrase 'self-government in industry' and so the pre-war record of pluralist corporatism – and this during the years of 1948 and 1949, when the neo-Liberal counter-revolution was in full tide. Inevitably, the Conservative image seemed self-contradictory. Since the controversy tended to merge with the early phases of the 1950 general election, it served as one of the reasons why observers doubted whether in practice the two major parties differed very much.

Some Conservatives saw steel as the Rubicon of British society – beyond it lay full socialism (or State capitalism, as Macmillan put it). Beside the alleged economic irrelevance of steel nationalization, such fears are difficult to appreciate. A more serious point at issue was a revival of the inter-war controversy between 'voluntary' and 'compulsory' reorganization; the British Iron and Steel Federation (BISF) defended the first, and so in practice defended the right of the larger firms to control an entire industry. In any case, since the Government explicitly denied any intention to reorganize the industry, even this issue seemed slightly irrelevant.

The Conservatives opposed nationalization of steel in principle, and did so for nearly three years before the Bill was published. There was never any doubt that, if able, they would denationalize it.[54] As in the case of transport, the case against nationalization was developed in close consultation with the major trade associations of the producing firms which created a Joint Policy Committee to represent their interests in Parliament and liaise with the Iron and Steel Consumers' Committee representing the major steel users.[55] In addition, the party had a number of members directly connected with the industry who could represent it in Parliament,[56] the best known being Sir Andrew Duncan MP, re-elected Chairman of BISF in September 1945. Ironically, the main source of information on iron and steel production for the Government was also the BISF, so that, at times, the Parliamentary conflict could seem like little more than elaborate shadow-boxing.

The case against the Bill resolved itself into a number of central points.

(a) The industry was already adequate in all respects

This point was made by many Conservatives, and expressed in Churchill's description of the industry as 'an island of peace and progress in the wrack and ruin of our times'.[57] However, the charge of monopoly complicated this. Churchill admitted the accusation,[58] as did many others, but argued that it warranted public control not public ownership. Thorneycroft suggested that if monopoly was proved by the existence of a trade association, then few industries could claim exemption from nationalization.[59] Others challenged the charge of monopoly, saying that substantial competition existed in the industry, that there were no signs of monopoly, that shareholders controlled the managers in the public interest, or that State control already checked the industry adequately but would not be able to do so under State ownership.[60] Many of these points usually went with praise for inter-war conceptions of pluralist corporatism – Eden praised the IDAC system as the model for State-industry co-operation; Hugh Fraser lauded it as 'a successful combination of private initiative and public interest;

the first example of self-government in industry under the aegis of State control'; and Selwyn Lloyd described the almost fully corporatist hierarchy of the industry as working 'extraordinarily well in practice'.[61]

(b) Nationalization would have adverse internal effects

The Opposition case here was a little weakened by the repetitive assurances of the Government that it did not intend to change the structure of the industry. To sustain certain points, Conservatives had to assume some hypothetical reorganization for which there was no evidence at all.

Some Conservatives suggested that nationalizing only part of the steel industry would divide necessarily integrated processes, but that the alternative, nationalizing the entire industry, would introduce the State into most sectors of the economy, so close was the industry's involvement in almost all the main industrial processes.[62] Others argued that the good labour relations said to exist in the industry would be disturbed – either because of limitations on managerial authority, or through the elimination of allegedly substantial worker shareholdings in steel, through the necessary destruction of independent trade unions following any wage confrontation between State and unions, or through the workers refusing to work or accept managerial authority because they felt they owned the industry.[63] Again, it was said State ownership (but presumably not large-scale private corporate ownership) entailed bureaucracy, which must reduce the efficiency of the existing industry, and make managers more devoted to political promotion than industrial production.[64] Some of these points were clearly arguments against nationalization *per se* rather than just the nationalization of iron and steel.

Finally, it was argued that nationalization would have adverse economic effects; it would dislocate expansion and recovery. Innovations in the industry would cease, and it would freeze into the shape it was when it was appropriated.[65] Further, if the industry were divided into private and public producers, the private would be at the mercy of the public steel suppliers; either there would be a disastrous price war between the two or a tacit price agreement that would permit prices to rise indefinitely.[66]

(c) *Nationalization would have adverse external effects*

Nationalization, it was said, would frighten away foreign capital from Britain and alienate the United States, Britain's major creditor.[67] Lyttelton was more concerned with the problem of an uncartelized steel sector; having a public and private sector would divide the voice of British steel abroad.[68] Churchill argued that bureaucratic control (that is, State control) would not be capable of competing abroad. Finally a wide variety of speakers warned the Government of the dangers of making economic relations between private firms in different countries into relations between States – war must replace ordinary competition.[69]

Within the domestic economy, nationalization would mean disorganization, introducing the State into hundreds of diverse industries. 'If the Government were to stop their projects of nationalisation', Lyttelton reflected . . .

it would be very difficult but not impossible for private enterprise to retain the initiative, contrivance and boldness with which the country would regain its position in the world. If the Government are to add steel, the principal raw material of industry, then I say that private enterprise cannot exist as we have known it.[70]

A backbencher added the interesting point that henceforth the State would have to bear responsibility for all errors, rather than diffusing it among non-public centres of power throughout society.[71]

A miscellany of other points was also made: that, for example, under the terms of the Bill, Parliamentary control was inadequate and ministerial power excessive. In this context Lyttelton praised the pre-nationalization system of public control; if the BISF did not know the national interest, the Government could direct it; if the BISF misused its position, Parliament could appeal for protection to an independent State. Under nationalization, however, there were no such checks, and the minister had absolute power to define the national interest as he saw fit. This was a somewhat academic point since 'the Opposition was itself committed to a system which involved choosing persons who would have power to determine the national interest (the IDAC) and would in turn be subject to Ministerial control'.[72]

There were additional complaints that the compensation terms were inadequate, the time inappropriate, the case for nationalization non-existent, and the Bill without any scheme for reorganizing the industry.[73] Consumer safeguards were inadequate, and the opportunity for a real State-industry partnership had been thrown away.[74] Committee amendments followed the pattern of earlier Bills – amendments to limit the scope of the Bill, the power of the minister, and to protect consumers. Under this last heading, amendments were tabled to permit dissatisfied steel-users the right of resorting to the courts for redress, and to create an independent Price Tribunal to regulate steel prices. A tactically astute aspect of Conservative opposition concerned the timing of the Bill, and involved an Opposition request that execution of the Act await another general election. This compelled the Government to consider constitutional reform to overcome opposition in the House of Lords, or, as Conservatives put it, to prevent the electorate 'having more time to consider the Bill'. Shrewd the tactic may have been, but it involved no point of principle.

The Conservative case against steel nationalization assumed and approved an industry which was in essence pluralist corporatist, while mobilizing various traditional corporatist arguments on top of that. The assumption was inconsistent with what it supported. The defence of 'free enterprise' and competition implied an industry with a reasonable number of actively competing firms, not a tightly organized cartel almost as remote from the implications of 'free enterprise' as was a State industry. The 'freedom' involved seemed no more than the freedom of shareholders to receive dividends or the freedom of existing producers to monopolize the industry. The neo-Liberal case made almost no impact in steel, and it was quite clear that the Conservatives did not envisage reforming the private steel industry so that competition would become effective. They were left with arguments which either contradicted existing practices in the steel industry or were directed against all nationalization without discrimination.

The word 'decentralization' did occur towards the end of the controversy, but again, it did not mean changing the structure of the private industry (which, as a structure, continued intact under nationalization), but merely returning it to the *status quo ante* in terms of ownership alone. Some Conservatives did accuse the Government of centralizing the industry excessively, despite the evidence that the Government intended no structural changes at all, and as a result urged as an alternative 'decentralization'.[75] However, Macmillan carefully clarified this point by arguing: 'The Opposition attempt to provide the maximum amount of decentralisation approximates as nearly as possible to the present set-up in the industry whereby the Iron and Steel Federation is merely a co-ordinating body and individual firms retain their own managements in entirety.'[76] That is, the Opposition did not refer to the organization of the industry at all in the word 'decentralization', but merely to the question of ownership; it did not therefore intend to break up the large corporations or their cartel arrangements, the heart of what organizational centralization there was in the industry.

Thus, in steel at least, the return to Liberalism had clear limits and was rather more verbal than practical. The role of the State in the steel industry was to remain as it had been before the war: mentor and guardian to watch over the possible lapses of a monopolistic industry. Implicitly, by accepting the need for such a guardian, Conservatives suggested the limits to their own proposed legislation on monopolies.

4. OTHER NATIONALIZATION MEASURES

The trends were reflected in varying degrees in other nationalization measures. For example, the Opposition did not oppose a public corporation assuming a monopoly of atomic energy; they argued this on the grounds that the scale of capital required in this field would make it unprofitable for private exploitation.[77] Again, no official opposition was offered to the nationalization of Commonwealth Cable and Wireless Services since this measure, it was argued, strengthened imperial unity.[78] The Conservatives initially accepted the nationalization of the Bank of England,[79] and then subsequently decided to oppose the measure formally on the grounds that it wasted time, not on the properly Liberal ground that finance should be independent of the State rather than a weapon of public policy.[80] None of these undertakings was scheduled for denationalization, nor even 'decentralization'.

In civil aviation, it was the Government, paradoxically, which sought some measure of decentralization in a Conservative-created monopoly,[81] and the Conservative radicals who opposed it (the year was 1946). The party divided into two – those who attacked the Government for perpetuating public ownership[82] (so condemning Conservative inter-war policy), and those who pressed for a single functional monopoly, a cartel of all forms of transport. On this last point, Macmillan argued that the Government sacrificed 'the advantages of genuine diversity without obtaining the full advantages of uniformity'; he went on to cite the impressive benefits accruing from 'a fully centralised single monopolist service' and from a cartel of all transport, the alleged aim of the Coalition 'Swinton Plan'.[83] The party did not, after this, commit itself to any action in the industry[84] until 1950, when *This is the Road* promised more private enterprise in civil aviation; the ideal of a transport cartel had by then faded.

The Electricity Bill of 1947 represented the turning-point in the field of nationalization from an implicitly corporatist policy to one more influenced by neo-Liberalism. The Parliamentary controversy was relieved by the absence of any major private pressure group,[85] and the alternatives were rather State or municipal ownership. Partly as a result, the centralization issue was deployed in genuine organizational terms with greater clarity, although with very much less Conservative involvement.[86] Although the Opposition case was developed in terms of the Government's 'passion for over-centralization', the party did not promise denationalization for electricity supply, nor even decentralization. The policy statements were silent on electricity.

Gas nationalization came too late to share fully in the corporatist genesis of earlier measures. The actual Bill's reliance on area rather than national boards as prime authority might be construed as symptomatic of the Government's parallel shift towards neo-Liberalism, although Conservatives tended to interpret this revisionism as a victory for their own ideas. However, this last comforting thought did not placate the Conservatives, but rather prompted them to even greater efforts to ridicule their former orthodoxy – namely, the case for functionally integrated industries and the co-ordination of all fuel and power production. *Only* competition, it was now alleged, would ensure maximum efficiency.[87]

5. THE CONSERVATIVE ANSWER: THE PROPERTY-OWNING DEMOCRACY

Hitherto, this account has been concerned with Conservative opposition to particular nationalization measures, and the ideological context which might be inferred from this. However, Conservatives did also argue that their particular opposition derived from a coherent, general political viewpoint that could be described independently. Many Conservatives propounded a wider solution for a wider problem, of which nationalization was only a part. The central problem, Conservatives said, was the issue of insecurity. Men felt themselves to be prey to the propertied, to powerful employers. What had been achieved politically in universal suffrage (namely, the claimed democratic participation by all and thereby the control of political decisions by a majority) must find equivalent expression in the economic field. The socialist response to this problem was to eliminate private property by giving it all to the State, so reducing all to a common servitude. The Conservative answer must be the reverse, to give property to all, and create conditions for participation by all in economic decisions. 'Both parties believe in a form of capitalism', a National Union report claimed, 'but whereas our opponents believe in State capitalism, we believe in the widest measure of individual capitalism.' The two antidotes to the two problems of unequal property distribution and unequal participation in economic power were summed up in the phrases, 'the property-owning democracy' and 'partnership in industry' (to be discussed later).

The first phrase had already occurred long before, and perhaps its intellectual origins can be detected in one form in the nineteenth-century suggestions that policy be directed towards the creation of a new class of independent peasants as a means of strengthening the *status quo*. The ethos of Young England stretched all the way from a romantic vision of a recreated medieval society to modest proposals for the creation or extension of allotments for industrial workers. Throughout, the justification of existing property rights played a major role in the argument. In 1945 and afterwards, the 'property-owning democracy' constituted similarly both a high ideal – for some Conservatives, standing as the Conservative alternative to socialism and covering the whole nature of society; and at the other extreme, a convenient phrase to describe the promotion of particular sorts of ownership among those who could afford its purchase, most notably here, private houses.

Eden revived the phrase after the war as an explicit alternative to nationalization. Macmillan, Butler and Eccles developed it, and some Conservatives tried to formulate practical measures, but of these, only house-ownership attracted much rank-and-file support.[88] The problem of inadequate purchasing power which underlay questions of wider ownership was said by Conservatives to be capable of solution through a policy of cheap loans and lower taxation (both of which would have had unequal effects on different social groups in the absence of other measures). In hard policy terms nothing was suggested, and it was possibly this which prompted Boothby to conclude in 1949 that 'the phrase "Property-owning democracy" has done good service for the Conservative Party during the past twenty-five years; but, like patriotism, it is not enough'.[89]

To define too clear an alternative to Labour had its dangers, since it might provide a focus for an intransigent opposition within the party. A minor sign of such a possibility can be seen at the 1949 Conference where Norman St John-Stevas attacked *The Right Road* for not saying that a property-owning democracy was flatly incompatible with the Welfare State.[90] In addition, too clear an alternative might have committed the party leadership to pledges, to specific economic policies that could embarrass the leadership in office and run counter to other economic purposes (as, for example, the housing programme, forced on the leadership in 1950, which did tend to run counter to general economic policy when the Conservatives came to office). In brief, the overall aim, in so far as it contrasted with the *status quo* or suggested a state of affairs unlikely to evolve unaided out of the *status quo*, was radical, and as such unlikely to achieve consistent Conservative support.

The leadership escaped from the dilemma of radicalism by redefining the implications of the phrase. What in *The Industrial Charter* was still an aspiration (implying that existing property distribution was unsatisfactory), had become in *The Right Road* a description of the existing *status quo*. Property, it said, had become much more widely distributed in the past fifty years, thereby implicitly tending to deny the existence of just the problem the 'property-owning democracy' was formulated to solve. The unexplained transition from normative to descriptive, always present in a phrase which serves both as an aim and as a means to justify what already exists (namely, property), was here at its clearest. This sort of transition always tends to make explicit general aims within Conservatism inoperative. However, the transition did not detract from Conservative rank-and-file enthusiasm for more houses, despite the opposition of the party leadership.[91] Neither side justified its attitude on this particular question in terms of the general ideal; no one explained how an extension of middle-class home ownership was an adequate reply to nationalization, and there was no appeal to society as a whole.

The problems of wider ownership seemed on the surface more intractable than most Conservatives admitted. The extension of house-ownership or small shareholdings would hardly give a majority of people satisfactory control of their own livelihood. It was not obvious from industrial history that there was a viable alternative to industrial concentration open to reformist achievement in societies dominated by either private or State ownership, with propertyless employment the lot of the majority. Wider share ownership, given the inefficacy of small shareholder control of firms, was no solution to the problem of the majority controlling its means of live-lihood, whatever help it might be to incomes or as a pre-requisite for a consistent gloss on conditions. The elision between 'capital' as an economic concept and 'capital' as merely person-ally-owned and used consumer durables could scarcely hold the long-term allegiance of the majority if put to the test.

The aspiration in practice was a middle-class one, and mildly Liberal rather than being a direct derivation from old Toryism and the landed interest's defence of large-scale landed estates. 'Property' for the middle class was merely a comfort without incumbent social duties, rather than a holding in the 'nation', entailing specific responsibilities to those without property. Conservatives argued that the possession of property reshaped the individual, fostering psychological attributes conducive to the stability of society. So desirable did these attributes seem that it was difficult to see why urging was needed, except to evade the economic problem underlying it. Conservatives tended to rest content with savouring the agreeable character-istics of their hypothetical individuals possessing property, rather than seeking either to offer a rigorous justification or to face squarely the problem of unequal incomes.

All this had little to do with actual Conservative politics. In practice, Conservative popular propaganda made virtually no use of the phrase, the 'property-owning democracy', for general election purposes. The significance of this phrase was essen-tially confined to party members offering the rank-and-file both a sort of ethos to counterpose to socialism and, if it was needed, a more general justification for immediate aims, decided on grounds other than those derived from the ethos.

One major difficulty in framing an alternative to socialism was that Conservatives were not unanimous in the analysis of the problem, in the explanation at an intermediate level of why nationalization had occurred. For some, it was the mani-festation of evil, stupidity or incompetence, and Churchill most frequently saw it as the result of the Government's addiction to 'political theory'. None of these explanations gave rise to a generalized case, and so the errors of the socialists seemed to be no more than unfortunate accidents. By contrast, some Conservatives did offer explanations in political terms.

Maclean saw nationalization as a means of strengthening the power of the trade union leadership against the workers.[92] Birch argued that it was merely part of the process of liquidating private capital, part of 'a great campaign . . . to persuade everybody to be a *rentier*. At the same time, he (the Chancellor) is crushing the life out of the *rentier*. There is to be no nonsense about euthanasia.' Macmillan did not develop any analysis but he did insist upon calling the emerging economic order 'State Capitalism',[93] with its underlying implication of a bureaucratic society operated solely in the interests of those who commanded the State. Hinchingbrooke took this element somewhat further by describing nationalization as part of the forward march of the managerial revolution. The Electricity Bill, he said, 'gives semi-political power to a new class of unrepresentative and uncontrolled scientific administrators. It gives pride of place to technical achievement, and dethrones economic needs.'[94] Similarly, the Iron and Steel Bill enthroned 'the applied scientist, the technocrat, the manager. . . . So much for fifty years after Keir Hardie.' Those who would lose by the change would include Parliamentary democrats, Bloomsbury intellectuals, Transport House and the workers: 'I challenge hon. Gentleman opposite', he concluded, 'to find in this Bill one thing which is good democracy or good Socialism, be it Guild Socialism, syndicalist socialism, or plain Christian Socialism. . . . Quis custodiet ipsos custodes?'[95] Perhaps there were distant echoes of the case that the State was being manipulated to establish and sanction the rights of a new vested interest in Churchill's 'Free the People' campaign, but it ill accorded with other Conservative complaints that, for example, management was not sufficiently independent under the terms of the various nationalization measures, or that technical autonomy was an aim insufficiently fostered under the Bills.

7

Organized Labour

The attitude of both major parties to labour questions up to 1951 was unspecific to the point of drift. Neither was sure whether full employment constituted a qualitatively new situation which had to be specifically reconciled with wage stability; nor, it could be said, whether full employment would even last indefinitely; nor, finally, what the role of trade unions in society should be. Neither had any clear policy on industrial conflict that went beyond mere expedients. The Government ended the period advocating to the TUC 'the familiar and essentially capitalist notion of profit-sharing'.[1]

Conservatism was related to industrial labour in a multiplicity of ways, many of them not necessarily separable in practice. However, three immediate points are relevant here. First, in general economic policy, general opinion was slowly moving towards the view that the role of wages was crucial. Second, trade unionism as a political force was in general inimical to the Conservatives. Finally, the existence of a Labour Government was at least in part seen to be a function of the peculiar position of organized labour, and Conservatism, to survive, was bound to try to provide some distinct alternative to 'Labourism', to offer some alternative conception of society in which labour would find what Conservatives considered a just and satisfying role.

The Conservative response in this period was mixed, and certainly more pragmatic or cautious than in other fields. Only in their approach to the first problem was the influence of neo-Liberalism discernible, but the second and third problems were seen as partial functions of the first: that is, economic expansion, the neo-Liberals said, would dissolve union loyalty to political solutions, and render Conservative trade unionism attractive.

Conservative policy on trade unionism aimed at making the unions 'non-political', and Conservatives usually denied that this was itself a political attitude. If trade unions were 'non-political', then they would presumably refrain from seeking to change the *status quo*. In political terms, Conservatives were accordingly concerned to persuade the unions to accept the existing structure of society, and in return, they promised a defence of trade unionism in its limited Conservative sense – that is, unions as 'purely industrial' organizations. It was not made clear what 'purely industrial' could mean, under what conditions it could hold, nor what a union response should be when it was clear that 'purely industrial problems' had no 'purely industrial solutions'.

It was earlier argued that much corporatist speculation saw the unions as vitally important institutions in the future society. They were to become the responsible agencies of either delegated State power or managerial authority, entrusted with the social discipline of labour (possibly along lines already established in, for example, the Soviet Union or Spain). That is, unions were to be not so much defenders of labour against capital, as, with capital, instruments for the control of labour, for the social organization production: administrative agencies of the *status quo*. If labour, capital and management were functionally rather than competitively related, they would share a common allegiance to the 'nation' and its supreme expression, the neutral State. The State would then be able, without controversy or challenge, to establish just wages for all in the most efficient relationship to production. In metaphysical terms where the Hegelian undertone becomes clear, the unions would necessarily will what was most appropriate for society through the State, and execute the public will amongst the different sections of labour. In milder terms, an agreed or 'voluntary' wages policy would maintain just income differentials between the rewards of different sections of the 'nation'. The role of economic growth in changing differentials was not generally considered at a time when depression rather than growth was seen as the main problem. It followed from the general scheme that there was no place for a separately political trade unionism. The unions were to receive explicit representation in (or the right of consultation by) the State or those whose organs (corporations) made up the State, so that they had no need to attempt to gain supreme control of the State. To do so was to jeopardize the stability of the 'balanced' society. In tactical terms, any attempt to establish a relationship between the existence of industrial problems and political solutions was inherently dangerous for social stability and the assumption that society, as given, was just and not even in principle amenable to anything except the narrowest practical improvement, let alone conscious radical political change.

By contrast, a Liberal position emphasized that the market was superior to the State, and that *only* the free competition of unions and employers could secure both the maximum rate of economic expansion and the most efficient allocation of rewards between both parties. Any idea that the factors of production could be functionally related to each other at the level of society could only be an illusion that would conceal inefficiency and protect the rights of established interests against competition. In contrast to the unanimity portrayed in corporatism, society was an arena for trials of strength, the results of which represented what was economically most satisfactory and the *sole* means available to allocate resources most efficiently. The State should not rig the contest between the competitors since the State could never know what was economically most desirable. This position accepted, indeed demanded, that the pre-eminent role of the trade unions was to defend the interests of their members, not to become merged with the managerial or State organization of labour. It accepted conflict as the desirable norm of society and the means to equilibrate the conflict of capital and labour. Against this, corporatism assumed a social harmony that eliminated the need for labour to defend itself as it eliminated the need for 'politics'. Both cases, it should be noted, assumed effectively non-political trade unionism, although in the Liberal scheme, since the State, the political organ, did not control the economy, the political views of the unions were of no significance; if the State was not of economic importance it was also presumed that the unions would not be political in an effective sense.

A priori, then, certain sorts of practical positions can be derived from this dichotomy. In fact, up to 1947 the Conservative party, while firmly adhering to the demand for non-political trade unionism, hardly committed itself on the freedom of the unions in wage bargaining; where members did commit themselves, radicals urged a strong wages policy. After 1947, by contrast, the party became firmly committed to entirely untrammelled trade unionism and completely free wage bargaining. It was added that given full employment, this position would be possible without inflation if there was continuous economic expansion; this would contain all possible demands on the economic product without such conflict as would jeopardize social stability.

1. TRADE UNIONS AS INSTITUTIONS

A number of problems, partly institutional in character, were of concern to Conservatives: for example, the practice of 'closed shop', unofficial strikes, contracting in or out of the political levy, the proposal that a secret ballot be held before every strike. To these can be added the partly economic problems of 'restrictive practices' and the need to increase productivity, the post-war need to redeploy labour or increase its supply and to counter the results of inflation in the labour market. The institutional questions were traditional to Conservatism, although not necessarily of great significance in the formulation of party policy. The partly economic questions were more closely related to particular post-war conditions, and have not been examined here except in so far as they are recurring problems.

Part of the Conservative critique of nationalization concerned its impact on labour and the need for statutory provision covering labour questions in public industries. Conservatives argued that in publicly-owned industries, independent trade unions must necessarily cease since the position of supremacy of the State could brook no direct opposition. The independence of unions was especially threatened where the State and unions were commanded by the same people (namely, the Labour party), who would therefore tend to operate as one, so depriving workers of independent defence. The case was fundamentally a Liberal defence of free trade unionism since it presupposed continuing conflict and rejected a corporatist subordination of unions to managers or State. It is of interest to note that the case began as early as 1945, was widely supported,[2] and provided subsequent strength to the neo-Liberal case as epitomized in *A New Approach*,[3] which urged unions to spur on industry and repudiate any idea of supporting a 'wages freeze'.

The group of institutional problems was high-lighted by the Government's proposal to repeal the 1927 Trade Disputes and Trade Union Act. This provoked initially strong Conservative opposition, including a campaign outside the Commons.[4] The opponents of repeal argued that the relationship between the State and the unions must remain clear (and a general strike illegal); the right of 'closed shop' was an intolerable infringement of individual freedom as was the intimidation of workers who continued to work during a strike; that the Civil Service must be prevented from adopting political loyalties; that the reintroduction of the 'contracting-out' means of making union contributions to the Labour party was an unjust tax on the unwary; and that the Bill as a whole was irrelevant to immediate economic problems.[5] The case followed the Conservative argument for non-political trade unionism, a legal limit on union activities, and a neutral State, the elements being complementary.

Whatever the importance of these issues to Conservative rank-and-file members, the actual course of the discussion is now of relatively limited concern, and attracted little sustained interest among Conservative MPs.[6] Conservatives did defend a particular notion of trade unionism and tended to do so in pluralist terms: 'We cannot maintain the position of private enterprise', one speaker argued, 'in which I believe, unless across the table there is a mighty trade union movement.'[7] However, Conservatives did not press the case consistently, and left the task of moving an amendment to the 1946 Loyal Address to the Liberals.[8]

The improvement in the economy from 1947 and the need to maximize output added restrictive practices to the list of outstanding issues. Conservatives veered between urging 'ruthless action' against such practices and merely exhorting or consulting with trade union leaders.[9] For the membership this issue was part of the purely institutional questions, and National Union Conference Agendas bear witness to rank-and-file frustration on this score.[10] The leadership did not respond to this pressure except to deplore the practices concerned and promise consultation with the union leaders.[11] Later policy statements said the problem of restrictive practices was serious, and *Britain Strong and Free* did go so far as to say restrictive practices would be made subject to an improved Monopolies Commission. This no doubt helped Labour critics argue that Conservatives were inimical towards trade unionists, and increasingly prompted the Conservative leadership to deny that it contemplated any action against the unions.[12] Electoral considerations tended to neutralize any efforts to satisfy the wishes of rank-and-file party members.

2. WAGES POLICY AND COLLECTIVE BARGAINING

The problem said by one school of thought to be of central importance in both the sphere of labour and general Government economic policy, one where many of the institutional problems were ultimately located, concerned the reconciliation of free collective bargaining in conditions of full employment with a non-inflationary level of prices. Whether or not this was a problem depended from which side of the *étatiste*-pluralist dichotomy the person concerned drew his arguments. The *étatiste* asserted that there was a problem and only a powerful wages policy as part of an overall national plan would solve it; the pluralist denied that there was any such problem in general except as a by-product of misconceived Government intervention in the economy, and if any such problem did arise, it could be solved only by restoring to the trade unions and employers complete independence from the State; the sole economically justified action permitted to the State should be generalized influences through monetary policy, related to changes in the balance of payments.

From 1945, there were observers who argued that unemployment had formerly disciplined wage negotiations and prevented an imbalance between prices and incomes; since full employment now existed, there must be new means to offset the effects of an alleged 'monopoly' of labour, or, as it became politically expressed, of the trade unions (the 'monopoly' here was not explained). Inflation and shrinking export markets must follow unless a wages policy could be defined which would prevent the trade unions using the strength they now possessed.[13] Stating the question was some advance for the *étatiste* case, but it did not help either party locate an answer. It was important for the general corporatist case that reconciliation, not defeat of the unions was the means to success. Labour's 'wage freeze' was partly ineffective and partly eroded free collective bargaining; the ultimate Conservative answer, completely free collective bargaining and trade unionism, allegedly eroded the stability of the currency.

As a party, the Conservatives straddled both strands of opinion. Some attacked Labour for having a wages policy and proclaimed the freedom of unions to set whatever wage level they could achieve in an open market (even though that market was supposedly rigged in favour of full employment). Others attacked the Government for *not* having a wages policy or any coherent alternative. Both positions appeared up to 1947, but with the spreading influence of neo-Liberalism the party came down in favour of the first alternative.

One of the firmest advocates of a wages policy was a back-bencher, Norman Bower. He argued that it was foolish to hope for spontaneous conformity to Government wishes by unions and employers, that a wages policy was the precondition of an effective national plan, and that the trade union leadership must be supported by 'some kind of agreed and concerted policy'.[14] Others acknowledged the problem without drawing such clear conclusions. Macmillan, for example, meditated: 'We cannot close our eyes to the necessity for some form of voluntary self-discipline to replace the harsh and cruel discipline of the days of unemployment.'[15] It was here, through the very unclear notion of 'partnership' between State and unions, that the two wings of the party found some sort of reconciliation, a reconciliation which, however, concealed rather than clarified the problem. The terms of the 'partnership' were never specified, nor how the Government would enunciate its side of the partnership without a formal wages policy.

R. S. Hudson, like Macmillan a member of the Conservative Front Bench, outlined the neo-Liberal alternative to these variants on the 'restraint' thesis: 'We believe', he said, 'in the system of private enterprise. Under such a system, an individual trade union is free to negotiate with the employers concerned, and reach such settlement as their respective strength allows them to reach.' And, as if to scotch any rumours to the contrary, he added, 'Under a system of private enterprise no Government wages policy is essential'.[16] It was still possible to argue in this way in 1946 without the threat of immediate inflationary pressure. In later years, those in the party who at this stage equivocated, felt themselves compelled by inflation to choose clearly between free collective bargaining and some form of wages policy, whether by edict or 'voluntary restraint'.

In the event, the party chose the first. However, *The Industrial Charter* in 1947 was still concerned with the notion of 'partnership', even though it also asserted that the existing negotiating machinery must be defended. Its only contribution to the reconciliation of these two apparently divergent ends was to urge that more information be published so that different negotiations could spontaneously be reconciled with the 'facts of the nation's health'. A failure to communicate between different parts of the economy (rather than divergent interests) was thus seen as the crucial source of difficulties.

The Conservatives' choice between the two aims came, as much as anything, through asserting their incompatibility – wages can *either* be fixed by the Government *or* be reached by free negotiation between both sides of industry.[17] Implicitly this formulation rejected the hint of an intermediate solution which had been the charm of the word 'partnership', and, given the neo-Liberal context, posed an obvious choice. 'We believe', Churchill boldly declaimed, 'in collective bargaining and the right to strike. We believe in the independence of the Trade Union movement from Government policy.'[18] The policy statements which followed reiterated this position, and the 1950 National Union Conference enthusiastically endorsed it.[19]

This was the final position of the party summed up in *The New Approach*, which asserted that 'the more money a man earns, for which he has honestly worked, the better for him and for society as a whole'. A 10 per cent per annum increase in productivity (with 15 per cent after the first year) would incorporate all possible demands on the national income without inflation. Freeing the market would solve the pseudo-problem of reconciling full employment and a stable pound. Some observers were sceptical as to how far this represented the view of the whole party, but they would shortly have the chance to find out.[20]

3. THE PARTNERSHIP

Faced with the general problem of the opposition of organized labour, Conservatives did seek a generalized answer, summarized in the word 'partnership'. In general terms, 'partnership' was said to exist between all the major sections of society – between the State and industry, and, what is of concern here, between the 'two sides' of industry. The argument turned entirely upon how Conservatives defined the problem and sought to explain its existence. The immediate questions covered two related fields: first, industrial conflict, ranging from strikes to political unionism, from economic irritations to broad social questions that endangered stability and the *status quo*; second, production problems, covering rates of output and restrictive practices, that is, economic questions concerning the maximum output at given cost. The two are separated here, although Conservatives did not separate them (and, in practice, the two cannot ultimately be separated). However, some proposals suggested by Conservatives in fact only affected one element – for example, the introduction of piece rates in industry, strongly urged by some Conservatives, might have increased output, but might also, given the well-known opposition of the unions, have exacerbated the first problem.

The reasons offered for the existence of any general problem at all ranged widely, but tended ultimately to reduce to the proposal that the problem was more ideological than real. Time and education were the only real remedies to the mistaken viewpoint which labour, or at least some workers, were said to have. Some Conservatives blamed fifty years of socialist propaganda for the problem; for example, Thorneycroft waxed eloquent on the history of South Wales: 'the story of a country in which there were many happy valleys, where honest God-fearing citizens tried to do an honest job until Mr Arthur Horner (Communist and miners' leader, NH) and his friends arrived and started to exploit every grievance, every mistake, to trade on bitterness and hatred and all the wicked emotions of mankind'.[21] Other Conservatives emphasized the faults of leadership, a criticism which presumed that the structure of industrial relationships was broadly adequate already. 'Good management is the key to most industrial problems, just as bad management is the cause of most individual evils.'[22] Some saw the attitude of labour as merely an intellectual muddle, an unfortunate confusion of political power and economic grievance.[23] Yet others reiterated the Baldwinian explanation that the growth in size of industrial units had reduced the status of the worker and depersonalized his relations with his employer; better communication between management and managed would overcome this problem.[24]

The New Conservatives incorporated most of these points, drawing on the suggestions of inter-war Conservative radical writing and the academic study of industrial psychology, in particular the work of Elton Mayo. This approach acknowledged initially that industrial conflict was a real problem (as opposed to one of faulty public relations or propaganda), and one which involved workers themselves as something more than passive respondents to positive forces (as was implied in, for example, explanations resting on bad management, bad communications, etc.). First, it was argued, attitudes bred in the bad conditions of the nineteenth century had persisted even though those conditions had gone forever:[25] there was an 'ideological lag', attitudes no longer matched circumstances. Second, the size of unit and a minutely differentiated division of labour had simultaneously depersonalized work, made it monotonous, and eroded its status; the worker did not feel responsible in his work, and, as a result, the insecurity of his job was uppermost in his mind.[26]

The explanation implicitly rejected socialist explanations of industrial conflict (including the attack on property), and, again implicitly, asserted that the existing structure of society was just. Problems which arose did not relate to the structure or cast its legitimacy in terms of popular interests into doubt. However, the explanation did admit that the problem was deeper, more closely related to the structure of industry – rather than its transitory practice, or the occasional mistake of the rare bad manager – than had been acknowledged hitherto. This was not used as an argument to justify reforming the structure of industry, but as a basis for exploring means to adjust men to that structure.

A psychological explanation of industrial problems limited the sorts of solutions thought relevant. The problem was, by definition, about individuals, not a collectivity related to a structure. The solutions Conservatives offered covered broad economic policy and suggestions to ease the actual conditions of work and make promotion for the talented easier (since the frustration of the unrecognized but talented worker was seen as a powerful incentive to revolt). However, measures advanced to ease specific material problems were less directed at those problems than at claimed psychological by-products: to make labour, regardless of any evidence to the contrary, 'feel it has the same purpose as capital'.[27] At this point, proposals tended to become identical to those solutions offered by Conservatives before the advent of New Conservatism – exhortation and example would induce a 'new spirit', and persuade industrial labour that things were not as they supposed: 'The first essential of real partnership is mutual understanding. The key to an enhanced and more individual status for the workmen in industry is knowledge.'[28]

It will be recalled that one element stressed in the inter-war Conservative writing was that of status in modern society. It was said that class conflict was in fact not a problem of collectivities, but one of individual status – class was merely the irrational reflection of individual grievances, grievances rooted in the individual feeling that one was not important in society. The society of the future must therefore guarantee to each member of society a given status which indicated how important he was to society, a status recognized in a public document or charter, in a sort of social constitution. The document would demonstrate the justice of the *status quo* in publicly acknowledged terms, would lay down a social hierarchy which all who were reasonable would accept as a truthful reflection of inherent social harmony.

The problem of 'status', explicitly counterposed to the problem of 'class', loomed large in Conservative thought, even though it was explicitly inconsistent with the Liberal stress on the freedom of the individual. The New Conservatives revived the inter-war suggestion for a clarification of minimum working conditions, a proposal that aimed both at corporatist status ends (its positive aspect) and at Liberal contract aims (workers could be penalized for not meeting their contractual obligations). The Workers' Charter[29] (part of *The Industrial Charter*) laid down that a statement of conditions should be presented to Parliament for ratification as a statement of principle, and should include a contract of service defining workers' rights and obligations.[30] Some provisions should also be made to introduce payment-by-results to increase incentives to work, and promotion should always be by merit. Joint consultation committees should be fostered throughout industry to raise workers' status, and, where possible, profit-sharing introduced. These aims were not pledges nor promises, but merely suggestions – the party accepted only to exhort employers, not to offer incentives or compel.[31] Appropriately, policy statements greeted the 'charter spirit' but said consultations with industry would be necessary before any action at all would be contemplated.

However, 'partnership' might suggest some equality between the partners, and commensurately, some abrogation of managerial authority, some opportunity for employees to change and possibly initiate policy within industry. Joint consultation certainly required the opinion of labour representatives but it did not affect ultimate authority. Some Conservatives went further still and spoke of 'industrial democracy' and the need to evolve an industrial structure consistent with political democracy. This was a dangerous line of argument since it might imply the periodic election of managers (from amongst any freely nominated candidates) and the periodic right of ratifying industrial policy with more than one alternative available. Aubrey Jones escaped the dilemma by redefining political democracy to mean no more than consultation.[32]

Others saw the dilemma as 'a challenge', 'a real opportunity to lead the country by reconciling individual leadership in industry and management, which is vital to efficiency, with the confident participation of the workpeople in consultation'.[33] Yet others refused to be tempted towards these dialectical syntheses, and firmly asserted the over-riding need to preserve full managerial sovereignty;[34] indeed, one speaker recommended joint consultation as the means to secure firmly managerial authority, rather than ameliorating the problems of labour.[35]

The Conservative alternative, then, consisted of a series of practical measures as well as the propagation of a general ethos, designed to convince the worker that in general the viewpoint of the manager was the one closest to the truth and in the best interests of the country, and therefore the worker should accept it. In addition, there were suggested means whereby grievances could be aired, and more responsibility devolved upon the worker. However, all concrete measures were designed less to answer specific problems and rather more to help create the ethos of co-operation. As will be clear, the proposals assumed a basic harmony in society, a harmony resting upon the validity of one point of view, in this case that of industrial managers, and currently obscured by relatively transitory phenomena. All men would see the validity of the management viewpoint if these phenomena could be removed. The phenomena were primarily psychological (that is, had no real basis in the nature of society or in the divergent interests of different groups) and individual, and therefore exhortation, propaganda, education, psychological 'reconditioning', were the appropriate means to restore unclouded vision to the infirm.

8

The Old Order: Private Business

The Conservative party had no official position on private business apart from general economic policy. General economic policy stressed the necessity of, and greater possibility for, expansion, the need for incentives (that is, lower taxes), the freeing of the domestic market as a necessary precondition for an expansion of exports, the need for general decontrol and an end to government trading. Occasionally, suggestions on particular topics were made,[1] but these did not constitute policy. Indeed, it was Conservative policy to persuade the State to leave private business alone.

However, by particular emphases the party could not avoid indicating some positions. Over nationalization, Conservative attitudes have been noted, as well as the parallels between the broad views of industrial interests and those of the party. Similarly, party economic policy showed close similarities with the views expressed by industrialists.[2] Again, in relationship to particular Government proposals, the Opposition adopted an attitude; for example, Conservative opposition to Government trading in raw materials, in particular cotton, expressed a demand to return distribution and merchanting to private hands.[3] Finally, general attitudes to competition in industry were revealed in relationship to two specific issues: trade associations and monopoly.

I. TRADE ASSOCIATIONS AND COMPETITION

The case for competition in industry did not initially loom large in Conservative statements, although there was possibly more acknowledgement of the dangers of monopoly. Up to 1947, while there were occasional statements praising competition, the emphasis was rather more on the need for stability,[4] on maintaining and justifying existing practices, epitomized by Lyttelton's easy assurance that: 'At the moment, I do not think restrictive practices on the employers' side are a serious bar to industrial production.'[5] The notion of 'partnership' between State and industry did suggest that the industrial side was worthy of complete trust, not suspicious scrutiny. Even relatively late in the period, Eccles could attack the 1949 Labour policy statement advocating that State firms be set up to compete with private industry as 'not fair competition . . . state trading, financed with money taken from private industry'.[6]

However, some younger Conservatives did emphasize more consistently the need for competition in and after 1947. Eccles himself argued that competition was the only means available to reduce 'excessive profits' too easily made by industry.[7] Nutting deplored the practices that permitted 'the slack and unenterprising (to) have it all their own way'.[8] And Thorney-croft mobilized a frontal assault on the assumptions of pluralist corporatism, urging more competition and an end to 'the fog of words like "co-ordination", "the elimination of wasteful competition", "cutting out unnecessary overlapping", "looking at the industry as a whole", "assuming the obligations of a public service" '; he went on to contradict Eccles' complaint of 'state trading' by urging the Government to initiate new firms if necessary to produce competition in uncompetitive in-dustries.[9]

The status of trade associations in industry did tend to render some of the case on competition ambiguous. 'Partnership' on the industrial side presupposed organized trade associations in each industry, co-ordinating all interests concerned. Effectively, 'partnership' required, if anything, a strengthening of trade associations with commensurate reduction in competition. This the FBI in 1946 urged most strongly, suggesting that the Government 'give official recognition to effective trade associa-tions and normally use them, and them alone, in dealing with the affairs of their industry as a whole'. There were relatively few Conservatives who challenged this viewpoint, but Eccles did warn against business collusion, asking the Commons to consider seriously whether it is wise to adopt the principle that an industry ought to think as an industry. To do that is to be on the road to monopoly. There is only one industry in this country which thinks as an industry today, and that is iron and steel, and Hon. Members must ask themselves whether that is a good example.[10]

However, this was a lone voice, and most Conservatives stressed rather the integration of the industrial partner, urging the Government to rely on trade associations to perform public duties, to plan and take over the operation of State controls in their industries, to allocate scarce raw materials within their industries, etc.[11] For radicals the model here was the French Monnet Plan, the merit of which was said to be in its dependence on 'voluntary' industrial organization.[12] *The Industrial Charter* upheld this ideal of delegated public power, which should include the right of trade associations to distribute scarce raw materials. And *The Right Road* clarified this still further by offering the relationship between steel and the pre-war IDAC as the model for controls; the reply of Eccles is not available in his public statements.

At other times, speakers were more concerned merely to keep the State out of industry, to oppose interference.[13] This defence of pluralist corporatism only partially met the Government's own *étatiste* version. The Government did seek to create statutory trade associations in approved industries, development councils, and did devolve extensive powers upon such bodies. Conservatives did not oppose the councils on the grounds that they would help to limit competition, but rather that they were either unnecessary to achieve co-ordination or displaced existing trade associations, or, by including one-third independent members on the councils, permitted employers to be outvoted in their own industries.[14] What they could not very well attack, however, was that the councils were not 'voluntary' for the Government insisted on avoiding all semblance of compulsion. No councils could be created unless accepted by a majority of the employers in the industry concerned. The Government insisted upon 'self-government', rather than being prepared to repeat Conservative inter-war precedents in railways and electricity or adopt the position of Mond or Macmillan in the early 1930s. While some Conservatives said they suspected the councils were the Trojan Horse of nationalization, all the evidence suggested the reverse: namely, State help to foster corporatist aspirations.[15]

2. MONOPOLY

In contrast to Conservative opinion on trade associations, the party did for the first time define a policy on monopoly, a policy which accepted that very large firms might occasionally act in ways inimical to the public interest. This position followed lines laid down in the 1944 White Paper and Conservative pledges made during the 1945 election campaign. The demand for a more explicit policy on this score was one of issues activating opponents to the leadership in 1945 and 1946.[16]

The party was a little ambiguous as to how strongly it felt about the monopoly question, and in this it was at one with the Government. Both used the word 'monopoly' as a convenient term of abuse for each other's supposed industrial ideals, nationalized industries or private corporations, without either being prepared to spell out any practical implications. However, the demand for the maximization of output as well as the influence of neo-Liberal thought, prompted for the first time an attack on the new problem of 'restrictive practices' on both sides of industry, a phrase which was conveniently subsumed under the term 'monopoly'.

The Industrial Charter contained a section, written by Maxwell Fyfe, repeating in somewhat sharper terms the position of the party and including some practical proposals. It was this section of the charter which Eccles subsequently attacked as being too weak.[17] These proposals were expanded by Maxwell Fyfe later in what became the standard Conservative statement on the subject.[18] He refused to prejudge the rightness or wrongness of monopoly *per se* (in contrast to a properly Liberal position) but urged that economic expansion rendered formerly justified restrictive practices redundant. Legislation would be needed to dissolve these, but it would not cover wages, hours of work or labour conditions (he did not explain why these were excluded). The body of the statement concerned proposals for discovering the extent of restrictive practices and how far they were consistent with the national interest. The initiative for action was to lie solely with the Government, and he estimated that merely inquiry, notice, publicity and persuasion would dissolve the vast majority of practices. As in the field of labour relations, bad communications, rather than a clash of interests, was seen as a primary cause of the problem.

This was a somewhat stronger position than the charter proposals, but still did not judge the issue of monopoly, nor set up any sort of institutional defence that was independent of a particular government. The American practice, whatever its failings (always strongly emphasized by Conservative speakers), seemed closer to a properly Liberal attitude. However, the Government did not disagree with Maxwell Fyfe since their own Bill a month later contained the gist of his proposals. As both parties were thus in such harmony, the Opposition case was reduced to relatively few points: namely, that nationalized industries and trade unions should have been included in the Bill, and that industry should be more carefully safeguarded against abuses of the Bill.[19]

The discussion of the measure – indeed, that it should have been tabled at all – was part of the already more Liberal atmosphere, even if its timidity and limitations reflected the survival of earlier attitudes. Later in the 1940s, Conservative criticism of monopoly tended to increase, but this did not prevent the party opposing an unqualified welcome to the 1950 Lloyd-Jacobs Committee Report on resale price maintenance,[20] on the grounds that the report did not acknowledge the usefulness and benefits derived from price maintenance. However, younger Conservatives did wholeheartedly support a Labour backbencher's motion urging the Government to accelerate the procedure of inquiry into restrictive practices.[21] E. H. C. Leather from the Conservative side remarked that 'we have today the unique situation that for the first time in fifty years really healthy competition seems to be welcomed from both sides of the House'. He did feel that most of the restrictions were on the trade union side, but felt it important that the Government should help management to 'put its house in order' first.[22] The policy statement of the same year promised to strengthen the Monopolies Commission.

The move away from *étatiste* corporatist practices and the more Liberal atmosphere were more ambiguous here – where existing producers were directly involved – than elsewhere. Since Labour was in power, the Conservatives seemed rather more defensive than creative. Doubts concerning the viability of post-war economic expansion lingered on much later in this field, and rendered the practices of defence against slump or recession much more resistant to change. The age distribution of the neo-Liberals and the pluralists might suggest some marginal correlation with the different views expressed – between those whose viewpoint was formed before the war, who were accordingly more sceptical of the possibility of indefinite economic expansion, and those whose optimism denoted a formative experience in the post-war world.

The full Liberal case on monopoly posed impossible practical problems for the current structure of industry. To achieve any approximation to a classical free market, even with the complete reduction of tariff protection (which was not at all suggested by Conservative speakers) required a counter-revolution. The compromise established was stronger in emphasizing the merits of competition than in attacking the question of how it could be created in the presence of uncompetitive corporations, trade associations, trusts and cartels.

9

Conservatism and the Social Democratic State

The wider implications of the post-war revival of Liberal thought cannot all be explored here. Most of this account will be restricted to a few issues. But this does not do justice to the comprehensiveness of the change. For example, the corporatist/Liberal dichotomy can be detected in discussions of the field of international economic affairs. The *étatiste* corporatist assumed a unified nation-State, with the Government ultimately controlling all domestic economic variables. Tariffs were a vital weapon in isolating the domestic economy from the unsettling intervention of foreign competition, and trade ought to be conducted on a bilateral basis with quota agreements to retain maximum State control. The home economy should remain autarchic, or, at most, part of an autarchic but limited regional trading group – Europe or the Empire or Commonwealth. It followed that attempts to liberalize trade were seen as both illusory and dangerous; discriminatory trade should be the norm. Occasionally, this case – justified on predominantly economic grounds – was presented in conjunction with a political argument that an independent country or group of countries, in the immediate conditions of the post-war world, was needed for world stability as a 'third force' between the two autarchic rivals, the dollar and rouble areas. This viewpoint was relatively strong in the Conservative party early in the period. It was shown, for example, in pressure within the party against British adherence to the General Agreement on Trade and Tariffs or American competition within the Commonwealth, and supported occasionally by prominent members of the party.[1] Some Conservatives were sensitive to the charge that trade liberalization was merely a cover for the United States to defeat its commercial rivals by using its position of overwhelmingly superior strength. By contrast, the neo-Liberal case urged that the overall expansion of world trade permitted all demands to be met and would permit the British to compete. Accordingly, multilateral trade, the progressive diminution of autarchic barriers to trade – tariffs, quota-agreements, discriminatory trade practices – would be the means for British expansion, not destruction. After 1947 the neo-Liberal case came to reign supreme, and only a decreasing minority continued to criticize it.

In domestic economic and fiscal policy, initially the Conservatives scarcely differed from the Government. The taxation level was accepted; the cheap money policy was needed as much as when the inter-war Conservatives introduced it; the height of the budget was only to be expected in the circumstances.[2] Even the Conservative case for increased incentives was accepted by the Government. The Opposition did, however, urge, more distinctively, that incentives should be more concentrated at the top of the income scale rather than spread evenly throughout.[3] This note of agreement was broadly sustained throughout most of 1946, with only Boothby and a few of the younger Conservatives attacking Labour's financial policy for 'pedestrian orthodoxy'.[4] In 1947, however, an attack began to develop, and included initially the demand for a lower level for the budget, drastically reduced taxation, a steady scaling down of subsidies, and an increase in the revenue derived from payments for welfare services: that is, a substantial decrease in the role of the State. Further, it was urged that the cheap money policy should be modified or ended, and more stress placed on the role of private savings and an open finance market – that is, a partial rejection of the 1944 White Paper in this respect, and a return to principles not seriously entertained since 1931. The *rentier* was to be resuscitated.

Conservatives spoke strongly of gross extravagance in Government expenditure, and implied that it would be relatively easy to reduce such expenditure with economies that would not necessarily reduce the effectiveness of policies. Churchill went so far as to say he could cut five hundred million pounds off the 1947 budget,[5] but subsequent policy statements refrained from specifying where these savings would be gained. Other Conservatives were less reluctant, and offered as targets for economies the Civil Service, defence, the nationalized industries, the Central Office of Information, subsidies and welfare services, the abolition of the Ministry of Civil Aviation and large sections of the Ministry of Supply. Others refused to be tempted into detail, and merely stated that a tolerable figure for the budget should be set firmly, and then the country must live 'down to it'.

An interesting theory evolved from the campaign against the height of the budget, even though subsequently the Conservatives in office chose almost completely to ignore it. It was argued that inflation was the direct result of the level of Government expenditure. A cut in taxation would therefore moderate inflationary pressure. Anderson hinted that higher income groups automatically increased their incomes in order to compensate for higher taxation, thus producing an inflationary spiral.[6] This case assumed that far from incentives being inadequate at the upper end of the income scale, they could never be rendered inadequate. Birch stated baldly that when total tax revenue took above 25 per cent of the national income, prices must necessarily increase. If the thesis were true, inflation during the period of Conservative office would suggest the height of the budget was still too high, but by that time the thesis had been forgotten.

Along with the development of a fiscal alternative came a revival in the belief in the efficacy of monetary weapons to maintain economic stability, and even a mild case for a revival in the quantity theory of money – the most powerful weapons available to the State then being control of the volume of cash and a balanced budget.[7] However, the party was still pledged to maintain high employment, a pledge which, in terms of State action, could run directly counter to the prescriptions of neo-Liberalism.

1. CONTROLS AND THE 'VOLUNTARY' ECONOMY

Only after 1947 did the Opposition attack the Government

consistently on the question of Government economic and industrial controls. The Conservative party in Parliament did not initially oppose Labour's renewal of wartime control powers, although there was criticism of the length of time the Government claimed to require the powers,[8] and a minority denounced 'dictatorship'.[9] The Government's efforts to secure control of the global level of investment received similar approval, although Boothby attacked Labour for effectively evading the need for investment control rather than for seeking control.[10]

The attack that developed from 1947 was much fiercer than formerly, and was grounded initially in a distinction between 'planning', which was approved, and 'controls', which were not: 'co-operative partnership' between industry and the State should replace the external discipline of the State over industry. Eccles, for example, argued that 'the better the plan, the fewer the controls; the more controls, the less flexibility'.[11] Official statements were more cautious, stressing the continuing need for some controls in the short term,[12] but not specifying which ones nor how long the 'short term' should be. Here to some extent the case rested, although Conservative attitudes to the term 'planning' continued to evolve. At the 1951 general election, the issue of controls played scarcely any role at all in the Conservative case.[13]

The post-1947 Conservative attack was only partly justified by the Government's actions. Indeed, some observers criticized Labour for *not* employing physical controls, but relying on 'voluntary co-operation' from industry, and staffing its control system from private business.[14] In terms of political ideas, economic controls were not at issue between the parties. Both had advocated or opposed particular controls in the past. However, the controls introduced by the wartime Coalition became by practice associated with Labour, which in its turn, consciously or not, associated at least some of these contingent wartime regulations with the practice of 'socialism' (as much through defending itself from the Opposition as from any clear theoretical preconceptions). After 1947, the Government itself was not immune from neo-Liberal currents of thought which stigmatized controls as inhibiting expansion rather than helping it. The 'bonfire of controls' proclaimed by the president of the Board of Trade in November 1948 might testify to the conversion of the Labour leadership. By 1951, scarcely any of the great web of 1945 controls remained. What was left, a series of broad powers, the Conservatives found inadequate in combating the crisis of 1951. Perforce they had to increase the controls available.[15]

However, the Government's evolution did not deter the Conservative critique, which stressed that industry would perform spontaneously what controls were inefficient in achieving if the Government first trusted industry and then used invisible global influences over the level of economic activity (*viz.* monetary and fiscal policy). Some trace of the 'invisible hand' lingered in the case, conjoined with what was inconsistent with it – namely, the contention that industry was 'responsible'.

2. PLANNING: PRINCIPLE AND PRACTICE

The issue of Government planning crystallized many of the problems considered so far, and was, for Conservatives, the most sensitive political question concerning the role of the State. Only rarely did Conservatives separate the different meanings of the word 'planning' as it was used in political controversy, but it is perhaps useful here to summarize three separate conceptions:

(*a*) the Government should seek to apply consistent and explicit principles to its global economic activities, with the overall aim of consciously sustaining proportional relationships between the different elements of its expenditure and treating the different elements of society equitably. At a minimum, 'planning' here meant little more than explicit accounting, or what Churchill liked to call 'good housekeeping';

(*b*) the Government, given that the situation outlined above in (*a*) existed, should manipulate the proportions of its expenditure or activity to achieve certain immediate ends, considered desirable by the State. The aim should be not so much to achieve over time an overall distribution of resources within the economy, but rather specific politically desirable aims, usually by compensating for either the deficiencies of private economic activity or the vagaries of international economic trends. The sorts of ends considered appropriate ranged from high employment or an increased volume of demand for, or decreased supply of, particular commodities, to the expansion of a particular industry;

(*c*) the Government should, in the most radical version of 'planning', seek what became known as 'economic growth'. The 'equilibrium' aspiration which underlies (*a*), and the periodically modified equilibrium aspiration of (*b*), is replaced by the attempt to achieve continuous economic expansion along specific lines. The State, to achieve this end, would have to discriminate between different sectors of the economy, fostering the growth of those sectors which it predicts will grow most quickly, and inhibiting the activity of sectors it estimates are limited in potential for growth. Thus it cannot treat the different elements of society equitably; it must discriminate, defending its discrimination by claims to expert knowledge of the future desirable proportions of the economy.

These roughly differentiated categories do overlap; partial modifications under (*b*) must inevitably affect the future pattern of the economy, and were partly justified in practice by the pursuit of economic expansion. It is, however, useful to locate some points along the spectrum of political conceptions of the role of the State, between the State as the passive chairman of the economy and the State as active director of the economy, pursuing a global end. Whereas the State is seen as only one important institution among many in society in (*a*), in (*c*) it has become the supreme embodiment of society; it has both the role of defining the 'national interest', and requires virtually unlimited power to pursue what it considers that interest to be.

In 1945, the Conservatives certainly accepted that the State should perform the functions outlined in (*a*), even if many of them wished to reject the word 'planning'. Both Labour and the Tory Reform Committee broadly accepted both the word and that the State should perform the functions suggested under (*b*). From 1945 to 1947, the Opposition was converted to the same position, accepting both the word and (*b*) as broad definition. But from 1947, the Conservatives moved in the opposite direction until, by 1951, almost the entire party

CONSERVATISM AND SOCIAL DEMOCRATIC STATE

rejected both the word and (*b*); that is, had achieved a position, in the terminology of the time, more 'diehard' than it had occupied in 1945.

The relationship between the word and the different practices subsumed under it is complicated, but certainly the fluctuations in the use of the word seemed more extreme than any practical divergencies in the policies of the two major parties. Labour's practice changed through the period so that Conservative practice on coming to power was hardly distinguishable. Indeed, an economic history could present a coherent picture of Government policy before and after 1951 without mentioning the change of government in order to explain what happened.[16] If what Labour was doing at the end of its term of office was 'planning', the Conservatives also 'planned' in office.

The failure to specify what was meant by 'planning' permitted at different times both more unanimity and more disagreement than was justified. The sole hint in much discussion of a determinate significance came through the citation of planning's opposite – for some, 'chaos', for others 'individualism' or 'flexible policy'; for some, 'planning' should mean 'partnership', for others who saw 'planning' as 'dictatorship', 'partnership' was the opposite of 'planning'. By the end of the period, the Opposition had established for itself that the true opposite was 'freedom', and the choice became easy. However, the party always reserved the right to put forward a 'policy' for the whole economy. By this time, the Opposition had ceased to distinguish between good and bad planning, between '*le plan concertée*' which they had formerly approved, and '*le plan dirigée*' which they abhorred as much as did the Labour Government to which they attributed the idea.[17]

Politicians interpreted public opinion in 1945 as favouring something called 'planning'. This accorded with opinion on the Left and Centre of Parliamentary politics. The Conservative party was less unanimous on this score, and its election campaign was fought on the basis of a rejection of planning by the leadership, despite the Tory Reform Committee. In Parliament two Conservative responses to planning were clearly demonstrated – those who approved the Government's pledge to plan[18] and, if anything, criticized Labour for not planning enough; and those who attacked the pledge, said it was unrealizable[19] or criticized Labour for overplanning. Wages should be included in the Plan through a wages policy, the Conservative planners urged; wages could not be included in the Plan, and therefore a Plan was impossible, the anti-planners argued.

These main lines held through 1946, and if anything were sharpened.[20] Macmillan did seek an agreeable compromise for the party by distinguishing good and bad planning: the first should be 'strategic', but the Government practised the second, 'tactical'. A good general, he argued, did not direct every soldier, but concentrated on the overall aim.[21] Despite the doubtful analogy with military autocracy, many Conservatives found this a useful distinction, even though it merely postponed defining which elements belonged to each class. Indeed, for Liberals, central planning (strategic) was probably more odious than planning tactical details or, as it was also called, 'planning at the periphery'.

By 1947, changes within the Conservative party seemed to bid fair to establish a commitment to 'planning' as axiomatic to British Parliamentary politics as was, say, the pledge of high employment. The former opponents of planning were silent or tried merely to neutralize the meaning of the word so that it became trivial – 'To say that the Government must not have a plan', Lyttelton argued in this vein, 'would be tantamount to saying we must not have a Government at all because plans are to Governments like eggs are to omelettes or treaties to Foreign Offices; they are the nature of the things.'[22] The ideal for many Conservatives had now become the Monnet Plan in France, the merit of which was said to be its synthesis of State policy and voluntary business participation.[23]

The charge against the Government was now that it *failed* to plan, that Britain was, in Boothby's words, 'the greatest deliberately unplanned economy in the world'. Boothby also claimed at this time that Lyttelton and Cripps were united in a belief in the possibility of democratic planning. But, he went on, 'if that planning is to succeed, the Conservative Party for its part must convince itself and the nation that it knows how to prevent a return to an over-privileged and under-employed society, and the Labour Party must abandon Socialism . . . we shall have to meet in the middle or we shall diverge in disaster.'[24]

The attack now focused on the Government's controls, while defending the notion of planning itself. Following from this, the Opposition demanded a national plan,[25] which they interpreted in a more overtly corporatist fashion: 'the Government and industry should work out together, at all levels, the national budget of our economy . . . and . . . the carrying out of that budget or plan should be left with confidence to the enterprise and spirit of industry'. This 'budget or plan' should be advised by 'the strongest possible committee of Government representatives, employers and trade union leaders' (*The Industrial Charter*). The failure in the charter to give more unequivocal prominence to the word 'planning' might suggest the continuing strength of opposition in the party and it was this point that Eccles criticized in his commentary: 'The authors of the Industrial Charter kept the word "Planning" out of their text. Perhaps it was tactful, but I prefer to call a spade a spade.'[26] The Design for Freedom group had no such reticence and its pamphlet of February 1947 firmly promised 'planning on the grand scale';[27] a further contribution in September sought to lay out more details on the same theme, proposing State compensation for the deficiencies of private industry primarily in the field of employment and social services; that is, planning as the Government understood it and in the second sense outlined earlier.[28]

Implicitly, however, the charter accepted that the market was not enough, and that State co-ordination was necessary to achieve the ends all agreed were desirable. Its omissions were filled in by Butler's commentary on it:

In my view, the many other important aspects of Government policy for industry, such as tariffs, legalisation for monopolies, private and public, taxation, controls and other matters are subsidiary to the issue of planning since they are the instruments of policy and we must first see that our policy-making is right.

Planning, he alleged, was at the heart of Conservatism, and he cited the inter-war tariff legislation as evidence of this. A planning period must be selected, and a grand target set in consultation with industry. Consultation, collaboration, 'voluntary' activity, were the keynote of the operation, not bargaining or competing.[29]

However, while it might seem that Conservatives were reaching unanimity in a pledge to some form of planning, counterforces were already discernible. In mid-1947, Churchill attacked the Government for *over*-planning and deliberately expressed his belief in competition as the mainspring of society.[30] In the same month, Marples meditated that:

> I am myself being driven to the uncomfortable conclusion that there are only two effective stimuli to production in any country, either the play of economic forces, however mitigated by social reforms, or the police. . . . It looks as though 'democratic planning' were a contradiction in terms and a directed economy not effectively compatible with a liberal system of law and government.[31]

Even as the planners pressed home their victory,[32] *The Economist* interpreted the movement of public opinion thus: 'while there has been a movement of opinion towards planning-in-principle, there has been an equal movement of growing doubts about planning-in-practice'.[33]

In the following year, both themes continued to struggle for supremacy. Some Conservatives maintained an attack on the Government for having 'no long-term planning',[34] and Orr-Ewing reprimanded those Conservatives who refused to accept that a government should be committed to making a 'broad strategic plan'. But Lyttelton asked baldly, 'Without planning the lives of people, what is the good of talking about planning production? It is a farce.'[35] Again, rising inflation demonstrated for him 'the failure of planning, as we have come to know the word'. From there it was but a step to a much fuller case:

> . . . the needs and wishes of other countries, the fashions of others, the course of markets, the success or failure of crops

in primary countries, the political pressure which determines whether this country or that country should protect its infant industries, and the wide and deep effects upon the rest of the world of the economic policy of the United States are so interlinked that they make it impossible for any central body to possess the foresight or the data in time to mould a detailed plan.

'Planning' necessarily destroyed the very indices requisite for forming a plan: free market prices and currency exchange rates. Again, 'The Socialist general in the Socialist-run battle commands everything except the troops'. The choice lay between Socialism and freedom, and until it was made, 'the abracadabra of economic planning are a waste of breath'.[36]

This formidable case was clearly directed against planning *per se*, but it was still not accepted as mandatory for all Conservatives (even though Lyttelton was a Front Bench spokesman), and Thorneycroft could still find it 'an astonishing feature of political life that there are still to be found a few who blame the Socialist Government for too much planning, when the real cause of their downfall will prove to be the fact that they failed to plan at all'.[37] The 1949 controversy had as one of its symptomatic themes, 'planning'. Boothby advocated it, Law denounced it, and Spearman sought to cling precariously to the middle ground of discriminating good and bad planning.[38] As if in answer to the same stimulus, the Government's own *Economic Survey for 1949* omitted many of its earlier planning aspirations.

The Right Road was indeterminate in its precise allegiance, but it still tended to lean towards Lyttelton rather than *The Industrial Charter*. The document carefully differentiated between a 'plan' which multiplied restraints, and a 'policy' which emphasized freedom and adhered to an ideal in which the individual was supreme. In October of the same year (1949), Churchill reiterated his belief in 'the laws of supply and demand', and the value of free individual choice to the efficient working of society.[39] Much had been made earlier of a possible middle way between freedom and order, between *laissez-faire* and totalitarianism, both sides being equally opposed, but now there was a perceptible attempt to admit the value of what had formerly been denigrated as 'chaos', namely a free market, and suggest that the two alternatives were mutually exclusive: a synthesis or middle way was impossible. In this vein, Law firmly asserted that 'planning by the State is the denial of (the expression of) the individual's personality, to the extent to which the State takes away from him the responsibility for the decisions affecting his life'.[40]

However, it was still necessary for Lyttelton to spell out this conclusion publicly. In November 1950, he argued uncompromisingly that the Government's problems arose 'from the fundamental fallacy of trying to combine a planned economy with a free society'. In some surprise, Silverman from the Labour backbenches intervened to ask whether Lyttelton was 'seriously arguing on behalf of his Party, that a planned economy is not possible in a free society?' The unequivocal reply reiterated that that was 'precisely my argument'. However, Lyttelton did preserve an escape route: 'It is possible', he said, 'to have a policy under which there is a great deal of freedom of choice and . . . it is possible to secure it without disorder.'[41] In embryo, this was a proviso that permitted Conservatives to behave in Government in much the same manner as Labour had done towards the end of its period in office. It also demonstrated how much of the campaign against planning was in fact opposition to the word rather than any varying practices subsumed under it.

Here the case rested, and the word 'planning' tended to die out of Conservative speeches except as a term of denigration for the Government's practice, or in a sense wholly innocuous. Churchill, for example, asserted that 'we Conservatives want the future planning to take place primarily in the individual home and family. If they do not plan for the future, no state organisation can.'[42] Some had to make their peace with the new line, and usually, like Macmillan, escaped through the policy reservation.[43] Yet a few others continued to the end to advocate planning; Watkinson again recommended the Monnet Plan as a means to achieve a 10 per cent rate of growth, but his explanation of his party's position on planning was a little lame: Britain needed 'a Government that does not talk about planning but sometimes does it, which is rather an important distinction'.[44] Almost alone, Boothby continued into the new era to hold fast to the beliefs which, in his youth, had symbolized all that was 'progressive'.

3. THE ROLE OF THE STATE

By 1945, the State, apart from its temporary wartime significance, was already overwhelmingly the major unit within the economy and society. Parliamentary radicals believed, rightly or wrongly, that this massive instrument created to defend the existing structure of society, was in essence neutral and could be as easily diverted to changing society as conserving it. Thus, for those who wished to conserve existing society, it was of paramount importance to control the State, for when the State was controlled by radicals it might be a profound threat to existing society, even if in ways not envisaged by the radicals. When in command of the State, conservatives (the Conservative party was not necessarily consistently conservative in this sense) would wish to sustain the power of the State and deny the distinction between State and society – the two were one and the same, or the one was merely the highest expression of the other. Certainly there could be no fundamental conflict of interest between them. When radicals commanded the State conservatives would have the reverse interest: stressing the distinction, and the consistent conflict of interest, between State and society. Only with conservatives in power would society be offered genuine leadership that fully expressed its highest interests (thus State and society at that moment became identified as the 'nation'), for only conservatives embody the permanent will of the nation, as opposed to society's passing whims. Paradoxically, each position tends to entail views which carry over into the opposite state of affairs – stressing the importance of the power of the State when commanding it, this conservative case can be invoked by radicals when in power as well; in opposition, conservatives tend to develop a radical programme to dismantle the State, tend to become radical simply because they now demand a change in the *status quo*, namely the ejection from power of the radicals. The conservative need, in opposition, for a radical programme pinpoints the dilemma of all principled conservatives in a changing society, and contrasts with those who merely acquiesce in change. The first aspire to some determinate state of society (usually in the past), the second defending some much more fluid notion of the essence of existing society. The Conservative party, which has included few systematic conservatives, has been concerned historically more to ride the tide of change than play Canute, but nevertheless, the formal structural conditions between conservatives and radicals suggested above have tended to influence its posture. The party escaped the grossest inconsistency both by refraining from committing itself too deeply on any given general question and by ignoring what commitments it had seemed to be making on this score.

For example, in the post-war period, Churchill's slogan 'Set the People Free' contrasted the interests of the people and the State, and was radical. But it was not, given the tradition of Conservatives in office, a Tory attitude. Indeed, Tories could argue that since the people were corruptible, subject to original sin and incipiently disobedient to the highest moral law,[45] the slogan was an invitation to promiscuity and anarchy. A powerful coercive State was always necessary, even when commanded by radicals.[46] The notion of 'balance' here did not help Conservatives since there were no clear criteria presented which could adjudicate rival attitudes. Churchill's slogan was much more consistently part of the Liberal tradition, a tradition which had relied heavily in its early history on the separation of social entities, on their consistent and beneficial conflict: 'individual' and 'society', 'individual' (or 'society') and State. Indeed, the separation of these concepts was explicitly contrary to a Tory refusal to separate them. The separation was a radical one, for radical purposes. The contrast to it was the necessarily conservative refusal to make such separation, to assume complete identification and harmony.

Thus, in formal terms, for the Conservative party in opposition, the Liberal tradition answered the conservative need for a radical programme. The tradition urged the minimization of State intervention and the defence of society against the State.

However, even more important than these historical elements

was the historical shift in opinion away from the precepts of *étatiste* corporatism in the late 1940s. In each ideological phase, some clung to the precepts of the preceding phase, carrying to their conclusion short-term prescriptions. And some tried to limit the implications of the new phase, lest they be found to be subsequently embarrassing. Neo-Liberalism did not seek to put the clock back in institutional terms, but rather to limit the radicalism of the Government by demarcating the area considered legitimately to be the State's, and restricting the State to that. The 'mixed economy' as an expression of the formal ultimate *status quo*, the 'final settlement' that some saw in the 1832 Reform Act, symbolized the neo-Liberal attempt in one way. But to limit the force of the neo-Liberal case in this way, to take for granted some institutional structure of society not necessarily consistent with neo-Liberal aspirations, did more than restrict the case. It crucially neutralized many of its claims. An economy which was pluralist corporatist rather than a real free market, tended to become the defended *status quo*.

By contrast, the *étatiste* corporatists showed relative indifference to the public-private distinction embodied in the idea of a 'mixed economy', and were thus at times much closer to the view of conservatives-in-office. In such a context, the 'mixed economy' is an irrelevant description, since it is wholly subordinate to the unified national economy: ownership is an irrelevance beside the demands for unified production, beside questions of industrial organization. In the machinery of State planning, private organizations perform public functions, and public agencies perform private services; the staff of both are recruited from the same sources and are interchangeable. Neither side is thought to have distinctive characteristics which require special treatment, and the pursuit of profit becomes scarcely distinguishable from the pursuit of the public interest. Here the State is, at all times, the most important organization *in* society, and its role should be beyond political question.

Actual general statements by Conservatives on the nature of the State and its relationship to society are relatively rare in any period, and when enunciated, are usually so vague or open to divergent interpretations that they do not clarify much. For reasons suggested, the party was likely to stress a Liberal conception in this period, but there are many different sorts of ways in which such a conception could be expressed. From a purely pragmatic viewpoint, probably the epitome of the Conservative attitude can be seen in Major Lloyd George's description, a statement which should stand as the text for this discussion:

> My idea is that when things are not going so well, the State should come in, but when things are going well, the State should keep out. In other words, it is a policy determined by the state of trade in the country.[47]

Other Conservatives expressed themselves in traditional metaphors which are loosely grouped below in terms of the positiveness of the role of the State envisaged:

(a) The State should set 'the framework' or 'climate' of society (in earlier terms, 'maintain confidence'),[48] act as 'overseer' or 'ringmaster',[49] as 'policeman',[50] as arbitrator, balancing divergent interest.[51] It should be noted that in each of these cases, what it is that is to be controlled is created by sources other than the State and the State is, largely, the creature of forces outside its purview. 'Balance' is determined by the nature of what is balanced.

(b) The State should collect and supply information, presuming, in the absence of effective planning, that society would spontaneously conform to the policy demands of the State. It should act as authority to establish minimum material standards, of social security, consumer protection, industrial welfare or safety.[52] It should seek to compensate for the deficiencies of society, for example, in the field of employment.

(c) Finally, two stronger conceptions were presented, one consistent with Toryism, the other of relatively recent origin. The State should act as the guardian of the national tradition, or morality, or national mission.[53] This somewhat Hegelian conception is not entirely separate from the State as a means to make men free (or good), the State as a means to offer people incentives,[54] the State presumably knowing in which way people should be encouraged. The more modern version suggested the State as supreme directing authority, guiding or leading society towards ends, usually economic, judged desirable by the State. Unlike the earlier version which tends to look into the past to see the nature of the national mission (the pursuit of which does not necessarily bring prosperity to all) and which is moral in essence, the later incorporates the notion of consciously pursued and fostered progress; progress as something the State can conceive and pursue. The modern version, including in itself the third sense of 'planning' cited earlier, receives brief mention and declining attention in Conservative statements through the period.

The Industrial Charter was a Tamworth Manifesto reconciling Conservatives to the new 'Social Democratic' State. It formally ended the resistance of the 'diehards' and abandoned what were thought of as the discreditable features of the Conservative inter-war record. Ironically, however, the charter was already too late. Whereas the industrial middle class continued to ascend after the manifesto, *étatisme* declined after the charter, and a neo-Liberal orthodoxy developed which was rather more rigorous than its pluralist predecessor. Neo-Liberal thought was certainly opposed by some Conservatives. Utley complained: 'The cant about a universal, ever expanding, trade, now talked of indifferently by the Liberal wing of the Conservative Party and the Conservative wing of the Labour Party, is all part of the attempt to discredit and destroy the national state.'[55] But the stress on expansion, on an 'open society' where opportunity and initiative received reward, swept all before it. The period is still a paradox, with *étatiste* corporatists defeating pluralist corporatists before 1947, and the defeated combining with the neo-Liberals (the radicals who had supported *étatisme* before 1947) to defeat *étatisme* after 1947.

Out of this flux, new Conservatism was born. In practice few of the key issues were actually settled, but the reform of the party organization as well as the confidence of the new recruits gave an impression of spirit. The electoral platform of 1951 had little new to offer over 1945, but at least the men who offered it seemed confident.

PART III
Conservatives Triumphant, 1951–64

The Phoenix Lives

Office tested the Conservative commitment to neo-Liberalism, and events, rather than a Labour Government, became the formative influence in Conservative responses. In times of relative stability, Governments tend to display a greater desire for peace than irksome change, and mere inertia itself becomes a factor of political importance. The pulls and pressures of problems, crises, agencies and groups that possess sanctions, are needed to make Governments more than mere 'administration', to stimulate innovation.

The main area of stimulus to Conservative Governments after 1951 derived from the economy and its context in the world. The central problem was initially the dollar problem, but this subsequently merged into the general question of British external payments and its relationship to domestic inflation. International competition for scarce resources and competing domestic demands on the national income repeated in a new form the two central concerns noted earlier. In grappling with these problems, the focus of Conservative attention shifted away from nationalization, where it had been between 1945 and 1951, and came – albeit slowly – to concentrate on the problems of labour and the trade unions.

The party took office at a time of crisis, and it responded exactly as its predecessor might have been expected to act – by tightening physical and other controls. For reasons mainly external to the economy, the crisis was overcome, and a period of unprecedented expansion followed. The Conservative response was cautious, but it did resume the process of de-control of the economy begun by the Labour Government. The results seemed successful, and as a result, the speed of de-restriction accelerated. The march back to a more Liberal economy seemed assured. As a result, neo-Liberalism itself was strengthened; indeed, the phrase 'sterling convertibility' was once more in the political atmosphere to startle those bred in the inter-war years. However, from 1955 domestic inflation became increasingly important for the Government, rather than being a tolerated weakness. In seeking to overcome inflation, much of the Liberal ethos disappeared, to be replaced by elements of *étatisme*, symbolized particularly by the return to planning.

However, the apparent fluctuations in terminology should not disguise the continuity in practice. The main lines of a corporatist economy were not dismantled during the Liberal phase. Liberal tendencies remained largely in the realm of aspiration rather than practice. The role of the State continued as before. Despite early attempts at decentralization, at more stress on a pluralistic society, the State finally resumed the effort to knit all elements in the public sector, and to a lesser degree, in the private sector, into one coherent instrument with which to control the domestic economy and thereby moderate inflation. The developments were pragmatic, and Conservatives argued it was only when free economic activity created more problems than it solved, when Liberalism 'failed' to achieve 'orderly' growth, that the only solutions seemed corporatist. The change was thus less a conscious calculation by the Government and more the sum of its separate pragmatic efforts to overcome recurrent difficulties. Combating inflation by Liberal means allegedly curtailed the rate of economic growth, so exacerbating Britain's long-term position relative to international competition; a corporatist solution to eliminate inflation 'voluntarily' seemed the sole alternative to a full Liberal counter-revolution.

The shifting economic relationships between Britain and markets in underdeveloped and developed countries were a powerful external imperative for Conservatives. The relative decline of the Commonwealth and the rise of the European Common Market ultimately prompted the first unsuccessful Conservative application to join the Common Market and a competing initiative in the creation of the European Free Trade Association. Even at the time these efforts were being made to make Britain 'part of Europe', yet others felt that the way forward lay in closer association with the United States. For some, entry to the Common Market promised antidotes to a very varied range of domestic problems. But in any case, these issues – and in particular, the growing rivalry between the United States and Europe, with Britain in an uneasy no-man's-land between – overshadowed domestic concerns. It is not possible to go into these issues here, despite their decisive importance for domestic policies, but the startling doctrinal implications for Conservatism of an application to merge British identity in a new federation – whatever its implications for the 'Nation', established institutions, the constitution and the Commonwealth – should be noted.

In general, the Conservatives acquiesced in the inherited Social Democratic *status quo*, so that five years in Opposition seemed to have generated no ideas identifiably different from Labour's.[1] 'Mr Butskell'[2] symbolized the lack of division between the parties. The electoral effect of this was not necessarily adverse since, in 1955, the Government's vote exceeded that of Labour despite the lack of explicit promises on the Conservative platform.[3] Unlike the first period in office, the second witnessed greater Conservative unpopularity – the Suez expedition and continued inflation were possible sources; the 'middle-class revolt' and a Liberal party victory at the Torrington by-election (1958) were some of the results. However, by 1959 a brief phase of relatively non-inflationary growth carried the Conservatives to office for a third time, the first occasion since 1832 that a governing party had increased its majority in three consecutive elections.[4] This success was but a prelude to the re-emergence of the same complex of problems as before, accompanied again by a Liberal party victory at the Orpington by-election in 1962. The reappearance of popularity which had saved the party in 1959 did not occur, and thirteen years of Conservatism gave way to a Labour Government.

Over the first two general elections in office, success moderated the criticism that might otherwise have occurred, and permitted major changes of policy to take place without much protest from the party. Fluidity of policy might have reflected fluidity in the composition of the party. Some did complain that the party contained none of those great interests that had formerly given it its character; it was now only a miscellaneous collection of journalists, lawyers, advertising executives and professional politicians,[5] united solely by fleeting grievances and the ambition of self-made men.

It was not clear, in factual terms, how far the change was a real one. Possibly some major economic interests had found Parliamentary representation of less importance than direct communication with the administration.[6] General prosperity meant that expanding industry had less need of State intervention, and, in any case, representation in the House of Commons seemed decreasingly effective in obtaining direct assistance. Nor was the Commons able to exercise any sort of control over public expenditure.[7] However, the point should not be laboured, for the Conservative party did retain a class homogeneity – 'Directors of public companies were in every sense a better entrenched and more well-established group within the Party'[8] than any other.

Yet something had changed. Where direct interest representation declines, the role of 'independent persons' rises, and the trend visible since 1945 (in the Labour party as well as the Conservative) of the accession to power of professional politicians specializing in administrative questions rather than the furtherance of interests, continued during the period of Conservative office. Men of high intellectual calibre had certainly been members of the party in the past, but the party had never stressed its intellectualism; rather had it rejected the claims of mere merit in favour of 'instinct' or 'prejudice'. The intellectualism of the Conservative enemy, Benthamite or Fabian, was a point of Conservative attack on 'abstract reasoning', 'dogma' remote from the concrete conditions of the real world of practical men. By contrast, the party in the 1950s praised 'equality of opportunity', the rights of mere talent, offering promotion to men without traditional qualifications for office; to recruits, for example, from the party's professional bureaucracy, Macleod, Maudling, Alport, Powell, Maude. Two of these formed a group of post-war Conservatives to formulate policy suggestions; One Nation published a modest series of pamphlets[9] of high quality which achieved some renown, particularly when, from its small membership, three became Cabinet ministers and two, ministers outside the Cabinet.

One Nation was very restricted in membership, reticent in activity and consciously limited in appeal. The Bow Group was a more ambitious junior parallel to link graduates under the age of 30 in research and work 'amongst those who manage our society'.[10] Members of the Group were flamboyantly opposed to 'prejudice' and any views 'politically antediluvian or financially unreal'.[11] They were not conservative, and thus made Conservative enemies.[12] Like the *étatiste* radicals of the Opposition period, they identified a European economy as the model for Britain; unlike those radicals who saw their ideal as Monnet Planning in France, the Bow Group praised Erhardt's 'social market economy' in West Germany. The Group was at one with One Nation in so far as both tried to create a meritocratic Conservatism, opportunities for a talented minority to be socially mobile, for 'new men' without traditional attributes for office to assume positions of leadership within the party. Of more interest, however, was the response of the existing party leadership which welcomed the new direction,[13] indicating the freedom it felt relative to the traditional groups of Conservative support.

The response of one of those groups of support might have caused the party leadership more alarm. Between 1955 and 1958 there was a disturbance of the political equilibrium, called at the time 'the middle-class revolt'. It was said to be the response of middle and white collar income groups to the effects of 'the credit squeeze' and the failure of the Government to restore them to what they claimed was their pre-war position. Whatever the basis, criticism did increase within the party, explicitly in the cause of the middle class. Backbenchers raised the issue in the Commons,[14] party conference agendas reflected the same concern. About a third of the 1956 resolutions on economic and fiscal policy made pleas for the same groups. After 1956, pleading of this form declined, although it was expressed on particular issues – for example, the demand for the abolition of Schedule 'A' tax on owner-occupied property.[15] However, no serious friction took place at actual party conferences despite the work of various organizations to focus this discontent.[16] The party leadership offered two answers to the challenge – first, the purely polemical point that the party was a national one and could not favour sectional groups;[17] the second, that since the Conservatives had come to office, major benefits had accrued to 'middle income groups'.[18] However, the revolt was temporary, failing to achieve either dramatic concessions or any sort of permanent life. Prosperity in 1959 and a successful general election closed the issue.

In general, then, party history was relatively tranquil, despite resignations over the Suez affair, the Central African Federation and the scale of public expenditure. Success underpinned the dominance of the centre of the party. Some saw this possibly temporary accident as the 'end of ideology', but this was a somewhat premature conclusion.

II

The Challenge of Organized Labour

The Conservative relationship to organized labour came to be the centre of the Government's preoccupations. Identified as the main source of national economic problems, labour was ultimately regarded as holding the key to British competitive performance abroad.

Even on first coming to office, some Conservatives saw inflation as being generated by wages competing upwards, by 'leapfrogging', and the trade unions as being capable of moderating this race. Officially, however, inflation was generated by employers competing for scarce labour, was a function not of trade union strength (which, in fact, might keep wages lower by delaying increases otherwise offered by employers to capture new labour), but of the general level of activity in the economy.[1] Cost or wage inflation demanded Government control of the unions (or union 'self-control' to the same end); demand inflation required broad economic changes to control credit, to make profit more difficult to achieve and labour less scarce. In practice, the Government did not choose between these two alternatives, even though some policies appropriate to each were mutually exclusive. It both preached 'restraint' by the unions (itself refraining from action that would irritate the unions and make restraint less likely), and relied in times of crisis on general deflationary measures; it both urged corporatist policies and practised neo-Liberal ones. To preserve the possibility of the first, the second was never pressed to the point where unemployment became severe. But sanctions were never added to the first so that the wage-inflation hypothesis could be tested. A full wages policy remained anathema to the Government until relatively late, and even then, what was introduced was rather a blanket prohibition than a detailed plan. In full pluralistic corporatism, the preservation of existing harmony required inaction by the Government on its own; and yet, in practice, the presumed harmony itself generated crisis; the antidote pursued by the Government only further eroded the 'harmony'.

The dilemma of wages remained unresolved, and the thirteen years of Conservative rule were impressive for the sheer continuity of unsettled issues. The 1964 debates on labour reiterated the same complex of issues as the 1951 discussions, and ministers repeated the same formulae, adjurations and observations in virtually identical phrases. In defence, it could be said that the Opposition had nothing more fruitful to offer; it concentrated on criticism of the execution of Conservative labour policy, rather than offering a critique of its aims.

As a result, the Conservatives were never pressed into adopting a more clear-cut attitude. The periodicity of crises permitted the Government's attention to wander between them, to welcome short-term expedients as ultimate solutions, even to congratulate themselves during periods of peace.

The Liberal ideal of a free market in labour, stressed by the Conservative Opposition before 1951, demanded that no restraints be placed on the unions; fair fight should be guaranteed by a neutral State, so ensuring maximum efficiency and progress. A nineteenth-century writer put it thus: 'a strike for wages is a clear case of a strife in which ultimate success is a complete test of the justifiability of the course of those who made the strife. If the men win the advance, it proves that they ought to have had it. If they do not win, it proves that they were wrong to strike.' However, stability was also said to be important, and where labour was scarce, the trade unions constituted a 'monopoly' (what this meant was rarely specified), and therefore could threaten stability. The State, as defender of society as a whole, or as major participant in the economy, could not remain neutral. Even if it sought to do so, its acts, proclaimed as neutral or not (for example, in freeing prices), would be seen as politically motivated. The economics of Liberalism in the early 1950s were seen by the unions as politically hostile to them, as open to political choice, not merely given by some autonomous market. It was quite clear that, whatever the economic rationale involved, different social groups stood to lose or to gain by adopting different responses to the problem of inflation.

The first Minister of Labour did seek consistently to fulfil a neutral role, almost independent of Government policy. Yet the simultaneous advocacy of 'wage restraint' tended to invalidate this neutrality. For the unions were not, it seemed, pawns of the market (as all economic institutions were supposed to be in Liberal theory) but able to vary their actions (and so the economy) according to their own or the Government's wishes. Corporatism did involve 'responsible' unions, not a free market, as one of the determinants of wages, and 'responsibility' was an aim the Government most consistently pursued. Indeed, at one stage it was suggested that the Government would guard sterling, leaving the unions to determine the level of domestic employ-ment.[2] In theory, the Government renounced responsibility for employment, even though it did it by placing that responsi-bility upon 'self-government in industry'. The theme recurred, emerging again under the following Labour Government. The threat of unemployment to secure trade union 'co-operation' rendered the 'voluntary' aspect of the scheme rather thin.

Overall, then, the Government adopted a compromise position between neo-Liberalism and corporatism, what has been called 'laissez-faire collectivism'.[3] In the first half of Conservative rule, this consisted in the explicit terminology of pluralistic corporatism ('voluntary self-restraint'), under-pinned by a Liberal deflationary policy. In the second half, a verbal defence of the principle of free collective bargaining went with more or less extensive attempts to evade the implications of that principle or to emasculate it; *étatiste* corporatism emerged with increasing force. The first targets for Government policy were the industries within the public sector. As many of these were also industries in long-term decline, the two factors combined to make the public sector and, in particular, the railways, the main scene of the decisive battles.

I. COLLECTIVE BARGAINING

Initially, the Conservatives came to power as the defenders of free collective bargaining, untrammelled by the State, but they needed and sought trade union co-operation to overcome the external crisis of 1951.[4] To this end, the first Minister of Labour appointed was not a professional politician and was permitted to remain fairly unimplicated in Government policy.[5] No attempt was made to legislate on those aspects of trade union organization which Conservatives criticized, nor on *The Industrial Charter* proposals. Monckton acted as a neutral arbitrator, 'to help industry help itself' as he put it,[6] and his two attempts to change wage settlements (deploring two Wage Council claims which were explicitly related to a cost-of-living sliding scale) were not repeated when resubmitted.

Restraint was the keynote of general Government statements:

'Prices cannot be kept down', the new chancellor said, 'if wages and salaries keep rising unreasonably. It would be foreign to our ideas and practice to attempt to curb wages and salaries by central direction and administrative fiat. Responsibility rests on both sides of industry to establish conditions under which the national wages bill will advance in step with national production.'[7]

But the means whereby the unions would ascertain what 'restraint' was in practice remained unclear. 'Restraint' was not achieved by clumsy attempts to curry favour with the unions – by appointing three steel trade unionists to the new denationalized Iron and Steel Board, or by introducing an Excess Profits Tax in the 1952 budget, a measure one Conservative regarded as 'economically harmful although it may be politically necessary'.[8] More specifically, Butler did suggest a tripartite representative body to consider how wage increases could be related to productivity, but the unions refused to participate.[9]

In the short term, the problem could be ignored, but 1953, 'very near the turning point in postwar industrial relations',[10] produced threats that could only be evaded with danger. Late in the year, the prime minister intervened in the existing negotiating machinery by offering railway workers a settlement well above an arbitration award in order to avert a Christmas strike.[11] In the following year, disputes in engineering, shipbuilding, docks, foundries, buses and oil refineries, again reiterated the need for a more coherent and less pragmatic approach. The Government's response was to appoint Courts of Inquiry, two of which (into disputes in shipbuilding and engineering) suggested the need for some 'authoritative and impartial body'[12] to relate particular wage negotiations to the state of the national economy. By implication, the Government was not performing this role. However, the opposition of the unions and the Government's wish for union goodwill, killed this proposal. The minister reiterated the complete freedom of unions to reach what settlement they could.[13] Yet the contradictory demands remained:

> 'There is a need', the junior minister argued, 'for a new conception of democracy in industry. The driving force of democracy is "self-government" . . . but "self-government" can only be successful if everyone recognises a personal responsibility – realises there are "duties" as well as "rights" . . . there is a gap in the structure, a gap caused by the difficulty of trying to relate the national interest to any particular industrial problem . . . I am not advocating any procedure which would in any way dictate wages policy.'[14]

But in general, if there were doubts the Government suppressed them, reiterating that 'we do not seek to impose a decision. We do not seek even to say what the decision ought to be.'[15]

However, a subsequent Court of Inquiry in late 1954 – appointed to avoid a national railway stoppage – produced a different sort of decision. The railways were established by statute, it said, and its employees must not thereby be penalized with low wages; railway wages must be comparable with those in other industries until such time as the State rescinded its decision.[16] This was a blow at the conception of a Liberal economy where wages were set by market demands, not comparability, and market demand for railway services was said to be demonstrated by the railway deficit.[17] However, the minister was morally bound to accept the recommendation of a body created by himself and guarantee any ensuing increase in the deficit on railway operations.

The strains of 1955, including transport and dock strikes, and a state of emergency, did not divert the Government's policy of refraining from action which might endanger union co-operation, a position strengthened by the proximity of a general election and the Conservative need to avoid trouble. After the election where success seemed to vindicate past policy, Monckton again repeated the orthodox position. In general, Conservative backbenchers seemed to approve, although some did warn that the trade union leadership would lose the support of its members if it became too deeply concerned with national economic policy. Walter Elliot revived the suggestion of an Industrial Parliament, but the minister said it already existed in the National Joint Advisory Council.[18] However, the prime minister did undertake talks with interested parties, without success.

The continued worsening of the situation in 1956, due, the chancellor said as he introduced his emergency autumn budget, to increasing wages, consumption, and industrial unrest,[19] did impel some shift in policy. Employers were requested directly to restrain price increases. The British Employers' Confederation replied by reminding the Government that the British Transport Commission had granted a seven per cent increase to railwaymen early in the year, so beginning the wage round in the economy, doubling the railway deficit so that transport costs to private industry increased and forced up general prices.[20] As if in reply, the Government refused the British Transport Commission permission to raise its rates, and brought pressure to bear on all the nationalized industries to declare a 'price plateau' for a certain period ahead, whether to combat inflation directly (the State presumably meeting the ensuing deficit) or to induce managers within the nationalized industries to resist wage claims. Steady exhortation was added, along with an appeal by the chancellor to the FBI for dividend restraint.

These signs suggested that the Government was opting for the cost inflation thesis and taking a firm stand on wages. The employers were assured of Government support in resisting union claims.[21] However, real policy to control inflation continued to rely on a 'credit squeeze' which did not require union co-operation. In any case, the Government persisted in urging restraint, a plea the TUC refused by accepting a resolution proposed by the general secretary of the Transport and General Workers Union, Frank Cousins, at its September Congress in Brighton. Cousins was becoming the best known opponent of Government intervention in the wages field.

The following year – which saw the highest post-war record up till then in numbers of days lost in disputes – brought matters to a head. Disputes on the railways, in shipbuilding and engineering, and at Briggs Motor Bodies, seemed to promise a major crisis, not made any easier by the aftermath of the Suez crisis. However, in the short term, State pressure was used to compel concessions: the British Transport Commission offered its workers an all round five per cent pay increase. Two more Courts of Inquiry were appointed. The reports of these two bodies criticized current negotiating procedure. The report on the shipbuilding dispute went on to note that in some industries other than shipbuilding, wages had risen by 5 per cent even though 'these include industries which are either not profitable or only barely profitable. Against this background, it is difficult to resist a claim for at least a similar increase in an industry which is enjoying considerable prosperity.'[22] With this implied criticism of the State, it went on to suggest an impartial body to bridge the gap between particular negotiations and general policy.

The Government took up this last suggestion by creating a Council on Prices, Productivity and Incomes, the Cohen Council, to examine the general role of incomes within the economy. The minister again carefully stressed that this was not a prelude to a wages policy, nor 'intended to interfere with the process of collective bargaining',[23] a qualification that did not reconcile the TUC to it. At the same time, the Government permitted fewer concessions, and positively ran the risk of destroying what voluntary collaboration existed by reversing its 'price plateau' policy of a year earlier. Price increases were sanctioned throughout the public sector, in coal, transport, gas, electricity, docks, canals and the post office. In addition the Government was prepared to infringe its own standpoint of neutrality. 'It is carrying that doctrine (free collective bargaining) too far', the chancellor said,

> to say that the Government should be indifferent to the relationship between incomes and production. It is really the task of the Government to say plainly that if higher wages are paid, unmatched by what we as a nation produce, we are quite deliberately creating our own inflation'.[24]

A new note of harshness infected ministerial statements. The chancellor, in presenting the second instalment of his autumn emergency measures, argued with uncustomary violence, 'there is in this country and among our people, a disorderly scramble for a foreseen and tolerated spoliation'.[25] He went on to outline the priorities of Government policy:

> First, the Government should state with absolute clarity their own view of the economic situation and where they consider the national interest to be. Secondly, they should, by their monetary, fiscal and spending policies, create conditions and an economic climate consistent with this view. Thirdly, they should not interfere with collective bargaining, and fourthly, they should, where they are themselves the employers, seek to follow policies similar to those which they urge upon others.[26]

What, from subsequent ministerial statements, this seemed to mean was that the Government would safeguard sterling as its main priority, leaving it to the unions to decide whether that priority was consistent with full employment. Unless there was 'voluntary' restraint the Government threatened unemployment, or rather, it was prepared to qualify its commitment to maintaining high employment. The TUC, not unnaturally, rejected the Government's request for restraint, and, as the year drew out, wage claims continued to accumulate.

Meanwhile the Government demanded, as employer, that wage increases in the public sector must only be conceded if matched by corresponding economies in the industry concerned, a principle which severely limited autonomous wage decision-making in the nationalized industries. Despite Government protests that this did not interfere in collective bargaining, it rendered it hardly effective, and, in advance, qualified any arbitration decisions.[27] In one pay claim, the Government was led so far as to propose a drastic reform in the existing negotiating machinery (the Whitley Council covering hospital employees), again denying that this might constitute 'interference', even though the reforms were suggested solely to prevent the existing machinery reaching certain sorts of decisions.[28] It seemed that a unitary State sector was replacing its pluralistic predecessor, and that therefore the unions were compelled to fight the State rather than groups of employers over every major wage issue.

However, no sooner had the Government armed itself than the external threats began to recede. The first report of the Cohen Council[29] was of less help than was intended, since the economy was already showing financial improvement. In the same month as the report was published (February 1958), the Treasury announced that departmental economies need not cover all Civil Service pay increases. Yet three major wage claims within the public sector – from miners, railwaymen and London busmen – were still outstanding, and although resistance to them was not now so much a matter of dire economic necessity, the claim from the London busmen seems to have been selected to demonstrate the firmness of the Government's new commitment and its authority relative to the union leader involved, Cousins. Whereas the two other claims were settled, both at levels of increase above the Government's specified minimum, and one obtained by the Government varying an arbitration award, the minister avoided implication in the third dispute and showed himself quite willing to face a strike.[30] Even if the Government did not in fact select the London busmen to prove a general point, it seemed so both to the press and to some Conservatives. For example, Thorneycroft saw the issue involved as 'not crucial simply to the busmen or the London Transport Executive or to the travelling public. In my judgement it is crucial to this nation . . . to the future of our economy and to the success or failure of the policies which, rightly or wrongly . . . Her Majesty's Government have been seeking to pursue.'[31] The strike was long and bitter, eventually ending in a partial defeat for the union concerned. The press praised the

Government's stand, not for its defence of the principle of free collective bargaining, but for its resistance to that principle – namely, to freely rising (or, theoretically, falling) wages. On its side, the Government stressed its defence of the existing negotiating machinery, which, it said, had not been exhausted by the parties to the dispute.[32]

The party broadly supported the Government's position, although some had urged policies of a more explicitly Liberal or more corporatist variety. Thus Denzil Freeth argued that the unions had a duty to maximize the return to labour, and to interfere was to miss the real cause of inflation: the employer's willingness to concede.[33] On the other side, some urged a conscious wages policy, with a figure for maximum permissible annual income increases. Horobin suggested 3 to 4 per cent, Craddock $2\frac{1}{2}$ per cent.[34] 'It is not possible', Horobin maintained, 'in 1957, with the Government so much in it, as employers, paymaster and controller, for them not to have a wages policy.'[35] Yet others urged a revival of the Workers' Charter (the minister did issue a survey of the best employment practices) or a capital gains tax to persuade the unions to be more co-operative.[36] However, in general there was no strong pressure for a markedly different policy, although some greeted the resignation of the chancellor and two Treasury ministers in January 1958 as opposition to pursuing full employment as well as the stability of the pound.[37] Despite a fall in output and employment, the party remained loyal.

1959 offered a pause in the continuing battle, a pause crowned for Conservatives by a general election victory, the third consecutive triumph. However, in the following year a report on railway pay (the 'Guillebaud Report'), the end-product of the 1958 dispute, once more threatened the new principles of wage negotiation that the Government wished to introduce, and substantially increased the deficit on railway operations. The report recommended, on grounds of comparison with other industries, an increase in railway pay between 8 and 18 per cent, a recommendation the Government was bound to accept although it promised as well a drastic reorganization of the industry.

However, this was only a prelude to the strains of midsummer, culminating in the following year in 'chronic cost inflation', as the chancellor put it. By February 1961, back-benchers were stirring uneasily, and Hinchingbrooke called the trade unions 'rogue elephants', demanding sanctions against them, whether this be unemployment or something else.[38] In the budget, the Government strengthened itself with two innovations, a payroll tax (to enforce employer resistance to retaining redundant labour, although it could merely accelerate price increases partly to the benefit of Government revenue) and a variable purchase tax to control consumption.

Inflationary pressure continued through the summer, and this provided the immediate pretext for the Government's most dramatic reversal of its previous claims: the creation of a planning mechanism. Partly as an inducement to the trade unions to collaborate in an explicit incomes policy, the planning body was to be quite separate from the Treasury and the Government. Alongside this innovation went a clear Government instruction to wage negotiators to limit income increases to a set figure, a 'pause' as the chancellor described it.[39] The policy which had been applied to the public sector in 1957 should now be carried out in the economy as a whole. Yet the Government again refrained from taking powers to penalize those who refused to conform to its policy. To work, the 'pause' needed the voluntary support of the employers. However, the policy was new and contrary to the former Conservative emphasis on free trade unionism. It was also a gamble, since, if it failed, the Government might suffer in terms of popularity. It might also do much damage in the interim to the existing arbitration machinery, since the Government might interfere in the independence of arbitration judgements to encourage preconceived conclusions, as the president of the Industrial Court subsequently complained.

The chancellor went on to promise that once the short-term remedy of the 'pause' had been effective, a 'new long-term policy' to relate wage increases to productivity would be introduced.[40] As in 1957, in the short term the public sector was to lead the way in enforcing the 'pause'. The State 'as employer intends the normal machinery to work to the greatest possible extent consistent with the pause'. Again, defence of the existing negotiating machinery tended to give way in some cases to urging its reform so that it might produce decisions consistent with Government wishes, in this case affecting the Burnham Committee negotiating teachers' pay. With some innocence, the chancellor said, 'It is not the powers (of the existing machinery) but the use made of them which I believe is really important'.[41]

The 'pause' placed severe limits on the idea of *voluntary* self-restraint, as did the Government's implicit contention that its support for collective bargaining went only so far as the decisions of that bargaining were consistent with its policy. In the short term, the TUC answered by refusing to join the Board of the new planning agency. The actual course of the 'pause' did not, from the Government's viewpoint, augur well for the new policy. Electricity workers early defeated it, followed by the railwaymen. The dockers exceeded the Government's global limit on income increases just after the 'pause' ended, and when criticized for this, the chairman of the National Association of Port Employers said that port employers refused to pay the cost of a strike, the price of a policy not their own but the Government's. In any case, the settlement, he said, merely followed a Government award to dockers in the National Union of Railwaymen just previously. All told, by May 1962, at least some seventy-seven industries had received increases above the global level permitted by the Government. However, the Government did refuse a claim from nursing associations – 'the meek, it appears, have no chance of inheriting the earth', the *Observer* said.[42]

In the interim, the Government defined what it said was its long-term policy, the 'guiding light' to relate wage negotiations to an overall national figure for wage increases. To establish the specific connection between the two, it created, in July 1962, the National Incomes Commission, a body of experts to examine particular settlements. However, the powers of the new body were limited to claims already settled (unless the negotiating parties agreed), and only to those the Government chose to submit to it, and even then, the new agency would not examine arbitration awards. Perhaps to try to induce trade union co-operation, the Government also promised strengthened consumer protection, increased security for workers, reform of the apprenticeship system and more stringent legislation on restrictive practices. However, this did not seem to secure the desired result. Railwaymen and post office engineers exceeded the 'guiding light' almost at once, and when the awards of Scottish building workers and plumbers were referred to the Commission, the unions refused to give evidence. When finally published (February 1963), the new Contracts of Employment Bill proved a modest measure and did not perceptibly increase trade union interest, any more than the favourable budget introduced the following April.

Other suggestions were made. Conservative backbenchers made formal proposals for a new arbitration, conciliation and collective bargaining machinery in October.

A year later, there was a party report which urged substantially increased and widespread payments for redundancy, a proposal the Government accepted in the Queen's Speech the following month. However, relatively high unemployment through the winter of 1962–3 probably helped trade union disinterest in these olive branches. In the press, the trade unions were the targets of sustained criticism. Conservative MPs also seemed much more critical, and all five resolutions on industrial relations on the agenda for the National Union Central Council meeting in March condemned trade union practices. The nearer the possibility of a general election came, however, the less inclined the Government seemed to try to enforce its policy. Again, the public sector led the way with increases well above the 'guiding light' for postmen, electricity workers and busmen. The chancellor's attempt in January 1964 to persuade the union leaders on the National Economic Development Council to join with managers in a statement condemning both unjustified price increases and inflationary wage claims, foundered on the refusal of the unions. The period of Conservative Government ended, its problems postponed for consideration by its successor.

However, the Government had made an incomes policy – whatever might be its form or practicability – central to its position, rather than continuing to pursue the defence of completely free collective bargaining, the centrepiece of a Liberal case. Demands for a wage policy occurred throughout the later 1950s,[43] and Heathcoat Amory, before his resignation as chancellor in July 1960, is said to have favoured the same innovation. Alongside such demands, others urged full Liberal freedom for the unions, disciplined solely by broad controls over the economy. Nigel Birch argued that union restraint would be inadequate to cope with inflation which arose from excess demand for labour, but that what would be achieved would be the discredit of union leadership in the eyes of its members.[44] Enoch Powell quite firmly rejected the idea of an incomes policy or co-operation by employers since 'wages, profits and prices are determined, always have been determined, and always will be determined until we go Communist, by supply and demand'.[45] The Government might legitimately have objected that such a policy demanded the completely free movement of labour between countries. Its own Commonwealth Immigration Act, limiting such movement inwards, accordingly rendered the market imperfect enough to demand other remedies. Such a reply would have been doubly illiberal.

The compromise position of the Government – support for collective bargaining in so far as its results conformed to the demands of Government policy – implied some detailed policy on wages long before global figures were actually made public. The compromise inevitably suffered from being neither fully Liberal – tending to reduce the flexibility of the labour market and 'distort' the strength of the parties to a dispute – nor corporatist – the structure of wages was not seen as a just one, and the trade unions were not invited to be responsible for the overall distribution of the national income, with guaranteed security for all their members. However, for the Government to lean further in either direction would only have increased the error from the opposite viewpoint. To have accepted responsibility with the unions for the details of wage differentials (a full wages policy, the justice of which alone guaranteed the effectiveness of the corporatist alternative) would have reduced the flexibility of the labour market in a growing and changing economy to the point where it could have become economically disastrous. To have increased trade union freedom, given the cost-inflation thesis, might have accelerated inflation.[46] *The*

Economist offered the Government some compromise thesis towards the end of its period in office. A 4 per cent growth rate in the economy, it said, entailed two sorts of income increases: a 2 per cent 'natural or autonomous' rate of increase in earnings in manufacturing, arising from local factors or employer competition for scarce labour, and increases above this level which merely followed from trade union bargaining power. The first should and, on economic grounds, must be permitted; the second, cost-push rather than demand-pull, must be prevented as inflationary.[47] The Government's own permitted rate for nationally bargained increases, 3 to 3½ per cent, was vastly above the permissible level, even though this margin had been greatly exceeded in some settlements. However, for the Government to have pursued this policy it would have had to launch a central attack not on income increases but on national trade union organization. In the event, the dilemma was not so much resolved as postponed.

The Government refused to take full responsibility for the justice of wage differentials (so leading to anomalies, as in 1962, where the strength of the dockers permitted them to violate Government policy with impunity, but the weakness of nursing staff prevented them gaining an increase) and yet continued to rely in part on the spontaneous conformity of unions and employers, resorting to straight deflation with disastrous effects on investment when conformity was refused. The dock employers stated their refusal to pay the costs of Government policy,[48] and particular groups of workers equally refused to pay the cost of Government priorities out of their standard of living. To ask them to do so amounted to sectional victimization on relatively accidental grounds. Only a more fully corporatist system might have justified temporary hardship.

The Liberal approach to labour relations never really advanced very far beyond the level of slogans. 'Restraint' was the persistent theme. The guarantee of Liberalism, a pluralistic structure of wage negotiations, was the first target in a crisis. The Government was compelled to seek to unify the negotiating structure in the public sector, to become itself direct employer of all public employees. The State assumed in the public sector a role of national direction rather than neutral arbitration. Of necessity, unions facing the State could only see the conflict as in essence political rather than economic (as was supposed in Liberal conditions).

It is surprising, not that the Government changed its approach, but that it adhered so long to Liberal slogans. Towards the end of its period in office, the Conservatives repeated again the two facets of its earlier policy that had proved ineffective – exhortation on a global income limit and an impartial body of experts. Between the Scylla of inflationary collective bargaining and the Charybdis of rigid bureaucratic wage-setting, between Liberalism and corporatism, the Government steered an uneasy course, tacking between one and the other according to the external winds of the world economy. The course it finally set steered towards increasing corporatism.

2. TRADE UNIONS AS INSTITUTIONS

A partial function of the climate of collective bargaining and the state of the economy was the Conservative concern with trade union institutional questions: the 'closed shop', the political levy, strikes and restrictive practices. However, while not condoning such practices, the Government resisted demands to take action against them. Reform, it argued, must come from the unions themselves, and the pursuit of 'partnership' or co-operation in industry necessitated that the Government take no action that might seem penal. Other Conservatives were divided over the degree of importance to be attached to these matters, particularly during the waves of criticism of the trade unions in 1957–8 and 1961–4. But in general, they accepted the Government's broad position. Outside the party, stronger action was demanded, and much stronger condemnation of the unions appeared. *The Economist*, entirely without humour, argued that: 'the trade unions have become the repositories of mighty social power and the beneficiaries of unusual legal privileges; it is not entirely a joke to say that the last group of people to enjoy a similar combination of great power and special privilege were the French aristocrats just before 1789'.[49]

Conservative proposals to combat practices considered undesirable varied from immediate legislation to inquiry, from sanctions specified in some bargain with the unions to merely increased publicity for union misdemeanours. Later, demands for union self-reform gave way to the proposal for an independent inquiry or Royal Commission on the unions.[50] The Government's reply was always unequivocal. At no time did it allow it to seem that it seriously contemplated action. The clash between advocates of reform and the Government was restricted to Parliamentary questions, and, for example, two 'half-hearted demonstrations' in 1959.[51]

Party conferences kept up a sporadic campaign on the issues of the political levy and the closed shop. There was one resolution on the first question, and two on the second, among the record number of industrial relations resolutions in 1958. In 1960, seven of the seventeen industrial relations resolutions were critical of the political levy, and three of the forty-one resolutions on the 1961 Agenda concerned the same topic; but the 'closed shop' received no mention.

Strikes were not *economically* important during the period. For example, in 1956 the time lost in strikes amounted to two hours per worker in manufacturing industry, one-seventeenth of the time lost through sickness. By international standards, Britain did not have a poor record at all. It will be recalled also that some Conservatives, consistent with a Liberal position, urged the right to strike as one of the most fundamental in Western society, on a par with the rights to free speech, assembly and press. Yet other Conservatives pressed on their own Government periodically for some limitation on the right to strike. It was proposed that strikes should not be permitted outside the existing union structure or without a waiting period, or only after a secret ballot. Other Conservatives urged that strikes in important sectors of the economy should be broken by moving in new workers, that social security benefits be denied, limited or made repayable where paid to strikers or their families; that unofficial strikes be declared illegal with statutory penalties for offenders. Others urged a Charter of Labour which would specify strictly the conditions of employment, with increased penalties if workers failed to fulfil their contractual obligations, a proposal partly incorporated in the first draft of the Government's 1963 Contracts of Employment Bill.

The Government's resistance to this general pressure was pragmatic. But in 1956, the Minister of Labour, Iain Macleod, did offer a more comprehensive justification of his policy when he replied to a conference demand for the introduction of the secret ballot: 'The idea, of course, is that the workers are less militant than their leaders. All I can tell you, speaking quite frankly, is that this is not my experience, nor is it the experience of any Minister of Labour.' Minorities, he went on, only rarely created strikes, and when they did, the response to the strike call was very poor. In fact, if ballots were held on every issue normally settled by negotiation, the number of strikes would increase.[52] This was rather a new case in the context of Conservatism. Union leadership, Macleod implied, damped down industrial conflict rather than stimulated it, and therefore the Government should support union leaders in the present circumstances. It was not the case, as some Conservatives argued, that workers were basically co-operative but temporarily misled by the manipulation of minorities.

'Restrictive practices' by the trade unions were said to be serious curbs to output, but neither major party was prepared to go beyond exhortation in treating the question. Conservative rank-and-file pressure continued throughout the period of Conservative government, but without compelling specific Government actions, except to create or consult committees on the subject. The Government argued that, given action to increase worker security, where expansion in the economy did not dissolve restrictive practices, legislation could not help.

3. THE CONSERVATIVE ANSWER

The two aspects of the ideal proclaimed by Conservatives as their answer to the 'Social Democratic' or 'State Capitalist State' – 'partnership in industry' and the 'property-owning democracy' – were much less clearly distinguished under a Conservative Government and are appropriately discussed together. Both aims remained more or less explicitly Conservative ideals, although they were not now radically contrasted with the existing *status quo*, and were rather cited as descriptive of it. The normative 'ought' merged with the descriptive 'is' to the loss of radical implications for Government policy. Certainly, some measures introduced might be cited as evidence of Conservative efforts to promote a property-owning democracy. The role of the private sector seemed to have been increased; the monopoly of public broadcasting and airways was ended; private welfare schemes were encouraged; private house building was stimulated, public housing curtailed, and rents for tenanted property partly decontrolled to encourage house ownership and private investment in housing. But these measures did not constitute a coherent and conscious pursuit of a plan, but rather limited and unrelated responses to particular problems and pressures. That Conservatives chose these solutions was part of their tradition and interests as was the idea of a property-owning democracy, but the two were not directly related. Indeed, if they had been there might have been legitimate doubts about the effectiveness of the measures involved, since most of them did not help mass property ownership so much as the already propertied industrialists, financiers and the middle classes. Again, despite appearances, the State suffered no real diminution in its role by these changes. State expenditure remained a rising element in national expenditure, and, in some years, advanced as a proportion of the gross national product. If these measures had been directed specifically at increasing ownership, that intention would have shaped the final result less ambiguously.

Conservative leaders continued sporadically to mention the 'property-owning democracy'. Discussions with committees were the main practical adjunct to exhortation[53] to achieve what one speaker called, 'the answer of the Western world to world Communism . . . we must continue to apply it rapidly if we are to keep ahead of Communism'.[54] The membership of the party continued to press for particular proposals: more house ownership, wider share ownership, the abolition of Schedule 'A' tax, a reduction on taxes for middle income groups,[55] and so on. Sometimes the demands were phrased in terms of the property-owning democracy, but the ideal seemed rather too vast to encompass straightforward middle-class claims. But if pressure to make middle-class ownership easier was moderately strong, pressure for some application of the

Workers' Charter was very slight. Indeed, sustained interest in the document, except as an illustrious historical exploit, was almost non-existent. The document had, the minister said, been placed before the National Joint Advisory Council which had advised the Government to leave the matter to industry itself. Speakers, at times of particular stress, sometimes returned to the subject, and pressures in 1957 prompted the minister to issue a factual survey of partnership measures in operation in industry.[56] Right at the end of the Conservative Government, with a particularly threatening general election approaching, the Minister of Labour did introduce a Contracts of Employment Bill, but this proved so modest a measure – 'a very poor, weak and puny child' one Conservative backbencher said – that it hardly lived up to the promise of the charter. Indeed, the same speaker saw it more as a means to prevent strikes than a genuine charter of labour.[57]

On those measures where some immediate Government action was possible, Conservative pressure continued. The demand for more houses declined somewhat after the Government's early efforts, reviving a little in the late 1950s, and culminating in the successful campaign to abolish Schedule 'A' tax, achieved in the budget of 1963.[58] Yet general interest was relatively low – only some five hundred delegates attended the debate on house ownership at the 1961 party conference. There seemed to be more interest in increased industrial shareholding, helped by the success of the unit-trust movement, rising middle-class incomes and enthusiastic promotion by two backbenchers, Gresham-Cooke and Maurice Macmillan. The case for an increase in shareholding was the orthodox one justifying a wider distribution of property, with the additional point that industrial investment needed to find alternative sources of capital. Pressure was exerted through Parliament and the National Union, and through the Wider Share Ownership Council (the 1962 chairman of which was Maurice Macmillan). In Parliament, however, enthusiasm was limited by the party Whip; Liberal party amendments to the 1956 Finance Bill to give fiscal help to share ownership were not supported by the Conservatives. Concretely, Conservatives urged the Government to reform the incidence of taxation to discriminate in favour of small savers, to abolish or reduce Stamp Duty on share transfers (the duty was halved in the 1963 budget), exempt small dividends from taxation, and make the National Savings Movement handle industrial securities.[59] In reply, the Government argued that workers had little surplus income for share purchase, that house ownership must be the first priority, that the expansion of industry would achieve the same results without State help, and that the cost of the proposed concessions was too great for the public purse.[60]

So far as industrial workers proper were concerned, relatively little happened. Mention was occasionally made of the desirability of profit-sharing, and the minister issued two statements on the subject. But, like co-partnership schemes, the Government did little and rank-and-file pressure was negligible. The Contracts of Employment Bill of 1963 has already been mentioned, and some Conservatives did raise the issue of a contract during the preceding twelve years, although it was not an important issue for the party generally. In 1960, the Government made the necessary amendment to the Truck Acts to permit wages to be paid by cheque. In one of the readings of the Bill, less than forty members could be obtained to consider it. The measure was offered as a means of reducing class differences, and, if the banks agreed to handle industrial shares, of widening share ownership.

Many measures which required Government help failed to get it. Even the last two measures were very modest in scope. The Government also continued to introduce various measures covering industrial welfare, even though the emphasis of policy was shifting towards Government disentanglement from public welfare and in favour of private welfare schemes.

There were other suggestions of a wider social significance made by Conservatives that explicitly did not require Government action. It was constantly said that a new spirit was needed in industry, that propaganda should be shaped to help achieve this: ideology was the problem. It was said that industrial conflict did not arise from structural problems of irreconcilable interests, but rather from ignorance or irrationality on one side, these two elements being related to either psychoanalytic roots (innate aggressiveness) or Christian ones (original sin). The

175

neo-Liberals, being relatively optimistic, stressed a modified form of the first rather than the second for which there was no conceivable remedy except the perpetual discipline of force or self-restraint. Overall, since the problem was at root psychological, no immediate action seemed appropriate: only exhortation, education and time. Earlier Tories would probably have regarded this view as utopian, since innate sinfulness could only be restrained by powerful authority, backed by unsentimental sanctions of maximum deterrence. The two views, persuasion or force, were perhaps reflected in a different way in the controversy within the party over penal reform and capital punishment.

However, the case did offer a justification for Government inaction since the new spirit needed would be created largely by prosperity, even if the Minister of Labour could, on occasions, foster a 'sense of responsibility' amongst workers and seek to persuade them that they were considered with sympathy and not merely as a means of production.[61] One measure that might help if employers adopted it was factory consultation, but little happened here so that one Conservative was prompted to hint darkly that 'if consultation is not treated co-operatively when offered, employers may become unwilling to consult at all'.[62] Part of increased co-operation was seen in the provision of more information by managers to show workers the problems management faced and educate them to the management viewpoint. Macmillan described it thus: 'The more the worker knows of the problems of management, and the more the management understands the individual needs of the workers . . . the less will be the danger of those irritations which lead to strife.'[63] The shift between the first two clauses is instructive. For Conservatism, there is only one true answer to industrial problems, and, as a collectivity, it is possessed by management which must, therefore, educate workers to its viewpoint. Truth in a dispute is not a function of the interests at stake, since implicitly the Conservatives are identified with one side in the dispute. Management, since it has the one correct view of the situation (although individual managers may indeed be in error from time to time), has as a group genuine problems with which the workers should sympathize, whereas workers as a group have no genuine problems, they have problems only as individuals, personal problems with which management should sympathize. The case closely follows that on status, where again workers have no genuine problems as a group, only problems of individual status.

The reasons for industrial conflict were seen largely as the result of a failure by management to communicate its necessarily reasonable and correct viewpoint, it being assumed that that viewpoint would be accepted by all if only presented.[64] Prominent managers sometimes argued in the same way. Sir Frederick Hooper maintained that 'During my forty years in business, I can recall no experience of labour unrest which could not ultimately be traced to a failure of communication on the part of the management'.[65] A similar case was used by Conservatives when the Government seemed to be unpopular in 1952 and 1956–8. It was unpopular, it was said, not because of its actions or inaction, its policies or politics, but because of bad public relations. The Cohen Council was one response to this problem. The general case on industrial relations was popular among Conservatives – 'What must be done', Monckton as Minister of Labour said, 'is to get the facts of the situation explained from the management side';[66] 'to get political and social prejudice out of industry and put patriotism in its place', added Robson Brown.[67] Sir Spencer Summers defined the division of labour thus: 'there is a good deal needing to be done to industrial relations to ensure that the policy of the employer is understood, and to eliminate any criticism of delay in dealing with matters brought forward by the trade union side.'[68]

The Conservative view of industrial relations, then, assumes a division not between equally valid interests, let alone between innocent workers and tyrannical employers, but between generally correct management and irrational or ignorant labour. Bendix comments on an identical attitude among American managers: it 'certainly takes the attitudes and feelings of workers into account, but it still is merely a "psychological" characterisation of the "great unwashed", who are unreasonable, sentimental, emotional, ignorant, intellectually incapable, and destined to follow the leadership of their betters'.[69] The role prescribed for labour is essentially a passive one. Successful labour relations, Monckton argued, required 'good-will and leadership on the part of management and full co-operation on the part of organized labour', a sentiment echoed by another minister in, 'When management gives the leadership, we look to the unions, both at national and perhaps still more, at branch level, to respond to the lead'.[70] As labour played the passive role, so management had a monopoly of legitimate activity. Management embodied something called 'leadership', and 'human beings need leadership, and it is upon the leaders of industry that the prime responsibility lies for good relations'; where relations were bad, therefore, management alone was responsible.[71] Leadership was a trust, an honour, a duty, but not a privilege; it – not luck – was the sole secret of present and future success: 'Management has made today's industrial climate and today's standard of living by its past decisions: and is today moulding the future climate and the future standard of living by the initiatives and decisions it does or does not take.'[72] In this self-eulogy, initiative and responsibility for society rested solely with management, not with society itself nor with the State.

The heavy Conservative emphasis on management in so clear a form (rather than upon general leadership or entrepreneurship) was indicative of, if not a new distribution of power, certainly a new way of describing it. But preserving managerial prerogatives for action and decision restricts Conservative responses to industrial disputes. For 'participation' by workers is defined as no more than a residual of managerial power. In practice, Conservatives stressed worker participation much less when in office, and references to the need for 'industrial democracy' were more rare. Democracy implies collective suffrage. In industry, it implies that workers as a group can change the course of industry, not that individuals may make marginal objections, air grievances over decisions already determined solely by management, or receive sympathy for their private problems. Indeed, it is a slightly impertinent assumption that managers are in any position to advise on personal problems. The two trends in Conservatism diverge, and, in practice, the party firmly made aspirations to 'partnership' subordinate to managerial authority.

However, this point is only of academic interest since the Government took few steps to pursue its aims. Indeed, the Conservative party hardly sought to verify the validity of its proposed solutions and incorporate answers to objections to them.[73] They had nothing to say on the steady long-term decline in individual share ownership, for example.[74] The property-owning democracy served its main function when the party was in opposition as a counter-ideal to the Labour Government's *status quo*. In office, the aim lost its radical connotation. It was assumed that in so far as the aim differed from what existed already, it would evolve out of society without State intervention. In so far as the essence of what existed corresponded to the ideal, the *status quo* itself was ideal. In office, the phrase did serve a marginal function as a convenient way to summarize a constellation of middle-class interests and it also offered some shadowy link with the past, with the landed property of the landed aristocracy. But the nature of 'property' had changed radically, and there was little of real substance left in the rationale of the landed interest for its broad acres. An at least tangible house or an intangible industrial share, carrying no great rights and scarcely any duties, subject to close State regulation and arbitrary revaluation, did not offer great security, let alone social independence, even though they might constitute something of a 'cushion'.[75] The State as State could not be defended by 'property'; managers do not need a defence in terms of property. Paradoxically, the Conservative defence of property became the defence of small property against the State, and when the State is Conservative, even this modest role for the defence of property is redundant. The aim could only be one for the middle class, and the aim shared some of the change in that class. Middle-class power had become vested not in its ownership, but in its social function and expertise, in its role within large bureaucracies. To that extent, the property-owning democracy had very little significance.

The Mix of the Mixed Economy:
Public Ownership

Conservatives accepted the broad structure of the public sector in 1951, and their response to recurrent problems within the sector was, after the two initial denationalization measures, not guided by any broad conception of what nationalization should mean. Sporadic problems in the wider economy prompted the Government to seek to shape the public sector into a single whole, both to use it as an instrument of public policy within the economy, and to prevent independent action by different parts of the public sector running counter to general Government economic policy. However, the precondition for effective centralization – planning – was not pursued until rather late in the period in office. Indeed, there were trends in the opposite direction. Decentralization within individual public industries proceeded almost simultaneously with centralization of the public sector. External centralization to control public expenditure with internal decentralization to secure profitable units within an industry, compounded the effect of centralization: it reduced the power of the intermediate national board level, leaving weaker regional boards exposed to the effect of State control.

The Government, on coming into office, had few attitudes to nationalization, but the pressure of supporters and associated interests prompted it to fulfil its promise to denationalize two public industries, steel and road transport. It had limited success. The sale of road haulage was difficult, and the Government was compelled successively to limit its aims, finally deciding to leave nationalized a major section of road transport. The restored industry, indeed of relatively small competitive units, was nevertheless dominated by the large State holding of the long-distance trunk services. The sale of steel companies was easier but still slow, and at the end of the Conservative administration, the State holding in steel was still substantial. In denationalizing steel, no attempt was made to foster consistent price competition between the new private companies. As a test-case for Liberalism, the Government's recreation of a private steel industry seemed to show it in favour of some variety of corporatist industrial organization.

Corporatist models for industry portrayed non-competitive monopolies, public or private, either as autonomous public corporations in pluralist schemes or as executive arms of Government in *étatiste* ones. The logic of Liberal theory rejected nationalization as a solution to industrial problems, but a modified version, given the *fait accompli* of some nationalization, might have urged complete independence for such industry (both from the State and from other industries), competition between industries and between units within each industry.

In the *étatiste* corporatist State, investment funds were granted to industry by the State as part of general economic policy, and prices were negotiated within that policy as part of economic administration. In the Liberal economy, investment came from the private capital market, loaned on the borrower's credit-worthiness (that is, without special privileges such as a Treasury guarantee). In the intermediate case, investment came from earnings within the industry, from the prices the industry charged for its products. Only in the last two cases, it was said, were there public criteria for judging an industry's prices and rate of investment, its internal efficiency. If either of the last two arrangements existed (or some combination of the two), the State would be relieved of its large financial commitments to public industry, thus easing pressure on public revenue and permitting lower taxation. It would be able to disentangle itself from much of its role as participant in the economy, so increasing the effectiveness of its policy in industry as a whole. It would establish conditions of competitive equality between private and public industry so that national investment was distributed between industries according to different profit margins; this would ensure conditions of maximum efficiency in the economy. More generally, the power of society over industry, expressed through the capital market and through the freedom of the consumer to choose between the products of industries competing vigorously for his custom, would be rendered supreme, and the dangerous growth of State power curtailed.

In effect, the neo-Liberal critique of the nationalized industries was an attempted counter-revolution, seeking to make public industries as similar to private firms as possible. The Government, by the sum of its *ad hoc* decisions, slowly moved in the opposite direction. In practice, it did not concede very much to the neo-Liberal case, and, as a consequence, back-bench opinion shifted to seeking Parliamentary, rather than financial, scrutiny of public industry. However, the complexity of these industries, the reluctance of Governments to accord any real power to Parliament, and the nature of the party system, rendered efforts to establish 'accountability' virtually impossible. Just as the aggregate of private shareholders exercised negligible power over private corporations, so Parliament could not control the State's industries.[1] The neo-Liberal case remained unanswered, despite Enoch Powell's continual reminders: 'We cannot', he urged, 'rest satisfied or persuade ourselves that we have realised a free economy in this country until the nationalised industries are reintegrated, not necessarily all in the same way, but reintegrated, with the economy of the country at large.'[2]

If accountability was not a success – indeed, had it been a success, centralization would have been increased even more (the Civil Service was the epitome of an accountable agency) – decentralization of public industry was hardly pursued far enough to make much difference. There was never any question of creating small competitive units[3] where the source of decisions was familiar to all participants. The area board was as remote from actual operations as the national, and even the powers devolved to that point were carefully circumscribed. Perhaps the modest aim of the first Speech from the Throne – to achieve 'flexibility' – was achieved, but this hardly accorded with the high hopes expressed for the reform of nationalized industry before 1951. Rather, over time the Government chose to use the public sector as an instrument of economic policy. Effectiveness in executing that policy became the criterion of efficiency in public industry, not what was supposed to be the normal commercial index of minimum-cost production at market rates of return on capital employed.

Forms of control, whether through direct Government management, accountability to Parliament, internal or external competition, or the check of independent agencies (for example, Price Tribunals, the Monopolies Commission, Consumer Councils) remained Parliament's main preoccupation. Whether such control was consistent with the original statutes[4] did not deter consideration. A key area for this controversy was public pricing policy. The Government at various times kept prices down, although it was agreed that not only did this produce under-cost pricing, but it also generated deficits the State had to finance (so increasing the dependence of public industry on the State) and prevented the accumulation of funds within the industry for investment. On the other hand, some backbenchers complained, when nationalized industries raised the proportion of their investment coming from internal revenue, that prices were too high, indicating exploitation of a monopoly position.

Neo-Liberal critics urged that public industries be permitted to set their own prices freely (checked only by, for example, the Monopolies Commission) and that prices should cover full costs, so enabling a reduction in taxation and a decrease in Government control. Within this financial complex, different considerations were at work – deficit financing by the Exchequer came in part from revenue on a progressively graduated tax scale (or interest on the sums borrowed by the Exchequer was paid from this source); self-financing by a nationalized industry came from revenue on the sales of its products – that is, a relatively regressive system where the customer with maximum demand (measured in terms of his available purchasing power) contributed the maximum finance. As described by Liberals, the first system carried a larger 'social' element, the second was wholly 'economic', in being subordinate to the existing distribution of income. Without free pricing, it was urged, no criterion for investment existed. State investment, independent of market considerations, could mean over-investment in the public sector, to the financial loss – in terms of the misallocation of resources – of the private sector and the national economy. Such State investment, either appropriated through taxation or borrowed under special privileges by the Treasury, would raise interest rates, the cost of borrowing, and so increase inflationary pressure without regard to the state of the economy. The economy would be 'distorted' in favour of its most regressive or declining parts, given the actual nature of the public sector. Some warned that if the State persisted in heavy borrowing, lenders would become increasingly reluctant to tie money up in Government securities, so rendering monetary policy ineffective. Continued massive borrowing would, in any case, exhaust the reserves of society for a crisis. Deficit financing, it was said, tended to accelerate demand inflation, whatever the purposes of the finance involved.

The material concessions of the Government to the neo-Liberal case were small, although certainly more information was made available. At key points, the pricing controversy tangled with conflicting theories of inflation which further involved policy for the public sector with the central concerns of economic policy.

I. GOVERNMENT CONTROL AND PARLIAMENTARY ACCOUNTABILITY

Like its predecessor the Conservative Government accepted the need for some Parliamentary accountability, and the inadequacy of current provisions in this respect. It also acknowledged at some stages the need for managerial autonomy in nationalized industry, without reconciling this with the first aspiration. However, in practice the Government delayed taking action on a Select Committee Report on the subject,[5] and when the new permanent Select Committee on the Nationalized Industries was finally set up, so circumscribed its scope that the Committee was forced to confess that it had no useful function to perform. After yet further delay, a new body was created with slightly wider terms of reference,[6] and it set about producing a series of reports. However, the inherent difficulty of the work along with the limitations laid down by the Government, made any attempt at real accountability out of the question: 'If the Select Committee works for ten years', one observer commented, 'and produces a heap of Reports, full of useful information, the nationalised industries will be no more accountable to Parliament than they were in 1950.'[7]

Meanwhile the lines of Government control had become clearer. The Government's view ranged between an assumption that chairmen of nationalized industries were little more than senior civil servants, and the contention that ministers should not interfere in so far as public industry was commercial, and it should be commercial.[8] Between the unchecked power of ministers and that of national boards, there seemed little place for Parliament. In practice, particular crises impelled the State to reject the second conception. Public criticism focused on the State, whether the State accepted or disclaimed responsibility for its industry. For example, in 1955, when the Government was grappling with inflation, it was blamed for an 18 per cent rise in coal prices, despite the neo-Liberal case that such an increase was necessary to absorb excess demand.[9] As a result, the State tended thereafter to intervene rather more in order to escape unpopularity. Price restraint, first fully demonstrated in the 'price plateau' in the public sector in 1956,[10] in its turn promoted an increase in State responsibility for the nationalized industries; successive chancellors were prompted to intervene to limit, rearrange, postpone or cut the capital programmes of nationalized industries,[11] not on grounds located in the economics of each industry, but in pursuit of national economic policy. Cuts in capital programmes, designed to curtail general economic expansion and so, it was hoped, moderate demand inflation, were followed in 1956 by the Government assuming responsibility for the direct supply of capital funds to public industry. It was said that this would safeguard monetary policy from being sabotaged by the issue of public industry securities of equal safety to the Treasury's at inopportune times.[12] Begun as a temporary measure, it continued up to 1964, thus making the dependence of public industry on the State complete,

necessitating much closer State supervision of capital programmes, and compelling the State to run very large surpluses
above-the-line with an overall – and inflationary – deficit on the
budget.

The moderation of inflationary pressure permitted the
Government to return to the question of accountability, and to
grapple with the problem of more formal and rigorous planning
of public expenditure. In 1960, it published the first statement
of public investment plans for a year ahead,[13] without indicating the specific sums involved nor reconciling its own intervention with its proclaimed adherence to commercialism in public
industry. More information was provided later, and finally, in
1961, *The Financial and Economic Obligations of the Nationalised
Industries*[14] laid down that public industry was expected to
balance its accounts over five-year periods with a rate of return
on invested capital, allowing for depreciation at historic cost of
between 5 and 8 per cent (compared to a 15 per cent return
said to be the average in private industry). However, the document also argued that all the nationalized industries 'have,
although in varying degrees, wider obligations than commercial
concerns in the private sector', but it did not say what non-
commercial expenditure was justifiable nor on what grounds,
nor did it seek to relate such expenditure to the commercial
criterion. Again, it did not describe the role of public industry
within general economic policy. Commercialism was not
explicitly synthesized with State intervention, the plannable did
not seem to meet the unpredictable. This was partly illustrated
in the divergences between planned public investment and
actual investment in real terms, a discrepancy that belied the
Government's claim that it was merely acting as an orthodox
banker in relationship to industrial borrowers.

2. DENATIONALIZATION

While the denationalization of road transport is instructive in
showing the links between the Conservative party and particular pressure groups, it is of less significance in the economy than
steel. Being more important, steel gives a better guide to Conservative priorities.

The curious circumstances in which steel was nationalized were repeated in its denationalization. Neither party seriously disagreed over the economics of the industry, and Conservative intentions for the private industry were hardly distinguishable from the *de facto* operation of the industry under State ownership:

> 'The opponents in the controversy over ownership and control', one leading authority argues, 'betrayed no great cleft of opinion as to what should happen, concretely, in steel-making. There was no conflict over the pattern of growth, and there was complete continuity of policy from one Government to the other in respect of price stabilisation, in whose pursuit the levy system (the price support system within the industry) reached its apogee in 1951–3, although the new Government was legislating nominally to provoke efficiency through competition.'[15]

The formal measure of denationalization was delayed,[16] and the case for denationalization added little new to what had already been said in the nationalization debates. The Conservative case was more narrowly restricted to opposing nationalization than citing positive economic benefits in private ownership or why these were unattainable under State ownership, although, again, Conservatives could say they were safeguarding against inevitable future State reorganization of the industry in ways detrimental to the economy. Independence, initiative, enterprise, were alone possible under private ownership, the minister said, but public supervision was still required. The new supervisory agency would veto 'ill-conceived schemes by the companies, undertake schemes the companies refused to develop, and maintain the pricing system'. The minister refused to say why the taxpayer should undertake what private shareholders refused, or on what criteria such a decision would be made.[17]

The readings of the Bill were uneventful, and provoked little sustained interest. The second reading was adjourned at one stage as less than forty members were present. The Government's final case stressed that the private industry under public supervision synthesized the benefits of co-ordination and private

COMPETITION AND THE CORPORATE SOCIETY

enterprise, and steered between the dangers of inevitable bureaucracy and unco-ordinated anarchy: the middle way was again the ideal. There was no attempt in the Bill to stimulate competition in the industry. The system of control maintained by the BISF, 'a system which damped down the forces which encouraged change, eliminated most of the advantage of low raw material costs and restored and reinforced the waning attractions of old sites and the power of the old to resist the advance of the new',[18] was retained intact, unbroken since its establishment in the 1930s. The Bill indeed specified that the new public board should supervise the industry 'under competitive conditions . 'The whole Committee must be aware', the minister said, 'of what "competitive conditions" mean, and I do not need to waste any more time on that point.'[19] 'There are degrees of competition', he said:

> The degree of competition in an industry of enormous plants such as this may well be less than in the engineering industries. . . . That does not mean that there is an absence of competitive conditions at all. For example, when maximum prices are fixed, there is still competition in quality, date of delivery, development and so on. . . . I hope the Committee will not over-estimate that because there *is* co-ordination and co-operation in this industry and because plants are sometimes very big there cannot be competitive conditions. . . . As in so many parts of our life in this country there is room for both freedom and order.[20]

The minister's hesitations betrayed the ambiguities of the case. 'One thing shone clearly', Mr Burn comments, '. . . in the Government's eyes all the practices established in the steel industry under the Federation could be accommodated within their concept of "competitive conditions".'[21] As before the war, the danger that public sanction might be utilized for excessive private profit by a trade association, without the application of rigorous economic criteria, did not appear to trouble the Government. 'I sympathise', the minister said, 'with those who are anxious to be protected against the man from Whitehall. . . . It is the very essence of this Bill that companies shall be free to manage their affairs with the minimum of control necessary to safeguard the national interest.'[22] The power to define that interest was left to the State's Iron and Steel Board, advised by the BISF; a point of Conservative attack on nationalization had been that that responsibility devolved on the minister alone.

The new Act, then, attempted to recreate the *status quo ante*, and revive the continuity of the tradition begun by the IDAC–BISF relationship in the 1930s. The economic practices embodied in that relationship and the Federation's supervision of the industry – a prime example of pluralist corporate industry – were similarly ratified. The sole change was the statutory formalization of public supervision, and the proviso that the State could enter steel production itself if it so desired.

The disposal of iron and steel holdings proved more difficult than the passage of the relevant statute. In the interim, the State was required to invest substantially in the firms remaining in its hands, so much so that Nabarro accused the Government in 1960 of retaining a holding in steel larger than it had held before nationalization.[23] Whether the State would ever have been able to divest itself of its holding was not clear. In the meantime, the main State holding, Richard Thomas and Baldwins, had to behave as an orthodox competitor. In 1963, it was involved in a takeover bid for Whitehead's Iron and Steel Company, a private concern, which prompted Nabarro again to criticize the Government for paradoxical behaviour – was Richard Thomas and Baldwins borrowing heavily from the State to extend nationalization under a Conservative Government, ostensibly dedicated to a private steel industry?[24]

Economically, the general course of world events – including the British industry's adjustments to the European Coal and Steel Community – probably stimulated more competition within the steel industry during the period of Conservative Government. But such changes were not part of the Conservative pursuit of a neo-Liberal economy. As a test-case for Liberalism, the Government achieved negligible results in the steel industry. Continuity of policy between the 1930s and 1950s was much more impressive than neo-Liberal innovations. The best the Government could do was to describe the corporatist conditions of the industry as the ideal of Liberalism.

3. NATIONALIZED INDUSTRIES

Two examples of State industry have been selected here although brief reference will be made to other industries. Railways remained the most serious problem in the public sector, a problem similar in essence to that of railway systems in many developed countries with important motor industries. Electricity seemed, to some, the most solid triumph of public industry. The two industries represent the minimum and maximum of Conservative achievement within the nationalized industries.

Railways continued their long process of relative decline, throwing up recurrent problems for the State to solve, both in the areas of finance and collective bargaining. Like the cotton industry, railways seemed to absorb major strain in the general economy at particular times. The crises of the industry occurred simultaneously with stress in the economy: in 1955–6, 1957–8, 1960–1. The reforms prompted by each crisis were promised as final settlements, but proved somewhat less than this as soon as the economy again exhibited strain.

As Courts of Inquiry were appointed in labour relations, sometimes as if to evade decisions incumbent on the State, so the railways were beleaguered with committees of inquiry, successive 'reorganization proposals' and 're-assessments'. These were to no avail, and finally the Government was forced to eliminate the existing structure of the railway system, rather than seeking to overcome the problems of the system. The railway mileage was reduced by one-fifth between 1950 and 1962. It seemed that the State's introduction of a major change in national communications was begun less in order to provide the most efficient transport system at economic cost, than to remove an embarrassment, whatever the further problems thereby generated: the rising cost of road development and maintenance, urban disorganization, road congestion, diversion of resources into the most labour intensive forms of transport, and so on.

When the Conservatives first came to office, public judgement on Government policy was reserved until the initial reforms were complete. The principle of this first reform was decentralization although the central authority was to retain control of most crucial elements (*viz.* charges, wages and standards); and the repeal of much of the legislation curtailing free railway competitive ability (including the instruction to charge uniform prices). The railways were also permitted to increase their charges by 10 per cent without prior recourse to the Transport Tribunal.[25] The Transport Commission, rejecting competition within the industry (competition with road transport being considered sufficient), created six regional boards, the members of which were appointed by the Commission and consisted of 'public men who enjoy the confidence of those who need to use the railways'.[26] With this form of regional corporatism went a series of modernization proposals which, the chancellor felt, would cope with the long-term situation satisfactorily.[27] The Government's commitment to general competition in transport was, however, qualified. The minister was explicitly critical of competition and suggested instead 'a plan whereby agreement can take place between road and rail based on the advantages each have to offer, and which will not run the risk of ruining the railways'.[28]

Sir Ralph Glyn went further and deplored the organization of the railways under private ownership: 'I would rather have nationalisation', he declared, 'than the humbug that we then had, of free enterprise controlled by politicians in the House of Commons'; neither private enterprise nor nationalization had 'failed' since neither had ever been allowed to work, and the new proposals destroyed any possibility of the railways being able to pay their way; if road transport was to be denationalized, then so should the railways.[29] Others viewed the proposals with moderate approval, although one Conservative felt 'the shadow of old gods lies rather heavily across this White Paper (the Commission's proposals) – all the old shibboleths and phrases – integration, wasteful competition, taking the cream of the traffic and all the rest'.[30] It was left to Powell to put the cost issue most strongly: 'It is a contradiction in terms', he said,

> to say that the railways cannot pay in an economy which is paying. It is a contradiction in terms to say that we can produce at a profit, that we can export at a profit, but that we cannot, at a profit, transport the factors of production or the finished goods.[31]

He urged the profit criterion on the railways 'whether this involves denationalisation or not'.[32] Aubrey Jones also criticized the railways for seeing themselves as a public service instead of a commercial enterprise; modernization, he said in 1955, was already too late to overtake the deficits, and only the drastic reduction of uneconomic services and switching traffic to the roads would solve the problem.[33]

Jones' point on the deficit proved correct, and the situation was exacerbated by the Government holding down transport fares during its 'price plateau' policy of 1956. Reassessment became necessary. The minister laid it down, however, that this should take place without 'the sterile business of putting up charges',[34] since, he argued, this would merely reduce traffic and total revenue. He did not say what the evidence for this was, nor why it was undesirable. The modernization plan was to be accelerated, leading to a financially viable commercial railway system by 1961 or 1962. Accordingly the Government extended short-term finance to the industry, confident that this was economically justified.

The Government's optimism lasted until the 1958 recession when a relatively small fall in heavy industrial production produced financial crisis on the railways. The minister reproved the Commission, appointed an auditor to check that the crisis really was the product of circumstances outside the Commission's control, approved a further increase in short-term finance, and announced that, in conjunction with the FBI and other industrial interests, another reassessment would be made.[35] This allowed the minister 'a note of satisfaction', and the following year he extended the 'interim period' before the railways became self-supporting to 1963.[36]

The proximity of the general election of 1959 muted Parliament's response, but after the election the critics re-emerged. Some pressed for more decentralization, some for 'ruthless' contraction of the industry until no further State finance was required. Subsequently, the Guillebaud Report's recommendations on railway wages threatened to expand the deficit even further, impelling yet more radical State intervention. 'The men in the industry', the prime minister said, 'must accept that the Government have a right, since they are now producing the only source of revenue, the taxpayers' money, on which the industry can run, to take a more direct part in the reorganisation of the industry than if it were prospering.'[37] He did not suggest that part, at least, of the responsibility for the deficit belonged to the Government itself.

A five-man committee, recruited from private industry[38] but not, the minister said, 'representative', was appointed to make a confidential report to the Government on the railways. The Select Committee on Nationalized Industries was considering railways at the same time,[39] and later in the year, yet a third inquiry was set up to consider the modernization programme: 'Appointing committees is no substitute for policy', *The Economist* commented.[40] Meanwhile, the 1960 budget acknowledged the gravity of the situation by accepting that payments hitherto made to the railways as loans were unlikely to be repaid so that sums paid in the future were better regarded as subsidies, above-the-line in the national accounts, rendering the Transport Commission, one observer said, 'an additional department of the Minister of Transport'.[41]

The Government's new reform proposals[42] included a drastic cut in the Commission's debts, the abolition of the Commission itself and the creation of separate boards for each branch of the Commission's work. Railways were to come under a new and separate board which would hold the assets of the industry, and would have, the minister said, complete control of its own pricing, investment and wages.[43] The new regional boards would have full-time members (unlike the previous area boards). The railways were too large, the minister said firmly, and must be contracted. In general, the response to these proposals was guarded, although some people were critical of the failure to decide unequivocally between commercialism and a public service, or between an independent corporation or a department of State.[44] Some Conservatives attacked the delay in reaching the present reforms, and Aubrey Jones criticized the Government's preoccupation with organizational questions: decentralization would not obviously help, and separating road and rail transport so sharply might conceivably ruin both through competition; however unpopular, increasing transport prices might help: 'Which of the two unpopularities do the

Government prefer,' he asked, 'the unpopularity of seeing fares and charges rise, or the odium of so mismanaging the railways that they have permanently to subsidise them?'[45]

Thereafter, the reforms began to take shape. The first of these brought two prominent businessmen to the new Railways Board (one as chairman), both at salaries equal to that which they had received in private industry and well above that given to other members of the board.[46] The new boards were statutorily created and new proposals for reorganization published. The board began the process of contracting the railways. The first results seemed, on the surface, to vindicate the Government's approach. In the 1964 budget, the chancellor said that the deficit on the railways was 29 million pounds less than was provided for in 1963, itself a year in which the sum allowed for the deficit had been underspent by 18 million pounds. However, the broader economic questions remained unanswered, and the effectiveness of the new railways was still dependent on the general course of Government policy.[47] But these were problems for the Government's successor.

The delay shown by the Government in reaching its final proposals was considerable, despite the wealth of information with which it armed itself over the years. The delay, as well as sporadic Government intervention in pricing and investment policy on the railways, exacerbated the problems of the industry, demanding increasing State subsidies, without there being any very clear criteria justifying such finance. The organizational proposals did not impinge on the basic question, the context of railway operations – dominated by both Government economic policy and the existence of a powerful motor industry – nor did they directly relate to the aim of providing efficient transport at minimum cost. Decentralization proceeded with increasing ministerial control and intervention which, in sum, intensified centralization and *étatisation*. Finally, compelled to intervene more systematically, the Government's policy was less to make transport viable and more to eliminate an embarrassment. Taking profitability as a criterion, it was still not absolutely clear at the end of the Conservative administration whether railways as part of the national transport system, including the direct and indirect costs of road transport, should be contracted, eliminated or merely modernized. To have answered this question would have required a much more consciously interventionist role by the State, including re-entry into the areas of transport planning and effective co-ordination, with the possibility of the State directing different forms of goods to different means of transport. Reducing the railways to units in the hope that the source of the deficit could be located at specific points within an interdependent system inhibited comprehension of the entire field of transport, the context of railway operation, which produced the deficit but which was not itself subject to economic scrutiny. It was not clear whether the deficit was a sign of 'non-profitability' or merely the cost of Government policy in holding down charges, or merely the reflection of an under-valuation of the full national cost of road transport. A muddled corporatist solution gained neither the benefits of freeing the industry within the neo-Liberal scheme nor the advantages of a consciously *étatiste* prescription.

Electricity

The Government's initial neo-Liberalism committed it against treating the fuel and power industries as a single unit, an attitude approved by the report of the Ridley Committee.[48] The minister, in accepting this general approach, refused a commitment to competitive pricing, however. The aim was, he said, 'to combine full-blooded competition with co-ordination in the national interest'.[49] The electricity industry received from Conservative Governments larger public funds for investment than any other single industry, and appeared to be 'massively successful', as the chairman of a Select Committee inquiry into electricity described it in late 1963. This surface attribute prompted less consistent Parliamentary scrutiny, even though the large sums involved occasionally gave rise to worries. For example, when the minister sought to extend the industry's borrowing power in 1954, two backbench Conservatives moved an amendment rejecting the Bill.[50] Hinchingbrooke argued that no criterion existed to appraise the proposed loan, since, unlike private firms whose output depended on consumer sovereignty, State industry was solely dependent on ministerial power. Since State funds were urgently needed to build roads among other things, and funds were available from the private capital market, electricity should borrow directly on its own credit.[51] To this Powell added a more general comment: there were only two ways of achieving economic ends, by allowing demand to express itself through prices as profitability, or by deliberate economic manipulation which must be centralized in a plan. Any compromise involved a sacrifice and the danger of getting the worst of both alternatives. The British economy was neither one nor the other – the private sector operated for profit, the public under statute, and the Government intervened, making 'a series of decisions which can be regarded either as part of what is at most a partial plan or arbitrary decisions taken *ad hoc* from time to time'. Investment in the nationalized industries, he went on, could not be judged until they possessed a rational price structure, reflecting true costs and real demand. Accordingly, the Government must work towards a position where the Treasury guarantee could be withdrawn 'and there will be open competition in the money market as between all the various national industries without a deliberate advantage being attached arbitrarily to one group of them'.[52]

Some Conservatives had less enthusiasm for competition, and pressed the Government to co-ordinate fuel and power,[53] and prevent electricity and gas competing with private manufacturers and retailers of plant and domestic appliances.[54] After a considerable campaign, the Government agreed in 1956 to prohibit the manufacture of electrical equipment by public industry except for research purposes. The decision was made shortly after a Monopoly Commission Report had argued that there was too little competition between private electrical equipment manufacturers.[55]

The Government's main innovation was based upon an inquiry into the industry by the Herbert Committee. This recommended that the industry should operate on commercial criteria (including the raising of capital on its own credit), and should be decentralized so that the National Board would have no other function except the formulation of general policy. The Government broadly accepted the report although it rejected the recommendation that Area Boards should raise their own capital. The Government's Bill replaced the existing national authority with a separate Generating Board and a Council responsible for policy, co-ordination, the raising of capital and research; Area Boards were henceforth responsible for covering their own expenditure. The minister did not commit himself on the question of commercial criteria.[56]

In 1959, the Government again sought to extend the borrowing power of the industry to cover its seven-year investment programme. Nigel Birch immediately raised the problem of Parliamentary control for such an enormous sum spread over a period so far ahead. By 1958, he said, electricity had borrowed more than all the other public industries combined. The House was now being asked to commit itself seven years in advance, to commit a Government as yet not elected for its entire period of office to a specific rate of investment and taxation: 'something very near', he said, 'the abdication of the traditional rights of Parliament to control expenditure'.[57] Since the Government did not plan so far ahead, why was it necessary for one industry to do so? Powell supported this critique by urging Parliament's right to deny finance; the Bill must be amended to include an annual maximum sum, which, if exceeded, would allow the House to check expenditure.[58] In the event, at the report stage the Government agreed to cut the total volume of funds permitted.[59]

When the Government presented a similar Bill to Parliament in late 1963, there was relatively very little criticism; the measure increased the borrowing power of the industry for three years, and then a further three years on a resolution from the House, covering the period up to 1970. The minister explained that there was co-ordination between the fuel and power industries, and also competition: 'But it must be fair competition, and have regard for the national interest.' It was the minister's task to see 'that the national interest is properly reflected in the factors which influence consumers in their choice', a revision of the idea of consumer sovereignty which he did not explain.[60] For the rest there was almost only praise, although one Conservative did say that the private American electricity industry had markedly higher productivity, and another urged that loans to the British industry should be on strictly commercial criteria.[61]

Again, the limits to the Government's neo-Liberalism in this, the most 'successful' nationalized industry, were more impressive than its innovations. Despite the appearance of reform at the top of the industry, there was still insufficient freedom to create clear criteria for investment and pricing. Parliament was asked to vote sums which it was impossible for it or, indeed, for the Government to appraise economically and independently of the industry itself. Similarly, there were no means of appraising the size or performance of the industry, or whether the State was victim or commander of its enormous ward. The lack of a deficit in electricity was no more an adequate guide to the economic performance of the industry than the existence of a deficit in railways. The backbench neo-Liberal critique of the Government's treatment of the electricity industry stood out in clear contrast to the muddled corporatism of the Government. But it was also clear that the neo-Liberal case was powerless to shape events, and Parliament was equally powerless to control public revenue. The management of the electricity industry felt the industry had to evolve smoothly into the future, regardless of the vagaries of party politics. As a result, the impression remains that the public sector had become almost autonomous, a concern as unlimited (given Government support) in practice as large-scale private corporations, part of pluralist, rather than *étatiste* corporatist, aspiration.

Other industries

Few conference agendas were without pleas to make the nationalized industries 'more efficient', to lower their costs, make them borrow from the capital market, subject them to the Monopolies Commission, or introduce further decentralization:[62] 'We must return these industries', one speaker said, 'to a state as near like private enterprise as it is possible to get them.'[63] Any 'social' element must be eliminated, compelling those industries in decline to release their resources for expanding enterprises.

However, critics were not unanimous on the means to control the monopoly power of nationalized industry. Indeed, the 'monopoly' power was not always self-evident, given the existence of a private oil industry, and the creation of private television and private airways. Nabarro saw the main safeguard as the power exercised by the capital market if public industry borrowed from it,[64] but Shepherd was sceptical, and urged higher prices to permit auto-financing.[65] An issue not always faced by neo-Liberals was the danger of State industries becoming properly competitive. The 'logic of commerce' suggested that the coal industry should shift resources into oil and chemicals, railways into road transport, electricity into equipment manufacturing. The public sector would then grow, particularly where it could concentrate large resources against private rivals. The experience of the Italian State Corporation, ENI, suggested some of the possibilities of public commercialism. Paradoxically, advocates of a fully competitive public sector should have been prepared to see that sector absorb an increasingly large part of the economy in pursuit of competition. In 1963, the contest between a State steel firm and a private one for possession of a third illustrated some of the likely anomalies, as did the agreement signed between BOAC and a private air company to share the Atlantic services.

In the coal industry, a pattern similar to that in railways developed. A 1955 report from the Fleck Committee both stressed the need for commercialism in the industry and criticized the *excessive* decentralization of the industry.[66] The Government did concede something to the neo-Liberal case when it permitted, after the general election of 1955, an 18 per cent rise in coal prices; it was only a temporary move, and much criticized. By 1958, of ten applications for coal price increases, the Government had refused one completely, reduced four and delayed five. In 1960, the refusal of an application to import coal from America showed the limits of the Government's commitment to competition for coal.[67]

The Government also tried sporadically to delay the contraction of the industry – what Powell called, 'naked and unashamed, a plea for the maintenance of a price system which will retain in production the uneconomic pits'[68] – only to find itself overwhelmed by the increasing consumption of oil or the exodus of labour from the industry. But not all backbenchers were critical from the neo-Liberal position. For example, in the aftermath of the 1958 recession, some Conservatives pressed for the overall planning and co-ordination of the fuel and power industries, and their further co-ordination with the railways.[69]

In civil aviation, pressure to permit private operators on major routes held by BOAC and BEA continued up until 1959, when the State finally conceded the principle of equality to private companies, permitting all operators the same opportunity to obtain a licence for all routes. The State, however, retained the right to judge appeals against the issue of licences by the new Licensing Board, and refrained from disturbing the cartel agreements its corporations had reached with foreign companies. Indeed, the minister specifically promised 'I shall do all I can to encourage further international co-operation of this kind.' He saw the new Licensing Board as created to encourage co-operation between private and public firms while improving services by 'organized' competition.[70] In the first test-case – an application from the private company, Cunard Eagle, to fly the North Atlantic in competition with BOAC – the Government accepted BOAC's protest and cancelled the licence issued by the Licensing Board. The stable North Atlantic cartel was not to be disturbed, even though BOAC was allowed to compete with Cunard Eagle's parent company, Cunard Shipping Lines, which had requested and had been accorded public finance specifically to build a further Queen liner for the North Atlantic route. The picture was not complete until, in June 1962, BOAC and Cunard Eagle (itself now subject to newly intensified competition from a merged group of private aviation companies, Air Holdings) agreed to form a joint company to operate in the western hemisphere, 70 per cent of the capital being provided by BOAC. BOAC agreed not to compete with the new company, and, more significantly, Cunard agreed not to compete with BOAC, an arrangement which, *The Economist* said, 'comes close to making a gift of public assets to private investors' since BOAC was paying much more to keep Cunard off its routes than Cunard would have won by straight competition.[71] This was not a Liberal solution to the problems of creating efficient North Atlantic transport, but a public-private agreement not to compete, a solution that the other public corporation, BEA (facing a deficit the same year) might even then have liked to emulate, perhaps.

The neo-Liberal case was counterposed to the dominant elements in Government policy. In airways, a 'young growth industry', the Government's main aim seemed to be to protect its own industries, accommodating private companies with the minimum disturbance rather than fostering genuine competition. The *modus vivendi* achieved could only be temporary as the private companies continued to seek to expand, thus further limiting the operations of the public corporations, themselves already under pressure from severe international competition.

Decentralization, the main Conservative proposal for public industry when the party was in opposition, was as close as the neo-Liberal revival came to creating a Liberal economy in the public sector. Even so, execution was limited. Investment and wages remained controlled at the national level in order to allow the State to influence the general economy. Trends towards centralization, as evident in the private sector as in the agencies of the State over the preceding fifty years, were not materially deflected. The context of operation of public industry was linked steadily more tightly to the State until finally a plan could be devised for the entire public sector. Far from moving towards Liberal arrangements for public investment by compelling its industries to borrow from the capital market without a Treasury guarantee, the State forced all public investment through its own hands, thus simultaneously seeking to exercise supreme control over a major section of national investment (in order to control inflationary pressures) and preserving it from market criteria. In so doing, the Government tended to delay the decline of its declining industries, and so impeded the redistribution of national resources towards new growth industries. In not pursuing a clearly worked out corporatist policy, however, the Government did not restore declining industry to a role appropriate to its existing size nor organize a planned and, for the participants involved, painless decline. The middle way lacked design and direction, sometimes getting the worst of both worlds; it seemed merely to postpone what would become necessary, sooner or later – a plan. Indeed, the elimination of the conventional criteria for evaluating the nationalized industries prevented outsiders being in any position to make informed judgements. Parliament became successively less relevant in determining the pattern of the public sector. Indeed, the Government itself, without major sources of information except from foreign examples, could be seen to be as much a victim in certain respects as Parliament. The State, it seemed, had assumed a life and an autonomy of its own, independent of the Government.

13

The New Capitalism

The private sector of the economy was simultaneously the practical embodiment of the neo-Liberal elements within Conservatism, and the prime target of Government policy if stable economic growth was to be assured. In the first respect, it was supposed to be an area outside the immediate jurisdiction of the State, independent and self-reliant, holding the secret of progress and prosperity for society. To pluralists and Liberals, Britain was a private or free enterprise economy, firmly part of 'capitalism' as Lord Hailsham declared.[1] The private sector was society, and the public, not so much an equal 'sector' as a marginal amendment to the basic system, and even something of an anomaly. For the State, however, the private sector limited its supremacy, posed criteria of performance independent of the State's, fostered disturbing change, and generated problems the State was required to solve, problems not least prominent in the public sector itself.

A comprehensive list of the links between State and industry would take this account too far afield,[2] but certain salient features should be noted. First, and perhaps most important, business and Government in the period considered here shared common assumptions. They tended to identify the same sorts of things as problems, to describe those problems in the same way, and to propose the same sorts of solutions. This is not to say that, from time to time, there were not differences in emphasis, nor that the Government did not diverge radically from opinion in one section of business or one company, but only that business, as a collective, was more often at one with the Government. Second, the State required, for much of its policy to be effective, the close and continuous co-operation of businessmen. For example, employers collected an important part of the State's revenue through income tax and social security payments. Broad economic measures required specific action by business-men: to resist wage claims or refrain from increasing prices, to concentrate attention in the export field, to vary investment, to merge with other firms or even suspend production, move factories into designated areas or refrain from building in other areas. Monetary policy enlisted the direct assistance of the private banking system to control credit, even when this ran counter to the apparent immediate interests of bankers. The conception of State-industry co-operation and partnership is, as described earlier, an important part of the transition to corpora-tism, and is contrasted with the clear separation of the public will and individual private interest in Liberal assumptions.

For its part, the State sought to foster industry: at a mini-mum, by disentangling snares, providing information or services (for example, credit terms for exports); at a maximum, by financing an entire industry, diverting industry to specific areas, discriminating between different sectors, protecting industry from foreign competition, and, ultimately, providing a general plan to co-ordinate all elements in the economy and reduce duplication and mis-estimation by firms. In addition, through its own industries the State provided basic raw materials and services at relatively low prices; in some cases it provided subsidies which permitted under-cost selling: to the relative cheapening, for example, of exports. Defence policy, while directed at problems outside this discussion, had a pro-found impact on the economy through direct military contracts, and even more, through the multiplier effect of this expenditure. The British economy is built round the activity of the metal-using industries, and it was upon these industries that defence policy made maximum demands. In some cases, those demands made an industry almost wholly dependent on the State (in aircraft, for example, whose main source of alternative work to defence was BEA and BOAC, both part of the public sector). There is little evidence that the State used its defence expendi-ture directly for economic purposes, although it did occasionally change parts of it – by advancing defence contracts for cotton, for example.

The State, then, acted almost as a national managing

director, supervising a series of subsidiaries which stood in varying relationships to it. Private industry needed the protective shell of the State to ensure stable production and defence against foreign competition. State welfare services smoothed some of the effects of economic change in order to safeguard social stability. Finally, international competition prompted the State to seek to focus all national effort on the foreign field, rather than permitting efforts to be dissipated in domestic competition and conflict. The foreigner should be the target, and the State became inevitably nationalistic.

The formal points of intersection between State and industry were very diverse. Firms and their federal organizations were consulted directly on matters likely to affect their interests, were invited to send representatives to attend inquiries, including inquiries into the State itself (for example, the Fleck and Stedeford Committees). Private firms tried to influence ministers by sending deputations to them, inviting them to meals and meetings, by creating pressure groups to work at influencing particular departments, by submitting memoranda or publishing statements on most major questions through their federal organizations (for example, annually on the budget), by circularizing ministers and MPs, and holding meetings to address them. The general climate of opinion was more important here than direct persuasion; the press – for the Government, the only immediate representation of public opinion most of the time – played an important role in creating as well as reflecting that climate.

The line between State and business was never very clear in terms of personnel. Businessmen were employed in public roles, on the boards of nationalized industries and similar agencies. For example, Lord Cromer, a merchant banker, became governor of the Bank of England, or Dr Beeching, a director of ICI, was made head of the railways. On the other hand, Conservative ministers were sometimes recruited from private industry, and, on retirement, returned to industry. Oliver Lyttelton (later Lord Chandos) was only one of the better-known examples of this. In Opposition, Conservative ministers similarly accepted positions in industry. Finally, friendships and personal relationships between prominent businessmen and politicians helped to keep the two united. Much of this was also true of the Parliamentary Labour party although this does not directly concern this account.

This multiplicity of links suggests that where the views of Government (of either major party) and the general business community diverge, they can be quickly reunified. It is unlikely, for reasons stated, that their views would diverge very far. The work of a diversity of committees, advising the Government and staffed by joint business-departmental representatives, smooths the course long before action or legislation is initiated: 'The Advisory committee is the means by which the pressure group has been given a place in the formal structure of Government,'[3] the embodiment of what Beer calls, 'the quasi-corporative State'.[4]

This picture, however, exaggerates the consistent unanimity and conceals the occasional strains. For example, the 1952 Excess Profits Levy excited wide business opposition, partly compensated, in 1953, by what the president of the Board of Trade called 'primarily an industrial Budget. Its purpose is to help industry and it is none the worse for that.'[5] The fluctuations of economic policy in relationship to international changes also prompted industrial criticism, particularly where this produced grave miscalculations in company finance due to an unexpected change in Government policy. The criticism culminated in the Government's readoption of State planning, itself a new effort to reintegrate business and the State.

The level of actual co-operation under Conservative Governments varied. For industry, dependence on Government intervention was a partial function of its own confidence, of business expectations. While a post-war slump was still feared, State help was retained even when irksome, and when international competition seemed to grow more intense, help was again demanded. The fate of the 1954 Industrial Organization and Development Bill is instructive in this respect. The Bill, to permit federal organizations to be created in badly-organized industries, and to make levies on constituent firms to foster efficiency, research and export efforts, was a direct descendant of the Development Council policy of the Labour Government and inter-war aspirations to 'self-government in industry'.[6] Any

co-operation between businessmen is of questionable value if
competition is the main end in view. However, the fear of post-
war slump was past, and the restrictions of organization were of
less value to industry than the opportunity for competitive
expansion. The Bill evoked sharp criticism within the party and
'determined opposition within industry',[7] so much so that it was
withdrawn. The curtailment of prosperity, however, could be
expected to revive the idea, and, indeed, as part of the planning
apparatus of the National Economic Development Council,
little 'Neddies' were set up to cover individual industries at
the very end of the period of Conservative administration,
although this elaborate innovation was not considered by
Parliament.

The Conservatives were pledged generally to assist small
business, but little specific was done, even though, presumably,
small business was closer to the ideal of the 'property-owning
democracy' than large. Stability and efficiency suggested that
the need for large firms was greater than that for small, a case
made more urgent by international competition between very
large firms, and the need for large-scale investment and research
in the new technologically intensive industries. One Conservative, indeed, urged that the State should use its purchases
to force amalgamations, ensuring that each industry possessed
one firm as big, and preferably bigger, than its foreign rivals.
Once one main firm was created, there was room for many
small ones.[8] The Government did not pursue the proposal
although one minister did believe that 'in many modern industries, an increase in the size of firms is an essential condition of
advance'. However, an attitude was suggested that small business was not the key element in the neo-Liberal economy, but
rather a tolerated luxury in the corporate society, a luxury
which should not be permitted to infringe the interests of the
major element in the economy, large firms. Small business
itself, traditionally united with large in a common defence
against socialism, showed, despite the brief activities of, for
example, the National Union of Small Shopkeepers,[9] no signs
of evolving a political case hostile to the Conservatives in
response either to the lack of attention shown them,[10] or to
measures they might see as directly hostile to their interests (for

example, the abolition of resale price maintenance), or to the decline in the challenge of socialism.

State innovations in assistance to business were directly related to the course of the general economy, and, as a result, Conservative Government action tended to be bunched at the later end of its period of office, and particularly from 1958. An important index of this help is the list of grants and loans to private companies. The specific figures are not satisfactory.[11] But in broad terms they do show that help was given during and just after the crisis of 1951, with a decline thereafter, and then during and after the recession of 1958. The principles on which the help was given were not clear, which prompted *The Economist* to protest that the Government had 'treated some nationalised industries almost as if they were its positive enemies, while a considerable pork barrel has been opened up for a growing number of private firms in cotton, steel, motors and other industries'.[12] Such help was small, however, beside the aid given to agriculture, and cannot really be compared to the flow of capital funds to the nationalized industries, since such industries had no other source of investment finance outside internal reserves. However, the repetition of inter-war precedents was of interest. The State could replace the capital market by offering investment funds at cheap rates to particular firms, and could directly subsidise industry, to the continued 'distortion' of the Liberal economy.

Only a few topics can be discussed here, and much is omitted in the interests of brevity. Distribution of industry policy, State action towards particular industries and towards restrictive practices, are cited rather as examples than as the substance of a complex relationship.

I. DISTRIBUTION OF INDUSTRY

Within a broadly corporatist framework, location of industry policy had an important role. General physical planning aimed to ensure uniform national development, uniform standards of livelihood without recourse to direct welfare measures, and the full utilization of social capital (for example, communications, towns, power supplies and so on) invested in formerly prosperous areas. By contrast, Liberals argued that such interference by the State distorted the working of the market and so the most economic distribution of resources as reflected in different costs in different geographical locations. Firms must be allowed to choose freely the site of their production on the basis of the real costs involved, on costs as accurate economic reflections of the real value of the sites concerned. If some areas allowed only high-cost production, labour should be encouraged to move away from them. In any case, most of the social capital there, it was argued, was obsolescent and had already paid for itself over the years of its use. To retain such capital in use 'artificially' was to impede progress as well as raise the costs of production or the cost of State subsidies to induce firms to move to such areas when there were alternative outlets of expenditure with higher rates of return.

In general, the Conservative Government leaned towards the first case (having any policy at all on location implied this), and some of its backbench critics towards the second. The general prosperity of the period reduced the importance of the topic, except when State intervention to secure deflation of the general economy had exceptional effects in particular areas. This became increasingly important towards the end of the Conservative administration. Economic expansion had a different impact on different areas, and Scottish and Lancashire members continually pressed the Government to take action on the problems of their own areas, helped by members from Northern Ireland whose situation was indeed the worst.

Up to 1958, the Government continued the policy of its predecessor, but emphasized that the overall cure for local unemployment was general economic expansion. The recession of 1958, however, promoted more vigorous action: budget concessions and a Bill to make current policy, the minister said, more flexible.[13] There was some opposition to this last proposal on the grounds that increased help in this form contradicted current deflationary policy (one critic said that current unemployment was merely the result of that policy).[14] At the same time, the Cohen Council criticized existing policy on the grounds that increased grants to unemployed workers would be economically more valuable. The new Bill was small comfort to

Conservatives from areas with relatively high unemployment, particularly as unemployment figures rose through the winter of 1958–9. Further concessions were added in the New Year, and the scale of advances to new industries increased. By March, however, employment figures were already returning to normal.

This brief episode had, however, shown some weaknesses in current legislation, and after the general election the Government introduced its only major innovation in the field, the Local Employment Bill. This was an opportunity to deschedule some areas (the proportion of the country covered fell from 19 to 14 per cent); it permitted action before unemployment actually appeared, and directed aid at relatively small areas. The minister justified the continuation of such help on the grounds that economic theory was inadequate, change had to be mitigated for social reasons not through the direction of industry but through regulating its plans where they clashed with social priorities.[15] It was more likely perhaps that the Bill was a concession to local interests. However, again minor opposition expressed itself. Hinchingbrooke, for example, was 'wholly opposed to the extension of the Welfare State from the individual to businesses in distress', and urged that direct State help should go only to individuals.[16] This 'old fashioned Whiggery'[17] was rejected by the minister and did not excite wide support.

The Bill was not an end to the problem, and complaints were resumed in the next recession.[18] The new Act was criticized for breaking interdependent planning areas into small pockets which ignored conditions outside. In late 1962 and 1963, the problems of the North-East loomed sufficiently large in this respect for a Cabinet minister to be charged with special responsibility for the area. In addition, special help was given to particular localities (for example Jarrow, Kirby and Hamilton) outside the terms of the Act, but in general the Government resisted the pressure of its members to do more than the legislation already specified and adjured its critics to await the effects of its general economic policy.

Overall prosperity reduced party interest in the problem during most of the period of Conservative administration, and did not provide an adequate basis either for a sustained neo-

Liberal critique of existing Government practice, nor more substantial corporatist innovations by the Government. However, a policy did continue, and to that extent infringed the Government's claimed return to a Liberal economy. A more serious recession might be expected to intensify the corporatist elements.

2. COTTON

The position of cotton in the private sector was comparable to that of railways in the public. Both were in a process of long-term decline and together reflected in a more extreme degree the strain periodically exhibited in the general economy. Like railways, the decline of the cotton textile industry was an international phenomenon in all developed industrial countries that had had a major textile industry. Perhaps the decline in Britain was more painful since it had been so important in the economy earlier, but the decline was marked. By 1963, the industry employed 28 per cent of the numbers employed in 1913, and 55 per cent of the total employed in 1950. The effects of general economic fluctuations were possibly even more disastrous in cotton than in railways, producing successive crises in 1951, 1955, 1958 and 1962–3. The Government's response was different, however. Simultaneously it sought to foster a neo-Liberal solution, leaving the industry alone so that foreign competition could reduce and 'reorganize' it into a viable form, and a corporatist remedy, first encouraging the industry to reach arrangements with foreign producers to control competition (but without lending the industry public sanctions to compel foreign producers to accept such arrangements), and secondly, financing an industry-wide contraction on the model of pre-war reorganization schemes. The second policy implied an overall directing role for the State which included determining the ultimate size of the industry and promising security to the millowners. The first policy worked in the opposite direction, placing sole initiative in the hands of the millowners. The confusion of the two policies both muddled the economic criteria involved and intensified bitterness among the millowners. The general case is instructive since it introduces an area of Government involvement, international trade, crucial for the full picture (and one where Liberalism achieved its major triumphs) but hitherto discussed only indirectly.

The general economic crisis of 1951, and, in particular, the strain on dollar reserves, prevented the new Government immediately fulfilling its Liberal pledges to free cotton trading. But once the crisis was past, the Government carried out the recommendations of its committee to end State trading in raw cotton. Its general view of the industry's prospects was optimistic, and its sole concession to current difficulties was to advance defence orders for textiles and make various purchase tax changes to help textile sales. Other Conservatives, however, continued to press for some form of protection. Julian Amery, for example, saw the major difficulty for the cotton industry as the increasing liberalization of world trade, eroding imperial preference and British defences against a world slump. The Government, he said, should consider whether Britain ought to withdraw from GATT.[19] However, the development of domestic prosperity perhaps moderated later criticisms.

1955 reopened the issue, but the Government refused to go further than undertake negotiations with the Indian Government to reduce its tariffs on textile imports (subsequently successful). Once again it cut the purchase tax rate on textiles. Japanese imports, the Government argued, were already very limited. To limit European imports would be to violate current attempts to liberalize trade. To limit Indian imports was simultaneously to take discriminatory action against an important buyer of British exports, as well as to violate existing Commonwealth and GATT agreements.[20] These concessions did not deflect the industry's pressure for increased protection. The Cotton Board urged quotas and increased tariffs on all textile imports, and, in particular, protection against imports from India and Hong Kong. Nor did they moderate party criticism.[21] A Lancashire Conservative backbencher, Richard Fort, advised Burnley manufacturers to invest elsewhere than in the cotton industry. The president of the Board of Trade took up many of these points in his reply to the industry at the 1955 Harrogate Cotton Board Conference. In a distinguished list of negatives, he firmly rejected both domestic protection and

Government responsibility for the internal conditions of the industry, its markets or its products. The autumn budget sweetened this homily by abolishing the special discriminatory system of purchase tax on textiles.

The industry did not improve substantially the following year, however, making it the fifth year in succession in which cotton's export performance showed a further decline. Britain became the fourth- instead of the third-largest cotton exporter. Party pressure at the Conservative conference reflected continuing dissatisfaction with what one delegate described as an industry 'battered and bemused by slave labour and subsidised oriental competition'.[22] The Government's suggestion this time was that the industry should make approaches to Indian producers to arrange some limitation of their exports to Britain. When it was found that Indian acceptance of such a limitation depended upon a like ordinance being accepted by Pakistan and Hong Kong producers, delegations were despatched there. Meanwhile, the fragile equilibrium of 1957 gave way to crisis in 1958. 'We watch', the minister said, 'with real anxiety the cotton industry, with its proud record, suffering these severe and continual amputations but . . . we are thankful that the younger operatives have so easily found work in other growing industries.'[23] The Government hoped that a voluntary world agreement in conjunction with its existing tariffs would protect the industry without State intervention, 'a slightly hypocritical and not particularly brutal plan for dodging Britain's obligations to the GATT', as *The Economist* described it.[24]

Backbenchers were less critical on this score, and rather attacked the Government's delay or refusal to force agreement internationally by threatening to raise tariffs against Commonwealth textile imports.[25] Fletcher-Cooke complained that 'over and over again in these debates we hear these phrases, many of them shibboleths, which arouse good emotions, such as Imperial unity, Imperial Preference, the open door, free entry, freer trade'.[26] However, additional Government action fortunately proved unnecessary, and Hong Kong accepted the principle of agreement. India and Pakistan, the prime minister said, had shown 'a statesmanlike and constructive attitude' in accepting detailed terms, and he hoped Hong Kong would now follow suit.[27] The minister was pleased that the agreement, reached 'voluntarily', had not compelled the Government 'to resort to unilateral restrictions on imports'. He felt 'a new lease of life (was) coming for British textiles'.[28]

However, in the following year – 1959 – a change of policy, hinted at in the previous October, was suddenly and with considerable speed announced and carried out. The Government offered the industry substantial financial aid to eliminate surplus capacity, offered now, the minister said, because a world producers' agreement had been reached and thereby stabilized the textile market.[29] Others, more cynically, saw it as an electoral tactic against Lancashire's Labour strongholds.[30] The Government's Commonwealth responsibilities, the minister argued, must not be allowed to compel domestic industry to bear the cost alone. The 'profit-and-loss' account could not be permitted to control cotton, since the Government were not old-fashioned Liberals, and, in any case, felt the envisaged expenditure to be economically justified: 'This is not a retirement pension that we are offering to an aged friend, but an advance payment to an enterprise of whose sustained capacity for expansion we have no doubt.'[31] A board, consisting of the chairman of the Cotton Board and two of its nominees, and two industrialists nominated by the Government, would supervise the expenditure. In general, Conservatives seemed, in an election year, to approve the measure. 'It is perfectly consistent with the philosophy of free-enterprise', Fletcher-Cooke maintained, 'that the State should help enterprises along their way.'[32] However, Powell interposed to warn that private industry whose taxes paid for this expenditure must see that it was an extraordinary and limited one; as the proposed contraction rate was little faster than the actual unaided rate in recent years, the onus of self-reform lay on the industry itself.[33]

The process of subsidized contraction was somewhat slow (the minister extended the time-limit), partly because it coincided with a revival in the world cotton textile market. There were complaints in 1960 of a shortage of capacity in the industry.[34] Industrialists also delayed re-equipment to see the impact of the expiry of the agreement with Hong Kong (on which the agreements with Pakistan and India depended) in early 1962.

By late 1961, production was again falling without any sign of long-term improvement: 'we have been lifted up and dropped', one manufacturer claimed, 'and were lifted up when, I believe, an election was just around the corner. Since then we have been ditched.'[35] The Government resisted pressure, and also advice that the industry be ignored,[36] and returned to seeking a renewal of the Hong Kong agreement, achieved in June 1962. This did not abate criticism – cotton operatives lobbied Parliament and demonstrated in Hyde Park, and Lancashire MPs organized a protest, four Conservatives voting against the Government; 'it is nonsense', one critic wrote, 'for the Government to say, as it has said, that it is up to the industry to determine its own size when the biggest single factor affecting the future of the industry is Government policy itself'.[37]

Under the first phase of the Government's scheme, applications for aid reached some 116 million pounds. The minister explained that the second phase of the scheme, modernization, would take place while imports were at a relatively low level since almost all exporters to Britain had agreed to limit their despatches. Pakistan had not agreed to do so, but the Government would ensure it did not exceed the ceiling laid down. As to complaints that the Government should take a more active part, 'how could we decide who to merge with whom?' the minister asked. The new chairman to the Cotton Board still demanded much more stringent control of Commonwealth imports, and Conservative MPs criticized the Government's inactivity over a protective wall which Fletcher-Cooke described as 'a few widely dispersed and rather low hurdles, with a great many gaps between them'.[38] The Government agreed to introduce category limits within the quotas and initiate discussions on lowering the quota ceilings; for the rest, it kept its peace.

Cotton did have special problems. Some 35 per cent of the home market was taken by imports, a larger proportion relative to the size of the British industry than most other developed countries. The 1959 Act had apparently seriously underestimated the scale of imports which subsequently entered the country. However, the Government's behaviour was still an uneasy compromise between neo-Liberal and corporatist tendencies. Exposure to foreign competition contrasted with piecemeal protection and partial State support. The Government was not Liberal in so far as it continued to protect cotton from non-Commonwealth competition, fostered quota agreements amongst Commonwealth producers as a means to evade responsibility for illiberal trade practices, and briefly financed part of the reorganization in the industry, rather than leaving it to competition and the capital market to tailor the industry to competitive size. On the other hand, it was not fully corporatist since it retained duty-free Commonwealth entry, did not systematically finance the industry nor establish clearly that the finance it gave would be of maximum use, and refused to alter its tariff policy to suit the existing size of the industry. There was little possibility of compromise between the variables of a Liberal trade policy, formalized in GATT, Commonwealth commitments, and the social costs of allowing cotton to decline 'naturally'. As it was, the Government tacked between different points without seeming to have consistent intention. Its efforts to achieve a producer agreement, for example, were clearly an evasion of the spirit of GATT, but were relatively weak because the Government refused to formalize the evasion by offering the Cotton Board a stiff tariff against Commonwealth imports if the Hong Kong producers refused an agreement. However, the Government did agree to take measures to compel Pakistan not to exceed its quota. Thus the 1959 Act, while expending a substantial sum of money, appeared to be relatively ineffective since the industry was not prepared to add its own funds to this sum in the conditions of overall uncertainty facing the industry. Perhaps the Government hoped that time would dissolve the problem somehow, and the movement of synthetic fibre manufacturers, ICI and Courtaulds, into the cotton textile industry did offer some hope of a new order. But this was not the result of Government policy or initiative which seemed to have failed to achieve any of its stated objectives.

3. OTHER INDUSTRIES

With the exception of aircraft, the Government did not intervene consistently in major industries, but some occasional involvements deserve closer attention. For example, jute, of little political significance, is a case where nearly all attempts to break down the inherited corporatist structure of the industry failed, despite the cogency of the neo-Liberal critique (partly expressed in a Restrictive Practices Court verdict in 1963) and its violation of both GATT and Commonwealth free entry.[39] Late in the period, substantial State loans to shipping and steel are of relevance to this account. More important, however, was the evolution of aircraft building.

The aircraft industry was heavily dependent on Government aid or contract work and could not have existed as it was without the Government. A Liberal policy was never seriously suggested for the industry, even though this might have stimulated the industry along quite different technical lines, concentrating on a low cost, low speed mass production output to reach a similar market to that supplied by the motor industry, instead of, for defence purposes, a very high cost, high speed output to supply the Government. As it was, the Government fully accepted responsibility for the industry and instructed it on the size it should be and the type of its main production. Between 1950 and 1964, Government payments to the industry covered 70 per cent of the industry's total output, and in May 1957, some 60 per cent of the industry's labour force was employed on defence work. Initially expanded by military commitments (the Korean War, followed by continued military innovation), the 1957 changes in defence policy – to replace manned combat aircraft with guided weapons – threatened to reduce the industry's activity very seriously. Accordingly, the Government instructed the industry to bear more of the costs of its own civil projects, to concentrate its activities (a recommendation of a Select Committee Report just previously)[40] in two to four airframe and two aero-engine firms, instead of fourteen and five major firms as hitherto, and thus contract its labour force from a quarter of a million in 1958 to 150,000 by 1963. Pre-war precedents were cited for this radical change, and the 'shot-gun marriages'[41] were duly consummated in five firms (two duopolies and one monopoly, of helicopters) under a Government threat that it would in future only issue contracts to the merged firms. Immediate sanctions operated through contracts for the

TSR2 project and a BEA liner. 'It is no part of the Government's business to try and tailor the aircraft industry to any particular size,' the minister reassured members at the same time.[42] In fact, the labour force in June 1962 was 293,000 although the proportion employed on defence work had decreased to 50 per cent.

However, it was clear that the State *did* make detailed and explicit economic and technical judgements concerning the size, structure, output and finance of the industry. The industry was 'an excellent example of . . . a monopsonist using its powers to change the structure of an industry according to its own definite criteria'.[43] Government responsibility also involved co-ordinating different parts of the public sector to dovetail with aircraft. BOAC complained in 1962 that it had been compelled by the Government to purchase uneconomic aircraft from the industry. Indeed, private purchasers from the industry depended upon Government decisions made under the 1960 Civil Aviation (Licensing) Bill, which in turn depended in part upon Government policy for its own corporations. Overall, the State was a precondition for the activity of the entire aviation industry and was clearly tending towards the role of national manager with private and public subsidiaries. Policy, not the independent initiative of the aircraft companies, was the key element in the industry. The corporatist and *étatiste* model remained scarcely influenced by neo-Liberalism. Whether the situation concealed excessive private profit at the expense of the State, or State administration disguised as private enterprise, whether, in any case, the production of aircraft was remotely 'economic', remained unclear.

The 1958 recession illuminated the problems of areas where shipbuilding was extensive. As, at the same time, Cunard Lines were considering the replacement of one of the Queen liners (originally financed largely by the State in the inter-war period), the Government agreed to finance part of the construction of the new ship. The minister justified this on the grounds that, on the North Atlantic run, the dollar earnings of such a liner would be substantial. The investment was economically justified and supported by the need to maintain British prestige (a case similar in essentials to that used to justify State

participation in the manufacture of the Anglo-French super-
sonic airliner, the Concorde). There was much criticism of the
decision,[44] particularly since it was known that Cunard was
moving its interests into civil aviation. One newspaper called
the relevant Bill 'the Selected Private Industry Benevolence
Bill'.[45] A Conservative backbencher, Sir John Vaughan-
Morgan, deploring subsidies in general, especially where they
were paid to a particular firm to build a 'white elephant', asked,
'is it really for the taxpayer to subsidise the transportation
across the Atlantic of tired tycoons?'[46] However, when the Bill
was in committee, Cunard announced, to the Government's
embarrassment, that the company had postponed the project
pending a full review of its North Atlantic services.[47] This was
not the end of the affair since the following year, the shipbuilding industry experienced a record decline in new orders, and in
May 1963 the Government announced a Shipbuilding Credit
Scheme to make loans to British ship-owners who agreed to
order from British shipyards. The initial sum offered, 30 million
pounds, was increased after two months to 60 million pounds,
and, with the inclusion of the new Cunard liner, to 75 million
pounds by October. However, again in an election year, when
the minister sought Parliamentary ratification for these innovations in the Shipbuilding Credit Bill, there was almost no party
criticism and certainly no Liberal criticism.[48] Without the Bill,
the minister said, the industry's labour force would contract
from 53,000 (June 1963) to under 30,000 (March 1965); with
the Bill, 70,000 could be employed between the spring of 1964
and that of 1965. This might have seemed less what the minister
claimed for the industry as 'a breathing space' and rather more
what he denied, 'to prolong artificially an excess capacity'.[49] At
best, it was a gamble.

No new attempts were made after denationalization to
increase competition in the steel industry, or break up its
corporatist cartel, although neo-Liberal criticism continued in
the party.[50] In 1957, the public Iron and Steel Board converted
the formal pricing arrangements, set by the State, into tacit
agreements within the industry to escape possible jurisdiction
under the 1956 Restrictive Practices Act.[51] In the same year,
the industry advised the Government that a new continuous

strip mill was required, and the siting of the mill immediately became a political contest between Welsh and Scottish claimants.[52] In the event, the Government compromised by agreeing to finance in part two economically less efficient semi-continuous strip mills, one each in Wales and Scotland. The minister justified this advance of State finance on the grounds that capital for such a project would be difficult to obtain as there would be no return for a long period ahead.[53] But the project, Nabarro claimed, was 'the subject of more criticism from every quarter than any Bill I can remember'.[54] Powell said that he did not believe that 'as a matter of settled policy, the borrowing of money on Government credit to be advanced to private enterprise on economic grounds can be justified or defended; other steel companies had borrowed amounts equal to the proposed loan recently, and in the previous week, the Governor of the Bank of England had complained publicly that too many funds were chasing too few good shares'.[55] The minister's defence stressed the exceptional nature of the present loan: steel was needed quickly, Scottish unemployment was serious, and pledges already made could not be broken; he said, 'we do not believe it wise to withhold State assistance from an industry when it is clear that that industry needs such help, that such help is in the national interest and that such help is not forthcoming from private sources'.[56]

Each of the minister's points was in doubt. Each was challenged. The division between a socially-concerned *étatiste* economy and a Liberal one, controlled at base by a freely operating and autonomous capital market, was not bridged. Neither in shipbuilding nor in steel was it clear that the proposed expenditure could be justified on Liberal economic grounds, nor what criteria were available in steel even to approach the question.

4. MONOPOLIES AND RESTRICTIVE PRACTICES

Neither major party was concerned with monopoly *per se*, although both used the term as one of denigration whenever it suited their purposes. For example, the campaign for commercial television was conducted almost entirely in terms of the

BBC's 'monopoly'.[57] Yet in practice MPs were rather more concerned with practices associated with cartels and oligopolies. Few Conservatives saw monopoly as intrinsically bad, regardless of the personal character of the people managing the firm: 'our view', Heathcoat Amory as chancellor said, 'is not necessarily that monopoly is a bad thing, but it is a bad thing if it abuses its powers as a monopoly.'[58] The properly Liberal view of monopoly would have seen it as not dissimilar to dictatorship: there were good dictators and bad dictators, but in essence dictatorship was, *ipso facto*, bad. However, Conservatives were generally prepared to trust large firms, checking only the formal external relations of such firms where they infringed legislation. Indeed, it was argued that the existing legislation, in attacking agreements between firms, stimulated monopoly formation by firms formerly linked by indictable agreements.[59] The American Anti-Trust legislation which, in principle, at least, attacked the question of monopoly as a structural problem (that is, not related to the practice of particular individuals) stood in Liberal contrast to the British approach, even if, in practice, the divergence was less clearcut.

Conservatives did not regard mergers as bad. 'We are a party of private enterprise', a minister said, 'and we must be a party of competition. You may find the number of competitors is reduced from six or seven to two or three, but as long as there are competitors there is competition.'[60] There seemed no obvious reason why, over time, the competitors should not be reduced to one, at which stage it was difficult to see whether the Conservatives would regard the situation as being changed in a retrograde direction or not. The commitment to competition, as earlier described, did not extend to the units of public industry nor to the steel industry. Nor did it impel the use of State firms to stimulate competition among private firms; indeed, in the electrical equipment manufacturing industry, the Government carefully prevented any such occurrence, despite a clear report from the Monopolies Commission that little competition existed in the industry. Again, the commitment did not reduce Government dependence on trade associations (despite the fact that formal and informal practices inimical to competition were sustained there). Some Conservatives were critical of such associations – for example, Shepherd argued that 'the greatest single cause of the lack of all dynamism in British industry' was the restriction of trade associations which kept prices too high and protected inefficient production.[61] Nor, finally, did the commitment permit restrictive practices legislation to be extended to the nationalized industries or the trade unions. Nationalized industry, the minister said, was statutorily created and part of Government policy, and neither factor could be made subject to outside check, a case that was legal rather than economic; on the other hand, labour was not susceptible to the 'legislative approach'.[62]

The effectiveness of the actual legislation was not clear. It did allow a series of exceptions; and procedure, even when reformed by a Conservative Government, was very slow. The execution of recommendations remained the sole prerogative of the Government which, persistently, seemed reluctant to accept the most radical proposals of its Commission. For example, the Government accepted all recommendations on both the match and oxygen industries except the proposal to impose price control on both; in addition, all major restrictions on oxygen were withdrawn in November 1962, although it was quite unclear what had changed in the industry to justify the decision.[63] Finally, the legislation had no provision for attacking tacit agreements, a loophole the iron and steel industry employed under the guidance of its public Iron and Steel Board. Formal agreements could escape indictment simply by being converted into undetectable informal agreements.[64] As a result, the overall effect of the legislation in economic terms was probably limited. Its impact on the retail price index seems to have been insignificant,[65] although this was not the sole criterion of effectiveness.

Conservative innovation in action against restrictive practices covered three measures. Initially, the Government expressed satisfaction with the procedure of its predecessor, and this perhaps helped negatively to gain industry's co-operation. The first change expanded the work of the Commission to examine general practices in industry rather than particular industries. Some criticized the change for its radicalism. Fletcher-Cooke felt monopoly was not necessarily a bad thing, and Reader Harris thought competition was not necessarily a good thing.[66] *The Economist* commented: 'It is as if the Government had talked of abolishing slavery but then introduced a measure under which the worst cases of cruelty to slaves might be investigated.'[67]

In 1955, the Commission, in a divided report, recommended further innovation. The majority report found collective price discrimination widespread and recommended it be declared, *prima facie*, pernicious, although justifiable exceptions could later be accepted. The minority report recommended the creation of a register of those agreements designed to foster given practices, those subsequently being found to be contrary to the public interest, being suppressed.[68] The Government tried to thread some middle way between the neo-Liberal maximum and the relatively acquiescent alternative. The practices were not to be declared criminal, the minister said, but all agreements would be registered and then examined by a separate tribunal on the assumption that they were against the public interest. The Government rejected collective resale price maintenance, but then offered legal sanction to individual price maintenance. Despite pressures both to strengthen these proposals and to weaken them,[69] the minister persevered in this approach which became the gist of the new Bill. The Bill enumerated seven categories of agreements to be excepted: one of which allowed an agreement where it helped to reduce local unemployment, and a second, where the agreement was necessary for other reasonable trade practices. The following year, the Register of Restrictive Practices was opened, and, by August 1960, some one thousand of the two thousand three hundred agreements on it had been ended or amended to meet the Court's specifications.

In formal terms, this was an encouraging development for neo-Liberal opinion, but a number of test-cases tended to limit its significance. First, in 1961 the Monopolies Commission reported on the tobacco trade, recommending that Imperial Tobacco Company divest itself of its extensive holding in its main rival, Gallahers. The Government delayed making any statement on this question until January 1962, when it announced that Imperial Tobacco would be permitted to retain its holding, first because of the 'responsible attitude adopted by Imperial Tobacco Company and . . . the special regard which the company had paid to the public interest'; second, because competition in the tobacco trade was very intense; and third, because the company had assured the Government that it regarded its decision not to interfere in the management of Gallaher's as binding in the future. The Government, then, refrained from ensuring that competition would be structurally assured in the tobacco industry because it trusted the individuals managing Imperial Tobacco to know and conform to the public interest. In Liberal terms, it trusted these individuals to be such bad businessmen that they would act, if necessary, contrary to their own interests. The Commission argued that competition between two clearly separate firms would improve the efficiency of Imperial, and that to prevent American intervention in the British market (as Imperial said its Gallaher's holding was designed to do) was not in the public interest. The Government's decision was a direct rebuff to the standing of the Commission and to neo-Liberal hopes.

The second case concerned the attempt of ICI to take over Courtaulds, potentially the largest merger in British industrial history up to that time, and designed to establish a virtual monopoly of many kinds of synthetic fibres in Britain. The struggle was protracted, and political opinion was exposed to what one newspaper described as 'two Property Owning Democrats of enormous significance . . . quarrelling like fish-wives over money'.[70] Under pressure, the Government said that the Monopolies Commission could not intervene in the negotiations since it could not foresee the possible effects of the merger and whether it might be undesirable, a point critics ridiculed on the grounds that the Commission was specifically instructed to assess the future effects of current or proposed agreements. Criticism prompted the chairman of ICI, Paul Chambers, to attack the dangers of competition, saying legislation against concentration of economic power was now out-of-date and what was needed was industrial planning to eliminate surplus capacity.[71] The situation was not improved by ICI's subsequent application to the Government for an increase in the tariff on ammonia sulphate imports, which, it argued, were being 'dumped' by East Germany. The tariff increase was ratified by a Conservative majority of only twenty-nine. However, the Government's embarrassment over the merger was relieved by the failure of ICI to absorb Courtaulds.

The incident, along with the approach of a general election, perhaps stimulated more reforming zeal by the Government, since it produced not only a White Paper covering future measures to increase competition generally, but also a Bill to abolish resale price maintenance, neither of which had featured in the preceding Queen's Speech. The president of the Board of Trade resisted considerable backbench pressure on behalf of small shopkeepers to preserve his original Bill, which, he said, was the logical result of the Government's experience over the preceding thirteen years in dealing with restrictive practices.[72] By the time the House came to consider the Government's White Paper, electioneering obscured most issues. However, the minister did deal comprehensively with the subject, saying again that the American Sherman Act was not 'appropriate' in Britain – 'In a market the size of the United Kingdom, the case against monopoly must be much less clear . . . public opinion here tends to be suspicious of the encroachment of the law against the freedom of action of individual firms except where there is the clearest evidence of need.'[73] The Government proposed to examine restrictions in commercial services, to expand the size of the Monopolies Commission which would consider monopoly situations presented to it by a new Registrar of Monopolies (subject to Board of Trade approval). Once the new machinery existed, the Government would keep a close watch on proposed mergers and refer to the registrar cases where it had doubts, although it would not prevent such mergers taking place. More Liberal criticisms came from backbenchers. Sir John Vaughan-Morgan criticized the delay in producing the White Paper, and William Shepherd declared that more severity, not less, was required in Britain relative to the United States.[74]

As a postscript to this account, it is instructive to cite a speech given in the later years of the Conservative administration by Oliver Lyttelton, Lord Chandos, a former Conservative minister, in which he urged price-leadership in industry or, as

225

he called it, 'discipline in the producers of certain products'. Industry, he said, was now operated by a new managerial class that had no incentive to make inordinate profit or exploit the community. Accordingly, the community should exercise care over legislation 'which was designed – a good deal of it at the expense of efficiency and order – to cure evils that were not going to exist except in very few cases'; the community should trust industrialists.[75] Appropriately, *The Economist* took up the gauntlet for Liberal opinion, replying both to Chandos and to Paul Chambers, head of ICI, together:

'No theory of "imperfect competition" or of "industrial self-discipline" yet evolved', it declared, 'has been able to suggest that this kind of real behaviour (as advocated by the two industrialists, NH) in a real world can be relied upon to bring about that rightness of price, that optimum efficiency, that ideal allocation of resources that the theories of perfect competition were so sure would arise from unreal behaviour in an unreal world. Remove the simplifying assumptions, and one removes the automatic acceptance of business behaviour too . . . its removal positively invites the intervention of society into the sphere of decisions many of his (Chandos') fellow-businessmen, less ruthlessly realist, still consider their own prerogative.'[76]

This was a strange but symptomatic reply, almost a plea for ideological innocence to protect an un-innocent world from acknowledging a corporatist reality, a practical defence of a Liberalism substantially weaker than its forebears. Pluralistic corporatism in industry which rejects the right of society to ensure corporatist responsibility through the State, however 'ruthlessly realist' in describing the world, has no defence against the demand for social responsibility if it once allows the decay of the 'unreal' theory of Liberalism. The weakness of the defence indicated the limits of Liberalism in contemporary British society, as well as the lack of any rigorous justification for corporatism.

The opening discussion suggested that State-industry partnership already approximated in important respects to a corporatist model. The general attitude of the Government – pragmatism on each separate industrial issue, with fairly heavy dependence on outside pressures to set the context of its own decisions (rationalized in a claimed adherence to 'balance') – rendered it subordinate to the trends in industry rather than the grand architect of those trends, as some Conservatives saw it. It was not consciously corporatist by persuasion, but actually corporatist by default, so throwing into sharp relief the Liberal critique from some of its backbenchers. Since it relied more heavily on the advice of parties to a dispute or problem rather than on an intellectual or political commitment of its own, its actions often seemed (as in the 1930s) merely to foster the interests of dominant vested parties rather than shaping events. Lord Chandos testified to the impressive continuity of attitudes between the 1930s and the 1960s, despite the successive economic changes and fluctuations in opinion that had taken place, and had seemed to transform the political climate. Practice remained in important essentials as it had been, and the aspirations of the neo-Liberals were unfulfilled. The middle way left things much as they had been. The Government's neglect of declining industries (relative to what could have been done) was some concession to the Liberal case, as were its attempts to strengthen the restrictive practices legislation. But, for Liberals, these concessions were limited by the intervention after 1958 and the qualifications attached to restrictive practices legislation. Conservatism seemed rather to have had expansion and prosperity grafted on to it than to have made a radical shift. Conservative caution and acquiescence in the existing *status quo* were quite inappropriate to the achievement of Liberal aims. The balance, sustainable in theory, between freedom and order, concealed rather more order than freedom.

The Conservative State

Throughout the period of Conservative Government, the State sector was by far the largest and most important single element in the economy, employing some six million people (nearly 25 per cent of the working population),[1] investing some 40 per cent of total national investment, and expending more than 40 per cent of the gross national product. Historically, State expenditure had risen almost inexorably, if not consistently, from some 9 per cent of the gross national product in 1890 to 37 per cent in 1955, an increase of forty-seven times in money, and ten times in real, terms.[2] Despite a check to this increase in the middle 1950s, it resumed its growth after 1958, reaching new peacetime records that a Conservative Government regarded apparently with relative equanimity.[3] Yet this scale of expenditure, this scale of participation in the economy, entailed a society which was markedly different from one in which the State could really seem to be outside the economy, a neutral arbiter. It also meant that to recreate a Liberal economy required a major counter-revolution, a structural transformation of British society and economy. Necessarily, very substantial limits were placed on neo-Liberal aspirations by the Government's acceptance of the *status quo* it inherited from Labour. In practice, the issue became not how to create a Liberal economy, but how to ensure economic expansion, an aim in the pursuit of which the Conservatives did not differ from the Opposition. The parties indeed changed places: as the Conservative Opposition had attacked the Labour Government for restricting expansion by its obsession with the balance of payments, whereas the true problem was to raise domestic production which would automatically take care of the external position, so the Labour Opposition mobilized the same case against the Conservative Government; the change of positions in 1951 was repeated in 1964, since both parties seemed equally expansionist in propaganda and restrictionist in practice.

However, in the first five years of Conservative Government, expansion did take place and, as a result, Liberal aspirations seemed stronger than later on. The key to the strength of those aspirations lay in success, and would not long outlast an appearance of failure. The 'liberal ideology of the market place',[4] as one observer called it, seemed to be strongest in the area of foreign trade and finance, and the domestic indices of State participation, taxation and public expenditure showed little significant decline after the burden of rearmament in the early years had been lightened. After 1955, problems accumulated, culminating in a series of economic fluctuations which reduced the rate of economic growth. Rather than press on into a more explicitly Liberal approach, the Government turned in the opposite direction, towards planning.

Even the more Liberal phase, however, did not end protection. Free trade and sterling convertibility, a wholly free domestic market in capital and labour, remained only aspirations, and hardly even aspirations in certain fields (for example, agriculture). Indeed, the success experienced seemed largely the result of relatively accidental factors outside the control of the Government: for example, a two and a half year decline in world commodity prices after the Korean boom, or, later, a 'remarkable recovery in personal savings', unprecedented since 1914, and substantial restraint in domestic consumption, 'almost certainly lower than in any peacetime year since 1914, and probably for many years before that'.[5] Once relatively favourable exogenous factors ceased to operate (or worked in the reverse direction), domestic inflation became a problem only exacerbated by the price increases suggested in a neo-Liberal approach 'to mop up excess demand'. Of necessity, optimism declined, and a retreat from even neo-Liberalism set in without a clear political alternative replacing it. The economics of neo-Liberalism diverged increasingly from the politics of government.

However, these groping steps in a different direction did not in the short term end neo-Liberal aspiration. Members of the

Bow Group continued to pursue 'the ideal of the free market economy',[6] Erhardt's aspiration for the West German economy and a model contrasted with pure *laissez-faire* by the State's retention of general economic guidance through fiscal and monetary policies. Pursuing this aim, it was urged that controls on capital be ended, taxation be sharply reduced and made more regressive, and the nationalized industries be put on the same footing as private firms.[7] In the first two proposals, the Government did go some way to meet the demands, but in a way not related directly to the overall aim. However, later, when doubts concerning economic growth were increasing, members of the Group pressed for *stronger* Government direction and later supported planning, without clearly reconciling this with the 'market economy'.[8] One writer regretfully admitted that pursuit of the 'market economy' had achieved few notable successes, that the State had increased rather than decreased its role, and that 'the free market philosophy (seems) ... to have come into direct conflict with other ideals'; pragmatism was no guide since 'the policies which seem to be the most reasonable and practical appear to diverge more and more from the principles in which they should be founded'.[9]

Not all Conservatives had, in fact, adhered to the Liberal trend. Sir Robert Boothby consistently deplored 'the gradual, steady, corroding conversion of the Tory Party to the fiscal doctrines of the Liberal Party' as 'the greatest grief of my declining years'.[10] Opposition to neo-Liberalism was most clearly expressed in the field of international trade and currency. The national control of trade and currency was essential for the autarchy implicit in corporatism. Arguments for discrimination or bilateral trade, and against liberal trade, the GATT provisions and sterling convertibility, were sustained by backbenchers throughout the Conservative administration. 'I joined the Tory Party', Boothby said, 'because I believed in discrimination. We called it Imperial Preference in those days.'[11] And Sir Victor Raikes suggested that the GATT 'is a very good instrument of trade for the United States of America, without the least doubt, and they are quite entitled to make what use they can of it, but we are also entitled to look after our interests'.[12] The case was initially mobilized against suggestions that the Government move towards freer international trade and sterling convertibility, the latter being known in its heyday as 'the dash for freedom'.[13] In fact, after the Commonwealth Economic Conference in late 1952, the Government modified its intentions by restricting efforts to reduce exchange control. 'With head tucked well into a new protective shell', *The Economist* commented, 'the objective is now to crawl like a crustacean to freedom.'[14] However, rumours of impending convertibility persisted in threatening sterling with speculative dealings up until 1955.[15]

The Government itself was primarily concerned with administration rather than political ideas or long-term policy. Inflation superimposed problems on those of administration which demanded extra-administrative responses, which, in their turn, changed the nature of administration, compelling further State innovation and ultimately increased attempts to make State direction coherent, explicit and consistent. The Government's main approach to inflation was primarily one of manipulating available economic mechanisms (even if buttressed with exhortation) rather than, in the short term, attributing praise or blame. But the moral undertone emerged more clearly as time went on, perhaps most succinctly summarized in a *Daily Telegraph* editorial which alleged that 'Inflation is a moral as well as an economic crisis . . . what we are suffering from, as a nation, is greed.'[16] Butler, in a similar vein, called for 'a lead to the country in calling for material values to emerge instead of materialist appetites', what *The Observer* called 'The Nanny Approach'.[17] Whatever the elaborate economic rationale, this accusation that the working class was greedy was likely to be more appealing to a middle-class party, arranged in battle order to protect its privileges. The moral element also brought the case much more firmly into an older tradition – income restraint replaced sexual restraint in the version put forward by, for example, Malthus.

Conservative use of fiscal and budgetary policy is not examined here, although the broad trends confirm the conclusions of this discussion. Attention is restricted to a brief account of Conservative attitudes to controls and monetary policy, the return to planning and the role of the State.

I. THE ECONOMY, CONTROLS AND MONETARY POLICY

Even before the change of Government, economic controls had ceased to be an area of crucial political controversy, although the Conservatives did retain some difference in emphasis. However, practice even eliminated much of this emphasis, and in 1960, Thorneycroft, a former chancellor, was arguing that physical control of building 'With all its difficulties . . . does have some merit as an instrument to use with others in seeking to check an inflation at an early stage'.[18] On monetary policy, however, the parties did seem more clearly separate. Some Conservatives saw the sole use of monetary means as restoring the former power of the City over the economy, although other writers viewed it as making the private banks an 'integral part of the State mechanism'.[19] The structure of the economy (the degree of State participation, the level of oligopoly and labour organization, and the degree of company financing not directly subject to a market) necessarily limited the effectiveness of monetary policy. Such a policy had to succeed against apparently insuperable odds to attain public approval. It did not succeed, and indeed some argued that the use of monetary policy was irrelevant to any of the few successes claimed for it: 'Orthodox management of the credit base played an insignificant part in the Government's program.'[20] The Government acknowledged this by its increasing use of other, more discriminatory and physical, controls, despite dark warnings from businessmen: 'these controls', Mr Paul Chambers of ICI claimed, 'are inconsistent with a free society with a healthy climate in which capitalism can develop. . . . There are many ways in which the spirit of enterprise can be killed; one is the continuation of socialist controls by a Conservative Government.'[21]

In any case, the Government never relied solely on monetary policy, but supplemented it, to a greater or lesser degree, with exhortations to employers and trade unions, and non-monetary controls. The impact of monetary policy was also not where it might have counted – on Government expenditure and on the largest companies – but rather on small firms dependent on outside credit, to the political loss of the Conservative party. However, Conservative policy, even in its anti-Liberal phases, did not return financial conditions to what they had been prior to 1947, or even 1939. The cheap money policy was not restored (it would have been irrelevant to the problems after 1951), and investment was not directly controlled, although influencing it was the main aim of Government action. To replace the controls relinquished after 1947, and in the absence of an autonomous Liberal economy, reliance perforce had to be upon 'co-operation' between State and industry, a national form of 'self-government in industry'.

Initially, in 1951, the new Government did utilize the physical and financial controls used by its predecessor to overcome the crisis of that year, and in doing so, violated agreed OEEC measures for trade liberalization. 'I do not believe', the chancellor declared, 'that in present circumstances monetary policy by itself will have decisive results, but I am sure that direct influence over the volume of credit can do much to support other measures to combat inflation.'[22] However, by the time of the budget the following year when the bank rate was increased to 3 per cent, *The Banker* estimated that 'Monetary policy is now elevated to be the main spearhead of Britain's disinflationary programme'.[23] However, the Government displayed initial reluctance to proceed towards decontrol of the economy. But once the process had begun, it gathered speed and seemed crowned with success, to the enhancement of general Liberal views. The annual statements of the six largest banks testified to their belief that 'monetary policy has been outstandingly successful in carrying virtually the whole burden of the fight against inflation in the past year'.[24] The chancellor was jubilant when, in 1953, he presented the most highly praised budget since the war: 'We step out', he said, 'from the confines of restriction to the almost forgotten but beckoning prospects of freer endeavour and greater reward for effort.'[25] However, although the external current account between the sterling and dollar areas was roughly in balance, the *Economic Survey* warned that falling British exports as the world sellers' market ended, could become a problem.

In 1954, the strains began, even though decontrol continued

(sweet rationing was ended). The chancellor continued to be optimistic, wondering whether Britain had at long last found the secret of full employment without inflation, and assuring the National Joint Advisory Council for Industry that 'In conditions of full employment, there is no need to be afraid of investing too much or of producing too much. . . . We must take the long view and plan for expansion.'[26] The continued stresses of 1955, a year of record world trade, produced the first doubts and qualifications,[27] but the chancellor continued to entrust the control of imports to monetary policy 'which, without cramping or distorting the natural vigour of the economy, maintains the disciplines which are essential to an expanding economy'.[28] He permitted substantial price increases in the products of the nationalized industries; he did also, however, ask the banks directly to limit their credit, and introduced more discriminatory hire purchase restrictions.

But all this was only a prelude to the range of new controls introduced to cope with the strain of 1956. 'There is a season of growth and a season of pruning', the chancellor said,[29] and the pruning included much heavier reliance on selective hire purchase controls, fiscal policy and direct instructions to the banks, a 'price plateau' for nationalized industry (with the State acting as price leader for the whole economy), and a propaganda war to achieve 'restraint' which implicitly rejected the right of the market to determine the right price. The bank rate, centrepiece of monetary policy, became less the main control in a mechanical system, and more a weapon in psychological warfare, a public index of Government estimates and an auxiliary element in persuading businessmen to defer investment decisions.

In 1957, the increasing doubts about monetary policy led to the appointment of the Radcliffe Committee to inquire into monetary instruments, but it was already clear that Government faith no longer rested on that policy. The 7 per cent bank rate of the autumn was only possible given that lack of faith, since so violent an increase would have been felt most dangerous if likely to be as effective as formerly thought. It took place at the same time as the chancellor curtailed public investment directly, and instructed the banks to reduce their advances. The

Report of the Radcliffe Committee[30] was indecisive, but its very indecisiveness strengthened Government fears, despite Powell's firm confidence in independent interest rates.[31] However, the Government was accorded some relief from these concerns by 1959, a year of moderate confidence and a favourable balance of trade with the United States, the first time since the Civil War, said the president of the Board of Trade.[32] Powell thought this provided a firm basis to press forward and overcome the last 'forty years during which the economic forces have, for one reason or another, been dammed and falsified by the intervention of the legislature and of the Government'.[33] However, the Government continued to urge restraint, even if with qualified optimism, and permitted substantial price increases in the public sector.

The return of external strain in 1960 was almost expected. The chancellor faced it squarely: 'our economic system', he said, 'has no inherent tendency to stability when left to itself'.[34] The following year, one of relative stagnation and the third in which the overall balance of payment was in deficit, prompted intensified criticism. *The Economist* looked back to see crises stretching away, 1960, 1957, 1955, 1951 and beyond, and the same thing could be expected in 1963 and 1965.[35] The stage was set for the Government's major innovation, the attempt to control imports and domestic consumption without affecting investment. This brought to fruition the policy of a propaganda campaign to secure 'voluntary' restraint, in the immediate context embodied in the pay pause, the National Economic Development Council and the control of public expenditure. But the idea of an autonomous, self-regulating market economy was now far away. The State had to assume the role of forcefully ensuring balance, whatever the means involved or whatever their discriminatory effects.

2. PLANNING AND GROWTH

Different routes back to the word 'planning' have been noted earlier: the need to induce the trade unions to accept an incomes policy with the promise of steady economic growth, the need for business to integrate its plans more closely with the

State's future policies to avoid miscalculations, the need to co-ordinate the investment plans of large firms and the State, the need to control and plan State expenditure to eliminate great fluctuations – the need, overall, to unite the independent units of the pluralist society so that its diffused efforts, partly dissipated by domestic competition, could be focused on a common national effort in the field of international competition. The index of national effort was seen in the newly fashionable measurement of comparative economic growth. However, it was not the intention of the Government that its own broad priorities for expenditure should be changed. Consumption had to be varied to permit both private firms to continue expansion and the Government to continue to pursue its central policy objectives.

During the entire period of Conservative Government, Britain was 'a planned economy in what would have been regarded twenty years ago as the most important sense of the term'.[36] Highly developed economies, whatever their apparent political colour, were, in an important sense, inevitably 'planned'. The three senses in which the term was used were noted earlier – planning merely as coherent administration; planning for specific purposes within an equilibrium economy; and planning for economic growth.[37] Conservatives always sought planning in the first sense; in the second, they also sought planning although less consistently perhaps (or rather, with more qualifications). However, it was the third meaning, the most radical, which provided one of the motives for the Conservative return to the use of the word towards the end of their period in office. The need for external stability in the economy constantly directed State restriction towards the point where expansion was generated, domestic investment. Compared to the growth rates of Western Germany, Japan, Italy, France and the Soviet Union, the British performance seemed poor, although it was considerably better than most of the economies in the world over the long period, and it was not remarkably poorer than the performance of the American economy, up to the early 1960s. However, the Government's attention was directed towards its immediate rivals and the need to prevent the devaluation of sterling. There is consider-

able doubt about the validity of comparing the economic per-
formances of different countries, but it was argued that Britain
could attain a growth rate comparable to its foreign rivals by
certain organizational adjustments. With astonishing speed,
'planning' suddenly became as fashionable as it had been in
1945. There were still a few sceptics who suggested that the
'plan', the attempt to organize unanimity within society as a
whole, was merely an evasion of the fact that bitter controversy
would be the inevitable result of the changes needed to foster
economic growth. The British, one critic wrote, 'are reluctant
to face up to the fact of conflict. . . . Rather than recognize that
a higher rate of growth represents a serious challenge to deeply
held values and customs (they) prefer the easy way out apparently offered by NEDC.'[38] However, this description rather
concealed the real problem since it omitted to note that different
people stood to gain and to lose by the changes needed, and in
the Government's attempt to stimulate growth while retaining
the loyalty, or at least indifference, of those who stood to lose,
was the appearance of evasion.

The new planning agency, the National Economic Development Council, reflected its diverse parentage. Corporatist
schemes cover both pluralist models which stress social stability
and the decentralized power of autonomous corporations
governed in a national assembly by 'representatives'; and
unitary models, stressing forced autarchic progress at the expense of foreign rivals and the highly centralized power of the
State over society, managed by an expert bureaucracy – the
meritocracy were to monopolize executive power by reason of
their acquired knowledge, and override the untutored wishes of
society. NEDC embodied both approaches, with more public
stress on the first. It was both a representative Industrial Parliament,[39] gathering together some of the most powerful figures in
industry, the unions and the State, and was designed to achieve
'consensus'; and, like the Cabinet itself, it incorporated an
expert staff with the key role of defining the nature of the problem for the Council and proposing alternative antidotes. The
Council reaffirmed aspects of Conservative thinking current
since before the First World War, 'voluntary partnership' and
'self-government in industry'; the expert staff was more closely

COMPETITION AND THE CORPORATE SOCIETY

related to the *étatiste* radical thought of the inter-war period. Out of its attempts to overcome inflation, then, Conservatism returned to planning. Financial interests and the middle classes, united in their hostility to the depreciation of the currency, joined the pursuit of industrial growth urged by industrial managers and forced what seemed, in terminology at least, a *volte face*. The change, unlike the earlier one in 1947, was more than semantics. However, particular Conservatives were not necessarily deeply affected, since historical slowness allowed apparently incompatible ideas to be gently smudged into each other. Enoch Powell, on the other hand, had quite clearly said that there were only two mutually incompatible alternatives: the free market or a planned economy; any attempt to evade choice between them could mean only a partial plan or muddled *ad hoc* decisions.[40] Yet, at the time of the return to planning, Powell was a member of the Government, and so can be presumed to have approved the change in policy.

More generally, men of radical temper rather than clear intellectual persuasion, those who pursued immediate short-term aims without seeking to reconcile those aims with wider and more consistent long-term purposes, tended to adhere to radical ideas, regardless of their incompatibility. Thus, some of the most enthusiastic former supporters of neo-Liberal aspirations became, after 1961, equally enthusiastic about planning, even though closer examination might have revealed contradictory aims: under planning, industry, with public sanction, might reap maximum benefits at minimum cost, with no assurance either of efficiency or social responsibility or that a redistribution of income from society to private businessmen would not take place; or, on the other hand, the actual dictatorship of the State would be disguised by the apparent voluntary adherence of business, and the defence against a totalitarian State would have been lost without it being publicly known that it was threatened. The Liberal had been clear in giving supreme power to the market (and thus, ostensibly, 'society') to regulate itself, sure in the knowledge that such regulation, and it alone, would ensure the maximization of production, efficiency and the most economically beneficial growth. The planning solution gave supreme power to the State which, utilizing the best expert knowledge and the co-ordinated effort of all, would design and direct society in the way it felt to be most desirable. Compromise must vest power somewhere and that point would determine how far the *status quo* was one that could be accepted by the majority as defensible.

The new panacea often concealed more than it clarified. The problems seemed clear, but the explanation of the problems and the formulation of politically equitable responses still remained obscure for both major parties. In the short term, for radical Conservatives the ideal of the West German 'free market economy' gave way once more to French planning, its immediate predecessor. The aims of short-term prediction, of co-ordinating the economy and improving industrial forecasts, were not easy to achieve in an international free market (or even, for that matter, in an organized international market) so that the achievement of a high rate of growth still remained only a statement of intention. However, the word and what it symbolized had returned to respectable political discussion, symbolizing the return of Conservatism to the path of its former evolution, a path broken temporarily by the peculiar circumstances after 1947.

The Conservatives did not altogether cease to use the word 'planning' after 1951, but it was mainly used in its first innocuous sense.[41] The first chancellor did pose what some saw at the time as a national target – that the national standard of living should be doubled in twenty[42] or twenty-five years.[43] But this was rather a happy aspiration than a serious statement of purpose or a promise. Macmillan, formerly one of the most enthusiastic proponents of planning, did not go beyond the generalities of the late 1940s,[44] although he did suggest the need for more statistical information to 'help industry help itself'.[45] Both he and his successor as chancellor stressed the need for expansion and the equal need for periods of 'pruning', and Thorneycroft introduced a two-year plan to control public expenditure.[46] On the other hand, the *Economic Surveys* eschewed all ambition to predict future trends, and rather became, as they had been in the closing years of the Labour Government, historical résumés.

Some backbenchers were less inhibited than their leaders.

Boothby, for example, continued to urge planning and its concomitants. In 1955, discussing investment, he said 'this direction (of investment) is the basis of strategic economic planning. We are all agreed that we must have a strategic plan for the economy as a whole. Investment policy is the core of this.' And in 1956 he suggested that both the United States and West Germany were planned economies, and Britain ought also to be so.[47] At the opposite extreme, Hinchingbrooke attacked what he called, in 1955, 'compulsive planning from our Government at present'.[48] In the middle ground there were diverse suggestions. For example, Craddock proposed a Minister of Industry to supervise 'Great Britain Ltd' in conjunction with the 'Director of Sales of Great Britain Ltd', the president of the Board of Trade.[49] Others saw desirable planning exhibited in the Government's actions before it formally returned to planning,[50] or demanded planning in particular fields.[51] Carr, on the other hand, argued that the Local Employment Act was the limit of possible planning without the direction of labour and industry.[52] Powell ridiculed pretensions that the Government could be, even in principle, able to control the economy except marginally; he denied that 'it is within the power of any Government to set a specific rate of advance and guarantee by their policies that it will be achieved'.

If earlier crises had not compelled the Government to seek more radical solutions to recurrent problems, the strains of 1960 precipitated more sustained complaints of instability and curtailed growth. In November 1960, a Brighton Conference of the FBI, in the presence of the chancellor, demonstrated deep dissatisfaction amongst a group of important businessmen. Large firms must plan five to ten years ahead, it was said, but the Government did not plan and was thus compelled to intervene in the economy suddenly so that company plans were disorganized.[53] The same theme was taken up in the correspondence columns of *The Times* at the turn of the year by industrialists and economists, and in a survey of growth.[54] This prompted the Government to admit that the subject was a problem although 'the idea that the production of a national plan is the same thing as the achievement of our objective of steady expansion is a dangerous fallacy'.[55] However, a minister did consult the FBI, and the chancellor did mention the need to know more about what was being planned in the private sector so that it might be possible to achieve a growth rate of 3 per cent.[56] The term economic growth had by now become a fashionable concern, only intensified by the external strains of the summer of 1961.

In late July 1961, the long-awaited Government proposals to combat current inflation were unfolded. Discussions with industry, the chancellor said, had suggested the need for more co-ordination in the economy, for 'consultation and forecasting' to achieve a 3 per cent growth rate. Such consultation should examine prospects for the economy five or more years ahead, surveying all elements in national expenditure to achieve growth. To this end, the National Economic Development Council was to be created.[57] In general, backbenchers approved the innovation, and, at the end, the prime minister appropriately summed up the auspicious occasion. He once wrote a book, he said, called *The Middle Way*, and observed innocently that 'I was happy to see when reading it the other day that nearly everything I had recommended has since been done'.[58]

Thus, 'sixteen years after the end of the war, and six years at least since it became clear that cost inflation could not be tackled by monetary measures alone',[59] Conservatism returned to planning. In general, opinion was favourable, although the trade unions refused to join the new body as reprisal for its companion, the 'pause'. The party conference made no protest,[60] and appointments to the NEDC staff seemed to suggest more importance was attached to the new agency than some of its predecessors. The chancellor said NEDC was 'a great opportunity for both sides of industry to influence policy at the formative stage',[61] without seeking to reconcile this with the doctrine of the supremacy of Parliament. Since the Commons had no immediate right to examine the working of the new body, nor supervise its deliberations, its constitutional position might have raised objections.

NEDC's role remained unclear, and particularly its contribution to wages: 'If wages become fully planned', one observer reasoned, '– assuming this can effectively be done in a fully-employed democratic society – it would be a logical step to planning the whole economy. This, one can assume, would be anathema both to industry and the Government.'[62] A maximum and a minimum of radicalism was tolerable within the elastic new proposals. Another critic suggested NEDC might become just 'one more instrument for industrial self-government by unathletic compromise',[63] and another as a convenient invention to escape a short-term crisis, a body which, like the Cohen Council, would be forgotten as soon as current strain eased.[64] The failure of the British application to join the Common Market perhaps added intensity to the demand that NEDC provide adequate economic substitutes, and its initial proposals, including a target growth figure of 4 per cent per annum, helped to encourage radical opinion. Yet the planning body seemed from the outside not to have changed the substance of the problem, whatever brave hopes its expert staff expressed in their documents. The stimulatory budget of 1963 was not directly related to its work any more than was the slightly conservative budget of 1964, except in the sense that the NEDC staff provided an additional source of economic estimates, sources which the Government was not particularly lacking. Ministers made obeisance to the Council in their speeches, but the severe strains of late 1964 and 1965 on the external account indicated that the NEDC had perhaps been primarily psychological and had not been particularly successful in this role.

Thus the Conservatives' volte-face was, despite appearances, mainly verbal, an extension of the conception of 'restraint'. Even so, however, it was not primarily the Government which promoted the innovation but rather industry, which forced the Government to offer some policy which would avoid fluctuating investment rates. The change was not surprising, given the nature of the problems, but it was perhaps surprising that the change was so long delayed and, having been made, continued to operate within the context of short-term pragmatic adjustments.

4. THE ROLE OF THE STATE

If the State had become so important within the economy and for the economy, what view did Conservatives hold as to its role? General statements on the State, or its relationship to society, were relatively rare with Conservatives in office. They took that role for granted and did not hazard definitions. Since the Labour Opposition was often more concerned to attack the Government for not using or expanding its powers, the Conservatives were devoted at most to defending a relatively modest approach. Most frequently, attempts at definition degenerated into a series of prohibitions that often had little relationship to actual policy. For example, Butler said Conservatives were always prepared to use the State but did not believe in State trading, State ownership, State monopoly, controls and a planned economy.[65] In practice, the role of the State tended to continue its relative expansion, particularly in 1962–4. All the elements of the economy were being more or less pieced together to form a single instrument of State.

Initially, Conservatives stressed a pluralistic society: wages, nationalized industries, private firms, Government expenditure, local authority expenditure, were all to be autonomous, disciplined into an efficient whole by the overall control of a market. One by one, the State found it necessary to seek to limit that autonomy. Public expenditure and (particularly) investment had to be controlled to combat inflation, and so the nationalized industries' finances had to be centrally scrutinized. In the field of wages, public employment had to be controlled; to do this required extensive intervention in the existing system of collective bargaining. The elements of the public sector had to act as price and wage leaders for the whole economy or compensate for the deficiencies of the private sector. Outside the public sector, wages and business co-ordination provided key targets for attempts at State control. Finally, planning – as an aspiration – sought to encompass all these elements into one State-supervised whole. The State as a minimum regulating agency had become both a participating system and a control system.[66]

However, with few exceptions, Conservatives were not apparently concerned by this vast change, and preserved for public use a doctrine of a State which no longer existed, presenting in their statements both that doctrine and later amendments that were implicitly inconsistent with it. Thus in Liberal terms, the State was the creation of society, and society was always superior to the State; a view that stands contrasted with an earlier Tory conception where the State was the embodiment of society's highest morality, to which all members of society owed complete obedience (Sir Thomas Moore accused the Labour party of holding this view).[67] It was part of the Liberal view that the State was necessarily economically incompetent and uncreative. 'State intervention', Sir William Darling said, 'has all along been quite disastrous at the worst, and at the best, very disappointing'; the State should never be given power to make economic decisions in the first place, and should be eliminated from the economic scene.[68] However, Conservative Governments continually made economic judgements of crucial importance – annually, in the budget, and, to cite only some of the more prominent cases, in railways, aircraft, cotton, steel and shipping. They judged the detail of economic problems, and so, in Liberal terms, deprived society of power to decide for itself. The 'national interest' had grown out of its narrow confines to a point where it touched any and every issue, and where it could not be at all comprehended by the overwhelming majority of the members of society as in any way related to their individual interests, except in the mythology of constitutional theory.

However, it was this Liberal position which provided one of the main sources for Conservative statements, despite its apparent unreality. The most consistent claim for the State was still that it 'set the climate' for industry, a claim fortunately elastic enough to stretch from determining the total ideology of society (and thus, all its activity) to merely sustaining business 'confidence'.[69] Other roles were occasionally suggested, and sometimes, unintentionally if more realistically, slipped into more extreme positions. For example, Selwyn Lloyd argued that 'The art of modern Statecraft is to give these individuals (society) the opportunity, to give them reward for effort and initiative, to create a social atmosphere in which saving seems worthwhile.'[70] This statement contained much more than 'climate setting' since it suggested that the secret of society's economic endeavour lay within the State's prerogative. A similar implication can be seen in another minister's aim of 'harnessing' industry to the State's purposes,[71] an aspiration which tilted the balance of 'partnership' firmly in one direction.

Others stressed the State's role in mitigating economic fluctuations or acting against particular by-products of economic change. Some demanded that the State establish a social context which would prevent sections of society diverging from what the State considered appropriate. Inevitably, the State should give 'leadership', but it was rarely specified what this entailed in practice. There were also those who urged specific proposals. De Ferranti, as mentioned, suggested the State should foster one very large firm in each industry.[72] David Webster, echoing an early Welfare State aspiration, said the Government should provide a ladder for industry to climb and a net into which it could fall,[73] a conception which relieved shareholders of all possible 'risk-taking' and therefore, presumably, any right to participate in the proceeds of industry. Yet others repudiated such views firmly. Pickthorn, for example, felt no man fit to govern another, and felt accordingly that Government should be minimized.[74] Enoch Powell sustained perhaps the most powerful case in this respect in his opposition to State aid in industry: 'consistent vigilance is necessary', he said, 'if we are not to slip from one industry to another, into a position where it is the Government that takes the vital decisions on development and in investment, thereby lifting these decisions entirely out of the plane of a free economy'.[75] During the phase of Conservative enthusiasm for planning, he specifically denied the relationship between Government action and its claimed results; he argued that the 1964 State increase in net borrowing and public share of national output 'represents the utmost limit to which prudence could possibly go'; the sole creative force was not the State but the nation, and only in so far as the nation decided to act could there be any economic advance.[76] For the rest of the party the matter remained one of emphases and images, tacking between the extremes of the Government as 'creatures of circumstance' and as 'architects of the situation'.[77]

Macmillan's attempt to unite theory and practice, like the earlier one by Major Lloyd George, stressed an open-ended pragmatism. Like the Conservative attitude to free trade, he said, 'our view about the position of Government in industry (is that) it is not a principle, it is an expedient'; no role could be defended absolutely since it must change as conditions did.[78] However, the Conservative attitude to free trade may have started as a pragmatic adjustment, but it certainly did become an article of faith;[79] indeed, most of the 'principles of Conservatism', or at least those that had any practical significance at all, evolved in the same way. Doctrines of the role of the State are not disinterested maxims that can be adjusted pragmatically, but are rather political weapons to establish and foster particular views and interests with wide repercussions outside the world of thought. That Conservatism reflected the concerns of an earlier age and the interests paramount then, and in practice reflected later incompatible interests and views, was not evidence of 'pragmatism' so much as, on the purely intellectual level, sheer muddle. But on the political level, the embodiment of a piece of social history within the Conservative party indicated that its leadership was unwilling to admit the nature of its own practice lest that alienate its political supporters who might expect other things. For example, small business had very little to look forward to in the new *étatiste* corporatist world. That theory and practice did not cohere within Conservatism, that knowledge of Conservative theory gave no information as to possible Conservative practice, was itself politically significant in a party drawing support from social groups with incompatible interests. The muddle could conceal the sacrifice of what many Conservatives thought they were dedicated to preserving.

PART IV

Competition and the Corporate
Society

15

Competition and the Corporate Society

The history of capitalism is also the history of the attrition of the capitalists. Even at the height of its success, the system was slowly extinguishing those who had built it. Indeed, even in the middle of the nineteenth century, perceptive observers already detected this paradoxical process at work. But it was in the twentieth century that the most dramatic phases of the transition were seen: the creation of a capitalism without – or, at least, only marginally assisted by – those who would, a century earlier, have been recognised unequivocally as capitalists. The change was not simply a question of the euthanasia of the *rentier*. The *rentier* was not the heroic entrepreneur of legend, and his murder – in so far as it indeed took place even temporarily – affected only one segment of the capitalist class. More important was the inner decay of the class itself in the historic heartlands of world capitalism – the European and American enclaves of 'free enterprise'. That peculiar alliance between the largest business concentrations – only in myth governed by the mass of shareholders – and the State – even less effectively curbed by the mass of voters – stealthily extended its power. At the end, the 'new' ruling class no longer needed to commit itself to the defence of private property as first principle, much less the defence of the mass of small private property owners.

The Social Democrats were right when they identified the overall process as a quasi-socialist one. It was partly the threat of the socialist which prompted the old capitalists to lift at least some of the Left's clothes, to imitate in form if not content part of the Social Democratic aspiration. And it was not entirely accidental that those who had been for much of the nineteenth century the most capitalist of parties, the Liberals, were, in the early years of the new century, the pioneers of collectivist innovation. But the Social Democrats were wrong when they identified the new society which they themselves had worked so hard to bring about as the socialism which had inspired the thousands in their worker armies. For whatever the efforts of the socialists, they were not decisive in the creation of the new order. The new order was not a response to the popular needs or demands of those oppressed in the old. It was created out of the involuntary mutation of business itself, a mutation precipitated by, and also exacerbating – cause and effect – the suicidal rivalries of the old world order, in two catastrophic world wars, a slump of unprecedented severity and the disintegration of empire.[1] That certain structural features of the new order might echo Social Democratic aspiration was almost fortuitous, a mockery of the socialists.

The peculiarities of the British situation made the long-term processes difficult to detect. For the British were more ideological than their European brethren. As was appropriate for a pioneer, the ideology of capitalism – sustained by the brief British monopoly of world trade in manufacturing – left a deeper mark in Britain. For the British middle classes, part of governing the world was an adherence to free trade and a lofty suspicion of economic activity by the State. When other 'middle classes' nudged them aside, the British could afford neither free trade nor a rejection of State intervention. In changing the world, the British had changed themselves. It was painful in the extreme to go back on the claims of Victorian capitalism, much more painful than the same revision was in Europe. Yet, when to foreign rivalry were added the threats of a generalized downturn in the world economy, systematic State intervention and tariffs became vital for the survival of British capitalism.

The changes in ideology were not forced just by changes in the foreign environment. Mediating between the two were important changes in the domestic industrial structure. Firms were compelled by the rise of foreign competitors to change themselves, to concentrate activities, to organize and regulate whole industries. Out of the mass of small businessmen who had made capitalism – the 'middle estate' so beloved of James Mill – emerged the nightmare of those pioneers: oligopoly or monopoly on the one hand and State capitalism on the other. Questions of individual private ownership were now lost in a fog of public and institutional ownership and control.

The walls of the old capitalism did not fall to external assault. The system, the interests of the mass of capitalists, was subverted from within by the largest owners and controllers of capital. Without that subversion, the largest concentrations of business power might also have been destroyed. Important though this was, however, it affected only one geographical part of a world system. Elsewhere, often not even a minority of capitalists survived, and where they did it was clear they were weak and ailing. At first in Russia, then throughout Eastern Europe and a major part of Asia, to force economic development became the task, not of the supposedly abstemious fanatical entrepreneur, but of the supposedly abstemious fanatical party cadre. It had been thought that the process of capital accumulation was impossible without a class of private capitalist accumulators, of Individuals. But now it was clear this was itself a private capitalist myth. State capitalist accumulators, at least in Russia, could do as well and as ruthlessly. Paradoxically, State capitalism became, not the graceful reform of 'mature' capitalism to soften the harsh outlines of an accumulating society, but rather a new and more effective means to create an accumulating society, the starting point for development. Yet this dramatic innovation was not, as the more passionate defenders of both Moscow and Washington claimed, the result of a Communist conspiracy. For even where the imperatives of Soviet foreign policy or the peculiarities of social collapse failed to propel a Communist party to power, native private capitalists remained weak, dependent upon foreign patronage and the local State. The capitalist Prometheus in the backward countries was a weakling, no match for the State or the foreigner. And the triumphs of 'free enterprise' in the developing countries, rare enough, were all based upon the existence of a powerful public sector and foreign pensions. Far from State intervention infringing the dynamism of entrepreneurial capitalism, without it, 'free enterprise' could scarcely exist.

Yet if the capitalists decayed, the system did not. Indeed, after the Second World War, the result of pruning the mass of capitalists seemed to be relatively high rates of economic growth and a spreading ripple of prosperity in the industrialized countries. The new oligarchy – a *troika* of State officials, representatives of the largest institutional owners of capital, and professional managers – in contrast to the old capitalist class in the inter-war years, seemed to be able to meet the immediate demands at least of a majority of the population. The triumphs of the 'new' capitalism seemed to vindicate the claims of the old that the system was capable of rational self reform.

Appearances were misleading. For although the internal reorganization of each economy assisted or restricted the degree to which a country shared in the world boom, it did not make the boom. Indeed, despite the confident assurances that politicians learned to make after the dispiriting pessimism of the inter-war years, the boom was not designed and made by anyone. For each individual economy, the boom was a *deus ex machina*. Its sources were, if not beyond explanation (although few tried seriously to explain it), certainly beyond the control of any particular government. The new system, like the old, was perpetually driven wherever it went by forces not susceptible to regulation, by the rivalry for profit or domination of a giant company or individual government. Crisis came upon each economy like a storm; the weather was not something the best intentioned or wisest economic planner could prevent or direct. Indeed, the more unified and planned each national participant in the world economy, the less planned, the more exaggerated were the effects produced in the international environment. Governments did try to offset the domestic impact of changes abroad, but this imposed even more adverse effects on all the other participants. When the other participants in turn reacted, the results were compounded.

It was not domestic planning, any more than the 'managerial revolution', which held disasters at bay, but the sheer scale of expansion which, at least in the industrialized countries, seemed to sweep all before it. But domestic planning had other important effects. In particular, the purposes which informed planning, encouraging and supporting detailed control by the sub-units of each economy, reshaped the industrial structure in important ways. Planning was a by-product of war and the need to unify entire economies and direct them towards certain pre-eminent ends. In times of peace, planning remained intimately related to the State's response to threats, economic, political or military, from abroad. The system after 1945 was new in so far as a significant proportion of its global economic activity was devoted to a permanent preparation for war, a permanent arms economy.[2] Defence expenditure was not susceptible to long-term economic planning, only to the short-term imperatives of fear and international conflict. Yet the cumulative effects of defence expenditure on civil industry were of a long-term kind. Expansion and contraction of public expenditure on military aircraft might have short-term effects, but any continuing expenditure tended to reshape the entire aircraft industry from its employment pattern to its technology. The effects of defence expenditure, working directly upon the civil economy in those countries which had a relatively large arms budget, redirected and partly determined the largest economies. The instability of arms expenditure affected the planning process, and exaggerated the economically irrational effects of planning. But through it all, the role of the State in defence and planning gave it a decisive leverage within the economy. The more vulnerable each national participant was to threats from abroad, the more the State was required to supersede private business. At the end, the State had emerged as head of a national conglomerate.

Yet even in the process of creating a national whole out of a disparate set of public and private firms, the State itself was being superseded. International firms spread beyond the power of the individual State. And some States assumed the posture of suppliant, of Oliver Twist pleading for more capital from the giant companies outside its borders. In terms of investment, many 'multinational' companies seemed much more powerful than any of the host governments in whose countries they operated. The State was equally being superseded by efforts to establish wider markets, wider regions of economic control.

Capitalism, having used individual States to cut the wings of the mass of small capitalists, now seemed set to abandon even the State and large national capital. The very largest companies were disentangling themselves from association with particular nationalisms. Such a major change has social and political repercussions at least as great as the preceding transformation of the system. Within each national business class, some aspired to supersede the individual economy and establish international independence; others leapt to the defence of their national power, seeking a popular alliance against the 'foreigner'. The rise of the international company and the creation of the European Common Market directly threatened British capitalism and the British State, yet it also offered ways of survival for the largest business concentrations in Britain, ways which could not be rejected with impunity. The concentration of power within the firm now received a further distillation beyond the national economy. Yet the implication of this change was the nullification of much that the old capitalism had stood for. The survival of Britain seemed to depend upon the liquidation of Britain.

2

For a party of capitalism, the major transformations of the system entailed grave dilemmas. The Conservatives tried to conserve. Yet what they tried to conserve was in continuous change. Conservatives could influence some of the changes, but they could rarely determine any of the major ones. It followed that those positions which Conservatives adopted at one time to defend the *status quo* were often rapidly outdated by a new *status quo*. The sacred principles of one era were inevitably the pernicious prejudices of another. What was at one time the last ditch, at another is the first position to be gracefully conceded. The party of land did nothing to prevent the disastrous decline of British agriculture from 1870 to 1914. The party of business admitted a degree of State regulation that, to an earlier generation of businessmen, would have appeared indistinguishable from a socialist nightmare. The party of the nation applied to submerge British political independence in a wider European federation.

Yet the past was never quite relinquished in the face of what was fashionable in the present. In Conservatism today, the shadowy fragments of a commitment to free competition coexist with continuing attempts to regulate and damp down competition; the defence of free enterprise coexists with the acceptance and even the desire to extend State ownership; of self-help with public welfare provisions; of imperialism with decolonization; of individualism with collectivism. Each fragment represents a different element in the party's history and a different segment of support. And each time a Conservative leader speaks, lovingly reciting these battle honours of the past, there are different emphases for different audiences. For the claims of politicians may represent at different times very different things – claims on other powers, on sections of the party, on groups outside the party, aspirations for the future or evocations of the past, or all these things simultaneously. But for a Conservative party with a history to present all its demands together, regardless of time and place, can only make a nonsense, a contradictory jumble from which an outsider can derive no coherent viewpoint, let alone suggestions which allow him to understand or predict future Conservative behaviour.

The appearance of muddle does not mean that Conservatives are muddled in practice, merely that what they do is only obscurely related to what they say they are doing. Nor does this mean that Conservatives are peculiarly insincere or dishonest, as Labour leaders choose most often to suggest. It means rather that, because of the role they play in society, they are unable to give a coherent account of what they do. Most of the argument about the defence of the *status quo* is assumed, not presented, and indeed most Conservatives probably cannot even put into words what the argument might be.[3] It is for this reason that what they say appears so unsatisfactory.

On occasions, under severe attack Conservatives are forced further than they would otherwise prefer to go in justifying their political attitudes. But almost invariably this does not lead to a coherent argument so much as a retreat into some ultimate mystery. Whether in the laws of the heart or the blood, in the exemplary loyalties made obligatory by the nation or by some hero, by family, clan or tribe, the sources which justify Conservatism are said to lie ultimately beyond either argument or rational thought. The sources can be detected only in the symbols, in the rituals, the stylized phrases, in the pageantry which adorns action. At an extreme, discussion and even systematic thought become dangerous enemies, threatening to dissolve the mysteries without which the *status quo* would be naked. If there is intellectual muddle in the mystery, it is of no great account.

But there are other, more mundane reasons for the toleration of muddle. The Conservative party is a coalition, within which some groups are rising, some falling. Muddle, ambiguity, allow the expression in elliptical form of contradictory interests without precipitating open conflict within the party. Muddle favours the leaders of a coalition at the expense of any internal opposition. It is rivals to the party leadership who need clarification. Clarity exposes the contradictory interests and challenges the existing distribution of power. In the late 1950s and the 1960s, it was the role of Enoch Powell to try and clarify, and in this way mount a generalized critique of the party leadership, presenting himself as an alternative. He did so, initially, not in terms of divergent political purposes so much as a general abstract desire for increased rationality (and opposition to 'the mysteries'):

> if government decisions are to be more than a series of unconnected expedients and party policies, more than an anthology of electoral bribes, those decisions have to be taken, and those policies framed, with reference to some general notions of what Government ought and ought not to do . . . there is no advantage in sloppiness over precision nor in bad logic over good.[4]

Yet more often, those who challenged the party leaders reached to the past for criteria with which to judge policy, rather than framing new general conceptions of the *status quo*. And this was so because usually the critics were associates of declining interests; their criticisms were reproaches for neglect or positive hostility. But locating criteria in the past, in some golden age, only tends to exaggerate the philosophic irrelevance of Conservatism, or indeed, its soulmate, British Social Democracy. Where both parties borrowed from the past in this way, Parliamentary jousting gave all the appearance of empty shadow boxing, play acting, far removed from the real issues. Lord Hailsham was not above participating with enthusiasm in such commotions, but in quieter moments he reflected on the barrenness of the parliamentary political heritage:

> Ever since I came back from the Army at the end of 1942, I have been obsessed with the sterility and irrelevance of the conventional argument between conventional socialism and conventional capitalism . . . are we bound to stick to the traditional case of the conventional capitalist – himself a character almost as rare as the great auk . . .?

What Hailsham felt was missing from the debate was some recognition of the massive role of the State in modern Britain, a role which seemed to make irrelevant the old aspirations. His anthem of praise for the State went far beyond what could be comfortably accomplished in the Conservative credo –

> What is new and is valuable is the use of the state as the initiator of new voluntary enterprises, as the developer of scientific invention, as the catalyst which brings change about in industry, in society, in science, in education – in things, in short, which it does not necessarily control . . . no new modern aircraft, though it is best built by private industry, can be developed without state money.[5]

The beginnings of a new rationale were perhaps being created. But it still provided no clear criteria with which simultaneously policy could be judged, the interests of the majority acknowledged, and Powell answered.

However, for most Conservatives it was clear that Conservatism must be valid, coherent and adequate in every way simply because the party was so successful. Like crude Marxists, success in practice demonstrated correct theory. And such views were not entirely incorrect when things were going well. Crisis would be the testing time, when some men are compelled to rethink their purposes afresh, and others are driven to soothe their anxieties with a zealous readherence to what they believe

saved them and their forebears in the past. If success muddles
the reality of Conservative activity, then lack of success would
find the party much more vulnerable than it would otherwise
be, much less able to overcome the lumber of the past.

The general truths enunciated by Conservatives suggest the
degree to which crisis would find them prepared. When Conservatives talked 'philosophy', however, it could only be to each
other, since no one who did not already share their perspective
could possibly be persuaded by the self-indulgent sentimentality
which so often passed among them for the higher political veri-
ties. The Conservative argument was too often reduced to the
form: We are, and therefore we should be; what is, ought to be.
Such a deduction offered no guide to tactics in a crisis. It did
not indicate what was important in what was, and what could
be abandoned; what was the essence of the *status quo*, and what
merely decorative form.

Yet, on the other hand, it was clearly true that if Conservative success did not lie in philosophizing it certainly did lie in
sheer survival; or at least in the survival of the name, of a
certain tradition and institutions, for in terms of people, of
social groups, the Conservatives also changed. To have made
the transition from a party of the landed interest to a party of
businessmen when the collision between land and business
threatened the fabric of British society was a major success for
that small group of people who constituted themselves the
Conservative party. Like a circus acrobat, the party was thrown
from one pair of hands to another. It crossed the abyss. And
indeed, once across, it was able to find even more useful work
for businessmen than it had performed for its previous patrons.
For business was not, as land had been, a relatively coherent
and stable interest. Different industries rose and fell, different
groups of businessmen acquired power and lost it. For land,
history was merely a background pageant, a context within
which eternal interests held sway. But business was 'historical':
its vicissitudes were part and parcel of perpetual change. For
the Conservatives, to stay at the top of this greasy pole required
a flexibility much greater than that demanded of the Country
party, much more opportunism, and, in the breach, less sentimentality about old clients. The problems of survival were

exacerbated because British business was, throughout the period in which it gave its fairly undivided loyalty to the Conservatives, in relative decline in the world. Not for the Conservatives the great dash for freedom which the Liberals led in the middle quarters of the nineteenth century, but rather a steadily declining British proportion of world trade, a steady withdrawal from domination of the world. Yet the party rode the storms, and above all, was able to survive the catastrophes of world wars and slump, to stifle the threat of the working class, which at each stage seemed to Conservatives likely to engulf the society they commanded.

One of the things which saved the party was its facility for disentangling itself from temporary association with any one group within the broad ruling class of Britain. For even the most successful groups declined as the British industrial structure changed. New groups rose (the change in groups did not mean necessarily a change in the leading personnel or families). Any party too closely associated with one group would tend to share in that group's inevitable decline. It was precisely the party's lack of 'principle', lack of a coherent political philosophy, which – in conditions of relative stability – safeguarded its survival. When Disraeli deserted what was left of the squires, when the Ulstermen stood opposed to King and Constitution, when the inter-war diehards went into battle in 1945 to refuse the price of the Second World War, it was certainly not a foregone conclusion that the party was capable of this 'flexibility'. Indeed, it seemed as if at last the Conservatives were withering away, were being snared in their own history. There were rivals eager and willing to offer themselves as leaders of the British establishment. In the nineteenth century, the Liberals did not abandon lightly a significant part of their business support to the Conservatives. And after the Second World War, Labour appealed consistently for support to professional managers, and attacked the mass of small owners of capital and the *rentiers*. It was not entirely foolish at that time to suppose that the Labour leadership might succeed in displacing the Conservatives as the natural governing party of the new Social Democratic society (as Hogg identified it). Labour offered a brand of peculiarly explicit managerial capitalism. But Labour was tripped by its class origins, by the class war which still tended to run through the party, rather than between the parties. Its policies might come much closer to the aspirations of the new oligarchy, but ultimately it could not be trusted to control its Left. The Conservatives, whatever their inter-war record and their association with the old capitalism, were always safer.

Other things being equal, the Conservative party could always be trusted. It might fumble, or cling to policies which aligned it with the interests of an earlier *status quo* rather than seek to accelerate the evolution of the future *status quo*, but at least it was free from those alarming adventures that occasionally afflicted Labour. Such calculations were possible provided Britain faced no crisis so great that its demands exceeded the limits of Conservative 'flexibility'. It was never necessary to create a new party of the *status quo* because the Conservatives could no longer fight the fight. Or rather, of the numerous parties created at particular moments, none was ever needed except as a temporary spur or reminder to the Conservative leadership. And this was so because of the sheer stability of British society, whatever crisis afflicted it, whatever scale of apparent oppression was visited upon its people. The social schisms never became so wide that the Conservatives could not make some attempt to straddle them. The pursuit of 'balance' was never forced to give way entirely to the struggle for 'order'.

Verbal continuities allow the party to change in practice without acknowledging that it is changing. But the cumulative practical changes then come to contradict the party's rhetorical stance. For example, the rhetoric of competition and free enterprise continues to this day, yet it is consistently contradicted by the party's practice in office. The party's rhetoric has never been properly reconciled with the administration of a corporate State, of a public domain which dominates, organizes and, indeed, partly activates a private sector. No easy pragmatic adjustment between these two doctrinal positions was possible, for the obverse of the creation of a new ruling class was the partial destruction of the old. Part of the clientele of the old Conservative party had to be abandoned if the new was to be created. Fortunately for the Conservatives, this brutal simplicity was blurred by the slowness of the transition from one to the other, by the fact that important elements of the old constituted the new, and by the absence of a coherent Conservative view of the changes taking place. Except for brief moments of public illumination – like the discussions surrounding the 1938 attempt to nationalize mining royalties – Liberal-Conservatism imperceptibly smudged into corporatism, and in particular, pluralist corporatism. The terminology of the old order has not disappeared to this day. Small business exists, and in post-war conditions of rapid economic growth, parts of it have flourished. As an element in the economy it is not decisive, but it provides some basis both for the rhetoric and for local Conservative associations.

The fact that so much of the old capitalism survived into the new, however, means that part of the debate never ended. If the new forces had led an open and public assault on the old, a sort of revolution, the new *status quo* could have been established with a clear doctrinal rationale, including a critique of the old order. This was what Hogg called for – in a mild form – in the late 1940s when he talked of a new Tamworth Manifesto. *The Industrial Charter* was intended by some to be just this: the Conservative reconciliation with the Social Democratic society. Hogg did not point out that the Tamworth Manifesto did not prevent the destruction of the Tories. But then those were genuinely revolutionary times. In the less heroic years after the Second World War, *The Industrial Charter* was not the culmination of a revolutionary process, so much as a substitute for it. And immediately after it, the anxieties of the 1940s dissolved in the optimism of the 1950s; the old nagging issues were forgotten in the concerns of economic expansion. In any case, it is absurd to suggest that the new forces could ever have undertaken a revolution, even of the most modest dimensions. Inter-war Britain was far too vulnerable for any section of the ruling class to have risked igniting a popular revolt by airing its grievances too loudly. Any kind of seditious talk would have threatened the whole social order, playing into the hands of those who opposed not just the old capitalism, but capitalism itself.

Yet without such a 'first cause' of the new society – as it were, a new 'Constitution' – Conservatives cannot come to terms with their own past or identify what is new and what needs to be defended in the *status quo*. They escape inconsistency by rewriting their own history in the light of the present, by obliterating the changes of the past and reducing it to a continuum in which Conservatism is unchanging. This again places a premium on muddle and confusion. Short-term administrative demands are substituted for the long-term purposes which should provide the criteria by which immediate policy is appraised. The rhetoric of nineteenth-century Liberalism soothes the anxious.

3

Conservatives would not agree that no coherent philosophy informs the behaviour of the party throughout its history. Indeed, they would argue that it is precisely in its philosophy that the continuity of British Conservatism lies. And that philosophic continuity reflects deeper continuities, in 'human nature' and in the 'British character'. Conservatives argue that the essence of Conservatism lies in the basic unchanging processes of human life as mediated by the national culture and physical nature of Britain.

But this does not help the sceptic. For the definition of what is 'human nature' or 'British character' changes with the context. In sum, the identification of these notions appears quite arbitrary, and their relationship to the history of Conservatism random. Conservatives choose anecdotes from the wealth of contradictory elements in the historical record to illustrate their argument. But they offer no serious demonstration that human nature or British character is more constant than changeable. An industrial society is one where historical change is continuously fostered, so that the people who inhabit such societies also seem continuously to change, to recreate themselves in new forms. And what can be said about the unchanging habits of such people turns out to be trivial.

Toryism did not have the same problem. For although society in practice did change, it was more plausible to argue that in essentials it was unchanging. A majority of men were concerned with tilling the soil, the rhythm of seasons, and had been concerned with this activity for all of recorded time. Even those activities not connected directly with cultivation were nevertheless governed by agriculture. And the minds of virtually all men could scarcely escape for long from the discipline imposed by the land. What is more, Toryism built an historical element into the very concepts with which the world, the universe and human nature were to be analysed. Brute passions, like the brute masses, demanded the moral restraint of the soul, a sort of aristocracy, just as unregenerate Man needed the scourge of an omnipotent God. Christian civilization was secured by the three elements, God, aristocracy and soul, retaining supremacy by the accepted subordination of Man, masses and passions. To reject these interdependent dichotomies was fundamentally destructive: at the same time blasphemous, rebellious against the social order, and immoral. The mere passage of time, history, could not change this system of logic. Human nature was fixed in a certain social and cosmological mould. Time might reveal the immutability of human nature, its fixed essence in thousands of very different circumstances, but it could not change it.

Traces of this conception of human nature linger on in the writings of modern Conservatives,[6] even though the validating conditions for it, a relatively unchanging society, have disappeared. The ideas, or fragments of them, are a comfort to the aging in a world apparently gone mad: all else may change, but at least certain basic characteristics remain the same. But these traces do not constitute a coherent philosophy. They do not assist the understanding of Conservative behaviour. They do not identify any serious continuities in Conservative history. And indeed they are not shared by even a majority of Conservatives. In particular, the young Conservatives are likely to reject these ideas with scorn.

In what does the party's continuity consist? Above all, in the role of the Conservative party within British society. The party exists as a means of unifying the political opinions of different groups within the ruling class, of different elites, and giving them political expression. Indeed, it is through the party that groups can secure entry to the ruling class, can secure identification with its general political interests as well as a means to modify those interests. The political – as opposed to electoral –

success of the party turns upon its ability to continue to recruit rising groups within society and represent them politically, at the same time resisting complete identification with declining groups. For example, in the years between 1945 and 1951, a vital Conservative task was to recruit professional managers in modern industry and jettison the railway stockholders and the mine owners.

To newcomers, the party offers an established institution, with powerful and ramifying influence throughout society. It also offers a rationale of leadership and a code of association. It gives manners to the uncouth and leadership to the anxious. It assists the newcomer in identifying his interests within the framework of the *status quo*. Integrating novices is a difficult and delicate task, for the old entrenched groups resent changes which might reduce their power. On the other hand, unless the newcomers are offered a perspective of gaining something worthwhile, they might well refuse to collaborate. Friction between old and new elites can produce far wider social repercussions and jeopardize the stability of society as a whole.

The fact that industrial society necessarily fosters change, which in its turn continuously reshuffles power within the ruling class, recruiting new elements and ejecting old, makes the role of the Conservative party very much more difficult than anything undertaken by the Tories. The Tories could remain unequivocally identified with the interests of the smaller landowners, the Church of England and the monarchy. The Conservatives necessarily have to be much more vague, identifying at most with a broad ruling class, not with the City, but with a millocracy, with steelmen or chemical managers. Disraeli is quite rightly the most famous Conservative leader because he made the transition from Tory to Conservative, from a narrowly specific Country party to a party whose purpose it was to provide political leadership for a vast heterogeneous industrial ruling class.

The party also provides a rationale for leadership throughout society. It offers a case designed to show the necessity and position of a ruling class as a key element in its own social role. It does not identify the form of leadership, nor who the leaders are or should be; only that leadership is the vital element in sustaining society. The criteria for membership of the ruling class may change – from ownership of land to business activity, from ownership of business assets to industrial management – but the central concern in conserving existing society and protecting the interests of those who command it remains the same.

The rationale of leadership for Conservatives includes a broader assumption about the nature of society. It is assumed, in any given social situation, that there is only one correct answer to a social problem, and that answer is in general possessed by the leadership group. God, the aristocracy and the soul cannot, by definition, be wrong. There is only one Reason, and society should be directed by it, not by the summation of many equally valid opinions. It follows in practice that men are divided into two groups, the active leaders, the 'aristocracy', and the passive led.[7] Each group has defined obligations; if it flouts those obligations, society and civilization are jeopardized. If the leaders refuse to lead, or if the led refuse leadership, there is chaos, out of which there will emerge yet again something of the old order. For the division is a function of human nature, the constitution of men, and therefore cannot be eliminated. The led are as children, who, if they knew their own best interests, would demand firm guidance, knowing they cannot guide themselves yet cannot survive without guidance. Sometimes, foolish members of the middle or upper classes 'endow the masses with virtues and will not see that among the masses there lurk passions that need to be contained'.[8] Upper class leadership makes revolt possible; without 'misleaders', without Satan and his horde of expelled angels, even the possibility of revolt is denied the passive. In its modern guise, 'outside agitators' are required to disorient the basic loyalties of the honest, simple masses. Yet revolt is illusory, for ultimately the basic nature of Man will reassert itself – and Man 'will be the same fretful, anarchic creature as before, still needing therefore rules to obey'.[9]

The only means to avoid the chaos which results from a breakdown in the natural social order is for each group to perform its duties loyally. The active must monopolize all important initiative within society; and in each social sub-unit leaders must be permitted to determine what shall happen;

from the ruling class within society, to the manager or business-man in his factory, to the priest in his parish and the father in his family, each must be allowed to fulfil his obligation to guide those dependent upon him. Without this, the leaders cannot preserve the essential justice and harmony of existing society, embodied in their own power and position.

This 'bi-partite' view of society is assumed by Conservatives in considering each aspect of society. Earlier, this account noted the attitude in Conservative discussions of industrial relations. But it is equally important in other areas. For example, consider this comment by a Conservative MP on the distribution of incomes: 'The whole principle of payment for top offices is that quality matters there, and the whole principle of payment on the works floor is that time matters there.'[10]

The division of men into active and passive is necessary, it is said, because the passive require it, because they demand leadership. But the stable establishment of the division is also the precondition for the active being active. Indeed, Aubrey Jones argues, 'the main purpose of the class system is not so much to grade people according to ability as to secure that the function of leadership shall be recognised and respected, to provide a training school in which the habits and duties of leadership are inculcated, to create a tradition in which certain rare qualities are sedulously sought after.'[11] The unashamed circularity of the argument only demonstrates that its validity is less important than the firm assertion of the conclusion.

Yet again this line of thought is shared only by some Conservatives. It has origins in Toryism, not in Liberalism, and its emphasis upon the need for stability in society rather than expansion and change contrasts it with more Liberal Conservatism. For the Liberals, the justification of contemporary society lies rather in the fact that it permits free competition between old and new, it permits social mobility, the conflict between ambitious individuals, all of which, it is argued, benefit society as a whole. An overt class system sacrifices the rights of the majority to the stability of society and the interests of the already privileged. Such a society is more vulnerable to criticism than one which permits the talented to rise to positions of power and wealth. In the second case, problems which arise can

be attributed to the mistakes of individuals, not to the fundamental structure of society.

Within Conservatism, the two positions coexist: the nervous
and the bold remain unreconciled. In particular, Conservatives
are ambiguous about how far social conflict is to be welcomed
as the expression of a dynamic expanding society, how far it is
to be suppressed as a fundamental threat to the existing social
order. Relatively few Conservatives openly embraced social
conflict in the period considered here, since the dominant
fashion in politics was for 'consensus', rather than the struggle
of the good and true against the bad and false. John Rodgers
went as far as most did in praising conflict: 'Conflict is the
normal healthy condition of living, and providing it is kept in
bounds, conflict can be used to keep a business healthy, vital
and progressive, that is provided the conflict is kept within
bounds and directed towards constructive ends.'[12] The reiterated qualification betrays a certain nervousness which robs this
statement of its full force, even though it goes much further than
most Conservatives were and are prepared to go. For the
majority, it was safer to condemn all conflict as dangerous to
social stability rather than tolerate it in any form.

Even for Rodgers, however, leadership was vital in determining whether conflict was destructive or constructive,
whether it affected the margins or the structure of society. For
Conservatism, conflict was a matter subordinate to that of
leadership; if the second was securely established, elements of
the first were tolerable. Leadership, for some Conservatives at
least, is linked directly to the mystery at the core of existing
society, the mystery of human nature, of blood and biology.
Disraeli's fascination with ethnic distinctions, with the racial
characteristics of leaders, is a direct product of this attitude. In
part, the magical powers of leaders, like the right to rule of
noblemen and monarchs in the *ancien régime*, is transmitted
through the blood. Strong leadership shapes the minds of the
led, creating inspiration, infecting all with the high social purposes of the leaders. In this way, the active need not be bound
by some abstract democracy emanating from the idle whims of
the passive; it can inspire the passive to sacrifice, shape their
preferences so that their wishes accord with what is required by

the leaders. 'Experience has proved', one contemporary Conservative boldly asserts, 'that government can allay discontent not by altering their policy in accordance with the wishes of their subjects, but by altering the wishes.'[13] Democracy is not, in the revised version, government in accordance with, or under the control of, the majority; rather is it government which consults the majority.

The elements of continuity in Conservatism, then, all support and affirm the necessity and prerogatives of a leadership class. The rest of society – indeed, the rest of the world – is redefined in accordance with the picture presented of the leadership. As a result, the 'masses' are – when not led by their legitimate rulers – anarchic; indeed, even when lawfully governed they are scarcely upheld in a civilized condition by the forces of order. Civilization is safeguarded only by the existing leadership class; its view of the world is Reason. Of course, particular members of the leadership class may make mistakes; but the class in aggregate defines what is or is not a mistake, and cannot therefore be wrong at any given moment of time. Once the question of leadership is properly settled, then there is room for divisions of opinion about how far independent activity is to be allowed to the passive, how far social conflict is to be tolerated.

4

The recurring tension between the demands of order and of progress in an industrial society were reflected in the different prescriptions for action examined in this account. The labels – *étatiste* and pluralist corporatism – have been applied to ideas, not to people, and this inevitably involves a distortion of reality. For while a few Conservatives were consistently *étatiste* or pluralist, the majority were not. They chose from one school of thought or another, without much consistency and mainly in response to changes of fashion in public opinion. To explain the changes in fashion takes us immediately into questions both of the structure of British society and its place in the world.

The change in the climate of thought within which Conservatives operated was far more important in understanding

Conservative changes than anything intrinsic to 'Conservatism'. The background changes promoted shifts in Conservative opinion which produced apparent self-contradiction. The neo-Liberals of the late 1940s and 1950s – shallow and limited though their Liberalism was – drew supporters from the *étatistes* of the immediate post-war years. Monnet planning was exchanged for Erhardt's market, apparently without indigestion. And at the other end of this period, some of the most enthusiastic advocates of a return to planning were just those who had most passionately demanded a short time before that the State withdraw from the economy. France returned to favour, Germany faded into its private and peculiar 'miracle'.

The tags of 'Right' and 'Left' were mystifying; for both *étatistes* and neo-Liberals considered themselves radicals, of the Left, even though they believed contradictory things. And, despite the terminology the neo-Liberals shared with the very unradical pluralist corporatists, the neo-Liberals were radical. In the cause of competition they attacked the inherited business conventions of the pluralists, as well as that favourite object of pluralist indignation, the defensive practices of labour. But in the curious circumstances of post-war Britain, the changes between radical and conservative were mystifying for many. In 1945, the defence of competition was Right-wing, and of State welfare schemes, Left-wing; in 1955, the Young Turks of the Conservative party regarded the pursuit of competition and a critique of State welfare schemes as Left-wing.[14]

What the signposts, Left and Right, omitted to indicate was that the geography also changed. From 1931 to 1948, slump, economic stagnation and the demands of war were such that radical aspiration was consistently *étatiste*. By 1948, indeed, it seemed that the *étatistes* had already created the new society, and all that was left to Conservatives was to make their peace with it. The Macmillan–Butler Social Democratic programme had been achieved by the Coalition and Labour Governments. Yet from 1948, the long economic boom of the world economy swept away these complacent assumptions. The aims of the diehards once more seemed to become strangely progressive, and the Social Democrats 'diehard'. Yet up to 1964 the Conservatives were, despite their adventurous rhetoric, very cautious.

They did not dismantle the order they had inherited. Indeed, probably the most radical breaks with Social Democracy came under the Labour Government itself after 1948. For the rest, the erosion of the Welfare State, the successive innovations in the public sector, these were tentative, experimental, and slow, not sudden, assaults.

The pace of change might have been even slower still if the external threat to the balance of payments had not added urgency to the situation from the mid-1950s. The centrepiece of the Social Democratic society, sustained by the Conservatives, was the alliance between the State and the trade unions. Yet the strain on the external balance was caused, according to the conventional wisdom, by labour's 'monopoly', by the behaviour of the trade unions. The contradiction was not solved by Conservatives up to 1964. Rather, labour, instead of being one of several concerns, became the core of Conservative anxieties, if not obsessions. Yet there was still apparently room to manœuvre, room to use credit policy to control the economy as well as to repeat wearisomely both adjurations and institutional innovations to persuade the trade unions to exercise 'self-restraint'. The alliance between State and unions remained the linchpin of the *status quo*, and it was the central guiding need to sustain that alliance which determined how far the Conservative Government made changes in all fields of policy. It was for this reason that there were no dramatic assaults on union power, on wage settlements, on the Welfare State or on the public sector, despite constant pressure and criticism from the neo-Liberals. Even the denationalization of road transport and steel were essentially symbolic exercises, and equivocal in practice.

The sheer inertia of the Social Democratic society was amazing. Long after the forces which had created Social Democracy had disappeared, its ethos continued. The Second World War created the necessary precondition for it in class collaboration, and this – along with the innovations of Labour – bequeathed an atmosphere to the Conservatives which persisted right into the 1960s. There were moments when it was threatened, when Conservative ministers lost their tempers, or Mr Macmillan decided to give a public drubbing to the London busmen. At such moments Conservative leaders seemed sorely tempted to declare the end of the long truce, the reopening of class warfare. But the cloying priorities of consensus politics and a temporary righting of the balance of payments drew them back from the edge.

Yet each crisis increased the sense of frustration of activist Conservatives. While the Social Democrat Conservative leaders fiddled, Rome burned. Or more prosaically, the British economic position continued to deteriorate. The room for manœuvre was shrinking. Britain was sinking down the lists of economies by size of income; its share of world exports inexorably continued to fall. Without this growing level of anxiety, entry into the Common Market would not have been invested with such apocalyptic hopes; becoming part of Europe seemed to be arranging a *deus ex machina* to spirit away Britain's economic problems without a direct head-on collision of classes.

Yet the Conservatives could not break out of their Social Democratic inheritance. Ironically, it needed the founders of Social Democracy, the Labour party, to declare the end of the Social Democratic society. The Labour Government tried to carry to its logical extreme the alliance between the State and the unions, but using the unions to control labour on behalf of the Government. Of course, elements of this had always been a vital part of Social Democracy, but the unions had made a bargain: in return for their loyalty, there were specific benefits for their members. Reformism worked within certain limits. But now the unions were expected to sacrifice more than before with little or nothing in return: a wages freeze, an incomes policy, and finally, proposals for a labour law which would permanently inhibit organized labour's power to challenge the Government. Labour demanded all of this and more, without any *quid pro quo*. There was no bargain. Indeed, when the unions organized opposition, the Labour leadership displayed bored contempt. In Social Democracy, in the corporatist society, the participants had to accept with respect the claims of established interests, capital or labour. To treat Estates of the Realm with contempt was to destroy the whole basis of corporate collaboration. If the TUC was a 'paper tiger', there could be no effective alliance. The mists of mythology rolled back to reveal the embattled classes; 'partnership' dissolved once more into class warfare.

Under Labour, the alliance between State and unions snapped. And by that rupture, the long thraldom of Conservatives to Social Democracy was ended. If the TUC was powerless, there was no longer any point in Conservative self-restraint. If the unions could not deliver worker loyalty, they were no longer worth cultivating, soothing, bribing. A whole strategy for conserving the *status quo* was no longer valid. If *The Industrial Charter* heralded the Conservative acceptance of Social Democracy, the Industrial Relations Act of 1971 proclaimed its rejection of it, its return to open class warfare in order to secure the survival of British business. And perhaps the most obvious and dramatic symptom of this was the Conservative Government's toleration of unprecedented levels of unemployment. The promises embodied in the 1944 White Paper on Employment policy – part of labour's reward for loyalty during the war, and tangible evidence of the justice of the *status quo* – were being nullified. The Conservatives no longer accepted that raising unemployment could not be used as an instrument of economic policy, a means to scourge labour, to punish the unions for disobedience.

The breakdown in Social Democracy does not, however, mean that the Conservatives are any clearer about where they are going. Through the 1960s, the centre of British politics moved imperceptibly to the Right, but few knew why, and few Conservatives knew whether they approved or disapproved of the drift. And the 'Right' was not a coherent political position, Liberal or otherwise. Certainly, as in Liberalism, there was much talk of freedom, but this was largely about freedom for the middle class to receive and spend its income as it thought best, regardless of the rest. And even this freedom was subordinate to spasms of fear, of defensiveness, of anxiety; it was not a new clarification of positive perspectives. Shipping arms to South Africa, gratuitous nastiness to foreigners or Commonwealth immigrants, inventing bogies – drugs, sexual licence, the crime rate – to frighten the comfortable citizens of the Home Counties, these are the marks of the new Conservatism of the 1970s. The anxiety pervading the British ruling class infects Conservatives with the same irrational terrors of a brown face or long hair. The irrationalities suggest that at least for some, the time for talk is past; the British establishment is girding its loins for war.

In the past, simple nationalism has provided a decorous setting for these kinds of anxieties. But a nationalist platform is very much more difficult today, simply because British capitalism is divided. The Trojan Horse of international business has secure and entrenched positions within the British economy, and important sections of British business want to become international. Simple economic autarchy, a return to protection, is no longer practicable without serious damage to the *status quo*. Only British entry into the Common Market could supersede this dilemma. But the losses for some sections of British business in this case could be severe. The debate between the 'Europeans' and 'British national' capital is still unresolved.

So far as the Conservatives are concerned, in the 1970s they are again seeking to straddle the increasing gap between an old declining segment of business and a new rising one. But this time, the rising sector is part of a world beyond Britain's boundaries. And the declining sector constitutes 'Britain', part of a heritage Conservatives are supposed to conserve. The leap from a party of small and large national business to one of international companies would be one of the most agile transformations of all for the Conservatives, for it would involve the dissolution of the national British State on which the Conservatives have been for so long dependent. Yet for many Conservatives there seems to be no viable alternative: either internationalization or suicide. It remains to be seen whether or not the Conservatives prove 'flexible' enough to preside over the one or the other, or both together.

Appendix

The Conservative Tradition from Burke to Disraeli

Conservatives claim a tradition which developed long before industrial society. Some trace that tradition back to Bolingbroke and earlier, but most Conservative writers take the work of Burke as being a convenient point from which to identify the main lines of Conservative thought. It is accordingly useful to make some brief reference to the work of Burke in order to test the hypothesis that his standpoint embodies some durable Conservative perspective.

The argument here, and in the rest of this work, suggests that Burke did indeed embody certain attitudes which are common to the Conservative tradition. They are not the elements normally identified by Conservative historians. His attitude to the State, his conception of an 'organic society', his assumption that society is basically static, agrarian and rural, all make his views very remote from urban industrial society. The nineteenth century eliminated most of what was basic to Toryism. Conservatism assumed a competitive society, individuals rather than organic groups, a moderately progressive economy rather than a static one, and it actively promoted a nationalism and imperialism quite removed from Burke's perspective. To have attempted to remain loyal to the views of the older Burke would have led the Tories into counter-revolution, into a radical rejection of Victorian Britain.

Where the tradition does survive is in two important and related respects. Burke and many later Tories were concerned with defining what was 'the aristocracy'; what were the characteristics, the rights and obligations of a leadership class, the 'active' element in society. The nature of society and of the non-aristocracy followed from this definition. Burke also assumed, like most subsequent Conservatives, that although leaders might easily make mistakes or, on occasions, be deliberately wicked, nevertheless the leadership class did and ought to have a monopoly of legitimate power; this class alone could make the right decisions. And if they were permitted to make the right decisions, the rest of society would, unless diverted by a malicious minority, instinctively recognize the wisdom of their choice. Burke assumed a basic harmony within society, which lay beneath the surface appearance of disagreement. Establishing the position of the 'aristocracy' beyond challenge would permit that harmony to be revealed. The substantive inquiry – into the 'aristocracy' – depended upon the methodological assumption that there was only one legitimately valid answer to any social problem, and that answer was, in principle, the one provided by the leadership class.

The two elements of continuity were often obscured. The 'aristocracy' disappeared into individuals, in the maintenance of authority, even into 'the role of managers'. Yet the concern, and what it assumed, proved viable over a very long period of time through successive transformations of British society. When in doubt, Conservatives looked again at the nature of leadership to see where they had gone wrong. Of course, at this level of generality there were no unequivocal answers. In the inter-war period, some wanted to strengthen the monarchy, some the State, some businessmen. But all prescriptions tended to circle the basic concern: the survival of a ruling class.

I. EDMUND BURKE

Burke's work is divided into contradictory elements. The beginning of mercantile economics – Burke accepted the maximization of economic satisfactions and elements of the market economy – is not properly integrated into his conception of an organic society. The co-existence of these two elements was not difficult since Burke tended to hold the full version of each at different times. As a New Whig, the early Burke favoured the power of Parliament and a 'balanced constitution', in opposition to the Tories who favoured a powerful personal monarchy and an organic and hierarchic society. He justified established institutions on almost quasi-utilitarian grounds, namely that time and experience had justified them (a more conservative writer would have refused to be drawn on what 'justified' the *status quo*). He satirized the justification of the aristocracy's claims and sympathized with the lot of the poor;[1] the later Burke firmly rejected any infringement of aristocratic prerogative.[2] Burke's work embodies the contradictions of two societies, uneasily co-existing. For Conservatives, it is the later Burke who is held in greater esteem.

For Burke, society was an integrated whole which included the State. As in Plato's work, the leading class constituted society's intellect, governing the led as the mind supposedly controlled the body.[3] In a society where the main occupation was agriculture, the leading class must necessarily itself be the leading class in agriculture, in land. With scorn, Burke pointed to the landless character of the French revolutionaries; they were not even part of the French nation.[4] Those who embodied society's Reason ought obviously to control the government, particularly since the primary purpose of government was to protect the nation, the body of which was landed property.

It followed that the 'People' should obey. The early Burke, an iconoclast, argued that the People were the masters of society, wise in their prejudices and not easily misled.[5] The later Burke, writing in the fiery light cast by the French revolution, was afraid that any concession to the 'mob' would release the innate evil of Man and endanger Reason.[6] He chose to call the 'People' only that group which was guided by Reason (that is, by the aristocracy), the two together forming a corporate unity in which there was 'habitual social discipline, in which the wiser, more expert, and the more opulent conduct . . . the less provided with the goods of fortune'.[7] Without the supervision of Reason, there was only a 'mob', given over to the unReason of pre-civilization barbarism, or a 'faction', devoted to a selfish partial interest rather than national interest. While Reason reigned, the poor were bound by their duties not to be interfered with but adjured to 'Patience, labour, sobriety, frugality, and religion'.[8]

In such a society, the individual as an important – less still, the basic – social unit did not exist. The basic units of society were corporate and timeless, not tied to the mortality of particular persons. The corporate whole had varying temporary human manifestations, but these were insignificant beside the historical continuity of the whole. It followed that the merit or value of existing institutions, of society and of the aristocracy, did not depend at all upon what particular people at any given moment of time represented them. Any government entrusted to individuals as individuals, to mere statistical units, would act without reference to the real purpose of government. For one wise man could more easily determine the national interest than a mere aggregation of indiscriminately selected men. Clear straight Reason was required, not the random results of a mathematical majority.

It followed that, where the aristocracy – natural or actual – commanded the government and, in guiding the non-aristocracy, thus fulfilled the validating condition for the constitution of 'Society', there could be no real distinction between the State and society. Such a distinction could only arise if the government could be legitimately commanded by a group hostile to the interests of the aristocracy, to Reason. By definition, this could not happen. There was no society if Reason was rejected; and if the government did become controlled by a group inimical to Reason, it was rule by a faction, not the 'State'.

But if the State could not properly be distinguished from society, nevertheless it did perform special functions: 'He who gave us our nature to be perfected by our virtue willed also the necessary means of its perfection: He willed therefore the State.'[9] It was the primary instrument to uphold the moral order. But in a healthy society, the moral order in essentials already existed. So the function of the State was essentially a disciplinary one to prevent evil. It could do little positive good, and certainly not 'provide for us in our necessities'.[10] In more specific terms, 'the State ought to confine itself to what regards the State, or the creatures of the State, namely, the exterior establishment of its religion; its magistracy; its revenue; its military force by sea and land: the corps that owe their existence to its fiat . . . to the public peace, to the public safety, to the public order, to the public prosperity.' But, 'Nothing, certainly, can be laid down on the subject that will not admit of exceptions, many permanent, some occasional.'[11]

Since Reason was embodied in the aristocracy, the protection of the aristocracy – and its material basis, landed property – was the primary function of the State.[12] The State indeed had been created by the propertied to defend property. Man's sense of duty, his 'natural' prejudice, supported this role for the State. Thus, defence of the *status quo* was supported by the consent of property and the 'presumed consent' of all others, for 'the presumed consent of every rational creature is in unison with the predisposed order of things'.[13] If that consent was withheld, the creature was no longer 'rational'.

Given the continued maintenance of this framework, Burke's views were pragmatic. He attacked attempts to change the form of society, while being critical of maladministration within that form. He was suspicious of increases in State power, upholding the counterweight power of great property. Any monopoly of power, he said, was repugnant to him, although on another occasion he praised the monopoly of capital.[14]

He assumed harmony within society, a presumed – in modern terms – 'consensus'. For example, he asserts of the relations between farmer and labourer that 'it is absolutely impossible that their free contracts can be onerous to either party'.[15] A Commons dominated by large property owners could not conflict with a society dominated by the same people. Reason could not conflict with the best interests of the non-aristocracy, for property was Reason. If a man recognized his best interests, it followed – as in Hegel – that what he willed individually accorded with the external repressive force of the State. Implicitly, Burke's argument is designed to prevent any possibility of seeing the landowners as themselves a separate interest. Their prerogatives are alone circumscribed by their duties to God.

However, society is afflicted by numerous dangers, it is delicate and its form cannot be altered except with great peril. This did not mean that the detail could not be amended – indeed, it must be amended to preserve the form – but amendments must be narrowly specified to a 'grievance'.[16] Narrow grievances could and should be answered provided they did not jeopardize the form of society. And change in the form was not feasible, since one such change would set up a whole wave of readjustments, the ultimate results of which could not be predicted. The very idea of changes in the form must be prevented, since ideas – rather than hardship – prompt men to irrational action.[17]

The framework of the writings of the later Burke assumed that political problems in so far as they concern the structure of society could have only one answer, that there was only one Reason to which all men, in principle, had access. There was no valid conflict between equally rational and experienced beings, only the conflict between those with the right answer and one of two varieties of error: the irrational or the selfish. A revolt could not therefore be the expression of interests in conflict with the governors, but was rather the reappearance of the irrationality which civilization normally curbed, of Hobbesian man, perhaps, stimulated by evil or selfish interests, 'agitators'. As Satan had once been a member of the Heavenly Host, so also the 'agitators' were often a 'misaristocracy'. The government should not attempt to understand what was in principle incomprehensible, but rather should use immediate force to restore what it knew to be true moral discipline.

What Reason was, was primarily a social matter. Once the 'reasonable' was clear, evil was identified. Once the aristocracy had decided what was reasonable, no one could then pursue other courses. For 'Men have no right to what is not reasonable, and to what is not for their benefit.'[18] The class of persons who owned land could define the reasonable as a class, not as individuals. For 'We are afraid to put men to live and trade each on his own private stock of reason; because we suspect that the stock in each man is small, and that the individuals would do better to avail themselves of the general bank and capital of nations and of ages.'[19]

Burke's defence of the landed interest primarily justified the existing distribution of power, rather than power in general. And he did this partly by rejecting the idea that force or mere individual choice maintained existing society. Conflict could not be valid or normal or social. To allow it to be social – a necessary part of the existing structure of society – would be to admit that there could co-exist more than one valid answer to a social problem, that Reason was not unequivocal and different interests could be equally 'reasonable'. That admission would have destroyed the unity of Burke's scheme by accepting divisions within society.

Burke was fortunate that the challenge to the British *status quo* was as mild as it was. In Europe, defence of a similar kind of position demanded that Reason retreat into a meta-world of validity, the noumenal essence beyond mere appearance. Here it was protected from the 'rationalist' Reason of the radicals. For the Romantics, Reason and what they felt to be 'intuitive certainty' were in conflict. For Burke they were one.

Society's existence, not its origin, is the justification for its form: what is, is. And its form is defined by custom and social position, embodied in 'prejudice'. One's relationship to unique objects, to the soil, establishes one's rights, not force, choice or 'human nature'. Friction arises from a failure to perform duties naturally incumbent upon one's social position, not from the structure of society or its institutions. Errors lie in the nature of man, in his fallibility, in his 'original sin', not in the world around him.

2. ROMANTICS AND CONSERVATIVES

The full impact of the social and economic transformation already in train during Burke's life only emerged later. Burke was able to assume that existing society was, in essentials, the best possible; the Tories who came after him were never in so fortunate a position. The cry of the dispossessed and the squalor of industrialism made any Burkeian approach hypocrisy for many Tories.

The aristocracy which had been the pivot around which Burke constructed Christian civilization was also in mutation. A new industrial middle class challenged the power of land, and socially, performed a role in society which seemed to supersede that of the landed interest. It seemed as if industrialism had impoverished large sections of the labouring population, had destroyed the stability of rural society and created – or recreated

– a hydra-headed barbarism excluded by the old order. The picture of the past was doubtful, but it served a useful function in contrasting with the present.

The confrontation of two kinds of power in the political field symbolized the changes in society. Between 1780 and 1832, the millocracy grew in strength to the point where, with much popular support, it could begin to attack the political order. But the consolidation of middle-class political power took much longer. Indeed, consolidation was only part of a process which included merging with the old order, so that businessmen acquired the titles and style of life of aristocrats, and aristocrats acquired – assisted by the 1862 Company Act[20] – a more lucrative financial basis by becoming *rentiers*. The peculiarities of the settlement left members of the aristocracy with a disproportionately important role in politics, provided they met the needs of their new supporters.

The initial impact of these changes scattered the forces of Toryism, separating Parliamentary and non-Parliamentary supporters, and further dividing each into sects. Outside Parliament, the Romantic movement itself was part of the Tory radical attempt to comprehend the industrial revolution, to identify and salvage what were presumed to be the merits of the past order of society. In opposition to what seemed to be the heartless calculations of business, the reduction of all to a calculus of profit and loss, the poets and the Christians rejected the 'rational' for the intuitive, the present for the past, the urban for the rural, and – in some cases – the Anglican for the Catholic (a change of some violence for the Tory tradition). In politics, the spectrum was very wide, ranging from wistful medievalists, from mystics and reactionaries, to popular radicals like Oastler, Sadler, Bull and Stephens who provided one of the tributaries for the later development of Chartism, to – later – devout and paternalistic humanitarians like Shaftesbury. None of these currents of opinion is representative of Parliamentary Toryism, although similar tendencies were occasionally apparent. Conserving the value of British institutions seemed to have become counter-revolutionary, to have become a radical opposition to the *status quo*.

If the pivot of the old society had been the aristocracy, the decay of the landed interest provided the key to understanding the decay of society. The decay of society was most vividly apparent in what occupied the central position in the attention of many non-Parliamentary Tories – from Cobbett, through Southey and Carlyle to Disraeli – the 'condition of the people'. Some directly attacked the middle class for causing the decay, for refusing to accept the obligations incumbent on its possession of wealth. Some urged that the middle class be absorbed into the traditional aristocracy so that it could acquire both rights and social duties commensurate with its actual power. Some argued the case for a new aristocracy, or a force capable of instilling, with a new moral sense, the existing aristocracy, the *de jure* landed interest and the *de facto* millocracy. Disraeli's 'Natural aristocracy' combined several of these elements. Coleridge's 'National Clerisy'[21] was designed to recreate the social discipline of society through a reconstruction of the medieval Church. Carlyle's heroes[22] outlined new qualifications for the members of a leadership class, new criteria to justify power independently of land. Where the aristocracy was not automatically accepted, the precondition for social stability lay – for both Carlyle and Disraeli – in the popular approval of outstanding personal characteristics rather than a social role. What 'natural' or 'organic' social subordination was supposed to produce, genius impressing itself on the inferior had to create.

But there was too little time and the problems were too pressing to wait for a new aristocracy to create itself. As the ideal aristocracy was slow in appearing, a revival of the paternalistic duties of the squire by default devolved upon the State. Tory demands for State intervention and coercion grew. For the errors now were no longer inherent in Man, in human nature, but in the structure – Burke's 'form' – of society.

All this was fairly remote from Parliamentary Tories. There, Peel – himself a child of the new industrial aristocracy – set out to court the middle class by accepting the 1832 constitutional settlement and making concessions on free trade. He tried to isolate the Wellingtonian image of diehard resistance to all change, emphasizing that the Tories could be as 'responsible' as the Liberals and Whigs, and more competent in administration of the new society. He introduced the name 'Conservative' to disentangle the Tories from their specific identification with land, and group all those with an interest in the maintenance of the *status quo*, regardless of the source of their income. The attempt to marry land and industry, or shift the basis of the party from one to the other, was embodied in the Tamworth Manifesto.[23]

The influence of Liberal thought on Peel grew to the point where he could envisage a frontal attack on the fiscal privileges of the landed interest, the Corn Laws, in order to end protection and enshrine free trade. For the squires, the Peelite strategy must have seemed less like arranging the marriage of land and industry, and more like staging the suicide of land. The attempt was premature, and broke the Tory party. But it gave an opportunity to a most unlikely Tory, Disraeli, to wage an impassioned defence of the landed interest against the Quisling Peelites. When Disraeli inherited power in the party, he was even more Peelite than Peel.

The opposition to the repeal of the Corn Laws was not the first blow in the revival of the landed interest. It was a rearguard action which ended in defeat for land and the exclusion of the Tory party from office for much of the following thirty years. When it returned, it was as a Peelite and 'middle-class' Conservative party rather than the landed Tories.

3. BENJAMIN DISRAELI

Disraeli is by far the most important Conservative in the 'Conservative tradition'. He is not on the same intellectual plane as Burke, but what he has to say is much more relevant to understanding Conservatism.

Like Burke, his views as a young man and as an old one are very different. The early Disraeli, an obscure outsider of doubtful birth and prospects, was a radical; the later, a satisfied conservative of illustrious achievement, was accepted as part of the British aristocracy. One of the links binding the two parts was an audacity and irreverence which frequently shocked his more staid contemporaries.

The early Disraeli was a member of Young England, a discussion circle of younger aristocrats concerned with the ills of the new society and the decay of their own order. The members were romantic, wistful and fascinated by a version of medieval society: 'half lamentation, half lampoon; half echo of the past; half menace of the future', was Marx's comment.[24] The later Disraeli mocked the ideas of Young England, and showed little sympathy with its sense of crusade or its wish to recreate medieval society even proposing to use the total social subordination of the mill system to achieve it.[25]

The younger Disraeli, following other Tory writers, identified the problem of 'two nations'. His answer to the problem involved delineating what type of aristocracy could reunify the two to create One Nation. Outside Parliament, Disraeli's argument was almost pure romance, utopian speculation. Within Parliament, the search for a new aristocracy dissolved in an acceptance and defence of the existing mixture of land and industry.

In his speculation, however, Disraeli did provide a basis for the claims of a new aristocracy. The justification for leadership was mysterious and ultimately not explained in a coherent way, but nevertheless, the explanation detached the argument from its Tory association with land. The account had several different levels. The justification of individual leaders proceeded in terms of 'character'; of a class in terms of the need for leadership by the led and a 'national tradition'; and of a nation in terms of a national mission and racial integrity. Leadership, whether of an individual, a class or a nation (in the creation of empire) was now detached from any particular aristocracy. The scheme made provision for an explicit nationalism and for imperialism.

If a leadership class was to survive, according to Disraeli, it had continually to rejustify its existence in terms of the interests of the led. Popular enthusiasm had to supply what the formerly accepted customs of an organic society were supposed to accomplish, the security of the *status quo*. Popular support was only possible if everyone was able to identify the leadership as 'national', not merely the representative of some subnational interest. And this would be possible if there was a proper national ideology which encompassed the population and was defined by the leadership, and if the leadership demonstrated concretely that it cared for the led by introducing welfare provisions and reform. The national ideology is the 'national idea' as enunciated by the great leaders of the 'natural aristocracy'. In practice, Disraeli did not divulge what the national idea was, and his own statements are little more than colourful rhetoric. He remained in the position of the hero of one of his novels: 'There are great truths to tell if we had either the courage to announce or the temper to receive them.'[26]

The 'natural aristocracy' in the early Disraeli was a radical contrast to the actual aristocracy. It was a whip to scourge contemporary inadequacies. But it also made possible a landless aristocracy. It legitimised 'talent' – such as Disraeli had – as well as 'industry'. Later in life, whether because he became used to the *de facto* aristocracy (including both land, talent and industry) or more anxious about the threats to the *status quo* than some speculative ideal state, the natural and actual aristocracies tended to coalesce. The ideal became the real, and the real the ideal. 'Charisma' had replaced land.[27]

While the possession of 'charisma' might subjectively justify leadership, however, the objective justification lay in the need of people for a leadership distinct from themselves. Hatton in *Sybil* demonstrated the collapse into bestiality that occurred when people were absurd enough to try and lead themselves.[28] Sidonia explained: 'Man is made to adore and to obey: but if you will not command him, if you will give him nothing to worship, he will fashion his own divinities, and find a chieftain in his own passion.'[29] Human nature was the bedrock which supported the aristocracy. The leaders themselves must be excluded from the generalization, members of a class of exceptions or leaders. Society is thus divided into active and passive sectors, leaders and led.

The justification of leadership covered elements both Tory and inimical to Toryism: land and talent, experience and education.[30] A major talent in leaders was to change popular opinions (in contrast to Burke's argument about 'prejudice'). For society had become institutionally unstable, and the stability of prejudice impeded the benefits of change. Changing opinion made the national press of vital importance. The press – governed, incidentally, by men with, in Burkeian terms, no 'interest' in the nation – represented popular opinion, and thus meant that there was no need of Parliamentary reform to increase representation.[31] Influence through and on the press was the first weapon of leadership,[32] a statement that was an early Conservative version of the need for public relations.

The final justification for leadership, however, remained mysterious, out of reach of ordinary mortals. Honour fell unsolicited upon the great, whether new or old aristocrat, absolute monarch, meritocratic or charismatic leader.[33] It has an ethnic or 'biological' connotation. At the point of greatness, several strands of justification coincide – Stephen Gerard is Saxon, 'natural' leader of the poor and descendant of an hereditary aristocrat.

The ethnic connotation is a subsidiary theme or implication in Disraeli's work.[34] Britain's ills derive from the influence of foreign practices or blood. Foreign 'races' are the necessary complement of domestic unity and strengthen nationalism. 'Two nations' is the highest sacrilege possible, for it implies one 'race' divided as if they were two. The two nations somehow disappeared in the later Disraeli. Two different 'nations', also at loggerheads, land and industry, did reconcile their differences, but in so far as 'the altar of Mammon has blazed with triple worship',[35] it was not clear how the situation had changed. Mammon had hardly disappeared, and Traffords were hardly more common. But the outsider had become the insider.

The practical by-product of Disraeli's speculation was more modest than might have been assumed from his early writings. He stressed the need for popular welfare, for the State to assume the former obligations of Christian charity – 'the maintenance of the poor', he said, 'is a social duty, a duty justified by high State policy, and consecrated by the sanction of religion . . . a duty of everyone according to his means.' Maintaining the poor – even if it had been undertaken – would have meant compensating the victims of the industrial system, that is, assuming the persistence of a situation which created 'two nations' rather than changing the system. The programme *Sanitas sanitatum*, 'part of the desire to improve and elevate . . . the multitude',[36] was to comprise 'almost every consideration which has a just claim upon legislative interference'.[37] It would make 'The Monarchy of the Tories more democratic than the Republic of the Whigs'.[38] In specific terms, attempts were made to improve the minimum conditions of work (the Nine Hours Act), of working-class living standards (the Artisan Dwelling Act; Public Health Act; Sale of Food and Drugs Act), and to strengthen the general legal and industrial status of labour (by legalizing picketing in the Employers and Workmen Act of 1875). In Disraeli's administration, the primary responsibility for these measures belonged to the home secretary, Assheton Cross. The prime minister was better known for his foreign policy. The outline of the 'national idea' – Monarchy and Empire – were more important than social reform. As Gorst says, Disraeli 'took no part in framing (these Bills) and they consequently lacked the broad scope and unity that he alone was capable of instilling in them'.[39]

Disraeli's significance – apart from the short run importance of his 'Tory radicalism' – lies in the transition he made between what was left of Toryism, an incipiently counter-revolutionary doctrine for the restoration of a traditional agrarian society, to Conservatism, a position much less clearly distinguished from Liberalism. Disraeli accepted, praised and administered a Peelite world. He accepted the claims of industry – and the 'talented' – and made no attempt to prevent the continued relative decline of agriculture. He was a moderate free trader, and formally accepted the validity of 'economic law'. He argued that the essence of defending the content of the *status quo* lay in yielding gracefully to changes in its forms (a position which is almost exactly the reverse of Burke's). Reform was the precondition for defence. What the content of the *status quo* was, what was valuable, the 'great principles', remained cloudy.

References

INTRODUCTION

1. This is discussed at greater length in the Appendix, p. 275.
2. E. W. Hawley, *The New Deal and the Problem of Monopoly, A Study in Economic Ambivalence*, Princeton, N.J. 1966, p. 484, quoting P. T. Homan in the *Political Science Quarterly*, June 1936, p. 181.

CHAPTER I

1. cf. the Appendix, p. 275f.
2. cf. generally R. B. McDowell, *British Conservatism, 1832–1914*, London, 1959.
3. W. D. Jones, *Lord Derby and Victorian Conservatives*, London, 1956, p. 230.
4. *Quarterly Review*, CXIX–CXX, 145, 1867.
5. See his letter to Lord Caernarvon, 24 April 1868, quoted by Lady Gwendolin Cecil, in *Robert, Marquis of Salisbury*, London, 1921, p. 294.
6. A. L. Kennedy, *Salisbury, 1830–1903: Portrait of a Statesman*, London, 1953, p. 148.
7. W. S. Churchill, *Lord Randolph Churchill*, II, London, 1905, pp. 223–4 (1952 edition).
8. cf. his 1882 programme, cited in Kennedy, op. cit., pp. 143–4.
9. HOL *Debs.* 22 February 1884.
10. Cecil, op. cit., p. 153.
11. Speech, Birmingham, 16 April 1884, in *The Speeches of Lord Randolph Churchill*, London, 1889.
12. Speech, Birmingham, 9 April 1888, in ibid.

13. cf. 'Elijah's mantle', *Fortnightly Review*, May 1883.
14. ibid.
15. Churchill, op. cit., pp. 771–2.
16. A point made by George Wyndham, in K. Hutchison, *The Decline and Fall of British Capitalism*, London, 1951, p. 136.
17. Hutchison, ibid., p. 98.
18. E. E. Gulley, *Joseph Chamberlain and English Social Politics*, New York, 1926, p. 321. For further discussion of this topic, cf. J. S. Saloma, *British Conservatism and the Welfare State: An Analysis of the Policy Process within British Conservatism*, unpublished Ph.D. thesis, Harvard, 1961, p. 307 *passim*.
19. John Morley, quoted in Hutchison, op. cit., p. 97.
20. National Union and Conservative Party Conference Minutes, *Clippings*, London, 1907, p. 12.
21. Robert Blake, *The Unknown Prime Minister*, London, 1955, p. 90.
22. Austen Chamberlain, *Down the Years*, London, 1935, pp. 223–4.
23. cf. his memorandum to the King, September 1912; his advocacy of a Referendum, Albert Hall, 29 November 1910; his advocacy of force, where necessary, whatever the constitution, Blenheim Palace, 29 July 1912.
24. Blake, op. cit., p. 140.
25. ibid., p. 138.
26. cf. generally, Lord Hugh Cecil, *Conservatism*, London, 1912.
27. cf. Lord Balfour's comment on the 1906 election, quoted in Hutchison, op. cit., p. 19; or S. W. Hills on Conservative social reform, cited by Beatrice Webb, in *Our Partnership* (ed. B. Drake and M. I. Cole), London, 1948.

CHAPTER 2

1. W. K. Hancock, and M. M. Gowing, *The British War Economy*, Official History of the Second World War, London, 1949, p. 3.
2. Compare the outbreak of the Second World War in Sir William Beveridge, *Some Experiences of Economic Control in Wartime*, London, 1940.

3. cf. Sir Norman Hill *et al.*, *War and Insurance*, London, 1927, *passim*.
4. C. M. H. Lloyd, *Experiments in State Control*, London, 1924, p. 321.
5. S. J. Hurwitz, *State Intervention in Great Britain, 1914–19*, New York, 1949, p. 157.
6. V. L. Allen, *Trade Unions and the Government*, London, 1960, p. 30; cf. also Citrine's comment, cited in D. F. Macdonald, *The State and the Trade Unions*, London, 1960, p. 115.
7. cf. Asa Briggs, *Social Thought and Social Action: A Study of the Work of Seebohm Rowntree, 1871–1954*, London, 1961, *passim*.
8. *Industrial Relations Handbook*, London, 1958, p. 123.
9. H. B. Grey, and Sir Samuel Turner, *Eclipse or Empire?*, London, 1916, p. 113.
10. *Report of the Committee on Trusts*, Cmd. 9236, 1918, p. 11.
11. G. D. H. Cole, *British Trade and Industry: Past and Future*, London, 1932, p. 175; also W. A. Lewis, *Economic Survey, 1919–39*, London, 1949, p. 78.
12. cf. *Industry and Action*, FBI, undated publication; also R. A. Brady, *Business as a System of Power*, New York, 1943, p. 158; and S. E. Finer, The Federation of British Industries, *Political Studies*, IV/I, February 1956.
13. *Industry and Action*, ibid.
14. cf. Sir Charles Wilson's reference to the 'mailed fist', *Debs.*, 29 March 1926, 193/1734.
15. Allen, op. cit., p. 54.
16. cf. W. S. Churchill, *Parliamentary Government and the Economic Problem*, Romanes Lectures, Oxford, 1930; also Sidney and Beatrice Webb, *Constitution for the Socialist Commonwealth of Great Britain*, London, 1920; the FBI originally invited TUC affiliation to itself, but when this did not occur, created a short-lived 'National Alliance of Employers and Employed'.
17. A Private Member's Bill in 1922, and four bills in 1923; the 1924 Election Pledge included a promise to reverse the 'contracting out' provisions, cf. A. W. Baldwin. *My Father: The True Story*, London, 1955, p. 132. Baldwin had

to make a special appeal in 1925 to prevent the passage of another Private Member's Bill, and the 1925 and 1926 conferences made 'furious demands' for action, see Harvey Glickman, *Tory Ethos and Conservative Policy in Britain, 1922–39*, unpublished Ph.D. thesis, Harvard, 1958, p. 201 *passim*.

18. In *The Mond Moonshine*, London, 1928.

19. K. B. Smellie, *A Hundred Years of English Government*, London, 1962, p. 321. cf. also, examples cited in L. S. Amery, *The Forward View*, London, 1935.

20. cf. Sir William Firth, *The Engineer*, March 1934, and A. Chamberlain, chairman of Tube Investment, to his Annual General Meeting, 7 December 1938, cited in E. Davies, *National Capitalism*, London, 1939, p. 47.

21. G. W. Stocking and M. W. Watkins, *Cartels in Action*, London, 1946, p. 195.

22. See G. M. Young, *Stanley Baldwin*, London, 1952, for Baldwin's comment; also *The Times*, 3 February 1938.

23. But cf. R. G. Stewart, *Changing Views in Great Britain as to the Role of Government in Economic Planning, 1931–1947*, unpublished M.Sc. thesis, London School of Economics, 1948.

24. Harold Macmillan, *Winds of Change, 1914–1939*, London, 1966, p. 371.

25. cf. the relationship between Macmillan, Melchett, Amery, and the FBI over the plan for an Economic Union, 1931; the subsequent research committees, the evolution of the 1932 Wheat Act, the proposed Enabling Bill and the Industrial Reorganisation League; L. S. Amery, *My Political Life*, Vol. III, p. 60 *passim*, and Macmillan, op. cit., p. 371. Macmillan was also involved in PEP, which published *A Self-Government for Industry Bill*, London, 1934; cf. also, *Report* of the Committee on the Organisation of Industry, FBI, London, 1935, pp. 6–15.

26. On the decline of 'old' industry, cf. H. M. D. Parker, *Manpower*, Official History of the Second World War, London, 1957, pp. 19–20; cf. also E. L. Hargreaves and M. M. Gowing, *Civil Industry and Trade*, Official History of the Second World War, London, 1952, p. 8.

27. Lord Beveridge, *Power and Influence*, London, 1953, pp. 296–7.
28. M. M. Postan, *British War Production*, Official History of the Second World War, London, 1952, p. 146; also G. C. Allen, 'Concentration of production policy', in D. N. Chester (ed.), *Lessons of the British War Economy*, London, 1951, pp. 175–6; G. D. N. Worswick, *The Raw Materials Control*, London, 1944, *passim*; Duncan Burn, *The Steel Industry, 1939–59*, London, 1961, pp. 5 and 42.
29. cf. H. Levy, *Retail Trade Associations*, London, 1942; *The Economist*, 15 February 1942, pp. 206–7.
30. PEP, *Industrial Trade Associations*, London, 1957, p. 33; J. Hurstfield, *The Control of Raw Materials*, Official History of the Second World War, London, 1953, pp. 67–8.
31. Burn, op. cit., pp. 62–9.

CHAPTER 3

1. cf. his sympathy at a local level with Labour aims and his rejection of 'Toryism', in Keith Feiling, *The Life of Neville Chamberlain*, London, 1946, p. 135.
2. cf. Bonar Law, Speech, Glasgow, 26 October 1922, in *The Prime Minister's Policy*, London, 1922.
3. cf. White Paper, Cmd. 2327.
4. cf. discussion in D. Abel, *A History of British Tariffs, 1923–42*, London, 1945, p. 61.
5. S. Salvidge, *Salvidge of Liverpool: Behind the Political Scene, 1890–1928*, London, 1934, p. 205.
6. Sir Charles Petrie, *The Life and Letters of Sir Austen Chamberlain*, London, 1939, p. 180.
7. J. M. Keynes, *The Economic Consequences of Mr. Churchill*, London, 1925, p. 23; cf. the comment of Vincent Vickers, who resigned on this issue from the Court of the Bank of England, in Robert Boothby, *The New Economy*, London, 1943, p. 13.
8. L. S. Amery, *My Political Life*, Vol. II, London, 1953, pp. 241, 479.
9. ibid., p. 489.

10. R. T. Mackenzie, *British Political Parties*, London, 1955, p. 119.
11. Amery, op. cit., p. 497.
12. cf. *The History of the Empire Free Trade Campaign*, unpublished document of the Conservative Research Department, anonymous and undated, NUCUA stamp for 11 June 1930.
13. cf. the memorandum passed on to Baldwin by Chamberlain, arguing that the party could no longer be held together under his leadership, reprinted in Iain Macleod, *Neville Chamberlain*, London, 1961.
14. 2 April 1938; cf. also N. E. H. Davenport, *Vested Interests or Common Pool?*, London, 1942, p. 44.
15. 23 October 1937, p. 155.
16. 15 June 1940.
17. cf. *Report* of the Balfour Committee, 1929; also *Report* of the Greene Committee on Restraint of Trade, Cmd. 662, 1931.
18. For example, cf. *The Times*, 10 March 1925.
19. 'The end of laissez-faire', Sidney Ball Lecture, University of Oxford, 1924, reprinted in *Essays in Persuasion*, London, 1931, pp. 41–2.
20. H. A. Clegg, and T. E. Chester, *The Future of Nationalisation*, Oxford, 1953, pp. 15–16.
21. *Vienna Freie Presse*, quoted in Sir Stafford Cripps, *National Fascism in Britain*, London, 1935, p. 5.
22. Feiling, op. cit., p. 160. Compare H. E. Molson, *Conservatism and the Future*, London, 1935, p. 220.
23. cf. W. H. Mallock, *Democracy*, London, 1924.
24. cf. H. G. R. Sellon, *Whither England?*, London, 1932, p. 61; Sir Charles Petrie, *The British Problem*, London, 1934, p. 12; F. J. C. Hearnshaw, *Conservatism in England: An Analytical, Historical and Political Survey*, London, 1935, pp. 302 and 394.
25. Lymington argued that Toryism was incompatible with democracy; Viscount Lymington, *Ich Dien*, London, 1931, p. 12.
26. cf. Hearnshaw, op. cit., last chapter; Sellon, op. cit., p. 61; Dorothy Crisp, *The Rebirth of Conservatism*, London, 1931, p. 168; Lymington, op. cit., p. 46.

27. Lord Eustace Percy, *Democracy on Trial*, London, 1931, p. 15.
28. cf. Amery, op. cit.; Anthony Crossley *et al.*, *Planning for Employment*, London, 1935. In particular, cf. the clearest and most radical plan in Harold Macmillan's *The Middle Way: A Study of the Problem of Economic and Social Progress in a Free and Democratic Society*, London, 1938; cf. his earlier writings, *The State and Industry*, London, 1932; *The Next Step*, London, 1932; *A New British Financial Policy*, London, 1932; *Reconstruction – A Plea for a National Policy*, London, 1933; his association with *Planning for Employment*, *The Next Five Years*, *An Essay in Political Agreement*, London, 1935, and the journal, *The New Outlook* (1936–7).
29. L. S. Amery, *National and Imperial Economics*, London, 1924, pp. 9–10, and p. 333 of his *The Forward View*, London, 1935; Robert Boothby, *Industry and the State*, London, 1927, pp. 28, 55 and 213 *passim*; Macmillan, *The Middle Way*, etc.
30. Amery, *The Forward View*, p. 331; Alfred, 1st Viscount Milner, *Questions of the Hour*, London, 1924.
31. Amery, op. cit., p. 323.
32. ibid., p. 331.
33. Macmillan, *The Middle Way*, pp. 258 and 231.
34. For shipping, cf. Alfred Milner, HOL *Debs.*, 35/648, 1924; coal and minerals, Milner, ibid., and 35/683–5; liquor, ibid., 45/1121–6; transport and public utilities, H. E. Molson, op. cit., p. 220; general growth in public sector, Macmillan, *Reconstruction*, p. 109; industrial insurance, food production, minerals, Macmillan, *The Middle Way*, p. 231; Bank of England, ibid., p. 258; 'rundown' industries, Percy, op. cit., p. 103, and speech reported in *The Manchester Guardian*, 11 November 1935.
35. Boothby, op. cit., pp. 157–8.
36. Macmillan, *The Middle Way*, p. 231.
37. (i) Alfred Mond, 'Liberalism and modern industrial problems', in *The Remedy for Unemployment*, London, 1925, p. 8. Mond, the 1st Baron Melchett, was a Coalition Liberal minister and founder and first chairman of the largest British industrial group, an

early prototype of new quasi-monopolitic industry, Imperial Chemical Industries. Converted to general protection in the mid-1920s, he joined the Conservative party. He advocated managerialism, although he himself was also an owner, and consultation in industry (he initiated the Mond-Turner talks in 1927). He urged industrial reorganization, and co-operated closely with Amery and the FBI in framing proposals to this end in 1930; cf. William Bolitho, *Alfred Mond, First Lord Melchett*, London, 1933; *ICI Magazine*; *Industry and Politics*, London, 1927; W. J. Reader, *Imperial Chemical Industries – A History*, London, 1970. For a contemporary fantasy, cf. Mustapha Mond in Aldous Huxley's *Brave New World*, London, 1931. The 2nd Baron Melchett was chairman of the Industrial Reorganisation League in collaboration with Macmillan, and sponsored an Enabling Bill in the House of Lords.

(ii) Petrie, *The British Problem*, p. 58.
(iii) Macmillan, *A New British Financial Policy*; *Reconstruction*, p. 25 *passim*; *The Middle Way*.
(iv) Amery, *The Forward View*, p. 410.
(v) Percy, op. cit., p. 40.
38. Boothby, op. cit. p. 41.
39. cf. footnotes 28 and 37; cf. also Macmillan, *Winds of Change, 1914–1939*, London, 1966, p. 371 *passim*.
40. Sir R. W. Banks, *The Conservative Outlook*, London, 1929, p. 75; also Marquess of Salisbury, *Conservative Policy*, London, 1924.
41. cf. W. J. Wilkinson, *Tory Democracy*, New York, 1925, p. 471, on earlier sources of this phrase; also Noel Skelton, *Constructive Conservatism*, London, 1924; and Lt-Col. Walter Elliot, *Toryism and the Twentieth Century*, London, 1927, p. 69.
42. *Religio Militis*, London, 1927, p. 149.
43. In *The British Problem, passim*.
44. In *Reconstruction*, p. 16.
45. cf. Macmillan, *Winds of Change*, p. 363.
46. Macmillan, *Reconstruction*, p. 25.

47. Macmillan, *The Middle Way*, p. 210.
48. *Debs*, 9 February 1943, 387/1212.
49. Sir William Beveridge, *Power and Influence*, London, 1953, p. 324; Churchill, *The Second World War*, IV, London, 1948–54, p. 959.
50. cf. also, debates on air transport (January 1943) on the Scott, Urhwatt, and Barlow Reports, Central Council meeting, 7 October 1943; H. E. Molson, 'The Tory Reform Committee', *New English Review*, 22 March 1943, p. 247; 'Tory Reform Committee', *Forward by the Right*, London, 1943.
51. C. G. Lancaster, Quintin Hogg, and Peter Thorneycroft, *National Policy for Coal*, London, 1944; cf. also, Sir Alfred Beit, R. Clyn, H. E. Molson and J. A. Cecil Wright, *Tools for the Next Job*, London, 1945, pp. 37–8.
52. cf. reports in *The Times*, 22 March 1943, and *The Economist*, 27 March 1943, p. 328.
53. Anthony Eden, *Freedom and Order*, London, 1947, p. 268.
54. 3 January 1944.
55. National Union, *Work, The Future of British Industry*, London, January 1944.

CHAPTER 4

1. Michael Kidron, *Western Capitalism Since the War*, London, 1968, Chapter 3.
2. cf. R. Evely and I. M. D. Little, *Concentration in British Industry*, Cambridge, 1960; cf. also P. E. Hart and S. J. Prais, 'The analysis of business concentration', *Journal of the Royal Statistical Society*, 119/150, 1956.
3. cf. Board of Trade, *Company Assets, Income and Finance in 1960*, London, 1962.
4. PEP, *Industrial Trade Associations*, London, 1957, p. 248; cf. also an FBI 1946 scheme in *Report of the Trade Organisation Committee*, London, October 1946.
5. P. Sargent Florence, *The Logic of British and American Industry*, London, 1953, p. 215.
6. P. Sargent Florence, *Ownership, Control and Success of Large*

Companies, London, 1961, p. 29; and J. H. Dunning and C. J. Thomas, *British Industry*, London, 1961, p. 67.

7. cf. on public intervention in transport, John Smith, 'The Rise of the Bureaucracy', *Transactions of the Third World Congress of Sociology*, II, London, 1956.

8. On the relationship between Unilever and the Ministry of Food, cf. A. A. Rogow, and P. Shore, *The Labour Government and British Industry, 1945–51*, Oxford, 1955, pp. 62–5.

9. ibid., p. 76.

10. ibid., p. 77.

11. 'Business', in Morris Ginsberg (ed.), *Law and Opinion in England in the Twentieth Century*, London, 1959, p. 153.

12. For more extended discussion of this, see the Appendix.

13. Tour du Pin, *Vers un ordre social chrétien*, Paris, 1907, and *Aphorismes de politique sociale*, Paris, 1909.

14. The phrase was the title of a book by one of the better known guild socialists, G. D. H. Cole, London, 1917.

15. *In Days to Come (Von Kommenden Dingen)*, London, 1921.

16. 'The end of laissez-faire', pp. 41–2; cf. also the excellent discussion in 'Hal Draper, neo-Corporatists and neo-Reformers', *New Politics*, I/I, June 1961, p. 87.

17. cf. also George Bernard Shaw, correspondence, *Bernard Shaw and Fascism*, London, 1937; Henri de Man, *Nationalisme et Socialisme*, Paris, 1932.

18. For example, Sidney and Beatrice Webb, *Soviet Communism: A New Civilisation*, London, 1935.

19. Gaetan Pirou, *Essais sur le corporation*, Paris, 1938, p. 72.

20. ibid., p. 24; cf. also Eugène Mathon, *La corporation, base de l'organisation économique*, Paris, 1934.

21. Pirou, op. cit., p. 59, Pirou's italics.

22. E. W. Hawley, *The New Deal and the Problem of Monopoly*, Princeton, N.J., 1966, p. 35.

23. Cited in ibid., p. 281.

24. ibid., p. 176.

25. cf. Peter Drucker, *The Future of Industrial Man: A Conservative Approach*, London, 1943; *The New Society*, London,

1951; *The Concept of the Corporation*, Boston, 1960; cf. also E. S. Mason, (ed.), *The Corporation in Modern Society*, Cambridge, Mass., 1959.

26. Drucker, *The Concept of the Corporation*, pp. 140–1.

27. In W. H. Ferry, (ed.), *The Corporation and the Economy*, Santa Barbara, 1959, p. 9; cf. also *The Economy Under Law*, Santa Barbara, 1960; and Scott Buchanan, *The Corporation and the Republic*, Santa Barbara, 1958.

28. A. A. Berle, *Power without Property*, London, 1960, p. 19. See also, the same author's *Economic Power and the Free Society*, Santa Barbara, 1957.

29. *The Corporation in Modern Society*, p. 9.

30. cf. Kerr Clark, *Unions and Union Leaders of Their Own Choosing*, New York, 1957, *passim*.

31. A. A. Rostow, 'To whom and what ends is Corporation management responsible?, in Mason, op cit.

32. cf. also, C. A. R. Crosland, *The Future of Socialism*, London, 1956, pp. 260–5.

33. cf. 'City of God', in *The Twentieth Century Capitalist Revolution*, London, 1955; also *Power without Property*, p. 11; Ferry, op. cit., p. 4.

34. *Economic Power and the Free Society*, pp. 13–14.

35. *Power without Property*, pp. 6–7. Compare Father P. P. Harbrecht, *Towards the Paraproprietal Society: An Essay on the Nature of Property in Twentieth Century America*, Santa Barbara, 1960.

36. Pirou, op. cit.; Franz Neumann, *Behemoth, The Structure and Practice of National Socialism*, London, 1942.

37. In *Thoughts on the Constitution*, Oxford University Chichele Lectures, London, 1947; cf. also the speech by Macmillan, Brighton, 5 March 1949.

38. *Essays in Conservatism*, London, 1949, Chapter 4.

39. But cf. P. Marriott, *Property and the Nation*, London, 1949, p. 26.

40. S. E. Finer, *Anonymous Empire: A Study of the Lobby in Great Britain*, London, 1958, p. 102; cf. also H. A. Clegg and T. E. Chester, *The Future of Nationalisation*, Oxford, 1943, pp. 15–16.

CHAPTER 5

1. cf. Werner Stark, *The Fundamental Forms of Social Thought*, London, 1962, pp. 196–7, for a discussion of a similar change in a different context.
2. cf. letters to *The Times*, 31 July, 3 August, 28 September 1945; the resignation of the East Edinburgh Conservative candidate, *The Times*, 11 September 1945, p. 2; and the contest to nominate a candidate for South Kensington, *The Times*, 21 September 1945, p. 2.
3. cf. debate on the King's Speech, 15 August 1945, *Debs.*, 413/87; R. A. Butler, ibid., 413/192; and Oliver Lyttelton, 9 October 1945, ibid., 414/127.
4. e.g. Churchill described Labour's first budget as merely a continuation of Coalition policy, 24 October 1945, ibid., 414/2026.
5. *Onlooker*, January 1946, p. 3 and *passim*, and *The Times*, 29 November 1945, p. 8.
6. cf. Eden speech, 1 March 1946, Kingston-upon-Hull, in *Conservative Policy*, 1946, and quoted in *Freedom and Order (Speeches, 1939–1946)*, London, 1947, p. 396; Macmillan, *The Conservative Approach to Modern Politics*, London, 7 May 1946; Lord Woolton, speech to the Royal Empire Society, reported in *The Economist*, 22 June 1946, p. 1000; David Eccles, two speeches, 21 and 22 June 1946, reprinted as *Conservatism after 1945*, London, 1946; Eden, Wrekin Speech, reported in *Notes on Current Politics*, 12 August 1946, *The Times*, 7 July 1946 and *The Economist*, 13 July 1946, p. 51; Macmillan, *Notes on Current Politics*, 12 August 1946; and Eden, Hatfield speech, reported in *The Times*, 2 September 1946.
7. At Hatfield, reported in *The Times*, 2 September 1946, and at Chatsworth, ibid., 16 September 1946; cf. also Ernest Marples, to Liverpool University Conservatives, quoted *Debs.*, 2 April 1946, 421/1167.
8. Reports in *The Times*, 4 October 1946, p. 2, and *Onlooker*, November 1946, p. 6.
9. No. 12, December 1946.

10. It was signed by 110 members and candidates of the Conservative and Liberal parties (including Hogg, Braine, Erroll, Lancaster, Maude, Selwyn Lloyd, Molson and Spearman).

11. cf. speech by Heathcoat Amory at Tiverton, cited in W. Gore Allen, *The Reluctant Politician, Derick Heathcoat Amory*, London, 1958.

12. *Onlooker*, April 1947, p. 2, and *Notes on Current Politics* (9), 19 May 1947.

13. From businessmen, cf. Glickman, op. cit., p. 490; and from sections of the press, cf. report and comment in *The Economist*, 21 June 1947, p. 970.

14. Ralph Harris, *Politics without Prejudice*, London, 1956, pp. 104–7 (cf. p. 110 for Churchill's letter to Butler).

15. 'Forward into battle', *Tory Challenge*, November 1947, p. 2.

16. For example, cf. Eden, Party Conference *Report*, London, 1947, p. 35, and Churchill, ibid., p. 115.

17. Broadcast, 16 August 1947, reported in *The Times*, 17 August 1947, and reprinted as a Conservative Central Office Pamphlet.

18. cf. Central Council *Agenda*, March 1949; H. G. Nicholas, *The British General Election of 1950*, London, 1951, p. 67; meeting of the 1922 Committee with Churchill, reported in *The Times*, 4 March 1949; report of the Central Council meeting, ibid., 19 March 1949, p. 3; also *The Economist*, 12 March 1949, p. 455.

19. The correspondence featured in *The Times*, 3 March to 12 April 1949; on the analogy with the Tamworth Manifesto, cf. ibid., 26 March; R. A. Butler, *Conservatism 1949–50*, London, 1950, p. 1; and *Tradition and Change*, London, 1954, p. 10; Ralph Harris, op. cit., p. 115, and Nigel Birch, *The Conservative Party*, London, 1949.

20. *The Right Road for Britain*, London, 1949, p. 6.

21. cf. *The Economist*, 30 July 1949, p. 225; *The Manchester Guardian*, 24 July 1949; *The Times*, 12 and 15 October 1949.

CHAPTER 6

1. *Debs.*, 29 October 1945, 415/120.

2. Report on the Central Council meeting, *The Times*, 19 March 1947, p. 3, and *Onlooker*, April 1947.

3. *Debs.*, 29 October 1945, 415/149.

4. Committee of Inquiry into the Gas Industry, *Report*, Cmd. 6699, 1945.

5. *Debs.*, 6 December 1945, 416/2572.

6. e.g. Sir Waldron Smithers, *Debs.*, 15 December 1946, 430/435; W. Robson Brown, report of the 1946 Annual Conference, *The Times*, 5 October 1946, p. 2.

7. e.g. Churchill, *Debs.*, 6 December 1945, 416/2535.

8. Boothby, *Debs.*, 6 December 1945, 416/2572; I. L. Orr-Ewing, 1947 Party Conference *Report*, London, 1947, pp. 47–53.

9. *Debs.*, 27 May 1946, 423/855.

10. *Debs.*, 24 January 1946, 418/333.

11. cf. 1948 Party Conference *Report*, London, 1948.

12. e.g. Lyttelton, 1949 Party Conference *Report*, London, 1949, p. 49.

13. cf. White Paper, Cmd. 6364, 1942.

14. cf. Churchill's statement, *Debs.*, 13 October 1943, 392/921–2.

15. Cmd. 6610, March 1945; cf. Major Lloyd George's statement, *Debs.*, 29 May 1945, 411/74–8.

16. cf. Debate on the Address, *Debs.*, 17 August 1945, 413/248; for example, C. G. Lancaster 268, Col. L. C. Ropner 528; also Eccles, *The Times*, 4 January 1946, p. 5.

17. *Debs.*, 29 January 1946, 418/716–17.

18. ibid., 753.

19. ibid., 910.

20. ibid., 766.

21. ibid., 905.

22. *Debs.*, 30 January 1946, 418/947.

23. Along lines very similar to those presented in the FBI *Report on Coal Nationalisation*; cf. *The Times*, 7 February 1946; cf. also the statement of the Associated British Chambers of Commerce, London, January 1946.

24. cf. Thorneycroft, Clarke, Macmillan, Gridley, Bower, *Debs.*, on 12–13 and 27 February, 5 March, and 14 May;

and HOL *Debs.*, Lords Balfour, Llewellyn and Swinton, 19 June and 2 July, 1946.

25. *Debs.*, 20 May 1946, 423/60.
26. ibid., 128.
27. cf., for example, H. V. Raikes, *Debs.*, 10 November 1949, 469/1517; or Lancaster, at the height of the 1947 fuel crisis, *Debs.*, 28 February 1947, 433/100.
28. 5th day of the Debate on the Address, *Debs.*, October 1947, 450/100.
29. The resignation of Reid from the National Coal Board in the summer of 1948 on the grounds that the board was over-centralized added weight to the Conservative case; cf. Lancaster's criticism of the board, *The Times*, 27 August 1948; his *About Coal*, Two Way Movement Series, February 1948; *The Organisation of the Coal Board*, London, November 1948; and *Coal*, Inside Industry Series, London, September 1948.
30. Resolution 35, 1949 Party Conference *Report*, London, 1949.
31. *Debs.*, 25 October 1950, 478/2814.
32. *The Times*, 4 January 1946, p. 5.
33. e.g. Churchill in 1918, Dundee, quoted in *Debs.*, 12 November 1946, 430/921; *The Times*, 12 April 1918, and *The Spectator*, 22 March and 26 July, 1919; cf. also, Macmillan, *The Middle Way*, and *The Next Five Years*.
34. Churchill, *Debs.*, 12 November 1946, 430/16–31.
35. e.g. the National Conference of Road Transport, 20 November 1945, at Caxton Hall, London, and statements by the Road Haulage Federation and the National Union of Manufacturers, February 1946.
36. Report in *The Economist*, 16 March 1946, p. 402; cf. also, *British Railways and the Future* by the four railway companies, 12 October 1946.
37. Speech, 7 May 1946, reprinted as *The Conservative Approach to Modern Politics*, CUCO, London, May 1946.
38. Report in *The Times*, 19 November 1946, p. 2.
39. cf. statements by the major shipping associations (supported by the FBI, the BISF, and the ABCC), 12 December 1946;

by the four railway companies, 12 December 1946; by R. Gresham-Cooke, later Conservative MP for Twickenham, on behalf of the Society of Motor Manufacturers, 12 December 1946; cf. more generally S. E. Finer, 'The political power of private capital', *Sociological Review*, II/2, December 1955, p. 279, and IV/1, July 1956, p. 2.

40. Report in *The Times*, 14 December 1946, p. 8.
41. S. E. Finer, *Anonymous Empire: A Study of the Lobby in Great Britain*, London, 1958, pp. 67–9.
42. For example, J. S. Maclay, a shipowner and MP, moved some of the amendments affecting shipping interests.
43. Finer, 'The political power', p. 27.
44. ibid., p. 11.
45. Compare, for example, Sir David Maxwell Fyfe, *Debs.*, 16 December 1946, 431/1638 or Viscountess Davidson, 431/1678, and Sir A. Salter, 431/2012, or Sir John Anderson of the Front Bench, 431/1994.
46. Thorneycroft, ibid., 431/2025.
47. Maxwell Fyfe, ibid., 431/1638.
48. ibid., 431/2025.
49. ibid., 2030.
50. *Debs.*, 5 May 1947, 437/55 *passim*.
51. *Debs.*, 30 March 1950, 473/674.
52. ibid., 478/2087; cf also Butler, *Debs.*, 25 October 1950, 478/2795, and 7 March 1951, 485/514, and 31 July 1951, 491/1187.
53. 23 February 1951, 484/1615.
54. cf. statement by Eden, *Debs.*, 26 October 1948, 457/22–3.
55. Duncan Burn, *The Steel Industry, 1939–59*, London, 1961, footnote 3, p. 303; and Finer, *Anonymous Empire*, etc., p. 49.
56. For example, W. Robson Brown MP, Major Peter Roberts MP, Geoffrey Summers, 1948 President of the National Union; on the Front Bench, Oliver Lyttelton was connected with major steel-using interests.
57. *Debs.*, 16 November 1948, 458/219.
58. ibid.
59. 27 May 1946, 423/999.
60. cf. J. G. Braithwaite, summing up for the Opposition,

Debs., 27 May 1946, 423/950; Roberts, 423/880; Lancaster, 423/894; Lyttelton, 423/838.

61. Eden at Leamington, 1 June 1946; Fraser, *About Steel*, Two Way Movement Series, London, January 1949, p. 14; Selwyn Lloyd, *Debs.*, 16 December 1949, 469/322.

62. Lyttelton, *Debs.*, 27 May 1946, 423/838, and 15 November 1948, 458/53; Erroll, 27 May 1946, 423/925.

63. Lyttelton, 1948 Party Conference *Report*, London, 1948, p. 74; or *Debs.*, 9 May 1949, 464/1507; cf. also Lindsay, 16 November 1948, 458/282.

64. Ernest Marples, *Debs.*, 17 November 1948, 458/421.

65. Hinchingbrooke, *Debs.*, 15 November 1948, 458/106.

66. Lyttelton, ibid., 100.

67. Erroll, *Debs.*, 27 May 1946, 423/925; and Strauss, 15 November 1948, 458/121.

68. *Debs.*, 27 May 1946, 423/878.

69. Hudson, ibid., 423/1095; Eccles, *Debs.*, 17 April 1946, 421/2697; Roberts, 27 May 1946, 423/878; Hinchingbrooke, 15 November 1948, 458/106.

70. *Debs.*, 9 May 1949, 464/1507.

71. Lindsay, *Debs.*, 27 May 1946, 423/919.

72. Duncan Burn, op. cit., p. 296.

73. Roberts, *Debs.*, 27 May 1946, 423/878; Lyttelton, 15 November 1948, 458/53.

74. Lyttelton, *Debs.*, 9 May 1949, 464/1507; Thorneycroft, 28 May 1946, 423/1041.

75. cf. Fraser, *About Steel*, and the reply, *What We Think* (About Steel), London, November 1949.

76. Report Stage, 27 April 1949.

77. cf. *Debs.*, 8 October 1946, 427/43.

78. *Debs.*, 21 May 1946, 423/213; cf. also *The Economist*, 25 May 1946, p. 832; and the opposition of the *Evening Standard*, 22 May 1946.

79. cf. Churchill, *Debs.*, 15 August 1945, 413/94, *passim*, and Lyttelton, 28 October 1945, 415/43.

80. Boothby refused the Party Whip and voted with the Government, *Debs.*, 28 October 1945, 415/110; cf. also Boothby, *I Fight to Live*, London, 1947, p. 381.

81. cf. White Paper, Cmd. 6712; and *Debs.*, 24 January 1946,

418/313; 6 May 1946, 422/596, and HOL *Debs.*, 6 November 1945, 137/623.

82. e.g. Lord Balfour of Inchyre, 6 November 1945, 137/651; also A. T. Lennox Boyd, 6 May 1946, 422/596–616.
83. *Debs.*, 24 January 1946, 418/313.
84. *The Industrial Charter* suggested changes were needed, but without specifying what they should be.
85. But cf. the statement of the Electrical Supply Companies, *The Times*, 20 January 1947.
86. cf. Hinchingbrooke's complaint, *Debs.*, 4 February 1947, 432/1523.
87. e.g. Rt Hon. Brendan Bracken, *Debs.*, 10 February 1948, 447/239; and N. Bower, ibid., 282.
88. cf. Eden, *Notes on Current Politics*, 20, 21 October 1946, p. 15; Macmillan, *Debs.*, 30 January 1946, 418/134 and *About Economic Recovery*, Two Way Movement Series, London, February 1948; L. D. Gammans, 1947 Party Conference *Report*, p. 97; Eccles, speech to the Conservative Candidates Association, reprinted as *Forward from the Industrial Charter*, London, 1948, and his *About the Property-Owning Democracy*, Two Way Movement Series, London, October 1948; and the reply, *What We Think* (About the Property-Owning Democracy), London, June 1949; cf. also, *What We Think* (About Economic Recovery), London, November 1948.
89. Letter, *The Times*, 8 March 1949, p. 5; cf. also A. V. Harvey, ibid., 19 March 1949, p. 5.
90. 1949 Party Conference *Report*, p. 93; cf. also P. Marriott, *Property and the Nation*, London, 1947.
91. 1950 Party Conference *Report*, London, 1950, pp. 56–65.
92. Letter, *The Times*, 25 October 1945, p. 5.
93. For example, in *About Economic Recovery*.
94. *Debs.*, 3 February 1947, 432/1523.
95. *Debs.*, 15 November 1948, 458/106.

CHAPTER 7

1. *The Economist,* 15 November 1951; cf. comment in the *Financial Times,* 6 November 1946.
2. cf. letter by Fitzroy Maclean, *The Times,* 25 October 1945, p. 5 and his speech, *Debs.,* 2 April 1946, 421/1169. Also Lyttelton, 5 December 1945, 416/2347; M. S. McCorquodale, 29 December 1948, 457/398; Maxwell Fyfe, 'Trade unionists and nationalisation', *Conservative Approach,* 6 April 1949, and 1940 Party Conference *Report,* p. 39.
3. By Ted Leather MP, Harold Watkinson MP, and others, London, 1951.
4. cf. speeches by R. A. Butler, reported in *The Times* throughout February 1946, and also *All You Want to Know about the Trade Disputes Act,* Conservative Central Office, London, 1946.
5. cf. *Debs.,* 12 February 1946, 419/192; 26 February 1946, 419/1759; and 2 April 1946, 421/1122 *passim.*
6. cf. *The Economist,* 16 February 1946, p. 249.
7. Beverley Baxter, *Debs.,* 2 April 1946, 421/1150.
8. *Debs.,* 15 November 1946, 430/386.
9. For example, compare *Design for Freedom,* Part III, London, February 1947, and D. Clarke, *About the Trade Unions,* Two Way Movement Series, London, February 1947, pp. 16–18.
10. cf. for example, resolutions 28–9, 1949 Party Conference *Agenda,* pp. 44–5, and *What We Think* (About the Trade Union), London, July 1947.
11. cf. *The Right Road for Britain,* London, July 1949, Section 2; the protest of Sir Herbert Williams, *Tory Challenge,* November 1949, p. 10, and 1949 Party Conference *Report,* p. 83; cf. also *This is the Road,* and *Britain Strong and Free,* London, September 1951.
12. cf. Maxwell Fyfe's introduction to Ted Leather *et al., A New Approach,* London, 1951; Churchill at Woodford, 9 October 1951, reported in *The Times,* 10 October 1951 and 14 October 1951; *The Times,* 15 October 1951; *Trade Union Bulletin,* 52, October 1951.

13. cf., for example, *The Economist* in 1945 and 1946; or *The Times*, 10 September 1945 and 4 September 1946.

14. *Debs.*, 15 November 1946, 430/419–21; also 27 February 1946, 419/1993; cf. also London Area Young Conservatives, resolution 29, urging 'a National Wages Policy', 1946 Party Conference *Agenda*, London, 1946.

15. *Debs.*, 20 November 1946, 430/874.

16. *Debs.*, 27 February 1946, 419/2195; cf. also Eccles, 9 April 1946, 421/2041.

17. Thorneycroft, *Design for Wages*, London, 1948, p. 5.

18. At Wolverhampton, 23 July 1949, reported in *Trade Union Bulletin*, 29 September 1949.

19. cf. *This is the Road*, point 3, and 1950 Party Conference *Report*, p. 52.

20. cf. J. B. Wood, *Employment*, CPC, London, 1951.

21. *Debs.*, 27 October 1948, 457/139.

22. *Design for Freedom*, Part II.

23. Marples, 'Co-partnership in industry', *Tory Challenge*, February 1948, p. 1.

24. For example, M. S. McCorquodale, *Debs.*, 5 April 1950, 473/1204.

25. Angus Maude, *The Conservative Way of Life*, Topic for Today Series, London, May 1951, p. 2.

26. For expositions of this, cf. 'The Workers' Charter', Section III of *The Industrial Charter*, London, May 1947; D. Heathcoat Amory, *About the Workers' Charter*, Two Way Movement Series, London, September 1947; Iain Macleod and Angus Maude, *One Nation*, London, 1950; Michael Frazer, *The Worker in Industry*, London, 1950; Bernard Braine, *Tory Democracy*, London, 1948; C. Hollis, *Debs.*, 27 October 1948, 457/103; cf. also, letter from R. A. Butler, *The Times*, 12 January 1947, p. 5, and the ensuing correspondence.

27. Aubrey Jones, *Industrial Order*, London, 1950, p. 29; cf. also L. D. Gammans, *Debs.*, 5 April 1950, 473/1302; Brendan Bracken, 10 February 1948, 447/254; John Boyd-Carpenter, 5 April 1950, 473/1310.

28. Eden, 'Conservatism and industry', speech at Plymouth, 26 October 1946, reprinted in *Freedom and Order* (*Speeches*

1939–1946), London, 1947, p. 425; cf. also Amory, *Debs.*, 20 November 1946, 430/955.

29. *The Industrial Charter*, p. 28.
30. For a long list of obligations, cf. *What We Think* (About the Workers' Charter), London, 1948, p. 10.
31. cf. the *Trade Union Bulletin*, 2 June 1947. But the Workers' Charter did hint at possible sanctions, *What We Think*, p. 29.
32. Aubrey Jones, op. cit., p. 31.
33. R. A. Butler, 1947 Party Conference *Report*, p. 53; cf. also, T. E. Utley, *Essays in Conservatism*, London, 1949, p. 30, and Christopher Hollis, *Can Parliament Survive?*, London, 1949, p. 100.
34. e.g. *What We Think* (About Coal), November 1948, p. 5; also Michael Frazer, op. cit., p. 7, and D. Heathcoat Amory, op. cit., p. 16.
35. M. S. McCorquodale, *Debs.*, 5 April 1950, 473/1223.

CHAPTER 8

1. For example, the Inside Industry Series, produced by the CPC, *Wool*, 1948; *Cotton*, January 1950; *Shipbuilding*, November 1950.
2. For example, cf. FBI statements, 28 September 1945; 23 January and 20 February, 1946; 20 January and 30 March, 1947; December 1948, etc., and NUM and ABCC memoranda to the prime minister, 12 December 1946.
3. cf. *Debs.*, 2 December 1946, 431/41; 18 March 1946, 421/591; Churchill, 12 November 1946, 430/5; Lyttelton, 10 March 1947, 434/963, 29 July 1948, 454/1570, and in *The Daily Telegraph*, 27 December 1946; cf. also policy statements, and *The State as Merchant – A Study of Government Bulk Purchasing*, CPC, May 1948.
4. For example, Walter Elliot, *Debs.*, 24 March 1947, 435/867.
5. *Debs.*, 13 February 1947, 433/547.
6. Speech, London, 2 May 1949, reported in *Notes on Current Politics*, 10, 1949, p. 17.
7. *Debs.*, 6 March 1950, 472/186.
8. 1947 Party Conference *Report*, London, 1947, p. 51.

9. *Design for Freedom*, Part II, London, February 1947.
10. *Debs.*, 13 February 1947, 433/656.
11. For example, Lyttelton, *Debs.*, 10 March 1947, 434/1007; R. S. Hudson, 27 January 1951, 489/1412; cf. also *Design for Freedom*.
12. Harold Watkinson, *Debs.*, 27 April 1951, 487/705; R. A. Butler, 10 March 1947, 434/1248; Lyttelton, ibid., 999.
13. For example, Lyttelton, *Debs.*, 27 May 1946, 423/869; C. G. Lancaster, 13 February 1947, 433/629.
14. Sir John Barlow, *Debs.*, 13 February 1947, 433/604; William Shepherd, ibid., 607–9; cf. also Lyttelton, ibid., 565.
15. cf. *The Economist*, 1 September 1945 and 26 April 1947.
16. cf. L. D. Gammans MP, and resolution 32, 1946 Party Conference *Agenda* and *Report*, London, 1946.
17. cf. *Forward from the Industrial Charter*, London, January 1948.
18. *Monopoly*, CPC, London, April 1948.
19. Lyttelton, *Debs.*, 29 June 1948, 452/2143; cf. also Maxwell Fyfe, 22 April 1948, 449/2041, and his amendment, 27 May 1948; Shepherd amendment, 1 June 1948; also HOL amendments, Viscount Mayham, 13 July 1948, and Lord Balfour of Inchyre, 13 July 1948.
20. *Debs.*, 16 June 1950, 476/721.
21. The Labour backbencher was C. A. R. Crosland, cf. *Debs.*, 15 June 1951, 488/2689.
22. ibid., 2727.

CHAPTER 9

1. For example, Eccles, *Forward from the Industrial Charter*, London, 1948, p. 8; Boothby, *Debs.*, 10 March 1947, 434/963; L. S. Amery, *The Conservative Future*, London, 1945, and *The Awakening*, London, 1948; cf. also Macmillan, *About Economic Recovery*, London, 1948.
2. cf. Churchill, *Debs.*, 23 October 1945, 414/1911; Sir John Anderson, ibid., 2023.
3. Anderson, ibid.
4. Boothby, 25 October 1945, ibid., 2213.
5. Speech, Blenheim Park, August 1947; and broadcast,

16 August 1947, reprinted by the Conservative Central Office, London, 1947.

6. cf. *The Industrial Charter*, London, May 1947, Part II; Anderson, *Debs.*, 15 April 1947, 436/199, and other economic debates; cf. also *The Economist*, 21 April 1951, p. 904.

7. Lyttelton, *Debs.*, 10 March 1947, 434/999.

8. cf. Eden's amendment, *Debs.*, 15 October 1945, 414/1003.

9. For example, Major Guy Lloyd, *Debs.*, 9 October 1945, 414/149–50; Sir William Darling, ibid., 157; compare comment in *The Economist*, 13 October 1945, p. 519, and Lord Brabazon, HOL *Debs.*, 136/564.

10. *Debs.*, 5 February 1946, 418/1637; compare Ralph Assheton, ibid., 1547; Braithwaite, ibid., 1600, or Bracken, ibid., 1651; cf. also Eden speech, March 1946, reported in *The Economist*, 9 March 1946, p. 371.

11. *Debs.*, 11 March 1946, 434/1216; cf. also A. C. M. Spearman, 27 October 1948, 457/168, and R. A. Butler, *About the Industrial Charter*, London, September 1947.

12. cf. *The Industrial Charter*, and *The Right Road for Britain*, London, July 1949, p. 17; cf. also Lord Woolton's reply to the 1948 Central Council meeting, reported in *The Times*, 18 March 1948, p. 2.

13. cf. the *Financial Times*, 18 October 1951; also One Nation Group, comment in *Change is Our Ally*, London, May 1954, p. 38.

14. For example, A. A. Rogow and Peter Shore, *The Labour Government and British Industry, 1945–1951*, Oxford, 1955, or R. A. Brady, *Crisis in Britain*, London, 1950; cf. also PEP, *Government and Industry*, XVII, 318, September 1950.

15. cf. G. D. N. Worswick, 'Direct controls', in *The British Economy 1945–50* by G. D. N. Worswick and P. Ady, London, 1952; cf. also PEP, *Government and Industry*, London, 1952, p. 73.

16. This point is made in the Introduction to Worswick and Ady, op. cit.

17. Rogow and Shore, op. cit., p. 12, *passim*.

18. For example, L. D. Gammans, *Debs.*, 15 August 1945,

413/127; Eccles, ibid., 210; Boothby, 5 December 1945, 416/2574.

19. Lyttelton, *Debs.*, 16 August 1945, 413/490; compare Lord Woolton's view of the pre-war situation, *The Sunday Times*, 2 December 1945.

20. Compare R. S. Hudson, *Debs.*, 27 February 1946, 419/2190–8; Macmillan, 20 November 1946, 430/864; Nigel Birch, 5 February 1946, 418/1630 and 28 February 1946, 419/2190.

21. In *The Conservative Approach to Modern Politics*, London, May 1946.

22. *Debs.*, 10 March 1947, 434/999.

23. cf. for example, Anderson from the Front Bench, 11 March 1947, 434/1176; Butler, ibid., 1248; Boothby, ibid., 1045; K. Hutchison, ibid., 1229.

24. ibid.; cf. also Eccles, ibid., 1214.

25. e.g. Eccles, *Debs.*, 16 April 1947, 436/264; Boothby, ibid., 278.

26. *Forward from the Industrial Charter*; an edited version of this speech to the Conservative Candidates' Association, omitting this criticism, appears in *Conservatism, 1945–50*, CPC, London, October 1950.

27. *Design for Freedom*, London, February 1947, p. 12.

28. Peter Thorneycroft and Lady Rhys Williams, *Design for Survival*, London, September 1947.

29. *About the Industrial Charter*, pp. 6 and 10. The reply, *What We Think* (About the Industrial Charter), London, June 1948, suggests that the opposition to Butler's formulation was not great.

30. Speech at Blenheim Park, August 1947.

31. Letter, *The Economist*, 30 August 1947, p. 358.

32. cf. Orr-Ewing, 1947 Party Conference *Report*, London, 1947, p. 47.

33. *The Economist*, 29 November 1947, p. 865; cf. also ibid., 1 November 1947, p. 705.

34. Eden at Sheffield, 19 April 1948, reported in *Notes on Current Politics*, 10, 17 May 1948, p. 5.

35. *Debs.*, 12 February 1948, 447/679.

36. *Debs.*, 12 April 1948, 449/631–8.

37. *Design for Wages*, London, 1948; cf. also Spearman, *Debs.*, 27 October 1948, 457/171; also Thorneycroft's *Design For Living*, London, 1949.
38. *The Times*, 11 March 1949.
39. 1949 Party Conference *Report*, London, 1949, p. 123.
40. R. K. Law, *Return from Utopia*, London, 1950, p. 80. For an academic anti-planning case, cf. John Jewkes, *Ordeal by Planning*, London, 1948.
41. *Debs.*, 2 November 1950, 480/320–1.
42. 1950 Party Conference *Report*, London, 1950, p. 109.
43. *Debs.*, 7 November 1950, 480/884.
44. *Debs.*, 27 April 1951, 487/705; cf. also, with Ted Leather, *A New Approach*, London, 1951, p. 11.
45. cf. T. E. Utley, *Essays in Conservatism*, London, 1949, or Aubrey Jones, *The Pendulum of Politics*, London, 1947, for not dissimilar views.
46. As argued by Quintin Hogg in *The Case for Conservatism*, London, 1947, or *The Conservative Case*, London, 1959, p. 52.
47. *Debs.*, 20 May 1946, 423/76.
48. cf. D. Clarke, *The Conservative Faith in a Modern Age*, London, April 1947; *The Right Road*, Part I; R. A. Butler, *About the Industrial Charter*, p. 16; *Design for Freedom*, London, February 1947, p. 19.
49. R. A. Butler, 'Conservative industrial policy', *Notes on Current Politics*, 9, 19 May 1947, p. 2; Anthony Eden, *Three Partners in Industry* (Speeches), London, 1946; cf. also Hinchingbrooke, *Debs.*, 15 November 1948, 458/114.
50. Clarke, op. cit.; Utley, op. cit. (Chapter 3, 'Conservative Economics'); Butler, 'Conservative industrial policy'; compare Lord Dunglass, *Onlooker*, April 1946, p. 5.
51. Butler, *Onlooker*, May 1946; Lyttelton, *Debs.*, 27 May 1946, 423/868.
52. Eccles, Speeches at Bradford, 21–2 June 1946, reprinted as *Conservatism after 1945*, London, 1946, especially p. 7; Hinchingbrooke, *Debs.*, 15 November 1948, 458/106; *The Right Road*, Part I(i); broadcast, Lord Woolton, 24 January 1948; Butler, 'Conservative industrial policy; Eden, Speech at Walthamstow, 1 August 1946, reprinted in *Freedom and Order*, London, 1947, p. 409.

53. Utley, op. cit. ('The Moral Basis of the State'); Hogg, op. cit.; R. A. Butler, *Fundamental Issues*, London, 1946, and *Onlooker*, May 1946, p. 3.
54. cf. Eccles, *Debs.*, 9 April 1946, 421/2041; and Hinchingbrooke, 7 April 1949, 463/2287.
55. *Essays*, p. 12.

CHAPTER 10

1. cf. *The Economist*, 12 April 1952, p. 78; 3 March 1952, p. 277; 17 May 1952, p. 422; also *The Sunday Times*, 16 June 1952.
2. *The Economist*, 13 February 1954, p. 439.
3. cf. the Conservative Manifesto, *United for Peace and Progress*, London, 1955; comments in *The Times*, 17 May 1955, *The Manchester Guardian*, 17 May 1955, *The Economist*, 7 May 1955; on the election, cf. D. E. Butler, *The British General Election of 1955*, London, 1955.
4. D. E. Butler and Richard Rose, *The British General Election of 1959*, London, 1960; also David Hennesy, 'The communication of Conservative policy, 1957–1959', *Political Quarterly*, 32/3, July-September 1961.
5. cf. for example, Henry Fairlie, 'Ten years of Tory rule', *Time and Tide*, 12 October 1961, p. 1680; for contrary conclusions, cf. *The Economist*, 25 December 1954, p. 1059, and 26 January 1952, p. 194.
6. cf. S. H. Beer, 'Pressure groups and parties in Britain', *American Political Science Review*, L/1, March 1956. Note his use of the term 'quasi-corporatism'.
7. cf. *The Times*, 5 November 1962, p. 7.
8. S. E. Finer, H. B. Berrington and D. J. Bartholomew, *Backbench Opinion in the House of Commons, 1955–1959*, Oxford, 1961, p. 85.
9. *One Nation*, London, October 1950; *Change is Our Ally*, London, May 1954; *The Responsible Society*, London, March 1959.
10. '. . . seeking not to convert them to the Conservative Party but to convince them that the Conservatives have an intelligent and valuable point of view', James Lemkin,

The Bow Group, *Objective*, No. 13, October 1952, p. 14.

11. *Crossbow*, New Year issue, 1958, p. 9; cf. also ibid., Autumn 1957, p. 3.

12. For example, T. E. Utley, in *The Daily Telegraph*, 18 February 1960; cf. also description by Richard Rose, 'The Bow Group's role in British politics', *Western Political Quarterly*, XIV/4, December 1961, p. 865.

13. cf. Julian Critchley, 'The intellectuals', *Political Quarterly*, 32/3, July–September 1961, p. 268; also, 'The affluent reformers', *New Statesman*, 3 February 1961, p. 169; 'Who is the cuckoo?', *The Times*, 6 February 1961.

14. For example, Dame Irene Ward, *Debs.*, 18 April 1956, 551/1111; Cyril Osborne, ibid., 1243; T. L. Iremonger, ibid., 1287; Nigel Fisher, ibid., 1268; Brigadier O. L. Prior-Palmer, 6 November 1956, 560/64; H. A. Price, 12 February 1957, 564/1159.

15. For a more general examination of conference agendas, cf. Richard Rose, 'Who are the Tory militants?', *Crossbow*, Autumn, 1961, p. 35; on the culmination of the campaign on Schedule 'A' tax, cf. W. J. Biffen, 'Party conference and party policy', *Political Quarterly*, 32/3, July–September 1961, p. 257.

16. For example, The Middle Class Alliance, formed by Conservative MP Henry Price, June 1956; and The People's League for the Defence of Freedom which contested the East Ham by-election in May 1958, receiving 12·2 per cent of the votes. T. E. Utley answers some of the criticisms made, in *The Conservatives and the Critics*, London, October 1956; cf. also his reference to the 'South Kensington Revolution' in *Not Guilty*, London, May 1957.

17. For example, cf. Butler's speech at Meriden, 30 June 1956, reported in *Notes on Current Politics*, 16 July 1956, p. 2.

18. Macmillan, Committee Stage of the debate on the Finance Bill, 25 June 1956; Oliver Poole (chairman of the party organization), 'Yes, I am angry with some Tories', *Daily Mail*, 19 June 1956, and speech at Ditchingham Hall, Bungay, Suffolk, reprinted London, 1956, and closing

speech, 1956 Party Conference *Report*, London, 1956, p. 121. For a more general discussion of the 'revolt', cf. four articles by R. Goold-Adams, *The Sunday Times*, 30 March to 27 April 1958.

CHAPTER 11

1. For a sophisticated account of this, cf. F. W. Paish, *Studies in an Inflationary Economy*, London, 1962.
2. cf. also F. W. Paish, 'Inflation in the United Kingdom, 1948–1957', memorandum to the Cohen Committee, November 1957, republished in *Studies in an Inflationary Economy*.
3. Otto Kahn-Freund, 'Labour law', in Morris Ginsberg (ed.), *Law and Opinion in England in the Twentieth Century*, London, 1959, p. 224.
4. cf. D. F. Macdonald, *The State and the Trade Unions*, London, 1960, p. 153; and T. E. Utley, 'The great soft centre', *Crossbow*, I/1, Autumn 1957, p. 15.
5. V. L. Allen, *Trade Unions and the Government*, London, 1960, pp. 64–5; various concessions were made to the unions; for an account of these, cf. L. D. Epstein, 'The politics of British Conservatism', *American Political Science Review*, March 1954, p. 47; the concessions included an 'Excess Profits Levy', discussed by Andrew Shonfield, *British Economic Policy since the War*, London, 1958, p. 181.
6. *Debs.*, 3 March 1954, 524/1220; cf. also Barbara Wootton, *The Social Foundations of Wages Policy*, London, 1955, p. 91.
7. Butler, *Debs.*, 17 March 1952, 497/2057; and speech to the NJAC, 15 May 1952.
8. Ralph Assheton, *Debs.*, 12 March 1952, 497/1417.
9. cf. comment in *The Economist*, 2 August 1952, p. 274.
10. *The Economist*, 19 December 1953, p. 864.
11. V. L. Allen, op. cit., p. 98, and *The Economist*, ibid.
12. Cmd. 9084, para 147; cf. also, Cmd. 9085, reports on the disputes in shipbuilding and in engineering, February 1954.
13. Sir Walter Monckton, *Debs.*, 3 March 1954, 524/1314/7.
14. H. A. Watkinson, speech at Buxton, 11 March 1954.
15. Monckton, *Debs.*, 3 March 1954, 524/1317.

16. Cmd. 9352.
17. cf. comments in *The Times*, 9 January 1955; *The Economist*, 8 January 1955, p. 88.
18. Watkinson, *Debs.*, 23 June 1955, 542/1624.
19. *Debs.*, 26 October 1955, 545/202.
20. Statement, British Employers' Confederation, 14 March 1956; cf. H. A. Clegg and R. Adams, *The Employer's Challenge*, Oxford, 1957, p. 54.
21. *The Problem of Rising Prices*, OEEC, Paris, 1961, p. 440.
22. *Report* on a dispute in the shipbuilding industry, Cmd. 160, para 54.
23. Iain Macleod, 20 June 1957, to the 40th session of the International Labour Organization, Geneva; cf. also his speech at East Ham, 20 May 1957, and Amory, to the American Bankers' Association, London, 7 May 1957.
24. *Debs.*, 25 July 1957, 574/650.
25. *Debs.*, 29 October 1957, 575/50.
26. ibid., 56.
27. *Debs.*, 30 October 1957, 575/340.
28. Speech by the Minister of Health, *Debs.*, 6 November 1957, 577/231.
29. *First Report of the Council on Prices, Productivity and Incomes*, London, February 1958; for criticisms, cf. G. D. N. Worswick and Thomas Balogh, *Oxford Economic Papers*, June 1958.
30. cf. the Minister's explanation, *Debs.*, 8 May 1958, 587/1440; press comments on the rail award, *The Daily Telegraph* and *Daily Express*, 16 May 1958; *Financial Times*, 17 May, and *The Sunday Times*, 18 May 1958; on the miners' settlement, cf. *The Economist*, 27 September 1958, p. 1008.
31. *Debs.*, 8 May 1958, 587/1461.
32. The Minister's speech, ibid., 1422.
33. *Debs.*, 18 April 1956, 551/1087.
34. Sir Iain Horobin, *Debs.*, 25 July 1957, 574/706; G. B. Craddock (who attributed the figure to Lord Chandos), 23 January 1958, 580/1324.
35. *Debs.*, 29 October 1957, 575/92.
36. On a Workers' Charter, cf. 1958 Party Conference *Report*,

London, 1958, p. 53; the Ministry of Labour's statement was *Positive Employment Policies, Examples of Management Practice Contributing to Good Relations in Industry*, April 1958; the Institute of Directors had issued a similar statement, *Understanding Labour Relations*, with an introduction by the Institute's president, Lord Chandos. On a capital gains tax, cf. D. Ovens, *Crossbow*, New Year 1958, p. 14.

37. cf. Nigel Birch's interpretation of the resignations, *Debs.*, 26 November 1959, 614/630.
38. *Debs.*, 7 February 1961, 634/283.
39. *Debs.*, 25 July 1961, 645/221.
40. ibid., 229.
41. *Debs.*, 23 October 1961, 646/625.
42. 20 May 1962, p. 11.
43. For example, J. Driscoll, *A National Wages Policy*, London, September 1955, p. 1; or M. Shanks, 'Towards a wages policy', *Crossbow*, Autumn 1958, p. 61.
44. *Debs.*, 26 July 1961, 645/457; cf. also Julian Ridsdale, 23 October 1961, 646/638; Maurice Macmillan, 18 July 1961, 644/1146.
45. *Debs.*, 15 April 1964, 693/477.
46. cf. graph opposite. The actual economic effects of Government policy are unclear.
47. November 1962, p. 545; cf. also, 1 February 1964, p. 392.
48. cf. letter from the Chairman of the National Association of Port Employers, *The Times*, 22 May 1962, p. 6; cf. also Henry Smith, *The Wage Fixers*, London, 1962.
49. 27 May 1961, p. 870.
50. For example, cf. resolutions 208–9 and 217, 1957 Party Conference *Agenda*, pp. 77–82; G. Fletcher-Cooke, *Liberty in the Modern State*, CPC, London, January 1957, p. 69; John Ward, *Crossbow*, New Year 1958, p. 15; M. Shanks, ibid., Summer 1958, p. 8; resolutions 108, 111, 1960 Party Conference *Agenda*, pp. 62–5; Inns of Court Conservative Association, *A Giant's Strength*, London, 1958; successive issues of *Crossbow*, (e.g. G. Medd, Summer 1958; Geoffrey Howe, ibid., etc.); A. E. Cooper, *Debs.*, 4 April 1960, 621/85.
51. S. E. Finer, H. B. Berrington and D. J. Bartholomew,

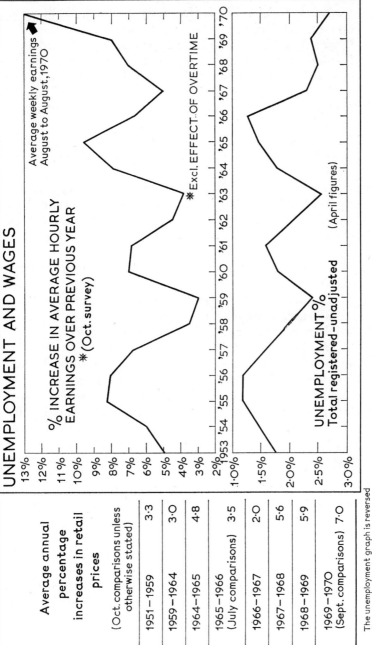

UNEMPLOYMENT AND WAGES

% INCREASE IN AVERAGE HOURLY
EARNINGS OVER PREVIOUS YEAR
* (Oct. survey)

Average weekly earnings
August to August, 1970

* Excl. EFFECT OF OVERTIME

UNEMPLOYMENT%
Total registered—unadjusted

(April figures)

Average annual percentage increases in retail prices (Oct. comparisons unless otherwise stated)	
1951–1959	3·3
1959–1964	3·0
1964–1965	4·8
1965–1966 (July comparisons)	3·5
1966–1967	2·0
1967–1968	5·6
1968–1969	5·9
1969–1970 (Sept. comparisons)	7·0

The unemployment graph is reversed

Source: The Financial Times, 11 November 1970, reproduced by kind permission.

Backbench Opinion in the House of Commons, 1955–1959,
Oxford, 1961, p. 124.

52. *Official Report* of the 76th Party Conference, Llandudno,
London, 1956, p. 85. Compare Kenneth Lewis on the
proposal for a contract: 'I hope the time will come when
strikes will be outlawed. Then justice and equity in industry
will be established by negotiation and adjudication', *Debs.*,
5 November 1962, 666/683.

53. For example, with the NJAC on first coming to office;
United for Peace and Progress, 1955, promised further discussions.

54. R. Gresham-Cooke, *Debs.*, 28 October 1958, 594/71, and
24 June 1960, 625/823; cf. also Eden, *Debs.*, 9 June 1955,
542/58; Boothby, 13 June 1955, 542/817; John Bevins,
speech at Leigh, Lancashire, 27 July 1957, reported in
Trade Union Bulletin, 117, August 1957.

55. cf. for example, Russell Lewis, *Industry and the Property-
Owning Democracy*, London, July 1954; also Maurice
Macmillan, speech, *Official Report* of the 1960 Party
Conference, London, 1960, p. 88.

56. Ministry of Labour, *Positive Employment Policies.*

57. Sir William Robson-Brown, *Debs.*, 14 February 1963, 671/
1550. For an academic comment, cf. Hilda Kahn's
Repercussions of Redundancy, London, 1964, p. 242: 'the
minima drawn by that measure (the Contracts of Employment Act) would seem excessively timid. It is questionable
whether a minimum period of notice of one or two weeks
can be regarded as conferring "status" on the worker in the
second half of the twentieth century, while it is unlikely to
lessen the both socially and economically harmful consequences of the fear of redundancy'.

58. cf. Chancellor's speech, *Debs.*, 3 April 1963, 675/454.

59. cf. Sir Toby Low, *Everyman a Capitalist*, London, April 1959;
Gresham-Cooke, *Debs.*, 24 June 1960, 625/827; Russell
Lewis, op. cit., p. 31; National Union speaker, *Official
Report* of the 1961 Party Conference, p. 60.

60. cf. for example, reply of the Economic Secretary to the
Treasury, *Debs.*, 24 June 1960, 625/823, and *Official Report*
of the 1961 Party Conference, p. 62.

61. Monckton, *Debs.*, 23 June 1955, 542/1526.
62. Sir John Barlow *et al.*, *Automation and the Consumer*, CPC, London, December 1956, p. 32.
63. At Stockton-on-Tees, 1 June 1957, reported in *The Times*, 2 June 1957.
64. For example, cf. resolution 179, 1956 Party Conference *Agenda*, p. 70; resolution 128, 1958 Party Conference *Agenda*, pp. 60–65; NJAC subcommittee report on human relations in industry, July 1954, and the Minister's Oral Answer, *Debs.*, 30 November 1960, 631/361.
65. In *The Director*, February 1962.
66. *Debs.*, 20 July 1953, 518/161.
67. *Debs.*, 20 January 1952, 495/323.
68. *Debs.*, 19 November 1958, 595/1216–17; cf. also Parliamentary Secretary, Ministry of Labour, 28 January 1955, 536/624, and 30 January 1952, 495/331.
69. Reinhard Bendix, *Work and Authority in Industry*, New York, 1963, p. 296.
70. Monckton, *Debs.*, 23 June 1955, 542/1527; Parliamentary Secretary, Ministry of Labour, 24 February 1956, 549/752.
71. Sir Halford Reddish, in *Prospect for Capitalism*, CPC, 191, London, 1958, p. 36.
72. *Automation and the Consumer*, p. 29.
73. For objections to joint consultation, for example, cf. G. B. Baldwin, *Beyond Nationalization: the later problems of British Coal*, Cambridge, Mass., 1955, p. 112; B. C. Roberts, *Trade Unions in a Free Society*, London, 1959, p. 56; also D. Ll. Davies, *Formal Consultation – in Practice*, London, 1959; on piecework payments systems, cf. Wilfred Brown, *Piecework Abandoned*, London, 1962.
74. The evidence during the period of Conservative Government was ambiguous, so much so that the Government might well have instituted an inquiry into the question if it had been serious. In 1966, the British Market Research Bureau undertook a survey for the London Stock Exchange which showed only $2\frac{1}{2}$ million personal direct investors on the stock exchange, a surprising conclusion in comparison to Conservative assumptions. Professor E. V. Morgan, *District Bank Review*, September 1967, derived a long-term

decline in personal share holding from the available figures; cf. also Michael Blanden, 'A decline of grass-roots capitalism in the U.K.', *Financial Times*, 26 November 1969.

75. Professor Burn notes in the 'Conservative tradition and its reformulation' (in Morris Ginsberg, ed., *Law and Opinion in England in the Twentieth Century*, London, 1959) that increasingly modest claims were made for 'property' and less and less effort devoted to its defence; in Hailsham's *The Case for Conservatism*, London, 1947, only six pages are devoted to the subject, pp. 97–102; for a justification of property, cf. Michael Fraser, 'The ownership of property', in *The Good Society*, 7, Oxford lectures, London, 1953.

CHAPTER 12

1. On the ownership prerogatives of Parliament, cf. Assheton, *Debs.*, 8 February 1954, 523/859 and I. J. Pitman, ibid., 903.
2. *Debs.*, 27 October 1959, 612/529.
3. Proposals for this purpose were not lacking – cf. I. M. D. Little on coal pricing in *Critique of Welfare Economics*, Oxford, 1958, Chapter XI, and *The Price of Fuel*, Oxford, 1953; also J. R. Sargent, *British Transport Policy*, Oxford, 1958; F. Cassell, 'Pricing policies in the nationalised industries', *Lloyds Bank Review*, October 1956; G. Walker, 'Competition in transport as an instrument of policy', *Economic Journal*, September 1956.
4. See the discussion in W. A. Robson, *Nationalised Industries and Public Ownership*, 2nd ed., London, 1962, p. 74; and Reuben Kelf-Cohen, *Nationalisation in Britain* (*The End of a Dogma*), 2nd ed., London, 1961, p. 166.
5. The creation of the new Select Committee was delayed 13 months, from 8 February 1954 to 16 March 1955; the original report was made on 23 July 1953.
6. cf. Prime Minister, *Debs.*, 10 May 1956, Oral Answers, 552/1417, and 29 November 1956, 561/590.
7. Kelf-Cohen, op cit., p. 185.
8. Compare the view of Lord Swinton, HOL *Debs.*, 12 March 1953, 180/1504, and paras. 495–6 of the 'Herbert', Report

Report of an Inquiry into the Electricity Supply Industry, Cmd. 9672, 1956.

9. Andrew Shonfield describes the rise in coal prices of July 1955 as a 'spectacular triumph' for 'doctrinal economic liberalism' and 'an act of bravado', cf., *British Economic Policy since the War*, London, 1958, pp. 226–7; for Conservative complaints against the price increases, cf. 1956 Party Conference *Agenda*, resolutions 286–8, 290, 293, 296, 301, and 308.

10. For example, in pursuit of the 1956 'plateau' policy, a proposed fare increase sanctioned by the Transport Tribunal was halved by the Government. Electricity boards were asked not to increase tariffs during the year. cf. John Hughes, *Nationalised Industries in the Mixed Economy*, London, October 1960.

11. For example, the 1955 crisis prompted the Government to postpone parts of the capital programme of public industry (cf. Chancellor's statement, *Debs.*, 25 July 1955, 544/826), and check closely plans covering other aspects of nationalized industries (Chancellor, *Debs.*, 26 October 1955, 545/202). In 1957 efforts were made to 'freeze' capital expenditure in the public sector for two years at its 1957 level (cf. Chancellor, *Debs.*, 29 October 1957, 575/46).

12. cf. *Debs.*, 17 April 1956, 551/852, and Committee Stage of the Finance Bill, 13 June 1956; cf. also 12 March 1958, 584/441, debate on extending Section 42 of the 1956 Finance Act.

13. *Public Investment in Britain*, Cmd. 1203, November 1960.

14. cf. also, Chancellor's statement, *Debs.*, 9 November 1960, 629/1057-8; *Government Expenditure Below the Line*, Cmd. 1338, April 1961, and *Public Investment in Great Britain*, Cmd. 1849, 1962, and *Debs.*, 27 November 1962, 668/214.

15. Duncan Burn, *The Steel Industry, 1939–59*, London, 1961, p. 153.

16. The intention to denationalize was announced on 6 November 1951 (*Debs.*, 493/53) but proposals were not published until July 1952 (*The Iron and Steel Industry*, Cmd. 8619), and debated on 23 October (*Debs.*, 505/1274); the second reading of the bill was on 25 November (*Debs.*,

508/266). cf. press comments – *The Times*, *The Manchester Guardian*, *The Daily Telegraph*, 29 July 1952, and *The Economist*, 2 August 1952, p. 296.

17. Note the question by G. Chetwynd, *Debs.*, 23 October 1952, 505/1285.
18. Burn, op. cit., p. 365.
19. *Debs.*, 29 January 1953, 510/1257.
20. ibid., 1269–70.
21. Burn, op. cit., p. 367.
22. *Debs.*, 13 January 1953, 510/1213.
23. *Debs.*, 27 June 1960, 625/1500.
24. *Debs.*, 29 January 1963, 670/759.
25. cf. the Minister's statement, *Debs.*, 17 November 1952, 507/1414.
26. Parliamentary Secretary to the Minister of Transport, *Debs.*, 1 November 1954, 532/39 *passim*; cf. the Transport Commission's *Reorganisation Scheme*, Cmd. 9191, July 1954.
27. *Modernisation and Re-equipment of British Railways*, British Transport Commission, 25 January 1955. cf. *Debs.*, 3 February 1955, 536/1280.
28. cf. *Debs.*, 21 May 1952, 501/482.
29. ibid., 516.
30. Geoffrey Wilson, *Debs.*, 1 November 1954, 523/75; cf. also Sir David Robertson, ibid., 87.
31. *Debs.*, 3 February 1955, 536/1328.
32. *Debs.*, 11 July 1955, 543/1654.
33. *Debs.*, 3 February 1955, 536/1351; cf. also David Renton, ibid., 1366.
34. *Debs.*, 3 December 1956, 561/897.
35. *Debs.*, cf. Minister's speech, 11 December 1958, 597/514. For a critical discussion, cf. also R. Molesworth, 'Railways at a profit', *Crossbow*, Summer 1958, p. 53.
36. cf. Cmd. 813, July 1959, and *Debs.*, 29 July 1959, 610/530.
37. *Debs.*, 10 March 1960, 619/647.
38. The chairman of the committee was Sir Ivan Stedeford (managing director and chairman of Tube Investments), and the members: the managing director of Courtaulds, the technical director of ICI (Dr Beeching), a partner of a

firm of Chartered Accountants, and a Government representative.

39. cf. its report, HOC 254, July 1960.
40. 29 October 1960, p. 483; cf. the Minister's speech, *Debs.*, 26 October 1960, 627/2358.
41. Kelf-Cohen, op. cit., p. 210; cf. the Chancellor's statement, *Debs.*, 4 April 1960, 621/49.
42. *The Reorganisation of the Nationalised Transport Undertakings*, Cmd. 1248, December 1960.
43. *Debs.*, 30 January 1961, 633/615.
44. cf. John Peyton, ibid., 680.
45. ibid., 646. cf. also the unpopularity of closing 'uneconomic' lines, *Debs.*, 20 December 1963, 686/1634.
46. Dr Beeching of ICI, and Mr P. H. Shirley of Unilevers; for comments, cf. *Debs.*, 15 March 1961, 636/1400 and 637/223; W. A. Robson, op. cit., p. iv; *The Times*, 29 November 1962, p. 8; cf. Minister's statement on the proposals, *Debs.*, 27 March 1963, 674/1319. More generally, cf. Anthony Lines, *Concerns of State*, Bow Group, London, October 1961, pp. 52–69.
47. cf. Chancellor's speech, *Debs.*, 14 March 1964, 693/239.
48. *Report of the Committee of Inquiry on National Policy for the Use of Fuel and Power Resources*, Cmd. 8646, 1952.
49. *Debs.*, 9 July 1954, 529/2512; cf. also 28 October 1952, 505/1749; for complaints on electricity pricing, cf. Economic Commission for Europe, *Report on European Coal*, March 1952, and for criticisms of the Ridley Report, I. M. D. Little, *The Price of Fuel*.
50. Sir A. N. Braithwaite and Hinchingbrooke, *Debs.*, 9 July 1954, 529/2512 *passim*.
51. ibid., 2529.
52. ibid., 2543.
53. For example, Gerald Nabarro, *Debs.*, 28 October 1952, 505/1795; cf. also, resolution 289, 1956 Party Conference *Agenda*, p. 90.
54. cf. resolution 233, 1955 Party Conference *Agenda*, p. 84, and resolution 298, 1956 Party Conference *Agenda*, p. 91; the campaign led by Nabarro during the readings of the

1956 Electricity Bill, *Debs.*, 17 December 1956, 562/938; resolution opposing the sale of appliances by nationalized industry showrooms, seconded by Nabarro, 1958 Central Council meeting, *1958 Annual Report* of the Conservative party, p. 24.

55. *Report on the Supply of Insulated Electrical Wire and Cables*, HOC 209, Monopolies Commission, 1956.

56. *Debs.*, 17 December 1956, 562/949.

57. *Debs.*, 27 January 1959, 598/70. The Government also committed its successors' public expenditure similarly by publishing a plan up to 1967–8, cf. Cmd. 2235, December 1963.

58. ibid., 98.

59. *Debs.*, 18 February 1959; cf. comment in *The Economist*, 21 February 1959, 'p. 709; for a neo-Liberal discussion of the electricity supply industry, cf. One Nation, *Change is our Ally*, London, 1954, and Anthony Lines, op. cit.

60. *Debs.*, 29 November 1963, 685/652.

61. cf. J. H. H. Skeet, ibid., 696, and Charles Doughty, 710.

62. In order, cf.:
    (i) resolutions 45–61, 1953 Party Conference *Agenda*, and *Official Report* of the 1953 Party Conference, p. 56 *passim*; resolution 231, 1955 Party Conference *Agenda*; resolutions 1, 11, 13, 14, 20, 24, 27, 29, 33, 47, 1957 Party Conference *Agenda*; resolutions 224–5, 230, 1958 Party Conference *Agenda*.
    (ii) resolutions 230–2, 1958 Party Conference *Agenda*; resolution 383, 1960 Party Conference *Agenda*.
    (iii) cf. report of the 1952 Central Council meeting in *The Times*, 22 March 1952, p. 3; resolutions 49–50, 1953 Party Conference *Agenda*.
    (iv) cf. citations in (i) above, plus resolutions 227–42, 1955 Party Conference *Agenda*; resolutions 381–2, 1960 Party Conference *Agenda*; cf. also Geoffrey Howe, 'Towards a more vital party conference', *Crossbow*, Summer 1958, p. 26.

63. *Official Report* of the 1953 Party Conference, p. 56.

64. *Debs.*, 12 March 1958, 584/460; also 15 April 1957, 568/1651; and 9 November 1960, 629/1112.

65. ibid., 15 April 1957, 1610; cf. also 10 November 1960, 629/1307; and D. Price, 23 January 1958, 580/1354.
66. *Report of the Advisory Committee on Organisation*, National Coal Board, London, 1955, p. 3; Dr Fleck, chairman of the committee, was also chairman of ICI.
67. The Minister's statement, *Debs.*, 24 October 1961, 649/766.
68. *Debs.*, 25 October 1954, 531/1676.
69. cf. Conservative backbench contributions, *Debs.*, 4 May 1959, 605/45, *passim*, and 23 July 1959, 609/1543 *passim*.
70. *Debs.*, 15 December 1959, 615/1232; cf. also Tony Lucking, *Wings over Westminster*, Bow Group, February 1959, and John Seekings, 'Britannia waives the rules', *Crossbow*, Summer 1959, p. 126.
71. 23 June 1962, p. 1234.

CHAPTER 13

1. Introduction, *Prospect for Capitalism*, CPC 191, London, October 1958.
2. For some classification of the links, cf. S. E. Finer. 'The political power of private capital', *Sociological Review*, Vol. III, 2.
3. J. D. Stewart, *British Pressure Groups, Their Role in Relationship to the House of Commons*, Oxford, 1958, p. 8.
4. S. H. Beer, 'Pressure groups and parties in Britain', *American Political Science Review*, L/1, March 1956, pp. 6–7.
5. *Debs.*, 20 April 1953, 514/671.
6. cf. Watkinson's discussion of this, *Debs.*, 10 April 1952, 498/3067.
7. PEP, *Industrial Trade Associations*, London, 1957, pp. 42–3.
8. Basil de Ferranti, *Debs.*, 2 November 1960, 629/201.
9. It demonstrated outside the 1960 Party Conference (cf. report in *The Guardian*, 12 October 1960); some saw in it the embryo of a British 'Poujadism'.
10. Very little on small business was published by Conservatives, but cf. T. Smith *et al.*, *Outlook for Small Business*, London, January 1961; cf. also Francis Boyd, *The Guardian*, 11 January 1961, also ibid., 19 May 1960. The Resale

Price Bill received its third reading on 1 May 1964, *Debs.*, 695/472.

11. cf. those given in *Debs.*, 6 May 1959, 605/55; 16 June 1959, 607/242; 25 February 1960, 618/68; 31 March 1960, 620/156. On payments to farmers 1951–9, cf. *Debs.*, 22 February 1960, 618/22, and Gavin McCrone, *The Economics of Subsidising Agriculture*, London, 1962.

12. 15 October 1960, p. 266.

13. *Debs.*, 30 April 1958, 587/423 *passim*.

14. Hinchingbrooke, ibid., 429.

15. *Debs.*, 9 November 1959, 613/31 *passim*.

16. ibid., 95.

17. ibid., 146.

18. cf. *Debs.*, 4 February 1963, 671/43; cf. criticisms by J. C. Rodgers, 88, and Sir John Gilmour, 55; Scottish Council, *Industry and Employment in Scotland*, London, November 1961 and complaints from Durham, reported in *The Economist*, 8 April 1961, p. 105.

19. *Debs.*, 26 March 1952, 498/628; cf. also Anthony Fell, ibid., 667.

20. *Debs.*, 9 March 1955, 538/464.

21. cf. Nelson and Colne, and Patwen, resolutions 10–11, 1955 Party Conference *Agenda*, p. 46, and resolution 12 from Clitheroe, ibid., p. 47; cf. also Nelson and Colne amendment to the resolution debated, seconded by Cheadle, *Official Report* of the 1955 Party Conference, pp. 33–7.

22. The representative for Nelson and Colne, *Official Report* of the 1957 Party Conference, p. 71; cf. also resolutions 345–6 by Accrington and Nelson and Colne, 1956 Party Conference *Agenda*, pp. 100–1.

23. President of the Board of Trade, *Debs.*, 30 June 1958, 590/894.

24. 5 July 1958, p. 10.

25. For example, Sir John Barlow, *Debs.*, 30 June 1958, 590/923; Richard Stanley, ibid., 914. See also resolutions 164–6 (Nelson and Colne, Blackburn, Middleton and Prestwich), 1958 Party Conference *Agenda*, and the Nelson and Colne amendment, *Official Report*, 1958 Party Conference, pp. 60–2.

26. *Debs.*, ibid., 980.
27. *Debs.*, 28 October 1958, 594/32.
28. *Debs.*, 4 November 1958, 594/786.
29. *Debs.*, 4 June 1959, 606/376; cf. *The Reorganisation of the Cotton Industry*, Cmd. 744, 13 May 1959.
30. cf. *Textile Weekly*, organ of the National Federation of Textile Works Managers' Associations, 13 February 1959.
31. *Debs.*, 4 June 1959, 606/384.
32. ibid., 427.
33. ibid., 464.
34. cf. report of the Harrogate Cotton Board Conference in 1961, *The Times*, 16 October 1961, p. 5; also the Rochdale resolution, 208, 1961 Party Conference *Agenda*, p. 40.
35. Chairman of Fine Spinners, one of the three employer members of the Cotton Board, reported in *The Economist*, 28 October 1961, p. 361.
36. For example, 'The case for letting cotton stew', *The Observer*, 20 May 1962; cf. reply by the Director General of the Cotton Board, ibid., 27 May 1962 and 10 June 1962, p. 5.
37. Letter, *The Times*, 14 June 1962; cf. correspondence in the rest of June on this issue.
38. *Debs.*, 1 July 1963, 680/110; cf. also 13 February 1963, 671/1443 and report of the Cotton Board Conference, *The Economist*, 26 October 1963, p. 393.
39. cf. *Debs.*, 17 June 1957, 573/1380; Gerald Nabarro, 9 November 1960, 629/1112; and 24 July 1963, 681/1680.
40. *The Supply of Military Aircraft*, 19 December 1956.
41. Guy Hadley, *The Making of Aircraft*, London, February 1961, p. 13; for Commons discussions, cf. *Debs.*, 13 May 1958, 588/226; 22 May 1958, 588/1498; 16 July 1959, 609/595; 20 July 1959, 609/949.
42. *Debs.*, 15 February 1960, 617/967–61.
43. Keith Hartley, 'The mergers in the United Kingdom aircraft industry, 1957–60', *Journal of the Royal Aeronautical Society*, 69/660, December 1965, p. 848.
44. *Debs.*, 29 April 1959, 604/1253; Anthony Fell, 30 January 1961, 633/93; Paul Williams, 1 May 1961, 639/956; cf. also discussion, 2 August 1961, 645/1467.

45. *The Guardian*, 24 March 1961.
46. *Debs.*, 1 May 1961, 639/945.
47. cf. Minister's statement, *Debs.*, 19 October 1961, 646/334.
48. *Debs.*, 15 January 1964, 687/232.
49. ibid., 237.
50. cf. One Nation, *Change is our Ally*, London, 1954; Russell Lewis, *Crossbow*, New Year 1962, p. 9, or Nicholas Garth, ibid., p. 19.
51. cf. *Annual Report*, BISF, London, 1957, pp. 35–6, and Duncan Burn, *The Steel Industry, 1939–59*, London, 1961, pp. 614–15.
52. cf. *Debs.*, 18 July 1957, 573/1365; 31 July 1958, 592/1722; Prime Minister's statement, 18 November 1958, 595/1016.
53. *Debs.*, 18 February 1960, 617/1443.
54. *Debs.*, 28 March 1960, 620/981.
55. *Debs.*, 18 February 1960, 617/1476; cf. also John Peyton, ibid., 1461, and Hinchingbrooke, 1584.
56. ibid., 1559.
57. cf. H. H. Wilson, *Pressure Group*, London, 1961.
58. *Debs.*, 3 November 1959, 612/891.
59. A point made by Basil de Ferranti, *Debs.*, 2 November 1960, 629/201; a similar view was attributed to Lord Chandos by *The Economist*, 25 April 1959, p. 356.
60. President of the Board of Trade, reported in *The Observer*, 3 December 1961.
61. *Debs.*, 10 November 1960, 629/1307.
62. *Debs.*, 20 March 1956, 550/1060.
63. Between 1956, when the report on British Oxygen was made, and 1962, the company's share of the British market fell from 98 to 95 per cent. More generally, cf. Sir David Cairns, 'Monopolies and restrictive practices', in Morris Ginsberg (ed.), *Law and Opinion in England in the Twentieth Century*, London, 1959, p. 173.
64. cf. the revised agreement of the Motor Traders' Association, reported in *The Economist*, 25 April 1959, p. 356.
65. cf. J. B. Heath, 'Freer prices – What progress?', *The Banker*, February 1960, and his 'The restrictive Trade Court on competition and price restriction', *The Manchester School of Economic and Social Studies*, January 1960.

REFERENCES

66. *Debs.*, 10 July 1953, 517/1611 and 1644 respectively.
67. 18 July 1953, p. 155.
68. *Report on Collective Discrimination,* Monopolies and Restrictive Trade Practices Commission, Cmd. 9504, 1955.
69. For example: (i) to strengthen the Bill, resolutions 251–6, 1955 Party Conference *Agenda,* pp. 87–8, and *Official Report* of the 1955 Party Conference, p. 106; (ii) to weaken it, cf. statements of the National Union of Manufacturers and the ABCC, reported in *The Economist,* 29 October 1955.
70. *The Observer,* 21 January 1962.
71. Speech to an American Chamber of Commerce luncheon, 10 January 1962.
72. *Debs.*, 10 March 1964, 691/255; cf. also 17 January 1964, 687/580.
73. *Debs.*, 6 July 1964, 698/36 (Debate on the White Paper, *Monopolies, Mergers and Restrictive Practices,* Cmd. 2299, March 1964); cf. also 14 November 1963, 684/326.
74. *Debs.*, 6 July 1964, 698/63 and 131.
75. *Jungle or Cloister,* Macmillan lecture to the Institute of Engineers and Shipbuilders, Glasgow, April 1962, reported in *The Times,* 11 April 1962.
76. 21 April 1962, pp. 263–4.

CHAPTER 14

1. cf. M. Abramowitz and V. F. Eliasberg, *The Growth of Public Employment in Great Britain,* Princeton, N.J., 1957, pp. 40–3.
2. A. T. Peacock and J. Wiseman, *The Growth of Public Expenditure in the United Kingdom,* London, 1961.
3. The case that the level of public expenditure directly caused inflation did not receive much airing until late in the period – cf. Selwyn Lloyd's resignation, and speech, *Debs.*, 8 April 1963, 675/921; cf. also the strange revival of the case on the return of the Conservatives in 1970, for example, the Wolverhampton speech of Enoch Powell reported in *The Times,* 7 January 1971.
4. Andrew Shonfield, *British Economic Policy since the War,* London, 1958, p. 182.

5. cf. F. W. Paish, *Studies in an Inflationary Economy*, London, 1962, pp. 80–1; on taxation, cf. introduction to G. D. N. Worswick and P. Ady, *The British Economy, 1945–50*, London, 1952; cf. comment in Enoch Powell, *Savings in a Free Society*, London, 1960, p. 134; also Bow Group, *Taxes for Today*, London, March 1958; and S. P. Chambers, *Prospect for Capitalism*, CPC 191, October 1958, p. 20.

6. David Howell, 'Our over-mixed economy', *Crossbow*, Summer 1961, p. 45.

7. cf. 'Policy Pointers' III, p. 31, and Geoffrey Howe, 'Towards a more vital party conference', *Crossbow*, Summer 1958, p. 86; John Chown, 'The use of capital', ibid., Summer 1959, p. 16.

8. cf. Editorial, ibid., Autumn 1961, p. 6.

9. David Howell, op. cit., p. 45.

10. *Debs.*, 31 October 1955, 545/736.

11. *Debs.*, 17 April 1958, 586/404.

12. *Debs.*, 18 November 1955, 546/924; cf. also 17 March 1952, 499/2022; 29 July 1952, 504/1339; also, for example, Julian Amery, 26 March 1952, 498/26; Antony Fell, ibid., 667; Wentworth Schofield, 4 November 1952, 507/58; A. V. Harvey, ibid., 690; Nigel Fisher, ibid., 860; Julian Amery, 10 November 1952, 507/829; Sir Charles Taylor, 18 November 1955, 546/915; R. H. Turton, 1 November 1960, 629/259.

13. cf. *The Banker*, January 1953.

14. 20 December 1952.

15. cf. D. B. Kenen, *British Monetary Policy and the Balance of Payments, 1951–1957*, Cambridge, Mass., 1960, *passim*.

16. 5 March 1956.

17. 16 July 1961, p. 2.

18. 'This statement is slightly heretical from a Conservative writer'; Peter Thorneycroft, *Not Unanimous*, London, 1960, p. 7.

19. L. C. B. Gower, in Morris Ginsberg (ed.), *Law and Opinion in England in the Twentieth Century*, London, 1959, p. 156, and Kenen, op. cit., p. 199.

20. Kenen, op. cit., pp. 42, 163, and 199; cf. also Paish, op. cit., p. 147.

21. In *Prospect for Capitalism*, CPC 191, October 1958, p. 19.
22. *Debs.*, 7 November 1951, 493/207; cf. also 29 January 1952, 495/40 and 11 March 1952, 497/1269.
23. April 1952, p. 183; but there were proposals simultaneously for an incomes policy even then: cf. the letter of Noel Newsome on Harry Ferguson's proposals of mid-1952, *The Times*, 12 March 1966.
24. *The Economist*, 24 January 1953, p. 228.
25. *Debs.*, 14 April 1953, 514/62.
26. 28 May 1954, London; cf. also speech, 14 May 1954, Sheffield.
27. cf. *The Banker* and *Lloyds Bank Review*, April 1956.
28. *Debs.*, 19 April 1955, 540/40.
29. *Debs.*, 20 February 1956, 549/41.
30. *Report of an Inquiry into the Working of the Monetary System*, Cmd. 827, August 1959. cf. also, *Debs.*, 26 November 1959, 614/574.
31. ibid., 650.
32. *Debs.*, 28 October 1959, 612/266.
33. ibid., 330.
34. *Debs.*, 11 July 1960, 626/1017.
35. 24 June 1961, p. 1342.
36. Thomas Wilson, 'Planning and growth', *Crossbow*, New Year 1962, Supplement No. 3.
37. cf. pp. 133–4.
38. John Brunner, 'The debate on economic growth; the dash for planning', *The Listener*, 10 May 1962, p. 817.
39. As was the National Joint Production Advisory Council for Industry; cf. comment by V. L. Allen, *Trade Unions and the Government*, London, 1960, pp. 35–6.
40. *Debs.*, 9 July 1954, 529/2543.
41. For example, R. A. Butler, *Debs.*, 29 January 1952, 495/61, or 29 July 1952, 504/1282.
42. To the NJAC, May 1954.
43. To the Party Conference, 1954, cf. *Official Report*, p. 66; repeated in *United for Peace and Progress*, CUCO, London, 1955, and *The Next Five Years*, CUCO, London, 1959.
44. cf. speech, 18 September 1954, reprinted in *The New*

Conservatism, London, 1955, pp. 63–5; and *Official Report* of the 1956 Party Conference, p. 74.

45. *Debs.*, 17 April 1956, 551/869.

46. *Debs.*, 29 October 1957, 575/55.

47. *Debs.*, 13 June 1955, 542/809; 21 February 1956, 548/2665; cf. also 3 July 1956, 555/1233.

48. *Debs.*, 28 October 1955, 545/583.

49. *Debs.*, 10 June 1955, 542/186.

50. For example, Spearman, *Debs.*, 20 May 1956, 550/1068; John Arbuthnot, 10 April 1957, 568/1178; Geoffrey Stevens, ibid., 1342.

51. For example, Sir James Henderson-Stewart, *Debs.*, 3 June 1959, 606/242, and 9 November 1959, 613/245.

52. *Debs.*, 9 November 1959, 613/127.

53. cf. Andrew Shonfield in *The Observer*, 15 January 1961; compare Nigel Birch's attitude to the long-term plans of Electricity Supply, *Debs.*, 27 January 1959, 598/70.

54. cf. letters by Lionel Fraser, an investment banker (4 January 1961 and 27 June 1961); Hugh Weeks, a company director active in the FBI (4 January 1961); W. Wallace and L. H. Trimby (20 January 1961); the survey of growth was by PEP, *Growth in the British Economy*, London, 1960.

55. Chancellor, speech, Leeds, 27 January 1961, reported in *Notes on Current Politics*, No. 12, 19 June 1961, p. 16; cf. also *Debs.*, 9 November 1960, 629/1343 (and comment by 'Beau Giles', *Crossbow*, New Year 1961, p. 51), and Chancellor's speech to the Liverpool Chamber of Commerce, 10 January 1961, reported in *The Guardian*, 11 January 1961, p. 18.

56. cf. *Debs.*, 6 February 1961, 634/52.

57. *Debs.*, 25 July 1961, 645/439; cf. also 18 July 1961, 644/1083.

58. *Debs.*, 27 July 1961, 645/723; cf. also Harold Macmillan, *The Middle Way: Twenty Years After*, London, 1958.

59. Economic editor, *The Observer*, 27 August 1961, p. 7.

60. cf. the amendment to the debated resolution, *Official Report* of the 1961 Party Conference, p. 90.

61. *Debs.*, 31 October 1961, 648/830.

62. *Financial Times*, 24 October 1961.
63. *The Economist*, 2 December 1961, p. 875.
64. Political Correspondent, *The Observer*, 14 January 1962, p. 11; cf. also 11 March 1962.
65. *Our Way Ahead*, London, 1956, p. 10.
66. The terms, *Anteilsystem* and *Kontrollsystem*, are those of F. Mann in *Die Staatswirtschaft unserer Zeit*, Jena, 1929, cited in Peacock and Wiseman, op. cit., p. 68.
67. *Debs.*, 7 November 1951, 493/290.
68. *Debs.*, 20 July 1953, 518/57.
69. For examples, cf. *Debs.*, Nicholson, 17 March 1952, 497/1999; Reginald Maudling, 3 March 1954, 524/1220; Hinchingbrooke, 9 July 1954, 529/2529; Thorneycroft, 25 July 1957, 573/643; Marples, 13 July 1961, 644/611.
70. *Official Report*, 1960 Party Conference, p. 101.
71. *Debs.*, 18 March 1959, 602/530.
72. *Debs.*, 2 November 1960, 629/186.
73. *Debs.*, 9 November 1960, 629/1086.
74. *Debs.*, 12 November 1958, 595/455.
75. *Debs.*, 27 October 1959, 612/320.
76. *Debs.*, 15 April 1964, 693/481.
77. The images are Thorneycroft's, *Debs.*, 5 April 1960, 621/430.
78. *Debs.*, 25 November 1952, 508/643; cf. also his speech at Luton Hoo, 23 June 1962, CUCO press release: 'In modern society, Government has to appear as the partner of industry, which shares its profits and losses, as its patron, as the user of its products, as the champion of the consumer, as the director of scientific research, as providing educational facilities for technical and industrial staff, as the initiator of new policies, as the creator of a spirit of confidence and enterprise.'
79. The point is made by W. L. Burn in 'English Conservatism', *The Nineteenth Century and After*, London, 1949, pp. 4, 1.

CHAPTER 15

1. For further exploration of this analysis, cf. Michael Kidron, *Western Capitalism Since the War*, London, 1968, and 'An alternative account', in Nigel Harris and John Palmer (eds.), *World Crisis, Essays in Revolutionary Socialism*, London, 1971, p. 129.
2. cf. Kidron, op. cit., Chapter 3, p. 38.
3. For further discussion of this, cf. *Beliefs in Society: The Problem of Ideology*, London, 1968 and 1971, Chapters II and IV.
4. 'The limits of laissez-faire', *Crossbow*, Spring 1960, p. 25.
5. Speech at Folkestone, 24 March 1963, reported in *The Times*, 25 March 1963, p. 6; an editorial in the same issue criticizes the unlimited power attributed by Hailsham to the State.
6. cf. for example, Aubrey Jones' definition of freedom as 'the state of heart, or of mind, which is reached when evil is held in check, when the ignoble and base, hurling themselves against the ramparts of the will, meet resistance and are thrown back', *The Pendulum of Politics*, London, 1947, p. 76; or T. L. Talmon's lecture to the Conservative Political Centre (published as *Utopianism and Politics*, London, 1957):

   man and society will never be able to save themselves solely by their own exertions, but that grace, coming from above or outside, is needed for salvation. Furthermore, men's unruly and weak nature requires Government from above, by a God, appointed Church, Divine Right of Kings, an aristocracy, or – in more abstract terms – ancient traditions, deep-seated beliefs, fixed habits.

7. John Stuart Mill gives an interesting account of the same division in the middle of the nineteenth century –

   the lot of the poor, in all things which affect them collectively, should be regulated *for* them, not *by* them. They should not be required or encouraged to think for themselves, or give to their own reflection or forecast an influential voice in the determination of their destiny. It is the duty of the higher classes to think for them, and to take the responsibility of their lot, as the commander and officers of an army take that of their soldiers composing it. This function the higher classes should prepare themselves to perform conscientiously, and their whole demeanor should impress the poor with a reliance on it, in order that, while yielding passive and active obedience to the rules prescribed for them, they may resign themselves in all other respects to a trustful *insouciance* and repose under the shadow of their protectors. The relation between rich and poor should be only partially authoritative; it should be amiable, moral, and sentimental; affectionate tutelage on the one side, respectful and grateful deference on the other. The rich should be *in loco parentis* to the poor, guiding and restraining them like children. Of spontaneous action on their part there should be no need. They should be called on for nothing but to do their day's work, and to be moral and religious. Their morality and religion should be provided for them by their superiors, who should see them properly taught it, and should do all that is necessary to insure their being, in return for labor and attachment – properly fed, clothed, housed, spiritually edified and innocently amused.

Principles of Political Economy, Boston, 1848, II, pp. 319–20.

8. Jones, *The Pendulum* . . . , p. 80.
9. ibid., p. 14.
10. I. J. Pitman, *Debs.*, 29 June 1959, 608/128.
11. Jones, *The Pendulum* . . . , p. 52.
12. In *Prospect for Capitalism*, CPC 191, October 1958, p. 46.
13. Diane Spearman, *Democracy in England*, London, 1957.
14. *The Economist* (29 May 1954, p. 689) made a similar observation: the evolution of the 'Liberal Left' out of the 'Fabian Left' was 'not a logical development of the slow post-war progress towards Tory reform that has been associated with the name of Mr Butler; indeed, in many ways, they (the Liberal Left) represent a sharp break from it'.

APPENDIX

1. cf. *A Vindication of Natural Society*, London, 1756; *Oxford Selections from Burke*, London, 1956.
2. *Reflections on the French Revolution*, 1970 Everyman edition, London, 1955, p. 240.
3. *An Appeal from the New to the Old Whigs*, 1791, World Classics Series, London, 1936, pp. 101–2.
4. *Reflections*, p. 48.
5. *Thoughts on the Cause of the Present Discontents*, 1770, World Classics Series, London, 1936, p. 6.
6. *Thoughts and Details on the Scarcity*, 1795, ibid., p. 22.
7. *An Appeal*, p. 100.
8. *Thoughts and Details*, p. 5.
9. *Reflections*, p. 107.
10. *Thoughts and Details*, op. cit., p. 3.
11. ibid., p. 30.
12. *Reflections*, p. 104; compare Viscount St John Henry Bolingbroke, 'Some reflections on the present state of the nation', *Works*, 1745, p. 174.
13. *An Appeal*, p. 94.
14. *Thoughts and Details*, p. 16.
15. ibid., p. 8.
16. *Letter to a Noble Lord*, 1796, World Classics Series, London, 1936, p. 35.
17. *Thoughts and Details*, p. 22.
18. *Reflections*, p. 60.
19. ibid., p. 95.
20. cf. E. A. Halévy, *A History of the English People*, I, London, 1937, p. 16; on the need for the new 'plutocracy' to merge with the old aristocracy and present a united opposition to democracy, cf. W. Bagehot, *The English Constitution*, 2nd edition, 1872, p. xxx. For Gladstone's 1896 statement about the seepage of businessmen into the Conservative party, cf. K. Hutchison, *The Decline and Fall of British Capitalism*, London, 1951, p. 49. For the decline of the landed aristocracy both absolutely and in politics, cf. H. A. Thomas, *The House of Commons, 1832–1901*, London,

1939, p. 18, and E. M. Ojala, *Agriculture and Economic Progress*, London, 1952, pp. 85 and 134–5; also S. H. Beer, 'The representation of interests in the British government', *American Political Science Review*, September 1957, p. 623.

21. cf. *On the Constitution of Church and State*, V, London, 1837.

22. *Heroes and Hero Worship*, London, 1840, p. 156.

23. In R. L. Hill, *Toryism and the People*, London, 1929.

24. cf. the 'feudal socialism' of the aristocracy, *Communist Manifesto*, III, 1a; also cited in H. W. J. Edwards, *The Radical Tory*, London, 1937.

25. Smyth and Manners of Young England visited mills in Lancashire in 1841. Manners commented: 'there never was so complete a feudal system as that of the mills; soul and body are, or might be, at the absolute disposal of one man, and that to my notion, is not at all a bad state of society; the worst of this manufacturing feudalism is its uncertainty and the moment the cotton lord is done, there's an end also to his dependents' very subsistence', cited in C. Whilley, *Lord John Manners and His Friends*, London, 1925, p. 106.

26. *Coningsby, or The New Generation*, London, 1844, p. 241.

27. ibid., p. 163.

28. *Sybil, or the Two Nations*, London, 1845, pp. 267–8; cf. also *Coningsby*, pp. 78 and 118.

29. *Coningsby*, p. 221.

30. cf. Benjamin Disraeli, *A Vindication of the English Constitution*, London, pp. 42 and 144–5, and Speech at Manchester, 3 April 1872, published in *Tory Democrat*, op. cit. But for cases where Disraeli emphasizes land as the qualification for leadership, cf. speech on Mr Miles' amendment (Corn Laws), 20 February 1846; also *Tory Democrat*, p. 42 and letter to Salisbury, cited in H. W. J. Edwards, op. cit., p. 199.

31. *Coningsby*, p. 316.

32. cf. his conception of statesmanship, *Selected Speeches*, I, 1882, p. 102.

33. On monarchical leadership, cf. Richard Faber, *Beaconsfield and Bolingbroke*, London, 1961, p. 26.

34. cf. *Coningsby*, p. 204; *Lord George Bentinck*, London, 1852, Chapter 24, pp. 323 and 330; on race and political

institutions, cf. his Manchester speech, 3 April 1872, op.
cit.; in *Sybil*, Sybil, Queen Victoria and the working class
are 'Saxon', St Lys Norman is 'Norman tempered with
Saxon'; in his Crystal Palace Speech, 24 June 1872, he
imputes 'cosmopolitan principles' to the Liberals, cf.
Tory Democrat; in the Trilogy, he says England has been
burdened with Dutch finance, Venetian oligarchy, French
wars and a German king.
35. *Sybil*, p. 40.
36. Crystal Palace Speech, *Tory Democrat*, p. 46.
37. Manchester Speech, ibid., p. 26.
38. *The Spirit of Whiggism*, London, 1834, p. 118.
39. H. E. Gorst, *The Fourth Party*, London, 1906, p. 76.

Bibliography

Books on Conservatism and Corporatism, and articles or periodicals cited
or consulted

I. WORKS BY CONSERVATIVES OR ABOUT CONSERVATIVES
OR CONSERVATISM (*including reprinted speeches, anthologies,*
etc.)

ALLEN, W. GORE, *The Reluctant Politician, Derick Heathcoat*
Amory, Christopher Johnson, London, 1958.
AMERY, L. S., *National and Imperial Economics*, National Unionist
Association, London, 1924.
Empire and Prosperity, Faber, London, 1931.
The Forward View, Bles, London, 1935.
The Framework of the Future, Oxford University Press,
London, 1944.
The Conservative Future, National Union, London, 1945.
Thoughts on the Constitution, Oxford University Chichele
Lectures, 1947, Oxford University Press, London, 1947.
The Awakening: Our Present Crisis, and the Way Out, Mac-
donald, London, 1948.
My Political Life, Vols I–III, Hutchinson, London, 1953–5.
A Balanced Economy, Hutchinson, London, 1954.
ASSHETON, RALPH, *Facing the Future*, CUCO, London,
1945.
AUERBACH, M. M., *The Conservative Illusion*, Columbia, New
York, 1959.
BAILEY, RICHARD, *Everybody's Economics*, 'BHT' publications,
London, 1949.
The Practice of Politics, CPC, London, January 1950,
revised May 1952.

BALDWIN, A. W., *My Father: The True Story*, Allen and Unwin, London, 1955.

BALDWIN, STANLEY, *Employment, Trade and Empire Development*, National Unionist Association, London, 1923.
Looking Ahead, National Unionist Association, London, 1924.
Peace and Goodwill in Industry, National Unionist Association, London, 1925.

BALFOUR, HAROLD, *An Airman Marches*, Hutchinson, London, 1933.

BANKS, SIR R. M., *The Conservative Outlook*, Chapman and Hall, London, 1929.

BARBER, D. H., *Stanley Baldwin*, D. H. Barber, London, 1959.

BARLOW, SIR JOHN et al., *Automation and the Consumer*, CPC 165, London, December 1956.

BARRATT-BROWN, MICHAEL, *Who are the Tories?*, Universities and Left Review, London, 1959.

BAUMANN, A. A., *Burke, the Founder of Conservatism*, Eyre and Spottiswoode, London, 1929.

BEGBIE, E. H., *The Conservative Mind: by a Gentleman with a Duster*, Mills and Boon, London, 1924.

BELL, DANIEL, (ed.), *The New American Right*, Criterion Books, New York, 1955.

BELLAIRS, CHARLES H., *Conservative Social and Industrial Reform*, CPC, London, December 1947.

BENTINCK, LORD, *Tory Democracy*, Methuen, London, 1918.

BEVINS, REGINALD, *The Greasy Pole*, Hodder and Stoughton, London, 1965.

BIRCH, NIGEL, *The Conservative Party*, British People in Pictures Series, Collins, London, 1949.

BIRKENHEAD, THE EARL OF, *The Life of Lord Halifax*, Hamish Hamilton, London, 1965.

BLAKE, ROBERT, *The Unknown Prime Minister: The Life and Times of Andrew Bonar Law, 1858–1923*, Eyre and Spottiswoode, London, 1955.
Disraeli, Eyre and Spottiswoode, London, 1966.
The Conservative Party from Peel to Churchill, Eyre and Spottiswoode, London, 1970.

BOLITHO, WILLIAM, *Alfred Mond, 1st Lord Melchett*, Martin Becker, London, 1933.

BOOTHBY, ROBERT, *The New Economy*, Secker and Warburg, London, 1943.
I fight to Live, Gollancz, London, 1947.

BOOTHBY, ROBERT; WITH HAROLD MACMILLAN, OLIVER STANLEY AND J. DE V. LODER, *Industry and State*, Macmillan, London, 1927.

BOUTWOOD, A., *National Revival: A Restatement of Tory Principles*, publisher not stated, 1913.

BOW GROUP, *Taxes for Today*, CPC 184, London, March, 1958.
Principles in Practice, CPC 223, London, February, 1961.
The Conservative Opportunity, Batsford/CPC, London, 1965.

BOYD, FRANCIS, *Richard Austen Butler*, Rockliff, London, 1956.

BOYD-CARPENTER, J., *The Conservative Case*, Alan Wingate, London, 1950.

BOYLE, SIR EDWARD (ed.), *Tory Democrat – The Speeches of Disraeli*, with an introduction by Walter Elliot, CPC, London, 1950.

BRACKEN, BRENDAN, *Enterprise can Do It*, CUCO, London, 1945.

BRAINE, BERNARD, *Tory Democracy*, Falcon Press, London, 1948.

BRINTON, C., *The Political Ideas of the English Romantics*, Oxford University Press, London, 1926.

BRITTAN, SAMUEL, *The Treasury under the Tories, 1951–1964*, Penguin, London, 1964.

BROGAN, COLIN, *Socialism Conquers All*, Hollis and Carter, London, 1949.
They are Always Wrong, CPC, London, March, 1949.

BRYANT, SIR ARTHUR, *The Spirit of Conservatism*, Hutchinson, London, 1929.
Stanley Baldwin: A Tribute, Hamish Hamilton, London, 1937.

BURKE, EDMUND, *A Vindication of Natural Society*, 1756, Oxford Selections, London, 1956.
Thoughts on the Cause of the Present Discontents, 1770, Oxford University Press (World Classics), London, 1936.
Reflections on the French Revolution, 1790, Dent, London, 1955.

343

An Appeal from the New to the Old Whigs, 1791, Oxford University Press (World Classics), London, 1936.

Thoughts and Details on the Scarcity, 1795, Oxford University Press (World Classics), London, 1936.

Letter to a Noble Lord, 1796, Oxford University Press (World Classics), London, 1936.

Thoughts on the Regicide Peace, 1796, Oxford University Press (World Classics), 1936.

BUTLER, SIR GEOFFREY, *The Tory Tradition*, John Murray, London, 1914.

BUTLER, R. A., *Fundamental Issues*, CUCO, London, 1946.

Our Way Ahead, CPC 169, London, October, 1956.

Tomorrow Our Responsibility, CPC 194, London, 1959.

CAMPBELL-JOHNSON, ALAN, *Sir Anthony Eden*, Robert Hale, London, 1955.

CARLYLE, THOMAS, *Past and Present*, 1843.

Heroes and Hero Worship, 1840, both in *Works* (Vol. X, and Vol V) Chapman and Hall, London, 1897–1901.

CARNELL, G., *Robert Southey and His Age: The Development of a Conservative Mind*, Clarendon Press, Oxford, 1960.

CECIL, LADY GWENDOLIN, *Robert, Marquis of Salisbury*, Hodder and Stoughton, London, 1921.

CECIL, LORD HUGH, *Conservatism*, Home University Library, Oxford University Press, London, 1912.

CECIL, LORD ROBERT, *The New Outlook*, Allen and Unwin, London, 1919.

CHAMBERLAIN, AUSTEN, *Down the Years*, Cassell, London, 1935.

Politics from the Inside, Cassell, London, 1936.

CHURCHILL, RANDOLPH, *The Rise and Fall of Sir Anthony Eden*, MacGibbon and Kee, London, 1959.

CHURCHILL, LORD RANDOLPH, *The Speeches of Lord Randolph Churchill*, 2 vols., Longmans, Green & Co., London, 1889.

CHURCHILL, WINSTON LEONARD SPENCER, *Lord Randolph Churchill*, Odhams, London, 1905, 1952 edition.

Parliamentary Government and the Economic Problem, University of Oxford Romanes Lectures, 1930, Oxford University Press, London, 1930.

Here is the Course We Steer, Declaration of Mr Churchill's

Policy, CUCO, London, 1945.

The Second World War, 6 vols., Cassell, London, 1948–54.

CLARK, G. KITSON, *Peel and the Conservative Party: A Study in Party Politics 1832–41*, Bell, London, 1929.

CLARKE, DAVID, *The Conservative Faith in a Modern Age*, CPC, London, April 1947.

COLERIDGE, SAMUEL TAYLOR, *On the Constitution of Church and State*, 1837, in *Works* (ed. R. W. Coleridge), Eyre, London, 1840.

COOK, A. J., *The Mond Moonshine*, Workers Publications, London, 1928.

COOTE, COLIN, *A Companion of Honour, The Story of Walter Elliot*, Collins, London, 1967.

CPC, Two Way Movement of Ideas Series:
What Do You Think (and What We Think)
  About Profit (Crump, N.), August 1946
  About Conservative Principles (Alport, C. J. H.) September 1946
  About the Trade Unions (Clarke, D.), February 1947
  About Taxation (Stanley, Oliver), September 1947
  About the Workers' Charter (Amory, D. Heathcoat), September 1947
  About the Industrial Charter (Butler, R. A.), September 1947
  About Economic Recovery (Macmillan, Harold), February 1948
  About Coal (Lancaster, C. G.), February 1948
  About the Property-Owning Democracy (Eccles, David), October 1948
  About the Nationalisation of Steel (Fraser, H.), January 1949
  More About the Trade Unions (Clarke, D.), November 1950.

The Industrial Charter, May 1947.
The State as Merchant; A Study of Government Bulk Purchase, May 1948. All London.

Inside Industry Series:
  Coal, September 1948
  Steel, 1948

345

Wool, 1948
Cotton, January 1950
Shipbuilding, November 1950
Distribution of Industry, December 1950. All London.
Conservatism, 1945–50, London, October 1950 (with an Introduction by Butler, R. A.).
Six Oxford Lectures, CPC 116, London, February 1952.
The Good Society, Seven Oxford Lectures, CPC 122, London, March 1953.
Great Conservatives, CPC 125, London, May 1953.
Tradition and Change, Nine Oxford Lectures, CPC 138, London, December 1954.
The New Conservatism, CPC 150, London, October 1955.
Liberty in the Modern State, Eight Oxford Lectures, CPC 166, London, January 1957.
Prospect for Capitalism, CPC 191, London, October, 1958. (Other CPC publications are cited under their authors or editors.)

CUCO, *Economic and Financial Steps to World Recovery*, London, March 1943.
Forty Years of Progress, London, 1945.
All You Want to Know about the Trade Disputes Act, London, 1946.
Co-Partnership Today, by the Advisory Committee on Policy and Political Education, with a preface by R. A. Butler, London, 1946.
Topic for Today Series: London, 1945–6:
  Man-Power
  Profits, Salaries and Wages
  Earnings in Industry and Commerce
  The Causes of Unemployment
  The Prevention of Unemployment
  Britain's Pay Packet.
Mr. Churchill's Statement of Policy (Manifesto), London, 1945.
The Right Road for Britain, London, July 1949.
This is the Road (Manifesto), London, 1950.
Britain Strong and Free (Manifesto), London, 1951.
United for Peace and Progress (Manifesto), London, 1955.
Onward in Freedom, London, September 1958.

The Next Five Years (Manifesto), London, 1959.

Industrial Change: The Human Aspect, September 1963.

CONSERVATIVE RESEARCH DEPARTMENT, *The History of the Empire Free Trade Campaign*, Unpublished document, anonymous and undated, NUCUA stamp, 11 June 1930.

CRANBOURNE, VISCOUNT, *A Time for Wisdom*, CUCO, London, 1945.

CRIPPS, SIR R. STAFFORD, *'National' Fascism in Britain*, The Socialist League, London, 1935.

CRISP, DOROTHY, *The Rebirth of Conservatism*, Methuen, London, 1931.

England Mightier Yet, The National Press Review Ltd., London, 1939.

CROSSLEY, ANTONY *et. al.*, *Planning for Employment*, Macmillan, London, 1935.

DAVIES, H. W. CARLESS, *The Age of Grey and Peel*, Clarendon, Oxford, 1929.

DEAR, DAVID, *Personal Savings*, CPC 127, London, September 1953.

DELAHAYE, J. V., *Politics, A Discussion*, Daniel, London, 1929.

DESIGN FOR FREEDOM, *Design for Freedom*, published by the same body, London, February, 1947.

Design for Europe, London, 1947.

Design for Survival (Thorneycroft, P. and Williams, Lady Rhys), London, September 1947.

Design for Recovery, London, January 1948. (cf. also entry under Thorneycroft, Peter.)

DICKINSON, C. L., *A Modern Symposium*, W. H. Allen, London, 1930.

DISRAELI, BENJAMIN, *The Spirit of Whiggism*, 1834, in *The Radical Tory* (edited by Edwards, H. W. J.), Cape, London, 1937.

Vindication of the English Constitution, Saunders and Otley, London, 1835.

Coningsby, or the New Generation, 1844, Lehmann edition, London, 1948.

Sybil, or the Two Nations, 1843, Penguin edition, London, 1954.

Tancred, or the New Crusade, Colburn, London, 1847.

Lord George Bentinck, 1852, Constable, London, 1905.

Lothair, Green, London, 1870.

Endymion, Longmans, Green, London, 1880.

Selected Speeches (edited by Kebbel, T. E.) Longmans, Green, London, 1882.

Whigs and Whiggism: Political Writings (edited by Hutcheon, William), John Murray, London, 1913.

Tory Democrat: Two Speeches of Disraeli (edited by Boyle, Sir Edward), CPC, London, 1950.

DOUGLAS, JAMES, *Restrictive Trade Practices*, CPC 155, April, 1956.

DRISCOLL, J., *A National Wages Policy*, Bow, London, September 1955.

DRIVER, C., *Tory Radical: The Life of Richard Oastler*, Oxford University Press, New York, 1946.

ECCLES, DAVID, *Conservatism after 1945*, CUCO, London, June 1946.

Forward from the Industrial Charter, CUCO, London, January 1948.

EDEN, SIR ANTHONY, *Conservative Policy*, CUCO, London, 1946.

Three Partners in Industry, CUCO, London, 1946.

Freedom and Order (Speeches, 1939–1946), Faber, London, 1947.

Full Circle, Memoirs, Vol. I, Cassell, London, 1960.

Facing the Dictators, Vol. II, Cassell, London, 1962.

EDWARDS, H. W. J. (ed), *The Radical Tory*, Cape, London, 1937.

ELIOT, T. S., *The Idea of a Christian Society*, Faber, London, 1939.

Notes Towards the Definition of Culture, 1948, in *Selected Essays* (edited by Hayward, John), Penguin, London, 1953.

The Literature of Politics, CPC 146, London, 1955.

ELLIOT, LT. COL. WALTER, *Toryism and the Twentieth Century*, Allan, London, 1927.

EMPIRE INDUSTRIES ASSOCIATION AND BRITISH EMPIRE LEAGUE, *Why?*, publisher as author, London, September, 1954.

FABER, RICHARD, *Beaconsfield and Bolingbroke*, Faber, London, 1961.

FEILING, KEITH, *The Life of Neville Chamberlain*, Macmillan, London, 1946.
What is Conservatism?, Faber, London, 1930.

'FOUR YOUNG CONSERVATIVES', *Forward from Victory*, Faber, London, 1943.

FRAZER, MICHAEL, *The Worker in Industry*, CPC 65, London, 1950.

GAMMANS, CAPT. L. D., *Facing the Facts*, CUCO, London, 1945.

GASH, NORMAN, *Politics in the Age of Peel: A Study in the Technique of Parliamentary Representation 1830–1850*, Longmans, London, 1953.
Mr. Secretary Peel: The Life of Sir Robert Peel to 1830, Longmans, London, 1961.

GLICKMAN, HARVEY, *Tory Ethos and Conservative Policy in Britain 1922–1939*, unpublished Ph.D. thesis, Harvard, April 1958.

GOLDMAN, PETER, *Some Principles of Conservatism* (News and Views Series), CPC 161, London, August 1956.

GOODHART, PHILIP, *The Moderate Alliance*, CPC 172, London, March, 1957.
et al., Choice – A Report on Consumer Protection, CPC 238, London, November 1961.

GORST, H. E., *The Fourth Party*, Smith Elder, London, 1906.

GRACCHUS, *Your M.P.*, Gollancz, London, 1944.

GREELAND, ANTHONY, *Fuel for the Future*, CPC 156, London, June 1956.

GRIFFITHS, ELDON, *The New Competitors*, CPC, London, 1965.

GRIGG, SIR E., *Three Parties or Two?*, Benn, London, 1931.

GULLEY, E. E., *Joseph Chamberlain and English Social Politics*, Columbia University Studies, CXXIII, No. 1, Longmans Green, New York, 1926.

HADLEY, GUY, *The Making of Aircraft*, CPC 222, London, February, 1961.

HARRIS, RALPH, *Politics Without Prejudice* (*R. A. Butler*), Staples, London, 1956.

HARROD, ROY, *Are These Hardships Really Necessary?*, Hart-Davis, London, October, 1947.

HAXEY, SIMON, *Tory M.P.*, Gollancz, London, 1940.

HEARNSHAW, F. J. C., *Democracy at the Crossways: A Study in Politics and History with special reference to Great Britain*, Macmillan, London, 1918.
Conservatism in England: An Analytical, Historical and Political Survey, Macmillan, London, 1935.

HEATH, EDWARD, *Parliament and People*, CPC 212, London, March, 1960.

HELY-HUTCHINSON, M., *Capitalism?*, Benn, London, 1933.

HILL, R. L., *Toryism and the People, 1832–1846*, Constable, London, 1929.

HINCHINGBROOKE, VISCOUNT, *Full Speed Ahead: Essays in Tory Reform*, Simpkin, London, 1944.

HOFFMAN, J. D., *The Conservative Party in Opposition, 1945–1951*, MacGibbon and Kee, London, 1964.

HOGG, QUINTIN (VISCOUNT HAILSHAM), *One Year's Work* (speeches), Hurst and Blackett, London, 1944.
The Times We Live In, Signpost, London, 1944.
The Left was Never Right, Faber, London, 1945.
The Case for Conservatism, Penguin, London, 1947.
Toryism and Tomorrow, CPC 181, London, October 1957.
The Conservative Case, Penguin Special, London, 1959.

HOLLIS, CHRISTOPHER, *Can Parliament Survive?*, Hollis and Carter, London, 1949.

HOPKINSON, AUSTIN, *The Hope of the Workers*, publisher as author, London, 1923.
Religio Militis, publisher as author, London, 1927.

HOWARD, C. H. D. (ed), *Joseph Chamberlain: A Political Memoir, 1880–92*, Batchworth, London, 1953.

HOWELL, DAVID, *Efficiency and Beyond*, CPC, London, 1965.

HUGHES, EMRYS, *Macmillan, Portrait of a Politician*, Allen and Unwin, London, 1962.

HUTCHINSON, JAMES, *The Great Betrayal*, CPC, London, January 1950.

INNS OF COURT CONSERVATIVE ASSOCIATION, *A Giant's Strength*, CPC, London, 1958.

JENKINS, ROY, *Mr. Balfour's Poodle*, Heinemann, London, 1954.

JENNER, R. V., *Will Conservatism Survive?*, Staples, London, 1944.

JONES, AUBREY, *Right and Left*, Signpost, London, 1944.
The Pendulum of Politics, Right Book Club, London, 1947.
Industrial Order, Falcon Press, London, 1950.

JONES, W. D., *Lord Derby and Victorian Conservatism*, Blackwell, Oxford, 1956.

KENNEDY, A. L., *Salisbury 1830–1903*, Murray, London, 1953.

KIRK, RUSSELL, *The Conservative Mind*, Faber, London, 1954.

LANCASTER, C. G., *The Organisation of the Coal Board*, CPC, London, November, 1948.
et al., *Structure and Control of the Coal Board*, CPC, London, June, 1951.

LAW, RICHARD, *Return from Utopia*, Faber, London, 1950.

LEATHER, TED, *et al.*, *A New Approach*, publisher not cited, London, 1951.

LEWIS, ROY, AND MAUDE, ANGUS, *The English Middle Classes*, Pelican, London, 1949.

LEWIS, RUSSELL, *Industry and the Property Owning Democracy*, Bow, London, July 1954.

LINES, ANTHONY, *Concerns of State*, Bow, London, October, 1961.

LOFTUS, P., *The Creed of a Tory*, Allan, London, 1926.

LONDONDERRY, MARQUESS OF, *Ourselves and Germany*, Hale, London, 1938.

LOW, SIR TOBY, *et al.*, *Everyman a Capitalist*, CPC 201, London, April 1959.

LUCKING, TONY, *Wings over Westminster*, Bow, London, 1960.

LYMINGTON, VISCOUNT, *Ich Dien*, Constable, London, 1931.

MCDOWELL, R. B., *British Conservatism, 1832–1914*, Faber, London, 1959.

MACLEOD, IAIN, *Neville Chamberlain*, Muller, London, 1961.

MACMILLAN, HAROLD, Collaborator in *Industry and the State* (cf. under Boothby), 1927.
The State and Industry in 1932 (unpublished, 1932).
The Next Step (unpublished), 15 June 1932.
A New British Financial Policy (unpublished), 1932.
Reconstruction – A Plea for a National Policy, Macmillan, London, 1933.

Collaborator in *Planning for Employment* (cf. under Crossley), 1935.

Collaborator in *The Next Five Years* (cf. under Next), 1935.

The Middle Way: A Study of the Problem of Economic and Social Progress in a Free and Democratic Society, Macmillan, London, 1938.

The Conservative Approach to Modern Politics, CUCO, London, May, 1946.

The Middle Way: Twenty Years After, CPC, London, March 1958.

Winds of Change 1914–1939, Macmillan, London, 1966.

Tides of Fortune, 1945–55, Macmillan, London, 1969.

MACNAMARA, J. R. J., *The Whistle Blows*, Eyre and Spottiswoode, London, 1938.

MALLOCK, W. H., *Democracy*, Chapman and Hall, London, 1924.

MANNHEIM, KARL, *Conservative Thought*, 1927, translated in *Essays on Sociology and Social Psychology*, I, Routledge and Kegan Paul, London, 1953.

MARRIOTT, P., *Property and the Nation*, Distributist Books, London, 1947.

MASEFIELD, MURIEL, *Peacocks and Primroses*, Bles, London, 1953.

MAUDE, ANGUS, *The Conservative Way of Life*, Topic for Today Series 26, CPC, London, May 1951; cf. also under Lewis, Roy.

MAUROIS, ANDRÉ, *Disraeli*, Bodley Head, London, 1927.

MAXWELL FYFE, SIR DAVID, *Monopoly*, CPC, London, April, 1948.

MAYBURY, MAURICE, *The Truth About the Interwar Years*, CPC, London, September 1949.

MILNER, VISCOUNT, *Questions of the Hour*, Hodder and Stoughton, London, 1923.

MOLSON, H. E., Contributor to *Conservatism and the Future* (cf. under Percy).

Collaborator in *Planning for Employment* (cf. under Crossley).

Full Employment and The Budget, Signpost, London, 1945.

A Report on Retail Distribution of Electricity, Tory Reform Committee, London, November, 1946. cf. also under Tory Reform Committee.

MOND, SIR ALFRED, BARON MELCHETT, *The Remedy for Unemployment*, Macmillan, London, 1925.
Industry and Politics, Macmillan, London, 1927.

MONYPENNY, W. F., AND BUCKLE, G. F., *The Life of Benjamin Disraeli, Earl of Beaconsfield*, 6 vols, Murray, London, 1910–20.

NABARRO, G. AND ALPORT, C. J. M., *Make Coal Work Harder*, CPC, London, December 1951.

NEXT FIVE YEARS, THE, *The Next Five Years: An Essay in Political Agreement*, Macmillan, London, 1935.

NICHOLSON, NIGEL (ed.), *Harold Nicholson: Diaries and Letters, 1930–1939*, Collins, London, 1966.

NORTHAM, R., *Conservatism the Only Way*, Right Book Club, London, 1939.

NUCUA (AND NATIONAL UNIONIST ASSOCIATION), *The Unionist Party and Future Policy*, London, 1922.
The Prime Minister's Policy, London, 1922.
Work: the Future of British Industry, London, January 1944 (publisher as author).

OAKESHOTT, MICHAEL J. (ed.), *Social and Political Doctrines of Contemporary Europe*, Cambridge University Press, Cambridge, 1939.

ONE NATION GROUP, *One Nation*, CPC 86, London, October, 1950.
Change is Our Ally, CPC 133, London, May 1954.
The Responsible Society, CPC 200, London, March 1959.

OSBORN, J., et al., *The Export of Capital*, CPC 239, London, October 1961.

PERCY, LORD EUSTACE, et al., *Democracy on Trial*, Bodley Head, London, 1931.
Conservatism and the Future, Bodley Head, London, 1931.
Collaborator in *Planning for Employment* (cf. under Crossley).
The Heresy of Democracy, Eyre and Spottiswoode, London, 1954.

PETRIE, SIR CHARLES, *The British Problem*, Nicholson and Watson, London, 1934.
The Chamberlain Tradition, Lovat Dickson, London, 1938.
The Life and Letters of Sir Austen Chamberlain, Cassell, London, 1940.

M

The Modern British Monarchy, Eyre and Spottiswoode, London, 1961.

PICKTHORN, KENNETH, *Principles or Prejudices?*, Signpost, London, 1943.

POWELL, J. ENOCH, *Savings*, Hutchinson for Institute of Economic Affairs, London, 1960.

RAISON, TIMOTHY, *Conflict and Conservatism*, CPC, London, 1965.

REES-MOGG, WILLIAM, *Sir Anthony Eden*, Rockliff, London, 1956.

ST JOHN, HENRY (VISCOUNT BOLINGBROKE), *Letters on the Spirit of Patriotism and on the Idea of a Patriot King*, Oxford University Press, London, 1926.

SALISBURY, MARQUESS OF, *Conservative Policy*, CUCO, London, 1924.

SALOMA, J. S., III, *British Conservatism and the Welfare State: An Analysis of the Policy Process Within the British Conservative Party*, unpublished Ph.D. thesis, Harvard, 1961.

SALVIDGE, S., *Salvidge of Liverpool: Behind the Political Scene, 1890–1928*, Hodder and Stoughton, London, 1934.

SCHWARTZ, G. L., *Why Planning?*, Signpost, London, 1944.

SELLON, H. G. R., *Whither England?*, Peter Davies, London, 1932.

SHORE, PETER, *The Real Nature of Conservatism*, Labour party, London, September 1952.

SKELTON, NOEL, *Constructive Conservatism*, Blackwood, London, 1924.

SMITH, PAUL, *Disraelian Conservatism and Social Reform*, Routledge and Kegan Paul (Studies in Political History Series), London, 1968.

SMITH, T., *et al.*, *Outlook for Small Business*, Bow, London, January, 1961.

SOMERVELL, D. C., *English Thought in the Nineteenth Century*, Methuen, London, 1929.

The Reign of George the Fifth, Faber, London, 1935.

Stanley Baldwin, Faber, London, 1953.

SOUTHEY, ROBERT, *St. Thomas More: or Colloquies on the Progress and Prospects of Society*, 2 vols., Murray, London, 1831.

Letters (edited by Fitzgerald, M. H.), World Classics, London, 1901.

SPEARMAN, DIANE, *Democracy in England*, Barrie and Rockliff, London, 1957.

STEED, WICKHAM, *The Real Stanley Baldwin*, Nisbet, London, 1930.

STELLING, D., *Why I am a Conservative*, Signpost, London, 1943.

STRACHEY, J. ST. LOE, *Economics of the Hour*, Hodder and Stoughton, London, 1923.

TALMON, J. L., *Utopianism and Politics*, CPC 180, London, December 1957.

THORNEYCROFT, PETER, cf. Design for Freedom Series.
Design for Wages, Eagle Press, London, May 1948.
Design for Living, Falcon Press, London, 1949.
Contributor to *Not Unanimous* (edited by Seldon, Arthur), Institute of Economic Affairs, London, January, 1960.

THORNTON, A. P., *The Imperial Idea and Its Enemies: A Study in British Power*, Macmillan, London, 1959.

TORY REFORM COMMITTEE, *Forward by the Right*, TRC, London, October 1943.
A National Policy for Coal (Lancaster, C. G., Hogg, Q., and Thorneycroft, P.). TRC, London, 1944.
Bulletin 2, *Employment Policy* (Thorneycroft, P. and Molson, H. E.), TRC, London, 1944.
What Shall We Use for Money? (Beit, A., and Molson, H. E.) London, 1944.
Air Transport Policy, London, July 1944.
Tools for the Next Job, London, January 1945.

TUGENDHAT, G., *Energy* (Men at Work Series), London, CPC 235, April 1961.

UTLEY, T. E., *Essays in Conservatism*, CPC, London, March, 1949.
Modern Political Thought, CPC, London, October 1952.
The Conservatives and the Critics, CPC, London, October 1956.
Not Guilty, MacGibbon and Kee, London, May 1957.
Edmund Burke, Longmans, Green, London, 1957.

WARDLAW-MILNE, SIR JOHN, *The G.H.Q. of £.s.d.*, Cassell, London, 1932.

WHILLEY, C., *Lord John Manners and His Friends*, Blackwood, London, 1925.

WHITE, R. J., *The Conservative Tradition*, Kaye, London, 1950. *The Political Thought of Samuel Taylor Coleridge*, Cape, London, 1938.

WHITMAN, G. E., *The Reform of Purchase Tax*, CPC 193, London, February 1959.

WILKINSON, W. J., *Tory Democracy*, Columbia University Press, New York, 1925.

WILLIAMS, SIR HERBERT, *The Case Against Socialism*, CPC, London, 1948.

WILSON, THOMAS, *Modern Capitalism and Economic Progress*, Macmillan, London, 1950.

WINTERTON, EARL, *Pre-War*, Macmillan, London, 1932. *Orders of the Day*, Cassell, London, 1953.

WOLFE, A. B., *Conservatism, Radicalism and Scientific Method: an Essay on Social Attitudes*, Macmillan, London, 1923.

WOOD, E., *Conservative Beliefs*, National Unionist Association, London, 1924.

WOOD, J. B., *Employment* (with a foreword by Harrod, R. F.), CPC, London, 1951.

WOOD, JOHN (ed.), *A Nation Not Afraid, The Thinking of Enoch Powell*, Batsford, London, 1965.

WOODS, M., *A History of the Tory Party in the Seventeenth and Eighteenth centuries with a sketch of its development in the Nineteenth Century*, Hodder and Stoughton, London, 1924.

YOUNG, G. M., *Ourselves*, Signpost, London, 1944. *Stanley Baldwin*, Hart-Davis, London, 1952.

YOUNG CONSERVATIVE AND UNIONIST ORGANISATION POLITICAL GROUPS, *Taxation in the Second Half of the Twentieth Century*, NUCUA, London, November 1961.

2. WORKS NOT EARLIER MENTIONED, CONSULTED OR CITED IN RELATIONSHIP TO CORPORATIST THEORY

BACCONNIER, FIRMIN, *Le Régime Corporatif*, La Production Française, Paris, 1935.

BENDIX, REINHARD, *Work and Authority in Industry: Ideologies of Management in the Course of Industrialization*, John Wiley/ Harper, London and New York, 1963.

BERLE, A. A., JUNIOR, *The Twentieth Century Capitalist Revolution*, Macmillan, London, 1955.
Economic Power and the Free Society, Center for the Study of Democratic Institutions, Santa Barbara, 1957.
Power Without Property, Sidgwick and Jackson, London, 1960.
with MEANS, G. C., *The Modern Corporation and Private Property*, Macmillan, New York, 1933.

BOULDING, K. F., *Organisational Revolution: A Study in the Ethics of Economic Organisation* (with commentary by Neibuhr, Reinhold), Harper, New York, 1953.

BOURGIN, N. GEORGES, *L'État Corporatif en Italie*, Montaigne, Paris, 1935.

BRADY, R. A., *Business as a System of Power*, Columbia University Press, New York, 1943.
Crisis in Britain, Cambridge and California University Press, London, and Berkeley, Calif., 1950.

BUCHANAN, SCOTT, *The Corporation and the Republic*, Fund for the Republic, Santa Barbara, 1958.

BURNHAM, JAMES, *The Managerial Revolution*, Penguin, London, 1945.

CROSLAND, C. A. R., *The Future of Socialism*, Cape, London, 1956.

CROSSER, PAUL K., *State Capitalism in the Economy of the United States*, Bookman, New York, 1960.

DRUCKER, PETER, *The Future of Industrial Man: A Conservative Approach*, Heinemann, London, 1943.
The Concept of the Corporation, 1946, Beacon edition, Boston, 1960.
The New Society, Heinemann, London, 1951.

FERRY, W. H. (ed.), *The Corporation and the Economy*, Center for the Study of Democratic Institutions, Santa Barbara, 1959.
The Economy under Law, Center for the Study of Democratic Institutions, Santa Barbara, 1960.

GALBRAITH, J. K., *American Capitalism: The Concept of Countervailing Power*, Hamish Hamilton, London, 1952.

357

The New Industrial State, Hamish Hamilton, London, 1967.

GRANICK, DAVID, *The Red Executive: A study of the Organisation Man in Russian Industry*, Macmillan, London, 1960.

HARBRECHT, FATHER P. P., *Towards the Paraproprietal Society: An Essay on the Nature of Property in Twentieth Century America* (introduced by Berle, A. A.), Twentieth Century Fund, New York, 1960.

HAWLEY, E. W., *The New Deal and the Problem of Monopoly; A Study in Economic Ambivalence*, Princeton, N.J., 1966.

HOROWITZ, I. L., *Radicalism and the Revolt Against Reason: the Social Theories of Georges Sorel*, Routledge and Kegan Paul, London, 1961.

KERR, CLARK, *Unions and Union Leaders of Their Own Choosing*, Fund for the Republic, Santa Barbara, 1957.

KEYNES, J. M., *The End of Laissez-Faire*, Sidney Hall Lecture, 1924, Oxford University Press, Oxford, 1926, reprinted in *Essays in Persuasion*, Macmillan, London, 1931.

LUCIUS, PIERRE, *Renaissance du Capitalisme*, Payot, Paris, 1933.

MAN, HENRI DE, *Nationalisme et Socialisme*, translated from Flemish by Kenis, Paul, L'Églantine, Paris, 1932.

MANOÏLESCO, M., *La Siècle du Corporatisme: doctrine du corporatisme, intégral et pur*, F. Alcan, Paris, 1934.

MASON, EDWARD S. (ed.), *The Corporation in Modern Society*, Harvard University Press, Harvard, 1959.

MATHON, EUGÈNE, *La Corporation, Base de L'Organisation Économique*, Berger-Levrauet, Paris, 1934.

MICHELIS, G. DE, *World Reorganisation on Corporative Lines*, (Le Corporation Dans Le Monde), Allen and Unwin, London, 1935.

MONSEN, R. JOSEPH JNR., *Modern American Capitalism: Ideologies and Issues*, Houghton Mifflin, Boston, 1963.

PIROU, GAETAN, *La Crise du Capitalisme*, Libraire du Recueil Sirey, Paris, 1934.
Essais Sur Le Corporatisme, Libraire du Recueil Sirey, Paris, 1937.

POLITICAL AND ECONOMIC PLANNING, *A Self-Government for Industry Bill*, PEP, London, 1934.

RATHENAU, WALTHER, *In Days to Come* (Von Kommenden

Dingen), translated by Eden and Cedar Paul, Allen and Unwin, London, 1921.

ROGGER, HANS AND WEBER EUGEN (eds.), *The European Right: A Historical Profile*, Weidenfeld and Nicolson, London, 1965.

SALVADORI, MASSIMO (ed.), *The American Economic System*, Bobbs Merrill, Chicago, 1963.

SHAW, GEORGE BERNARD, et al., *Bernard Shaw and Fascism*, Correspondence Favil Press, London, 1937.

SHONFIELD, ANDREW, *Modern Capitalism: the Changing Balance of Public and Private Power*, Oxford University Press for the Royal Institute of International Affairs, London, 1965.

TOUR DU PIN, *Vers un Ordre Social Chrétien*, publisher not cited, Paris, 1907.
Aphorismes de Politique, publisher not cited, Paris, 1909.

3. ARTICLES

BEER, S. H., The Conservative Party in Great Britain, *Journal of Politics* 14, 1952.
The Future of British Politics: An American View, *Political Quarterly (PQ)* xxvi/1, January-March, 1955.
Pressure Groups and Parties in Britain, *American Political Science Review (APSR)*, March, 1956.
The Representation of Interests in British Government, *APSR*, September, 1957.

BOOTHBY, ROBERT, The Economic Policy of the Conservative Party, *PQ* xxiv/2, April-June, 1953, p. 154.

BRADY, ALEXANDER, The British Governing Class and Democracy, *Canadian Journal of Economics and Political Science* xx/4, November, 1954, p. 405.

BURN, W. L., English Conservatism, I and II, *The Nineteenth Century and After*, January and February, 1949, pp. 1 and 67.
The Conservative Tradition and its Reformulations, in Ginsberg, M. (ed.), *Law and Opinion in England in the Twentieth Century*, Stevens, London, 1959.

BUTLER, R. A., Conservative Policy, *PQ* xx/4, October-December, 1949, p. 317.

CAIRNS, SIR DAVID, Monopoly and Restrictive Practices, in Ginsberg, M. (ed.), *Law and Opinion in England in the Twentieth Century*, Stevens, London, 1959.

CASSELL, F., Pricing Policies in the Nationalised Industries, *Lloyds Bank Review*, October, 1956.

CATLIN, GEORGE, Contemporary British Political Thought, *APSR* xlvi/3, September, 1952.

CRITCHLEY, JULIAN, The Intellectuals, *PQ* 32/3, July-September, 1961, p. 267.

DRAPER, HAL, Neo-Corporatists and Neo-Reformers, *New Politics* 1/1, Fall, 1961.

ECCLES, SIR D., Popular Capitalism, *Objective*, January, 1955, p. 3.

EPSTEIN, L. D., The Politics of British Conservatism, *APSR*, March, 1954.

EVELY, R. AND LITTLE, I. M. D., Some Aspects of Concentration in British Industry, *Proceedings of the Manchester Statistical Society*, February, 1958.

FEILING, KEITH, Principles of Conservatism, *PQ* xxiv/2, April-June, 1953, p. 129.

FINER, S. E., The Federation of British Industries, *Political Studies* iv/1, February, 1956.
The Political Power of Private Capital, *Sociological Review*, Vol. III, No. 2, and Vol. IV, No. 1, December, 1955, p. 279, and July, 1956, p. 2.
Transport Interests and the Road Lobby, *PQ* 29/1, January-March, 1957, p. 47.

GLICKMAN, HARVEY, The Toryness of English Conservatism, *Journal of British Studies*, No. 1, November, 1961.

GOOLD-ADAMS, R., The Conservative Dilemma, *The Sunday Times*, 30 March, 6, 13 and 27 April, 1958.

GOWER, L. C. B., Business, in Ginsberg, M., op. cit., pp. 143–72.

HART, P. E. AND PRAIS, S. J., The Analysis of Business Concentration, *Journal of the Royal Statistical Society* 119/150, 1956.

HARTLEY, KEITH, The Mergers in the United Kingdom Aircraft Industry, 1957–60, *Journal of the Royal Aeronautical Society* 69/660, December 1965.

HEATH, J. B., Freer Prices – what Progress? *The Broker*, February 1960.

The Restrictive Trade Court on Competition and Price Restriction, *Manchester School*, January 1960.

HENDERSON, H., The Pricing of Public Utility Undertakings, *Manchester School*, December 1947.

HENNESSY, DAVID, The Communication of Conservative Policy, 1957–59, *PQ* 32/3, July-September, 1961.

HINCHINGBROOKE, VISCOUNT, The Course of Conservative Politics, *Quarterly Review* 581, July 1949, p. 279.

HOGG, QUINTIN, British Industry After the War, *New English Review* 1/xi, May, 1945.

HOLLIS, CHRISTOPHER, The Conservative Opportunity, *New English Review* 2/xi, June 1945.

HUGHES, JOHN, Steel Nationalisation and Political Power, *New Reasoner* 2, Autumn, 1957.

KAHN-FREUND, O., Labour Law, in Ginsberg, M., op. cit., p. 215.

LEWIS, G. K., The Present Condition of British Political Parties, *Western Political Quarterly* v/2, June 1952, p. 231.

LIPSON, LESLIE, Common Ground and Emerging Conflict between the British Parties, *PQ* xxvii/2, April-June 1956, p. 182.

MACMILLAN, HAROLD, Self Government in Industry, *Service* 1/4, 1932.

MAUDE, ANGUS, The Conservative Party and the Changing Class Structure, *PQ* xxiv/2, April-June 1953, p. 139.

MOLSON, H. E., The Tory Reform Committee, *New English Review* 3/xi, July 1945, p. 245.

OAKESHOTT, MICHAEL J., Rationalism in Politics, *Cambridge Journal* 1/2, November 1947, p. 81.
Scientific Politics, *Cambridge Journal* 1/6, March 1948, p. 347.
Contemporary British Politics, *Cambridge Journal* 1/8, May 1948, p. 474.
Political Education, 1951, reprinted in *Philosophy, Politics and Society* (ed. P. Laslett), Blackwell, Oxford, 1956.

PAISH, F. W., Taxation and Investment, *Objective*, May, 1954.

POWELL, J. ENOCH, An End to Charter-Writing, *Crossbow*, Spring, 1958, p. 23.

Treasury Control in the Age of Inflation, *The Banker*, April, 1958.

The Limits of Laissez-Faire, *Crossbow*, Spring, 1960, p. 25.

ROBERTS, B. C., Trade Unions and Party Politics, *Cambridge Journal* vi/7, April 1953.

Trade Unions in the Welfare State, *PQ* xxvii/1, January-March 1956.

Industrial Relations, in Ginsberg, M., op. cit., pp. 364–90.

ROBERTSON, D. J., Trade Unions and Wage Policy, *PQ* xxvii/1, January-March 1956, p. 19.

ROSE, RICHARD, Tensions in Conservative Philosophy, *PQ* 32/3, July-September 1961, p. 275.

The Bow Group in British Politics, *Western Political Quarterly* xiv/4, December 1961, p. 865.

SAVASTANO, LUIGI, *Contemporary British Conservatism: Its Nature and Content*, MA thesis, University of Nebraska, published Vantage Press, New York, 1951.

SMITH, JOHN, The Rise of the Bureaucracy, *Transactions of the Third World Congress of Sociology*, 1956.

STREETEN, PAUL, Government and the Economy in the U.S.A., *Rivista di Diritto, Finanziario e Scienze Delle Finanze* xvl/1, Parte 1, March 1957.

TIVEY, L. AND WOHLGEMUTH, E., Trade Associations as Interest Groups, *PQ* 29/1, January-March, 1957, p. 59.

UTLEY, T. E., Principle and Empiricism, *Cambridge Journal* vi/4, January 1953.

The Great Soft Centre, *Crossbow*, Autumn, 1957, p. 15.

Should the Tories Try to Win the Next Election?, *Crossbow*, Summer, 1958, p. 12.

WALKER, G., Competition in Transport as an Instrument of Policy, *Economic Journal*, September 1956.

WILLENZ, ERIC, The Conservative Party in Great Britain Since 1945, *Social Research* 16/1, March 1949, p. 12.

WILSON, H. H., Techniques of Pressure – Anti-Nationalisation Propaganda in Britain, *Public Opinion Quarterly*, Summer, 1951, p. 225.

YOUNG, G. M., The Conservative Attitude to the New World, I and II, *The Listener*, 13 and 20 July 1950.

4. PERIODICALS AND NEWSPAPERS CONSULTED OR CITED

(A) CONSERVATIVE PUBLICATIONS, *Notes on Current Politics*, 1945–64.
Weekly Newsletter, 1945–64.
The Onlooker, 1943–June 1947 (ceased publication).
Tory Challenge, July 1947–September 1953 (ceased publication).
Onward, October 1953–June 1957 (ceased publication).
Objective, January 1950–58 (CPC quarterly).
Conservative Approach, November 1948–September 1951 (ceased publication).
Industrial Outlook, July 1960–Summer 1961.
Trade Union Bulletin, May 1947–61 (monthly notes for Conservative Trade Unionists).
Crossbow (Quarterly Journal of the Bow Group), Autumn 1957–Summer 1964.
PARTY ORGANIZATION DOCUMENTS, *Central Council Agendas*, 1946–64.
Report to Annual Conference and Agenda, 1947–64.
Annual Conference Reports, 1947–64.
(1946 report was not published and exists only in minuted form.)
(B) DAILY NEWSPAPERS, *The Times*.
The Manchester Guardian and *The Guardian*.
Financial Times.
The Daily Telegraph.
News Chronicle.
Daily Express.
Daily Mail.
Evening Standard.
(C) WEEKLY PRESS, *The Economist*.
The Sunday Times.
Observer.
New Statesman (and Nation).
The Spectator.
Tribune.
The Listener.

The Statist.
Time and Tide.
(D) PERIODICALS, *The Director.*
The Manager.
Cambridge Journal.
Oxford Economic Papers.
Three Banks Review.
The Banker.
Lloyds Bank Review.

Index of Names

(Names are listed as they first appear in this text; no attempt has been made to trace changes in titles.)

Subject Index

accountability (in the nationalized industries), 182, 183,
184-6
active (*v.* passive), 265-8; in
Disraeli's work, 286; in industrial relations, 177-8
agrarian society, 12, 275, 288
agriculture, 43, 208, 229, 254,
263, 277, 288, 339
Aims of Industry, 95
airways, 44, 55, 63, 173, 201;
private, 198; *see* aviation,
civil
amalgamations, 43, 44, 57, 59;
compulsory, in coal, 92; in
railways, 93; *see* mergers,
concentration
arbitration, 37, 38, 44, 158, 163,
165, 166, 167, 169
aristocracy, Burke and, 275,
277 *passim*; and corporatism,
65-6, 68; landed – , 12, 13,
179, 263, 265; leadership,
aristocratic, 23-6; 'natural' – ,
283, 285-6; oligarchy of, 27;
power of, 30
atomic energy (industry), 63, 87,
103
aviation, civil, 40, 87, 200;
abolition of the Ministry of,
131; aircraft industry, 63,
216; air transport, 297; Civil
Aviation (Licensing) Bill

(1960), 218; Government assistance to, 217-18; inclusion of, in transport cartel,
94; reorganization of, 104;
see BEA, BOAC

balance of payments, 115, 228,
235, 243, 270, 271; external
payments, 149
Bank of England, 54, 56, 293,
295; nationalization of, 86,
104, 205, 220
bank rate, 233, 234
banks, bankers, 29, 52, 205;
and role in Government policy, 204, 233, 234
bargaining, collective, 115, 116,
117, 157-70; in railways, 190;
see industrial relations, labour,
wages
Beveridge Report, 59; *see*
Beveridge, Sir William, in
Index of Names
Board of Trade, 133, 297
Bow Group, 153, 315, 343
Britain Strong and Free (1951),
115, 307
British Employers' Confederation (BEC), 82, 160, 317
British European Airways
(BEA), 200, 204, 218
British Iron and Steel Federation (BISF), 43, 46-7, 98, 99,

British Iron—*cont.*
101, 103, 188, 189, 303, 330;
see iron and steel
British Overseas Airways Corporation (BOAC), 199, 200,
204, 218
British Transport Commission,
160, 161
budgets, 56, 205, 231, 233, 244;
(1945), 130, 300; (1947),
131, 137; (1952), 158, 233;
(1953), 206; (1955), 213;
(1956), 160, 161; (1958), 209;
(1961), 165; (1963), 174,
175, 186, 242; (1964), 167, 242
Burlington House Conference
(Mond-Turner talks), 41, 296
buses and busmen, 158, 163–4,
167, 270
business and the State, relationship of, 204 *passim*
business, small, 207–8, 246, 327
'Butskell', Mr, 151

capital, 34–5, 41, 53, 56, 57, 103,
108, 109, 181–2, 183, 220, 229,
230, 253, 271; as an Estate,
66, 67–8; – exports, 64; foreign – , 101, 111, 120, 174; in
nationalized industries, 185,
186, 196–7, 198, 199
Capital Gains Tax, 164, 318
capitalism, 16–17, 31, 32 *passim*,
35, 36, 37, 46, 62, 63, 105, 203
passim, 208–9, 232, 249–54,
257, 260–1, 290, 292, 297,
322, 327, 332, 336, 337, 338;
challenges to, 66 *passim*;
State – , 62, 98, 105, 109, 172,
251
capitalist, 35, 57, 110, 200, 249,
252, 299, 320

cartels, cartelization, 33, 42, 45,
48, 49, 53, 57, 63, 69, 70, 97,
128, 221; in coal, 90, 92;
international – , 59, 63, 200;
by statute, 89; in steel, 98,
101, 102–3, 219; in transport,
93–4, 104
Catering Wages Bill (1943), 59
Central Committee of Transport
Users, 95; *see* transport
Chancellor of the Exchequer,
158, 160, 162, 165, 166, 167,
185, 191, 194, 221, 232, 233,
234, 235, 239, 240, 241, 320,
323, 334; resignation of, 164
chemicals (including petro-
chemicals), 34, 41, 47, 50, 55,
63, 199; *see* Imperial Chemical Industries
Christians, and corporatism, 68;
and the industrial revolution,
282, 287
Civil Service pay, 163, 182
closed shop, right of, 57, 113–14,
170, 171
coal, 34, 39, 40, 41, 43–4, 45,
49, 56, 161, 199–200, 295;
centralization of, 89, 302–3;
miners' pay, 163, 317, 321;
nationalization of, 86, 88, 89–
93; prices of, 185; Tory
Reform Committee and, 59,
61, 62, 297
Coalition Government, 41, 50,
51, 77, 295; and transport,
104, 132, 169
collectivism, 13, 14, 17, 36, 56,
69, 71, 250, 255
Commonwealth, 129; – Cable
and Wireless Services, nationalized, 103–4; – Conference
(1930), 52; – Economic Con-

monopoly—*cont.*

in civil aviation, 104; in coal, 90–2; and corporatism, 181; and labour, 116; Liberal attitudes towards, 221, 243; in nationalized industries, 183; in railways, 93; in steel, 98, 99, 102, 103; in transport, 96

motor industry, 34, 39, 45, 69, 190, 194, 208, 217, 330

National Economic Development Council (Neddy), 167, 207, 235, 237, 241, 242, 243

National Incomes Commission, 166–7

National Industry Recovery Act (U.S.), 18, 69, 70

National Interest and National Idea, 67

National Joint Advisory Council (NJAC), 46, 160, 174, 234, 320, 321, 333

National Union (of Conservative or Conservative and Unionist Associations), 26, 29, 52, 105, 115, 117, 167, 174, 290, 293, 295, 300, 307, 320

National Union of Manufacturers (NUM), 303, 309, 331

nationalism, 27, 67, 298

nationalization, 40, 42, 49, 53, 55, 56, 83, 85–109, 113, 123, 126, 149; capital supply to, 208, 221, 230; Conservative attitude to, 85–6; Conservative Government and, 180–202, 322, 323; and ownership, 73, 127, 131; price restraint and, 160, 321; Social Democrat argument against, 71, 299; Tory

Reform Committee and, 59–60; *see under* individual industries; *see also* property ownership, State, de-nationalization, public sector

Nazi-ism, 68, 72

New Approach, A, 114, 117–18

New Deal (U.S.), 53, 69–70

Next Five Years, The, (1935), 295, 352; (1959), 333

oil, 34, 63, 158, 198, 199

oligopoly, 39, 53, 92, 232

One Nation, 152–3, 314, 326, 330

oxygen, 222, 330

Parliament, 45, 56, 58, 101, 104, 121, 132, 135, 141, 152, 174, 182, 184–5, 192, 197, 198, 202, 215, 219, 241; Burke and, 276, 282; reform of, 287

participation (by workers), 57, 178

partnership, 57; State-industry–, 64, 82, 106, 132, 135, 170, 172 *passim*, 175; State-trade unions – , 116, 117, 118–22, 124, 178, 204, 226, 237, 245, 272; *see* co-operation

pay pause, 235, 241; *see* incomes, wages

payroll tax, 165

political levy, 113–14, 170, 171

planning, plan, 35, 44, 53, 56, 58, 59, 60, 66, 70, 79, 132, 133–41, 144, 145, 150, 196, 197, 204, 245, 252–3, 292, 295; – apparatus, 70, 73, 207; Churchill's Four Year – , 59–60; Conservative post-war